war against war

F. L. CARSTEN

war against war

British and German Radical Movements
in the First World War

UNIVERSITY OF CALIFORNIA PRESS
Berkeley and Los Angeles

© F. L. Carsten 1982

First published 1982

Printed in Great Britain
for the publishers
University of California Press
Berkeley & Los Angeles

Library of Congress Catalog Card No. 81-69892

ISBN 0-520-04581-5

CONTENTS

PREFACE

Many monographs and learned articles have been written on certain aspects of the British or the German Left in the years of the First World War, as well as many biographies of the leading politicians concerned. But to the best of my knowledge there has been no modern study of the Left as a whole in either country during these years, and certainly no comparison of the two. Yet comparisons can be made, for example between the British Independent Labour Party and the German Independent Social Democratic Party which adopted very similar attitudes towards the war, or between the shop stewards' movements in the two countries which again showed certain similar traits, or between the many strikes which threatened the production of armaments. It also seems important to try and establish in which of the two countries the anti-war movement grew stronger and for what reasons. These are some of the problems which have induced me to write this study, which throughout is based on new archival sources or on collections of printed documents which have been published above all in the German Democratic Republic, but to a lesser extent in Britain and in West Germany. It turned out that far more archival material on this subject is available in Germany that in this country. For this there is one very obvious reason, and some much less obvious ones. In Germany during the war years, at least three separate authorities reported regularly on political and social events within their districts: the police, the civil administration, and the military district commands. The detailed monthly reports of the latter were printed in a limited edition and are available in several archives (although nowhere complete). They are a mine of information, as are the reports of the police and the civil authorities. In Britain, no such regular reports were rendered. The police and the chief constables only wrote to the Home Office if anything of special importance occurred in their areas. The Ministry of Munitions collected material on the strikes, but only in particularly important instances. Regular monthly reports simply did not exist. Two other difficulties arose which could not be foreseen. A prolonged search for the 'lost' archives of the ILP succeeded in tracing them, but only to a publishing company which refused me access, because, it seems, they intend to publish parts of them. In addition, certain files in the Scottish Public Record Office in Edinburgh are still closed, and all efforts to obtain permission to use them proved to be in vain. For these reasons, the following pages contain on the whole less material on British left-wing and anti-war activities than on German ones. This is very regrettable, but it also seems that much more happened in Germany on the anti-war front. The German Labour Movement split on the issue of the war, the British Labour Movement did not.

My thanks are due to many archivists and historians who helped me to find material for this book or drew my attention to rare pamphlets and collections. The Historische Kommision zu Berlin assisted me by photocopying a number of rare pamphlets from the war period. The Department of Sound Records at the Imperial War Museum put at my disposal transcripts of their recordings of interviews with former conscientious objectors. Lord Brockway – one of the few survivors of these battles – was good enough to grant me an interview in 1978. Above all, my thanks are due to my wife who helped me throughout with her advice and who commented on the first draft of the manuscript.

The following abbreviations have been used throughout (some only in the notes):

A.K.   Army Corps, always preceded by a Roman figure to indicate what German Army Corps is meant (there were 21, plus three separate Bavarian Army Corps)

bayer.   Bavarian

BSP   British Socialist Party

ILP   Independent Labour Party

KPD   German Communist Party

NAC   National Administrative Council of the ILP

PRO   Public Record Office

SPD   German Social Democratic Party

UDC   Union of Democratic Control

USPD   German Independent Social Democratic Party

F.L.C.

London, January 1981

war against war

I

The opposition at the beginning of the Great War

The First World War was the great watershed of European history. In August 1914 a world came to an end, a world that seemed very stable and secure, a world firmly dominated by the old ruling circles, whether from the aristocracy or the middle classes, a world in which the lower classes, in spite of all their strivings, were kept down with a firm hand. Indeed, the working classes, too, benefited from the progress of industrialization; and in the major countries of western and central Europe the socialist parties were not revolutionary but endeavoured to achieve political and social reform within the existing capitalist system, bearing testimony to its progress and stability. The war of 1914-18 changed this fundamentally. It brought about revolutions in eastern and central Europe. It also brought forth revolutionary parties which aimed at the violent overthrow of the existing political and social system. The war created violence on a colossal scale. Above all, it was accompanied by an outburst of nationalist passion in all the belligerent countries such as Europe had never seen. The end of the war saw further outbreaks of violent nationalism, especially in the defeated countries, but also in Italy, which culminated in the growth of fascist movements. The old stability was destroyed for good, the European currencies lost their value, there was unemployment, hunger and inflation on an unprecedented scale. None of this could be foreseen in August 1914 when most people thought that the war would be over within a few months and everybody was hoping for a speedy victory. Thus the old Europe went to its destruction. It was to be replaced by a Europe beset by fears and crises, by violence and hatred. At the end of the war socialists found themselves in positions of power and influence in many countries, but they were to derive little benefit from these gains. Yet they did not enter the war to achieve greater influence: they too were engulfed by the wave of national enthusiasm which permeated the whole continent.

This wave affected Germany – a country where nationalism had been virulent ever since the mid-nineteenth century – perhaps more than any other European country, and it also strongly affected the party which was famed for its internationalist outlook, the German Social Democratic Party. On 3 August 1914 its parliamentary faction – which with 110 members was by far the strongest party in the German parliament – decided in a private meeting by 78 to 14 votes to approve the war credits demanded by the Imperial government, to desist from a debate on the issue in the public meeting, but to explain their affirmative vote by a declaration which was to be read by the chairman of the parliamentary party. Accordingly in the public session on 4 August, Dr Hugo Haase, a left-wing lawyer from Königsberg, read the declaration which committed the SPD to the support of the war and the parliamentary party, without a single dissenter, voted in favour of the war credits. Among the 14 dissenters of the previous day, who thus in public preserved party discipline, there were, apart from Haase himself, many who in later years became prominent opponents of the war – Friedrich Geyer, Alfred Henke, Georg Ledebour, Karl Liebknecht, Otto Rühle.[1] Many of them represented in parliament strongholds of the party's left wing, such as Berlin, Bremen or Leipzig, but for the moment the left wing had no voice and was submerged by the tide of patriotism which engulfed the whole country.

This national enthusiasm also affected the ordinary members of the SPD who were called to the colours. Two socialist deputies who travelled from Dortmund to Berlin to attend the Reichstag session met at the station groups of reservists who urged them, as one of them reported later, to do the right thing in Berlin: 'see to it that we have all we need; don't be stingy in voting money'. The deputy was deeply impressed by these voices, and his left-wing colleague confessed that he had had similar experiences. If the party should vote against the war credits there would be a storm of indignation at home and at the front; 'the socialist organization would be swept clean away by popular resentment'.[2] According to an account given by Karl Liebknecht, the arguments put forward by the adherents of the majority on 3 August emphasized that the party could not possibly swim against the popular current, could not allow itself to be pushed aside at such a moment, or to be treated as standing outside the law by the government; the defeat of

Russia would bring the overthrow of tsarism and would liberate France from the Russian alliance; Social Democracy would emerge much stronger from the war. But if the party voted against the war credits its organization would be annihilated. The arguments of the minority were listened to with impatience and amid many interruptions. The left-wingers were convinced that the party, in spite of the vote for the war credits, would continue its policy of opposition and class struggle during the war. They were afraid to reveal an open split in the party ranks in a situation fraught with such dangers; and the left-wingers were themselves disunited, some of the former radicals siding with the patriotic majority. Thus Liebknecht's efforts to persuade them to show their dissent in the public session of parliament failed completely.[3]

The vote in favour of the war credits has often been pilloried as a betrayal of socialist ideals; and indeed the Social Democrats in the Reichstag had always voted against the budget which sanctioned Germany's vast military expenditure and proclaimed their opposition to war from the rooftops. Every year May Day was celebrated with a demonstration for peace and proletarian unity against all warmongers. In 1912 the Socialist International held a special congress at Basel because of the threat of war. The congress issued a manifesto which bound the working classes and their parliamentary representatives 'to do everything to prevent war by the means which seem the most effective to them'; but if a war should break out, nevertheless, 'it is their duty to promote its speedy end' and to bring about the abolition of capitalist class rule, making use of the economic and political crisis caused by the war. Because the SPD feared the arrest of the party leaders and the suppression of its organizations in case of general mobilization, the leaders decided during the Morocco crisis of 1911 to send the party treasurers with the funds to Switzerland to prevent their seizure: a precaution that was to be repeated. Yet in April 1913 in a secret meeting of the Reichstag budget committee the Social Democrats present did not protest when the army's plan of an offensive in the west at the beginning of a war was revealed to them. They only demanded a declaration that in this case Germany would respect the neutrality of Belgium as long as other countries did the same. But the Prussian Minister of War, as the representative of the government, replied that such a declaration would only arouse hostility against Germany, and there the matter was left.[4] The Social Democrats preferred not to press the issue and did not insist on a declaration in favour of Belgian neutrality.

When – after the murder of Archduke Francis Ferdinand at Sarajevo by young Bosnian nationalists – the Austrian ultimatum was sent to Serbia and war in the Balkans threatened once more, the German Social Democrats reacted to the threat with total opposition. A prominent right-wing leader, Philipp Scheidemann, noted in his diary: 'I consider the ultimatum a monstrosity and am absolutely certain that Austria wants war.' *Vorwärts*, the Social Democratic paper, published a special party manifesto which protested sharply against 'the frivolous war provocation of the Austro-Hungarian government'; 'the demands of this government are so *brutal* as they have *never* been put to an independent state in the history of the world, and they can only have been calculated so as to *provoke a war*... A *serious hour has struck, more serious than any of the past decades. There is danger ahead! World war threatens!* The ruling classes which in peace-time gag, despise and exploit you want to misuse you as cannon fodder. Everywhere you must shout into the ears of the rulers: *We do not want war! Down with the war! Long live international solidarity!*' On the same day, 25 July, the party's leading theoretician, Karl Kautsky, wrote to the Austrian socialist leader Victor Adler that this surely was the moment to protest against the war in Austria by a mass strike, but that there was not the smallest sign of any mass protest. 'We must be glad', he added prophetically, 'if we succeed in this situation in preserving the unity of the party.'[5]

Three days later, on 28 July, socialist mass meetings adopted strongly worded resolutions against the Austrian policy and in favour of world peace. 'The warmongers must realize that, if a world war breaks out with all its suffering and atrocities, the political and economic crises caused by it will inevitably... powerfully accelerate the development of the capitalist social order towards socialism... Exactly like the French workers, those of Germany have at this moment the special task of exercising pressure on their governments so that the peoples of these countries are not sacrificed to an Austrian or Russian policy of prestige and conquest. Down with all incitement to war!'[6] The Social Democratic papers stressed that the Austrian government wanted war and that in an Austrian-Russian war Germany was not bound to help Austria by the terms of the Dual Alliance because Austria had attacked Serbia. In Berlin's most fashionable street, Unter den Linden, the socialists clashed with nationalist crowds. The police intervened with their sabres in favour of the chauvinists and arrested 28 socialist demonstrators. 'A wave of fury against Austria', on account of its Serbian ultimatum, permeated the German Left. At Leipzig, the party organized a colossal demonstration for peace at which the people shouted 'Down with the war!' and the socialist youth groups sang the Workers' 'Marseillaise': 'We do not count the enemy, nor all the dangers looming...'[7]

The Social Democratic leaders were not satisfied with anti-war protests, but they took positive steps to save the party funds from confiscation and to coordinate their protests with those of their French comrades. The party treasurers, Friedrich Ebert and Otto Braun, both later leading politicians of the Weimar Republic, were sent to Switzerland with the party chest, where the surprised Angelica Balabanov met them at Basel station on the morning of 31 July. The Free trade unions transferred large sums to private accounts because they too feared government seizure.[8] On 31 July the party leaders met. Several, among them Haase and Ledebour, spoke against the war credits, others were wavering, and a small minority was in favour of an affirmative vote. It was then decided to send Herman Müller (later twice a chancellor of the Weimar Republic) to Paris so that the French and the German parties would speak with one voice, and a decision on the war credit vote was postponed. Müller arrived in Paris, where general mobilization was taking place, on 1 August, accompanied by Henri de Man, at that time working as an interpreter for the International Socialist Bureau in Brussels, as well as by its secretary, Camille Huysmans. To the French socialist leaders Müller 'declared in the most formal fashion and several times over that a vote of the Social Democratic group in favour of the war credits would certainly not take place'; among the deputies, he said, there were 'only two appreciable currents of opinion: the one in favour of a vote *against* the war credits, the other in favour of *abstention*', with the opponents in the majority. His listeners were thus left with 'this very clear impression;

(1) that the majority of the German Social Democratic group was in favour of voting against the military credits;
(2) that if, in spite of that, those in favour of abstention were to prevail, it would be above all in order to safeguard the unity of action with the French Socialists;
(3) that the only hypothesis not to be considered was that of a vote of the German Socialists in favour of the war credits...'

Some of the French Socialists present, however, remarked that, if France was attacked and invaded, they could not avoid voting for the war credits, whereupon Müller replied that it was always difficult to determine who was the attacker.[9]

Yet as early as 31 July, the Prussian Minister of War was able to inform his Bavarian counterpart that 'the Social Democratic Party was firmly resolved to conduct itself as befitted every German in the present circumstances'. And by the beginning of August it had completely reversed its attitude. On 1 August another monster demonstration took place in Leipzig, but this time the main square was filled with an enthusiastic crowd clamouring for war, and among them were many members of the Social Democratic Party. One of the Leipzig radicals indeed thought that the whole world seemed to collapse around them. A socialist deputy who had contemplated either abstention or voting against the war credits found his own arguments so artificial that he quickly changed his mind although he still considered the war 'the greatest misfortune', but to him the worst of all possible results was 'the rule of tsarism over Europe'. Indeed, it seems to have been the general mobilization by Russia and the threatening invasion of East Prussia by the Russian army which induced many German Social Democrats to support the government and the war. For many decades tsarist Russia had been the arch-enemy of the whole European Left, and suitable quotations from Marx, Engels and Bebel could be adduced to underpin the hatred of autocracy. Hatred of Russia could, under the impact of the prevailing hysterical nationalist mood, easily be transformed into hatred of 'the enemy'.[10]

As far as the German socialists were concerned, there were other reasons which helped to explain the extraordinary change of mood within 24 or at most 48 hours. On 1 August the news of the murder of Jean Jaurès reached Berlin – the venerated leader who had moved the Basel resolution of 1912 – and 'vengeance for Jaurès' was a slogan that appealed to many Social Democrats and enabled them to combine the hatred of Russia with the hatred of France. A war of defence had never been repudiated by Social Democracy: now the Russian army was threatening German soil and in the eyes of the vast majority its defence became a sacred duty. Some years later the official report of the SPD parliamentary party emphasized that, as it had been unable to prevent the war, at least it had to prevent the victory of the hostile powers; nothing must be done to facilitate their plans, and that would have been the effect of a vote against the war credits. For decades the Social Democrats had been ostracized by the government and society, treated as outside the pale. They had been called a 'gang of traitors', 'enemies of the Empire', 'who do not deserve the name of Germans', who must be 'rooted out', by no less a person than Emperor William II. Now this would change almost overnight and, as a left-winger wrote in 1915, 'suddenly the terrible tension was resolved' and for the first time 'with a good conscience and without any fear to appear a traitor by doing so, we could join in the thundering battle song: 'Deutschland, Deutschland, über alles!'[11] At last there was national unity, and the Emperor proclaimed that he no longer knew any parties.

Apart from all national idealism, there were weighty material arguments for a vote in favour of the war credits. As a left-wing deputy reported in 1915, the Social Democrats feared the fury of the populace which might storm the party houses and demolish them. They equally feared the dissolution of their organizations and trade unions, the prohibition of their newspapers, the seizure of their publishing houses. As Otto Braun, the party treasurer, explained to a conference of socialist editors a few weeks later, 20 million marks were invested in the enterprises of the party and it employed about 11,000 people; all that was suddenly threatened with destruction. This fear alone can account for the dispatch of Ebert and Braun to Basel to save the party funds. The party leaders rightly expected the worst from the military authorities who took over power when a state of war was declared and who were bitterly hostile to any socialist. They knew full well that any new persecution would be far more severe than it had been under Bismarck's anti-socialist law. The same fear influenced the leaders of the Austrian Social Democrats. Their leader, Victor Adler, emphasized in July at the meeting of the International Socialist Bureau that, in view of the Austrian ultimatum to Serbia, the party was completely powerless: in this situation all that could be done was to try and save the existing organizations.[12].

Thus the causes of the sudden change of policy by the SPD leaders are very complex, and the usual explanation that they were simply swamped by the flood of nationalist enthusiasm has to be modified. The desire to save the socialist organizations, the press and property seems to have been equally influential. Finally, in the hour of 'danger of the fatherland' they wanted to prove themselves good Germans, as good as any. As one of the socialist poets put it, they had to show 'that the fatherland's poorest son was also its most loyal'. Thus the SPD came in from the cold. It is perhaps not surprising that, in the emotional and hysterical atmosphere of August 1914, the party decided to support the war and to conform to the vast majority of the nation: exactly as the French Socialists and the British Labour Party did. What is really surprising, however, is that the SPD leaders and the large majority of the members

17

loyally adhered to this policy during the later years of the war, when the atmosphere changed, when the opposition to a war which demanded such vast sacrifices from the German people grew by leaps and bounds, and when it became crystal clear that the German government continued the war as a war of territorial conquest. A decision of the SPD to oppose the war in 1916 or 1917 would have had momentous consequences for the whole course of German history, for in that case the German labour movement could have remained united, and the German Communist Party would not have got off the ground. Thus the whole history of the Weimar Republic might have been very different.

On the local and practical level cooperation between the socialist and the bourgeois organizations replaced the previous hostility. When a National Women's Service was launched by the authorities and the voluntary women's organizations to help in the war effort, Luise Zietz, (later one of the USPD leaders) as the representative of the Social Democratic women and the organized women workers, expressed her readiness to 'work hand in hand', and the chairman replied that her words gave 'the best impression of the unity of the German nation at this fateful time'. Even the German Peace Society issued a leaflet on the duty of national defence: 'Now that the issue of war or peace is no longer dependent on our will and our nation threatened from east, north and west is engaged in a fateful struggle, every German friend of peace must fulfil his duty towards the fatherland exactly as any other German. In patriotic ardour he will not be surpassed by those who, when there was still time, had nothing but derision and sneers for the idea of peace...'[13]

Yet from the outset there was dissent from the official policy of the SPD and it came from the left wing of the party. In the evening of 4 August the small circle of friends of Rosa Luxemburg met in her flat to discuss what might be done. Among them were the venerable historian of the party, Franz Mehring, one of the editors of *Vorwärts*, Ernst Meyer, and others who like him later became prominent leaders of the KPD, Wilhelm Pieck, Hugo Eberlein, Hermann and Käthe Duncker. They decided to send more than 300 telegrams to prominent left-wingers asking whether they were willing to sign a declaration 'Why we have not resigned from the party'. But the echo was entirely negative. From Stuttgart even the leaders of the local left radicals, Clara Zetkin, Friedrich Westmeyer and Arthur Crispien, replied that no one would understand such a protest; it would only show 'how totally isolated we are and how small and impotent'; it would separate them from the masses and increase disunity on the Left.[14] But as early as 6 August a meeting of the functionaries of the Stuttgart SPD with an overwhelming majority passed a motion of no confidence in the parliamentary party. At Bremen, the left radicals protested in front of the party premises against the policy of the leaders. At Dresden, several members went to the party offices to hand in their membership cards. In August, in several suburbs of Berlin, the opposition tried to mobilize the members but with small success. In Hamburg, three well-.known party intellectuals protested against the pro-war articles of the *Hamburger Echo*: 'The present world war is not a war of the people against each other and is not waged in the interest of the people, but it is a war in the interest of international finance capital. Basically it is a war between the young and expanding German and the firmly established but menaced British imperialisms...'[15] Yet these few signs of protest were drowned in the general chorus of consent which permeated the SPD – a party that had always been proud of its strict discipline and a strong sense of loyalty. During the years to come this spirit deeply influenced the majority of the members.

In the autumn of 1914 Rosa Luxemburg and her friends increased their efforts to win adherents in the Social Democratic organizations of Berlin and other towns. In September Liebknecht classified the vote in favour of the war credits as 'treason towards the International' and was supported by a few other deputies. Eduard Bernstein, hitherto the leader of the right-wing 'revisionist' wing of the party, passionately protested against the drowning of 150,000 Russian soldiers in the Masurian lakes: if the party did not protest Germany would cease to be a civilized country. In October a right-wing deputy reported that not only Rosa Luxemburg, Mehring and Duncker, but also Haase and Ledebour were conducting 'an intensive subterranean campaign to influence people against the decision of 4 August'; allegedly they had great success in the small conventicles in which they spoke, either members' meetings or educational groups; as thousands of such meetings took place every month, it was very difficult to combat these activities, for 'the few reasonable people cannot possibly be present everywhere'. The Berlin police also reported that in the members' meetings of the Berlin constituencies held in early October the radicals acted 'rather provocatively', that Ledebour again fulminated against the landlords and the police and even demanded – clearly a cardinal sin – pressure on the government for the introduction of the free, equal and secret franchise for the Prussian Diet as well as the vote for women and those between the ages of 20 and 25.[16] These were old socialist demands, but under the terms of the political truce declared at the outbreak of war they were shelved for the time being. The *Burgfriede* thus condemned Social Democracy to passivity in all matters of internal politics, however vital they might be.

During these months it was above all Karl Liebknecht who emerged as the spokesman of the radical Left. After a visit to Holland and occupied Belgium he protested to the party leaders that its emissaries had defended the German invasion of Belgium in foreign countries and 'in fact acted almost as the heralds of German imperialism', while the whole party got 'more and more deeply embedded in the Masurian swamps of a shallow nationalism and illusionism'; it was, he declared, the duty of every member to oppose 'the highest organs of the party in the interest of the party'. In November Liebknecht formulated several theses: 'This war has not been undertaken to promote the welfare of the German people. It is not a German war of defence and not a war of liberation, but a war of capitalist aggression and conquest... We oppose in principle and decisively any annexation because it violates the right of self-determination of the people and only serves the interests of capitalism'. At the end of November Kautsky informed Adler in Vienna that Liebknecht was apparently determined not only to abstain from the vote on the new war credits – which he was fully entitled to do – but also to oppose them publicly. Adler, in his turn, told Kautsky that Liebknecht 'together with the three old women' (apparently meaning Luxemburg, Zetkin and Mehring) was committing 'treason, not against Germany, but against the German party', so as to appear 'as the only just man in this chauvinist Sodom'. Kautsky feared that Rosa Luxemburg was trying to bring about a party split, though her following was still 'very small', and even Ledebour was now her bitter enemy. Within the party, Kautsky added gloomily, clashes were occurring everywhere, from Stuttgart to Hamburg.[17]

On 30 November the SPD parliamentary party decided by 82 to 17 votes to vote for the new war credits. The left-winger, Henke, moved to allow the minority to vote against the war credits and to state publicly their reasons for doing so, but this motion obtained only seven votes. Once more the large majority of the left-wingers kept party discipline, and on 2 December only two SPD deputies, Liebknecht and Rühle, voted, independently of each other, against the war credits. Several others left the hall so as not to participate in the vote. Liebknecht gave as the reason for his dissent that the war was 'an imperialist war, a war for the capitalist domination of the world market... The war is not a

German defensive war...' Henceforth his name became the symbol of opposition to the war, not only in Germany. As a left-wing journalist who knew Liebknecht well described him, he was virtually impossible to argue with; 'but he had an intensity of feeling with the victims of any tyranny which made him ready to make any, really any, sacrifice...' One might add: ready too to face martyrdom. Liebknecht was not a logical Marxist theoretician, but a warm-hearted and passionate socialist, with a deep sympathy for the underdog and the downtrodden, for many years prominent in anti-militarist propaganda. This sentiment also extended to 'the enemy'. As Liebknecht informed the party executive in October: 'the Belgian comrades are for me still comrades, friends, brothers, as previously, without any reservation. My feelings for our comrades in the poor, unhappy Belgium have become only more cordial, exactly as those for our French comrades...'[18] He was convinced that this feeling would find an echo among the German Social Democrats. That it found an echo in Britain is shown by the fact that his declaration against the war credits was printed in full in *The Labour Leader* of 17 December 1914.

Two weeks later *The Labour Leader* published greetings from the four most prominent leaders of the German extreme Left, Liebknecht, Luxemburg, Mehring and Zetkin. Rosa Luxemburg wrote: 'Upon the terrible ruins of civilization which imperialism has created the resurrection of the International as the only salvation of humanity from the hell of a degenerating and outgrown class rule shall take place. Already, after a few months of war, the Jingo intoxication which animated the working classes of Germany is passing away, and although they have been deserted by their leaders in this great, historic hour, their sense is returning, and every day the number of workers who blush with shame and anger at the thought of what is going on to-day grows...' This somewhat optimistic view was supported by Liebknecht: 'Already among the German workers there is far greater opposition to the war than is generally supposed, and the louder the echo of the cry for peace in other countries, the more vehemently and energetically will they work for peace here...' Clara Zetkin expressed the thanks of the German Left for the stand taken by the ILP 'against Imperialism and for Socialism. You have preserved the honour of the International, your attitude is a lofty example of faith and strength in the present, a hope and warrant for the future.' Yet their conviction that the number of determined opponents of the war was growing 'every day', that there were 'thousands upon thousands in Germany' who shared their views,[19] was only very partially supported by the facts. In the early months of the war opposition was on the whole limited to the old centres of the Left, to Berlin, Bremen and Stuttgart.

Before the war it had been above all the Socialist Youth groups of Stuttgart which occupied the attention of the authorities on account of their radicalism. The editors of the local SPD paper, *Schwäbische Tagwacht*, also belonged to the left wing of the party. In September 1914 they met Rosa Luxemburg in the house of Clara Zetkin, and some days later Liebknecht addressed a meeting of the party functionaries in Stuttgart. In the discussion they sharply criticized him for preserving party discipline in the vote on 4 August; the minority, he was told, had failed in an historic hour and done serious damage to the cause of peace and revolutionary socialism. This was the first time, Liebknecht replied, that he was criticized for not being sufficiently radical; he was deeply moved and pleased by this criticism which he considered entirely justified. He promised that in future he would fight against the war and the party leaders without any compromise. Conflict soon broke out about the political line followed by the *Schwäbische Tagwacht* when it began to attack more and more openly the attitude of the party leaders and the parliamentary party. At the beginning of November the SPD regional leadership for Württemberg and its press committee decided against the vote of the Left to appoint a new editor-in-chief, a prominent right-winger, to rectify the political line of the paper and to curtail the rights of the previous editors. But a few days later a large meeting of the local party members adopted a motion demanding the immediate dismissal of the new editor-in-chief and the restoration of the rights of the previous editors. An appeal was made to the party executive in Berlin which did not approve the intervention of the regional leaders and tried to arrange a compromise. But before negotiations started the Left urged its followers to cancel their subscriptions to the paper, and the local SPD organization of Stuttgart decided to retain the membership dues and, in spite of many reminders, not to transfer their share to the regional party funds. At the beginning of December an open breach occurred. The right-wing minority left the meeting of the local SPD members, and the majority decided to publish their own weekly paper and elected their own regional party leaders. The moderate minority then founded their own separate organization. From Stuttgart the conflict spread to a few other towns in Württemberg, but the reaction outside Stuttgart remained very limited. This was the first split in the ranks of the SPD.[20] Exactly like the later ones it led to bitter personal recriminations and hostility on both sides.

At Bremen, too, the Left had been strongly entrenched since pre-war days, and – as at Stuttgart – was supported by the editors of the local paper, the strangely named *Bremer Bürger-Zeitung* (not precisely a bourgeois paper). The editor-in-chief was the local member of parliament, Alfred Henke, the son of a poor cigar-maker, and his deputy was Johann Knief, a teacher of working-class origin. Two foreigners contributed their share to the radicalization of the Bremen SPD in the early years of the twentieth century: Karl Radek, who came from the same Polish left-wing party as Rosa Luxemburg but had fiercely quarrelled with her, and Anton Pannekoek, a Dutchman and noted Marxist writer, who was employed in Bremen to give courses on Marxist subjects. The radicals enjoyed the support of the dock workers and other large enterprises and used the columns of the *Bremer Bürger-Zeitung* to oppose the pro-war policy of the party leaders; there Henke argued for a revival of the International to overcome the quarrelling of the socialist parties. At Hamburg, the party paper, *Hamburger Echo*, supported the official party policy but was for that reason sharply attacked by members of the Left who argued that it was betraying the principles of socialism and following a chauvinist line. There two socialist intellectuals published a pamphlet on 'Imperialism and Democracy' which strongly opposed the political truce and the alleged political unity of the nation; as long as imperialism existed, they argued, there would be war, and only socialism could establish world peace; the organization of the proletariat must be opposed to the organization of capitalism.[21]

This pamphlet was legally published in Hamburg in 1914, but confiscated in the following year on the order of the military authorities. At the outbreak of war executive power in Germany passed into the hands of about 25 military district commanders, the so-called *Stellvertretende Generalkommandos,* who were solely responsible to the Emperor. According to a Prussian law of 1851, they could issue directives to the civil authorities, suspend the basic rights of the citizen, curtail the rights of free assembly and association, commit people to 'protective custody', exercise censorship over the press and other publications and even promulgate decrees contrary to the existing law. In Bavaria, however, the provisions of the law of 1851 did not apply so that there the powers of the military authorities were somewhat more circumscribed. But to what extreme even the Bavarian military would go, was demonstrated in November 1914 when they prohibited the publication of the *Fränkiche Volkstribüne*, the SPD paper of Bayreuth. The offence committed was the republication of an article circulated by the SPD press bureau and already published in the *Bremer Bürger-Zeitung*, which criticized the bitter polemics against Britain in the German press as 'a witchhunt against a great nation and a serious danger to the civilizing interests', and which the *Fränkiche Volkstribüne* had failed to submit to the military censors in Bayreuth.[22]

In the later months of 1914 the German pacifists too showed some signs of renewed activity. In the middle of August some of them met to discuss what might be done; but they believed then that the war would be over by the autumn. After the battle of the Marne, however, they began to form an opposition group and later they decided to found a new organization. This was done in November under the innocuous name of Bund Neues Vaterland which proclaimed that it was essential to break with the existing system and 'to achieve a political and economic understanding between the developed nations'. The founding group was very small and largely academic. It contained well-known pacifists such as Professors Quidde and Schücking, Dr Lehmann-Russbüldt and Albert Einstein. The new association tried to establish links with conservative circles so as to gain influence on the peace negotiations to come and had close connections with some former diplomats who were critical of German foreign policy, such as Prince Lichnowsky, the former ambassador to London, and the former ambassadors to Rome and Stockholm. Information supplied by them was used to write a memorandum on the foreign policy of Prince Bülow. Its author was the young Ernst Reuter (after 1945 the lord mayor of Berlin) and it was circulated privately. The 'Bund' also had contacts to prominent Social Democrats critical of government policy, such as Bernstein and Haase. But its membership remained very small,[23] and it soon suffered from persecution by the military authorities. It aimed at bringing about vital internal reforms and a negotiated settlement of the war.

In Britain, opposition to the war before it was actually declared came from the Liberal as well as the Labour side, and from influential sections of the City. On 1 August, the most important Liberal paper in London, the *Daily News*, carried an article by the editor: 'If we crush Germany in the dust and make Russia the dictator of Europe and Asia, it will be the greatest disaster that has ever befallen Western culture and civilization.' The paper also published numerous letters protesting against the possibility of British participation in the war. On the same day the British section of the International Socialist Bureau issued a manifesto signed by Keir Hardie and Arthur Henderson: *Down with the war!*. It declared:

> You have never been consulted about the war. Whatever may be the rights and wrongs of the sudden crushing attack made by the militarist Empire of Austria upon Servia, it is certain that the workers of all countries likely to be drawn into the conflict must strain every nerve to prevent their Governments from committing them to war.
>
> ...Hold vast demonstrations against war in every industrial centre. Compel those of the governing class and their Press, who are eager to commit you to co-operate with Russian despotism, to keep silence and respect the decision of the overwhelming majority of the people, who will have neither part nor lot in such infamy. The success of Russia at the present day would be a curse to the world.
>
> There is no time to lose. Already by secret agreements and understandings, of which the democracies of the civilized world know only by rumour. steps are being taken which may fling us all into the fray. Workers, stand together therefore for peace!...
>
> Down with class rule! Down with the rule of brute force! Down with war! Up with the peaceful rule of the people!

On Sunday, 2 August, the Labour Party organized mass demonstrations against the war which demanded that Britain should not participate in it. The crowds heard the leaders of the party denounce war and the alliance with tsarist Russia. The miners' leader Robert Smillie even exclaimed that, if a strike of the workers of Europe were to stop the war, the miners would take part in this strike.[24]

On 4 August, the day war was declared, the *Daily Herald* still stated: 'We believe in International Solidarity. For us it is no mere phrase, no vain and empty symbol... We need peace; we must have peace; our children will thank us if we make possible the realization of its promise.' On that day too, the German Social Democratic deputies unanimously approved the war credits and Belgium was invaded by the German army. But in Britain opinion remained divided. Five members of the Liberal government resigned rather than support the war, and within the Parliamentary Labour Party a minority of about six continued to oppose it. On 7 August Ramsay MacDonald resigned the leadership of the parliamentary party because his attitude to the war conflicted with that of the majority. For the large majority of the Labour movement it became the foremost duty to defeat German imperialism and to defend western democracy against its onslaught. Hence later in August the British trade unions accepted an industrial truce and the National Executive of the Labour Party agreed to a political truce for the duration of the war and to participation in the national recruiting campaign.[25]

Thus the attitude of the large majority of British Labour corresponded to that of the German trade unions and Social Democrats, exactly as the industrial and political truce corresponded to the *Burgfrieden*, although British Labour did not have to fear the seizure of its funds and the destruction of its property if it had opposed the war. All over Europe, the socialists found it virtually impossible to withstand the official propaganda and the national enthusiasm which pervaded the continent. For the Belgian and French socialists this was clearly a war of defence, the German invasion threatened the very existence of their countries, and in both, leading socialists joined the government. But the attitude of British Labour is less easy to explain. In Europe as a whole, only very small socialist parties, such as the Russian and the Serbian, maintained their opposition to the war, and the Russian Social Democrats were deeply split on the issue. The only mass party which continued its opposition to the war was the Italian Socialist Party, and for the time being Italy was neutral. The Italian Socialists remained bitterly hostile to the fiery nationalist propaganda which aimed at bringing Italy into the war on the side of the Entente.

In Britain, it was the small Independent Labour Party which saved the honour of the International and opposed the war from the outset. On 6 August *The Labour Leader* carried at the top and bottom of the front page in large letters the slogan '*Down with the War!*':

Workers of Great Britain, you have no quarrel with the workers of Europe. They have no quarrel with you. The quarrel is between the Ruling Classes of Europe.

Don't make their quarrel yours.

...This is not your war. It is not the war of the German working class, or of the French working class, or of the Austrian working class, or of the Russian working class...

This is a war of the Ruling Classes, But the Ruling Classes will not fight. They will call on you to fight.

Your fathers, your brothers, your sons will be called upon to shoot down the German workers. The German workers will be called upon to shoot down your fathers, your brothers, your sons. You have no quarrel. But you will have to suffer.

Why should you?

You will have to pay for the war. You will hunger and starve. Your wives will hunger and starve. Your children will hunger and starve. *Why should they?*

... the future is dark, but in the solidarity of the workers lies the hope which shall once again bring light to the peoples of Europe.[26]

A few days later, on 11 August, this was followed by a manifesto of the National Council of the ILP which once more stressed internationalism and solidarity with the workers of Germany and Austria:

To us who are Socialists the workers of Germany and Austria, no less than the workers of France and Russia, are comrades and brothers; in this hour of carnage and eclipse we have friendship and compassion to all victims of militarism. Our nationality and independence, which are dear to us, we are ready to defend; but we cannot rejoice in the organized murder of tens of thousands of workers of other lands who go to kill and be killed at the command of rulers to whom the people are as pawns...

Out of the darkness and the depth we hail our working-class comrades of every land. Across the roar of guns, we send sympathy and greeting to the German Socialists. They have laboured unceasingly to promote good relations with Britain, as we with Germany. They are no enemies of ours, but faithful friends. In forcing this appalling crime upon the nations, it is the rulers, the diplomats, the militarists who have sealed their doom. In tears and blood and bitterness the greater Democracy will be born... Long live Freedom and Fraternity! Long live International Socialism!

The manifesto further emphasized the danger of Russian militarism and of the alliance with Russia: 'If Russia is permitted to gratify her territorial ambitions and to extend her Cossack rule, civilization and democracy will be gravely imperilled. Is it for this that Britain has drawn her sword?'[27] The proclamations proved that the spirit of internationalism was not dead, that the ILP at least kept alive the message of the Socialist International.

Yet the ILP was not a Marxist party; many of its members opposed the war on pacifist grounds, others because it was an imperialist war, others still favoured a war of national defence but were against a war conducted to maintain the 'balance of power', and a minority were eager to support the war and the government recruiting campaign, while in Scotland the members were considerably more militant that in England. The ILP officers also realized their impotence in view of the prevailing nationalist mood. In August the Divisional Council of London thus informed the branches and members: 'We cannot at the moment take steps to stop the war, but we can help create a public opinion which will make another war an impossibility. This can be done if the ILP remains strong by each member maintaining their membership and each branch official remaining in office. We will then come out of the struggle prepared to use the new opportunities for the further service of Socialism...' These were rather modest goals which in fact postponed the struggle to the end of the war. According to a statement issued in October 1914, the large majority of the branches and numerous conferences 'practically covering the entire country' had endorsed the attitude of the ILP National Council. Only seven branches – mostly small ones – expressly dissented from it, above all from the refusal to support the recruiting campaign for the army, and only two branches repudiated the anti-war manifesto of 11 August. In Glasgow, as early as 9 August, the ILP, together with the British Socialist Party and the Peace Society, organized an anti-war demonstration to demand an armistice and to protest against high food prices.[28]

How much the Labour movement was split by the issue of the war and that of the recruiting campaign also emerged at the meeting of the Executive Committee of the Labour Party at the end of August when the Prime Minister's invitation to participate in the campaign was discussed. The two ILP members of the Executive, Keir Hardie and W. C. Anderson, strongly opposed participation, but before the vote was taken, Keir Hardie left. The invitation was accepted by a majority of seven to four – thus apart from Anderson there must have been three more dissenters. Two days later the National Administrative Council of the ILP met and unanimously endorsed the opposition to recruiting. The Labour Party was informed that the ILP could not accept the decision to join the recruiting campaign; it was decided to inform the branches accordingly and to advise them not to take part in it. But on the issue whether the statement should include 'a demand for an immediate truce and arbitration' to terminate the war the National Administrative Council was almost evenly divided and the decision in favour was only taken by six votes to five. The much smaller British Socialist Party, on the other hand, which was officially a Marxist party, supported the recruiting campaign and advised its branches to participate; but this attitude caused strong protests from many of its members.[29]

At the outbreak of the war the Executive of the BSP – like the ILP –

issued a manifesto that the workers of Europe had no quarrel with each other and that the war was due to the struggle for the domination of the world market. But it also recognized that Britain's freedom and national independence were threatened by Prussian militarism and that therefore the war must be brought to 'a successful issue'. Many party members joined the army as volunteers. In September the Executive came out in favour of the war and the recruiting campaign. But in London 15 out of 18 branches demanded a withdrawal of the statement and other branches followed suit. In Scotland John Maclean declared: 'It is our business as socialists to develop a "class patriotism", refusing to murder one another for a sordid world capitalism... Let the propertied classes go out, old and young alike, and defend their blessed property. When they have been disposed of, we of the working class will have something to defend, and we shall do it.' He advocated that any method, from strikes to insurrection, should be used to end the war.[30] But he was an isolated figure and the attitude of the BSP to the war remained ambiguous for some time.

During the later months of 1914 the views of the ILP leaders, too, were somewhat ambiguous. In September the party's City of London branch congratulated Keir Hardie and MacDonald on 'their courageous stand for peace against a hostile House of Commons' and expressed the hope that the party 'at the earliest suitable opportunity will take steps to inaugurate a great national campaign in favour of peace'. But, as one of its strongest supporters wrote as early as November, 'the ILP has not sufficiently declared its message to the world at large; it has not accepted the admittedly grave responsibility of a public and fearless campaign against the war...' The party chairman, F. W. Jowett, repeatedly declared that he desired Britain to win the war. Keir Hardie and MacDonald were willing to support the war as long as it was fought for a 'just' cause; they accepted that war had become inevitable with the German invasion of Belgium and must be continued until a 'just' peace became possible and Prussian militarism was destroyed, as they hoped, by the German people. In December Keir Hardie stated that none of the ILP pamphlets or statements demanded that the war must be ended immediately.[31]

In November MacDonald wrote to an American socialist to clarify his attitude to the war, pointing out the 'enormous differences' between it and the Boer War which he had violently opposed. By contrast, now 'everyone feels that there is nothing sordid or chauvinist about our intentions. It is a war for liberty and democracy as far as the man in the street is concerned... So far as Socialists are concerned, they must continue their efforts to keep the foundations of the International intact... Above all, they must cooperate to put an end to secret diplomacy and to the handing over of foreign policy to a handful of men drawn from the aristocratic and plutocratic classes. The one danger which the war has revealed is not that of militarism, because that is secondary, but that of class diplomacy, for upon that all militarism, both German and British, rests. On this point I differ from some of my Socialists colleagues who regard wars as inevitable under our present industrial order...' It was a strange analysis as far as militarism, and especially German militarism, was concerned, for it had little to do with 'class diplomacy', but rested on the weight of the Prussian army and of Prussian institutions in the united Germany. About the same time MacDonald also outlined his position in a special leaflet. He believed that the war might have been avoided; but once it had started, 'We must see it through. Every step to that necessary end must be taken... Prussian militarism must be broken, and the Russian people freed from Russian persecution...' As to the war aims Britain should pursue, all armaments should be limited, the small nations of Europe be 'properly protected' and Poland be freed. In general, 'democratic freedom and an unarmed peace in Europe' must be established and secret diplomacy be brought to an end.[32] The message was quite clear: the western powers must win the war, even in alliance with Russia, but the war should be used to free the Russian people and to establish democracy and a lasting peace. He did not indicate how these aims were to be achieved. Even if his attitude was somewhat ambiguous it was much appreciated by his constituency party at Leicester and numerous ILP branches throughout the country, which sent him congratulatory messages and reaffirmed their faith in him 'in spite of the reviling attitude of the Press'.[33]

MacDonald's stand against 'secret diplomacy' and 'class diplomacy' echoed that of an organization founded soon after the outbreak of war, the Union of Democratic Control. In August 1914 a number of prominent intellectuals and pacifist politicians met in the house of the Liberal MP Philip Morrell. The group included Norman Angell, MacDonald, Arthur Ponsonby, Arnold Rowntree, a prominent Quaker, Bertrand Russell and Charles Trevelyan, who had resigned from the government when Britain declared war on Germany. Several of them were Liberal MPs. Trevelyan contacted E. D. Morel who ten years earlier had organized the Congo Reform Association to stop the atrocities committed in the Congo by white colonizers and inaugurated the campaign to remove the Congo from the control of Leopold II, King of the Belgians. During this campaign Morel became deeply suspicious of the conduct of British foreign policy by the Foreign Office and very critical of its policy towards Germany. He was appalled when war was declared in 1914 and eagerly accepted Trevelyan's suggestion that he should become the group's secretary. But he quickly became much more than its secretary; he made the Union of Democratic Control, he was its heart and soul and dominated its policy.[34]

Trevelyan – the brother of the famous historian G. M. Trevelyan who had very different views on the war issue – drafted a circular with three proposals: the prevention of secret diplomacy through parliamentary control of foreign policy; peace terms which neither humiliated the defeated powers nor arranged frontiers likely to cause friction between the nations; and, after the end of the war, negotiations to achieve 'an international understanding depending on popular parties rather than on governments'. The draft was signed by him, Angell, MacDonald and Morel and privately circulated. In September the *Manchester Guardian* published a manifesto setting out the aims of the UDC: no province should be transferred from one country to another without a plebiscite, no treaty be concluded without parliamentary sanction, and the 'balance of power' policy be renounced; armaments should be reduced drastically by the belligerent powers, the manufacture of arms and their export be controlled and the armament industry be nationalized. The manifesto emphasized that the UDC was not a stop-the-war movement and did not intend to urge peace negotiations at this stage. 'The whole emphasis of our effort is laid upon indicating clearly the fundamental principles which must mark the final terms of peace...' But if an opportunity to bring about a negotiated peace should arise it should be used.[35]

Most of the leaders of the UDC believed that the war could only be brought to an end by negotiation and a compromise settlement as military victory eluded both sides. But its principal attack was directed at secret diplomacy which in its opinion was responsible for the war. As MacDonald put it in a pamphlet published by the UDC: 'The exclusion of public opinion from responsibility in foreign affairs provides the conditions under which classes dangerous to the public peace arise in all countries. Secret diplomacy allows the dangerous country to do evil. In every country there is a military faction which wishes for war either because it believes that an occasional war is good for humanity and keeps it from getting too slack, or because it sees an enemy in some other

31

Power. What is known as Prussian militarism differs only in degree from British militarism. They are all strengthened by secret diplomacy.' It was a rather simple view, taking no account of imperialism and the economic causes of war; but it was a view that quickly found an echo among members of the ILP as well as pacifists and Quakers. At its inaugural meeting the UDC had 5000 members, mainly ILP and trade union branches which had affiliated to it. By July 1915 the number of individual members was given as 6000, about a quarter of them in London. By the autumn of that year the UDC claimed to have 300,000 affiliated members.[36]

Even the most ardent pacifists were in two minds about the outcome of the war. At its outbreak the National Peace Council put on record its utter rejection of war, 'its utter detestation of the renewed resort by the Powers of Europe to the barbarous arbitrament of war, which, whatever the result, must inflict untold suffering upon, and blight the hopes of, the peoples in every country concerned...' A few days later the Society of Friends declared the conditions that had caused the war 'un-Christian', but many of its members supported the action of the government and rushed to enlist. Bertrand Russell has described in moving words how he was torn between opposing feelings: 'I was myself tortured by patriotism. The successes of the Germans before the battle of the Marne were horrible to me. I desired the defeat of Germany as ardently as any retired colonel... I hardly supposed that much good would come of opposing the war, but I felt that for the honour of human nature those who were not swept off their feet should show that they stood firm...' But many other Cambridge dons who had joined the UDC obtained commissions in the army.[37]

Yet some voices were raised in open condemnation of the war. The ILP issued a 'Road to Peace' leaflet which stated quite unambiguously: 'In the long run it is the workers who lose and suffer most from war. Whoever stand to gain from the war, the financiers, the armament firms, the ship owners and food contractors, at any rate, the working people do not stand to gain... Every day of this cruel conflict adds heavily to the price that must ultimately be paid. Is it not time we called a halt, is it not time we put an end to this criminal carnage?' The Scottish ILP maintained that the war was caused by capitalism and imperialism; its leaders were willing to fight, but only in defence of socialism.[38] *The Labour Leader* printed messages of solidarity from the most prominent members of the German Left. And a few underground leaflets against the war made their appearance. At Looe in Cornwall one such was distributed which proclaimed:

> Go forth, little soldier! Though you know not what to fight for – go forth! Though you have no grievance against your German brother – go forth and kill him! Though you may know he has a wife and family dependent upon him – go forth and slay him; he is only a German dog. Will he not kill you if he gets a chance? Of course he will. He is being told the same story! 'His King and Country Need Him!'

On the Clyde, there circulated the 'Clyde Workers Hymn of Battle':

> War is in Europe, toiler, blasting the land,
> Workers stand facing workers, rifles in hand,
> Your masters have quarrelled, toiler, loud their cannon roar,
> Slaying slaves in millions, therefore, go to the war.
>
> Go to the war, toiler, go to the war,
> Heed not the Socialist, but wallow in gore,
> Save not your helpless children, care for them no more,
> Leave your wife and family and go to the war.

By the end of 1914, thus William Gallacher reports in his autobiography, the 'campaign against the war, against high prices and rents and for increased wages was in full blast...The Clyde area was beginning to wake up.'[39]

In London too, the ILP had some success with its anti-war propaganda. In November its City of London branch recorded: 'Our second meeting with Normal Angell was a great, enormous, astounding, colossal, epoch-making and unparallelled success (sic). We packed 250 people into a room intended to hold 100', and the rather modest sum of £3 was collected from the audience, who also bought 7s. worth of literature. But in the same month Clifford Allen sadly wrote: 'The International Socialist Movement has crumbled at the first really critical strain put upon it... The German Social Democrat is butchering the French Socialist. The British Socialist hears the cry of anguish and hatred of the German comrade he is bayonetting to a fearful death. Where is now our proud boast of the solidarity of the workers? The battle cry of the International is silent...'[40] In the circumstances of 1914, all that he and like-minded British socialists could register was a protest against the war – exactly as Karl Liebknecht did in the Reichstag on 2 December.

In 1914 the ILP was virtually the only socialist party of a belligerent country – except the very small Russian and Serbian parties – to come out in opposition to the war, 'the despised ILP, the "umbrella" party, with its curiously mixed membership of Christians and Atheists, Socialists, Anarchists and Humanitarians'.[41] It is not easy to see why this was so. Unlike France and Belgium, Britain was not invaded, and did not have the excuse of fighting against tsarist autocracy which the German Social Democrats had. On the contrary, that Britain was allied with the most reactionary power in Europe no doubt influenced the attitude of large sections of the ILP. Founded comparatively late, in 1893, it never became a mass party. In 1900 it had only 51 branches with fewer than 4,000 paying members, according to its annual report. But in the following year it returned the astonishing figure of 13,000 members, which was clearly exaggerated, at the first annual conference of the Labour Representation Committee.[42] Whatever may have been the correct figure of the ILP membership in 1914, it cannot have been very large. It was much easier for a small party to withstand official pressure and nationalist enthusiasm than for mass organizations like the trade unions or the German Social Democratic Party. Quite apart from that, even if some of the party leaders wavered, they showed great personal courage in making their stand, as did Liebknecht and Luxemburg and their small circle in Germany, who in their turn felt inspired by the example set by the ILP. It is important too that the attitude of the ILP leaders was immediately backed by the large majority of the rank and file – a backing that was sadly lacking in Germany. If Ramsay MacDonald carefully collected all the letters and resolutions supporting his stand, this was not only done for the sake of posterity, but it also had an immediate purpose. He and others no doubt felt encouraged by this support.

At the end of 1914 the number of determined opponents of the war in Britain as well as in Germany was still very small. No action had as yet been taken to revive the defunct Socialist International, or to bring together opponents of the war from both sides of the great divide. For the moment, the opponents of the war were still condemned to silence, but this silence was not to last very long.

II

First stirrings of organized opposition

With the outbreak of war the Socialist International, founded at Paris in
1889, ceased to function. As all the major socialist parties supported the
war policy of their own governments, the famed international solidarity
of the workers proved unequal to the demands of the hour, and the
'Internationale' no longer 'united the human race'. In a Europe divided
by bitter national hatreds there were no contacts between the socialist
parties of the belligerent countries. Significantly, the first attempts to
revive such contacts came from the socialist parties of two neutral
countries, both opposed to the war and critical of the pro-war attitude of
the major parties: the Italian and the Swiss socialists. From the outset a
leading part in these endeavours was played by Robert Grimm, leader of
the Swiss Social Democrats and editor of their paper, the *Berner
Tagwacht*. At the end of 1914 Clara Zetkin wrote to him from Germany,
after the large majority of the SPD parliamentary party had once more
voted for the war credits, that this vote was worse than that of 4 August,
for then all sorts of 'extenuating circumstances' could be pleaded, but
that was no longer the case and the parliamentary party had 'not recoiled
from compounding a mistake by a crime'.[1]

As the president of the international organization of socialist women
Clara Zetkin took the initiative to summon to Bern a conference of
women's representatives. It met in March 1915 and was attended by 28
delegates from Britain, France, Germany, Italy, Poland and Russia. The
resolution proposed by her condemned the war but did not call for a
break with the Socialist International and did not state specifically that it
had collapsed ignominiously at the outbreak of war. For this reason it
was sharply attacked by the Russian and Polish delegates present who
followed the instructions of Lenin, then living in Switzerland as an exile.

As he put it soon after, the conference saw a clash between two different *Weltanschauungen*, two different views of the war and the tasks of proletarian parties. In one view, the International had not collapsed and 'no direct, undoubted, manifest betrayal of socialism' had occurred; in the other (his) view, nothing was 'more damaging and pernicious for the proletarian cause' than the adoption of diplomatic tactics towards 'the opportunists and social chauvinists'.[2] For this reason the minority declined to vote for the resolution proposed by Zetkin and moved their own which emphasized that revolutionary methods must be used in the fight against the war. The majority in their turn declared that the conference was not a tribunal entitled to judge actions which went undefended; the attack on the pro-war attitude of the socialist parties should take place at the national party conferences and the international socialist congress. Yet the minority of about six delegates refused to budge and to accept the majority resolution because it was 'insufficient and incomplete'.[3]

The manifesto of the socialist women's conference declared in favour of 'a peace without annexations, without conquests, a peace that recognizes the right to independence of all nations, even the smallest', a peace that does not impose any humiliating conditions on any country. It ended with the slogan 'Down with the war!' It was printed in Switzerland, and according to the Bavarian military authorities, posted in Germany as printed matter 'in largish quantities'. The post offices were ordered to confiscate it – apparently this was the first instance of underground leaflet propaganda. The same division occurred a few weeks later at an international youth conference, held in Bern in April 1915. It was attended by only 14 delegates, several of whom were – as at the women's conference – émigrés living in Switzerland. The Entente countries were not represented at all. As Angelica Balabanov recounts, after long debates and several interruptions the delegates repaired to Lenin's flat and there a resolution was adopted which he approved: 'War against the Imperialist War! War against the Political Truce!' Lenin masterminded the youth conference from a nearby café where he discussed matters with the delegates of his side who one after the other came to consult him.[4]

Thus the battle lines were clearly drawn when a much more important anti-war conference met in Switzerland a few months later, in September. This time there were 42 delegates, ten from Germany and two from France, but the British delegates were refused passports by the government. Grimm, the organizer, took the delegates from Bern by a circuitous route to a little mountain village, Zimmerwald, and took the additional precaution of blocking all outgoing mail. At Zimmerwald too, there were open clashes between the majority of the delegates and Lenin and his six or seven followers from the Russian and Polish emigration and a few neutral countries. The ten Germans present were divided into three political groups. The most important consisted of Social Democratic parliamentary deputies who so far had not voted against the war credits and among whom Georg Ledebour and Adolph Hoffmann were the most prominent. The middle group belonged to the circle of Rosa Luxemburg and included Ernst Meyer and Berta Thalheimer. A single German delegate sided with Lenin, Julian Borchardt, who represented a minute group from Berlin formed around his journal, *Lichtstrahlen*. Lenin soon moved that it was the task of the opposition 'to summon and to lead the working masses to the *revolutionary struggle* against the capitalist governments for the conquest of political power... The revolutionary Social Democrats have to tell the masses time and again that only the *social revolution* can lead to a lasting peace and the liberation of mankind.'[5] He also made it clear that he considered the Socialist International defunct and that he aimed at the foundation of a new, revolutionary International.

Lenin's principal opponent was Ledebour who stressed that his comrades in Berlin had given him a mandate to achieve the tasks which the Socialist International had failed to achieve, but not to found the Third International. Perhaps revolutionary actions which they all desired would take place, but not because they called for them in a manifesto; whoever signed such a manifesto, he continued amidst applause, had the duty to lead such actions, but some of the signatories – an obvious dig at the Russion émigrés – were living in safety; certainly, agitation in the trenches was desirable, but it must be carried out in a more practical fashion than Lenin envisaged; in the belligerent countries the signatories of such a manifesto would be immediately finished, so that whoever wanted real action could not possibly agree to it; all they could do was to resume the class struggle and continue it by the customary methods. Lenin, however, found it 'an old and shabby argument' to claim that it was impossible to summon the masses to revolutionary action if the people issuing the call were unable to participate in it; if the German Left was in favour of such action it was impossible to proceed legally but legal and illegal methods must be combined; in the present situation the old ways were no longer sufficient and the methods of the struggle had been spelled out 'in all revolutionary situations'.[6]

Clearly, in 1915 no revolutionary situation existed in any European country, nor even a situation that seemed likely to develop in that direction. But Lenin foresaw that the misery and suffering caused by the war would eventually open up such possibilities. Above all, he wanted to separate not only from the 'traitors' and 'social chauvinists', but also from the moderate leftists such as Haase and Kautsky. He wanted a split, on the national as well as on the international level, the same as he had brought about in the Russian Social Democratic Party. In his view, Ledebour and his friends were simply wavering between Liebknecht and Kautsky. When Ledebour rejected as unacceptable Lenin's demand that the deputies must vote against the war credits, Lenin was convinced that in fact they held almost the same views as Kautsky; in any case, they were so burdened with the heritage of the past, so much vacillating towards the 'Centre', that they could never be the leaders of a new International.[7] The French trade union leader Alphonse Merrheim put it very clearly at Zimmerwald: the majority wanted a manifesto to promote the cause of peace; Lenin, however, was not dominated by a desire for peace but by the wish to found a new International. They should stress, Merrheim declared, what united them, and not what divided them. Ledebour in his turn objected to the long speeches and recriminations which made them lose sight of their real goal; they were reprimanded for being too legal, but by coming to Zimmerwald they had broken with the legality of their country and the discipline of their party; they would use illegal methods where and when this was necessary, and did not need any lessons on the role of the party.[8]

For the German minority Berta Thalheimer declared that they were entirely willing to use illegal methods and were trying to mobilize the masses, but their most energetic leaders were imprisoned. She claimed that Liebknecht had a large following, 'the whole South German opposition stands behind him' – as she came from Stuttgart where a split had already taken place perhaps not too surprising a statement. In Ernst Meyer's opinion, Lenin and Ledebour understood different things by 'revolutionary struggles'; in Germany the term 'social struggles' was more customary; at the moment, no significant section of the German proletariat was prepared to take actions such as those envisaged by Lenin. Trotsky stressed the great importance of Liebknecht's vote against the war credits which 'had made an enormous impression on the public', but to have an effect it required others to follow suit. To avoid an open split among the delegates Lenin's amendment, which was to bind the participants to vote against the war credits, was withdrawn and the resolution proposed by him was rejected by 19 to 12 votes.[9]

The conference ended with the unanimous adoption of a manifesto which declared that the signatories did not accept 'the principle of national solidarity with the exploiters, but only that of the international solidarity of the proletariat and the class struggle'. They had met to renew the ties of internationalism and to summon the working class to fight for peace, 'for a peace without annexations and indemnities': 'No annexation, neither an open nor a hidden one, nor a compulsory economic incorporation which would become even more unbearable through political enslavement. The self-determination of the peoples must become the indispensable principle for the ordering of international relations... To all those who suffer through the war we call: across the frontiers, ...across the destroyed towns and villages: Working men of all countries, unite!' It was the first time that the slogan of peace without annexations and indemnities was issued by representatives of the French, German, Italian, Polish and Russian socialists, to echo across the trenches and the battlefields. It was equally significant that the French and German representatives issued a common declaration that the chauvinists of each nation were aiming at the conquest of whole countries or parts of countries: if successful this would contain the germs of future wars. They strongly condemned the violation of the neutrality of Belgium and demanded that Belgium be restored 'in its entire integrity and independence'. They renounced the political truce and affirmed their loyalty to the class struggle. The war 'disgraces humanity' and must be brought to a close: '*This war is not our war!*' The declaration was signed by the German Social Democratic deputies Hoffmann and Ledebour and by the French trade unionists Bourderon and Merrheim. Yet when Bourderon at the end of the year, at the congress of the French Socialist Party, moved a resolution which criticized the party leaders and called for greater efforts to bring about peace, it was defeated by 2736 votes to 76, a tiny minority.[10] For the time being, the call emanating from Zimmerwald had largely a symbolic value.

In Germany too, the reaction to the Zimmerwald conference was weak. Only a few opposition groups, especially in Württemberg, passed resolutions of approval. According to a report sent by Mehring to Switzerland in November 1915, this was due to the immature state of the opposition in Germany; they expressed their discontent with the attitude of the SPD majority, but did not have the initiative to take up an independent position and to draw a sharp dividing line between themselves and the party executive; the local minority groups were still 'rather isolated'. Another criticism of the conference was voiced by a radical socialist newspaper, the *Volksfreund* of Brunswick. The paper noticed in the decisions of the conference 'a certain pusillanimity' because they respected the limits observed by 'the rather halfhearted opposition' of the minorities within the German and French parliamentary parties, an opposition that clenched their fists against imperialism 'out of principle', but kept them in their pockets in parliament 'out of discipline'; the conference, while erecting a warning sign against 'the eddies of Bolshevist sectarianism' on the Left, had failed to put up a corresponding sign against the Right, towards 'the fluid frontiers between the opposition and the swamp'.[11]

Difficulties also arose because of the differences among the German radicals. At Zimmerwald, only Borchardt sided with Lenin and the Bolsheviks. Thus after his return to Germany he claimed a kind of leading position which was sharply contested by the followers of Rosa Luxemburg. As Berta Thalheimer informed Grimm in November, Borchardt's following in Berlin was very small, and 'our opposition' there was much stronger and refused to accept him 'as their leader' because they disagreed with him. She also reported that the German opposition was still without a firm basis and consisted of several 'independent currents' without any common ground; no regular contact between the different opposition centres existed so far; it was nonsensical if certain people delegated themselves for international purposes without possessing a firm base.[12] Borchardt in his turn emphasized the differences separating him from the other opposition groups by empowering Lenin, Zinoviev and Radek to receive all communications addressed to him and transferring his vote at the next conference which he did not expect to attend to any of those three who had no other mandate. According to Radek's version, he alone was thus empowered by Borchardt; thus the old quarrel between the Luxemburg circle and Radek found a new focus. At the beginning of 1916 Berta Thalheimer told Grimm that Borchardt rejected any compromise and that an open conflict must be expected. The followers of Ledebour in their turn refused to recognize any other groups 'and thus intend to push us to the wall': Grimm should take a firm line with them, even at the risk of a clash.[13] Deep rifts appeared in the groups of the German 'Zimmerwaldians' – rifts that were to continue right to the end of the war and beyond. Their disunity prevented the formation of a united front against the war and the Imperial government and absorbed the energies of the opposition leaders.

In Britain, the echo evoked by the Zimmerwald conference was even more muted. In September 1915 the ILP was invited by the Italian Socialist Odelino Morgari to appoint delegates to Zimmerwald and two of its leaders, F.W. Jowett and Bruce Glasier, were actually nominated but refused passports by the government. After the conference the National Administrative Council of the ILP declined to appoint a representative to the International Zimmerwald Commission which was to continue the work of the conference – on the grounds that he would be unable to obtain a passport. They also refused to pay any contribution to the Commission although they welcomed the Zimmerwald manifesto and published it in *The Labour Leader*. As the ILP leaders explained to the representatives of the Zimmerwald Commission, they 'disapproved of those passages condemning other Socialist groups for the action they have taken in connection with the war'. They believed that bitter controversy would result from 'any attempt to apportion responsibility or blame among the Socialist Parties'; this would only hinder the efforts to restore peace.[14] The ILP leaders still put their hope in a revival of the Socialist International and were determined to preserve their fraternal relations with the Labour Party as well as the Belgian and French socialists. Their attitude was similar to that of Haase, Bernstein and other moderates in Germany who, for the time being, put the unity of the party above all other considerations.

All that the ILP was willing to do was to affirm its loyalty to the Socialist International and to express its admiration for those on the other side of the trenches who did the same. As its chairman, F.W. Jowett, put it at the annual conference of 1915: 'We hold in profound respect that section of the German Socialist Party which has stood true to the International, as we are trying to do. We send our thanks to Liebknecht and his comrades who are trying to stem the tide of hatred against the British people, and to 'Vorwärts' and the other socialist newspapers likewise engaged...' The Executive Committee of the small British Socialist Party, on the other hand, decided in December 1915 to send the materials issued by the Zimmerwald conference to its local branches and to leave it to them to decide whether the party should join the Zimmerwald Commission. When the large majority voted in favour the party nominated a representative. But as he was unable to reach Switzerland this remained a platonic decision. Some BSP members went further and adopted Lenin's view that the Socialist International was dead and that a new International must be founded.[15] The only major legal European socialist party which fully supported the Zimmerwald movement and adopted its manifesto was the Italian party and its central organ *Avanti*.

While the military situation continued to be favourable the opposition inside Germany was bound to remain small. Any mass action was much more likely to be caused by food and other shortages or by demands for higher wages than by left-wing propaganda. From the beginning of 1915 onwards, indeed, the food situation caused growing concern. As early as January Walther Rathenau from his vantage position in the Prussian Ministry of War wrote to Maximilian Harden that the situation was 'very serious'; five-eighths of the reserves of cereals had been used up; fodder, especially oats, was lacking; it would be necessary to ration bread, and the same ought to be done with potatoes; it was a long time till the harvest, and 'unfortunately we will feel the pinch'.[16] But it was only in the autumn of 1915 that the first food riots occurred in the working-class districts of Berlin, and only during the following winter that food became so short that riots, local disturbances and protest meetings took place in many German towns. There was so little meat that the Prussian Ministry of Agriculture issued a circular pointing out that young crows were a good meat substitute and had a pleasant taste. In spite of the official maximum prices all prices continued to mount, reaching 143 per cent of pre-war prices in 1915, and doubling by the end of 1916. Yet during the whole year of 1915 only 141 strikes took place in Germany, with fewer than 13,000 participants.[17]

Rising food prices and scarcities were beginning to cause political demonstrations and a growing demand for peace. In Berlin several hundred women demonstrated in front of the Reichstag in March 1915 for peace and against the shortages. In May the demonstration was repeated by over a thousand people, mainly women, and the police arrested two dozen demonstrators. Much bigger peace demonstrations took place in November in the fashionable street of Unter den Linden. The crowds shouted for bread and peace, and against the food profiteers, and again there were many arrests. In October a large group of enraged women invaded a meeting of the SPD executive uttering invectives against the 'scamps' and 'knaves'. One of the women voiced their complaints about the high prices which caused deep embitterment among members and non-members of the SPD. 'Above all', she exclaimed, 'it is necessary to gain control of the spontaneous mass movement against dearth, to organize and to lead it. Then it may develop into a powerful popular movement against dearth and for ending the war... The best defence against further price rises is a quick end to the war. We demand from the party leaders that they must do everything to terminate the war...' Throughout the war, the growing food shortages and ever rising prices provided the opposition with ample ammunition, and women remained in the fore-front of the working-class militants. In November the women members of the Stuttgart SPD presented an address to the government that the war had caused enough suffering and sacrifices; without the war, there would be no state of emergency; peace must be sought immediately and was not to be delayed by a single day by demands for annexations.[18]

Anti-war slogans and leaflets began to appear elsewhere. At Dresden small red posters were displayed in the streets on May Day 1915: 'Is the mass murder going to continue? In the name of humanity raise your voices and demand peace! peace! peace!' In the same month a leaflet was distributed in Frankfurt which appealed to working-class women: 'Not the defence of the fatherland, its aggrandisement is the purpose of this war... The workers have nothing to gain from this war, but everything to lose that is dear to them... Down with capitalism which sacrifices hecatombs of men to the wealth and the power of the property owners! Down with the war! Long live socialism!'[19] That the war was not a war of defence but a war for annexations was recognized by many ordinary members of the SPD as well as by some of its parliamentary leaders. At the end of the year Haase declared at a meeting of the parliamentary party that for him the war had been a war of conquest from the first day; he might have been mistaken then, but now no doubt was any longer possible; many old and active comrades were on the verge of leaving the party because they despaired of it. Dittmann emphasized many party comrades were forcefully demanding that the deputies must vote against the war credits because the war had become a war of conquest. Ledebour seconded: in his opinion, the situation was the same as during the Franco-Prussian war of 1870: when, after the battle of Sedan and the collapse of the French Empire, the Prussian plans of annexation became known, Social Democracy protested, and today the same situation existed; it was impossible to support the war effort any longer. That Haase was right about members resigning from the SPD is shown by a police report from Düsseldorf of March 1915 according to which more than a hundred members had left the party, among them comrades of 20 years standing. In party meetings there the Reichstag deputies who voted for the war credits were called traitors and Judases. The local deputy, a moderate, was sharply attacked and stormy scenes took place at the meetings where only Liebknecht's attitude was praised.[20]

In the course of 1915 the clashes inside the SPD became considerably sharper, the opposition demanding that the party change its policy, renounce the political truce and oppose the war credits in parliament. In June the opposition submitted a memorandum to the party executive which severely criticized the policy of 4 August 1914 and the passivity of the SPD since that date. It urged that the SPD should break the political truce and resume the class struggle according to its programme and inaugurate a socialist campaign for peace. The memorandum was signed by 729 functionaries of the SPD; 40 per cent of them came from Berlin and its immediate neighbourhood, and strongly represented were the principal opposition centres, such as Bremen, Brunswick, Düsseldorf, Gotha, Hanau, Stuttgart and several towns of Saxony. In Berlin meetings of the party members and functionaries in several districts sharply attacked the official party policy during the winter of 1914-15. In March a large majority of the delegates to a party conference of the district of Niederbarnim near Berlin condemned the attitude of the parliamentary party and of their local right-wing deputy. In June a party meeting in north Berlin, attended by about 400 people, was addressed by Dr. Duncker who called for an energetic protest against the policy of the party 'which has shown us up before the whole world'. A resolution of no confidence in the party executive was adopted unanimously, as was another which demanded 'bread, freedom and peace'. In the discussion eight members expressed their whole-hearted support for the speaker and demanded above all the lifting of the state of siege. In October a meeting in the working-class district of Neukölln strongly protested against the new vote of the parliamentary party in favour of the war credits which 'once more promotes a lunatic war which is contrary to the interests of the proletariat of all belligerent countries...and to the principles of the Social Democratic Party'; in addition, this vote was taken when the state of siege was smothering any movement in favour of peace and the party members who supported the peace movement were thrown into prison; the minority among the deputies should state the case for socialism publicly in the Reichstag, for the party's principles came before any party discipline.[21]

At Zimmerwald Ledebour reported that on the Lower Rhine, in East Saxony and in Stuttgart the opposition already was the majority. This was correct for Stuttgart, for Düsseldorf on the Lower Rhine and for Leipzig in Saxony, but an overstatement for these areas as a whole. Ledebour further mentioned 'strong opposition' in Frankfurt and Hamburg; but his claim that the opposition would win the majority in the party within three months if free debate were allowed was far too optimistic. Clara Zetkin, too, mentioned Frankfurt and Hamburg as opposition strongholds in a letter to Grimm of April 1915. In Frankfurt, she wrote, 'things are going well and getting better all the time'; Haase had spoken there to the members 'very clearly and sharply'; 70 per cent of those present sided with the opposition and the agitation in the factories was bearing fruit, while at Hamburg too the opposition was growing in strength. But according to a police report of about the same time, it was only 'a small minority' at Frankfurt which favoured the radical tendencies and tried to make life difficult for the local SPD leaders. A meeting of the members in May unanimously accepted a resolution that the workers by their own strength must try and bring about an early peace based on international solidarity, and not based on the suppression of other nations. Similar resolutions were passed by meetings of SPD members at Hanau, Wiesbaden and other towns of the area.[22]

At Brunswick a small conspirative circle was formed by left-wingers against the local party leaders. After a speech by Haase the members passed a resolution in favour of immediate peace without any annexations and of an international proletarian action for peace. At the same time, the local socialist paper demanded the introduction of the equal franchise for the Diet of the duchy: 'the people are allowed to defend the fatherland, but not to have equal rights in it'. As the Diet consisted of a mixture of deputies elected by the three-class franchise and representation of Estates, the Brunswick SPD had a radical tradition which became evident before the war in large popular demonstrations for the equal franchise and in bloody clashes with the authorities. During the war this radical tendency revived strongly and made the town of Brunswick – if not the duchy – a stronghold of the extreme Left.[23]

Early in 1915 a rather worried Kautsky wrote to Adler that party unity was not getting stronger but weaker. A few months earlier the greatest danger to party unity came from the Left, the 'Rosaurians' (meaning the followers of Rosa Luxemburg), now the danger came from the Right, for David and the trade union leaders thought the moment opportune to cleanse the party of all 'Marxism'; they took over one position after the other and for this purpose 'use terrorism with no holds barred'. In June Bernstein, Haase and Kautsky published a manifesto, 'The Demand of the Hour', which for the first time dissociated the authors publicly from the policy of the majority. Pointing to the enormous sacrifices which the war demanded from all the nations involved, the cruelty and devastation caused by it, the bankruptcy that would result from it, they declared that a stronger and stronger longing for peace was coming to the fore among all the belligerent nations: 'while the ruling circles hesitate to fulfil this longing for peace, thousands and ever more thousands look to Social Democracy which used to be considered the party of peace and expect from it the word of delivery... As the plans of conquest have become public knowledge, Social Democracy has gained full freedom to make clear in the most explicit fashion its opposition point of view, and the present situation makes this freedom a duty...' During the same month even the official party leaders protested sharply 'against all tendencies and announcements in favour of the annexation of foreign territories and the violation of other nationalities', as they had appeared in the demands of large economic associations and the speeches of prominent politicians: 'the people do not want annexations, the people want peace!'[24] But this was a mere declaration and was not followed by any action such as voting against the war credits, which alone might have made an impression on the Imperial government.

This passivity led to new angry debates in the SPD parliamentary party, and finally to an open defiance of the party whip. In February 1915 Liebknecht once more declared in the party caucus that the war was not a war of national defence but had 'imperialist causes and aims'. Wolfgang Heine replied that his agitation was caused by enmity towards Germany, that in Berlin conventicles the slogan was coined: 'We desire the defeat of Germany because then we can make a social revolution.' In August Haase moved in the party caucus that Social Democracy decisively rejected the violation of the independence of any nation and any policy of annexation, 'in particular any attempt, in whatever form, to ravish Belgium'. But his motion was rejected by a majority of 59 to 37. A few days later the parliamentary party decided by 68 to 31 votes to approve the new war credits; any abstention, it was added, must not be accompanied by a public demonstration. By December 1915 the number of opponents of the war credits rose to 38, and that of their defenders declined to 58, a significant change. It was then that 20 SPD deputies decided to break party discipline and to vote publicly against the war credits, while 24 more left the hall before the vote was taken. In the name of the dissenters Friedrich Geyer – the SPD leader of Leipzig – read a declaration that peace could only be concluded on the basis that no nation was wronged, that the political and economic independence of every nation must be guaranteed, that all plans of conquest must be renounced; if the war went on Germany and Europe would get impoverished and their culture devastated; Germany, being in a militarily favourable position, must take the first step towards peace. It was impossible for his friends, Geyer added, to support a policy which openly clashed with the interests of the people, which did not try everything to stop 'this unspeakable misery': their determination to bring about peace could not be reconciled with a vote for the war credits.[25]

Liebknecht's comment on the vote and declaration of the 20 was that all depended on what further steps they would take. Only if their future policy was shaped by a determination to renew the class struggle, to destroy as a matter of principle the parliamentary truce, would it be more than a *beau geste*: the 'demand of the hour' was unrelenting opposition in parliament, '*against* the wishes of the majority of the parliamentary party'. He considered that the minority, 'the Men of December 1915', was not a homogeneous group, but an 'oddly assorted group of different elements, a group with such contradictory opinions on theory and tactics, of such different degrees of energy and fortitude, that from the outset they will be unable to carry out together a consequent socialist policy'. In his opinion, 'any policy that adopts the confusing phrase of the defence of the country and makes the support or opposition to the government and the war dependent on the current military situation or on a declaration of war aims, differs only by a lesser degree of consistency from the policy of the majority...' In May 1915 Liebknecht composed a leaflet 'The principal enemy stands at home: German imperialism, the German war party, German secret diplomacy. This enemy the German people must fight, fight in a political struggle, in cooperation with the proletariat of the other countries who must oppose their own imperialists... Stop the genocide!'[26] This leaflet was written in honour of the determined anti-war attitude of the Italian Socialists, on the occasion when Italy entered the war on the side of the Allies. Two months before, in March, the followers of Liebknecht and Luxemburg held their first conference in Berlin, in the absence of Rosa Luxemburg who was in prison for having publicly encouraged disobedience to the law in case of war, many months before its actual outbreak. Present were Liebknecht, Mehring, the two Dunckers, Pieck and representatives from Berlin, Dresden, Düsseldorf, Frankfurt and Stuttgart, the few centres of left-wing influence. Those present were instructed to act as liaison officers for their areas and to establish further contacts. The group was still very small but the first organizational links were established.[27]

The most important decision taken was to publish legally a journal, *Die Internationale*, with articles by the leading left-wingers. Pieck went to Düsseldorf and arranged with the manager of the *Volkszeitung* to print 9,000 copies. In Berlin alone, 5,000 were sold within a few days. Then the authorities stepped in and confiscated what was left and imposed preliminary censorship on any further issue: none appeared while the war lasted. Rosa Luxemburg contributed an article, 'The reconstruction of the International', which contained sharp attacks on Kautsky and emphasized the collapse of the International: 'Never, since there was a history of the class struggle, since there were political parties, has there been a party which dissolved so completely into thin air as a political factor as did German Social Democracy within 24 hours, after a continuous growth through 50 years, after conquering a most powerful position, after winning over many millions... There is only one alternative: either Bethmann Hollweg or Liebknecht, either Imperialism or Socialism as it was understood by Marx...'[28] From that time onwards her followers became known as the Group Internationale.

The members of the group, however, did not resign from the official SPD but worked inside it with the aim of conquering the party; and they cooperated at first with the leaders of the moderate opposition, such as Ledebour or Hoffmann who led the German delegation at Zimmerwald, and even with Haase, in spite of all misgivings about their wavering attitude. The left radicals strongly objected to the declaration of the 20 deputies in parliament in December 1915 which in their opinion was not based on socialist principles. Therefore the Group Internationale, at a conference held in Liebknecht's office on New Year's Day 1916, decided to separate from the moderate oppositionists so as to gain 'freedom of movement in propaganda and agitation'. This time more towns were represented at the conference, among them Berlin, Bremen, Brunswick, Chemnitz, Dresden, Duisburg, Erfurt, Frankfurt, Hamburg, Leipzig and Stuttgart. It was decided to issue underground letters of information. The majority of those present expressed their readiness to face a split of the existing organizations if this should become necessary in the interest of the class struggle, but rejected the proposal of Otto

Rühle to make propaganda for such a split:[29] an issue that was to divide the extreme Left in the years to come.

The moderate oppositionists too felt that cooperation with the radicals was becoming difficult as their views more and more diverged, and decided to separate from them. Thus by the end of 1915 there existed at least two – and counting the fringe groups of the extreme Left more – different opposition groups, increasingly hostile to each other, and the vote of the 20 against the war credits had not helped to heal the breach. Further to the Left than the Group Internationale there was the nucleus of yet another group. At Düsseldorf, revolutionary workers dissatisfied with the passivity of the trade unions in war time, founded a General Workers' Union which had clear syndicalist tendencies. At Bremen, Johann Knief, released from the army, formed an extremist group, the so-called Bremen Left whose views began to influence the local SPD members. Elsewhere, there were mutterings about withholding the party dues from the executive because it used them to fight all radicial opinions, 'and rather to face the worst'.[30] Any such action, of course, would have given to the party bureaucracy the opportunity to expel the opposition and thus to rid themselves of all troublemakers.

In the Reichstag, Liebknecht made use of his independent position to ask awkward questions and to insist on an answer. Ledebour in his turn used the debate on the budget in March 1915 to defend the persecuted national minorities and to pillory the punitive actions decreed by the High Command of the army. The measures taken against the minorities, he averred, were driving the inhabitants of Alsace and Lorraine into the arms of the French and made bitter enemies of the Poles and Danes. If the government suppressed them by its language decrees, its policy was similar to that of the tsarist government; if the slogan 'against tsarism' was to be taken seriously, they should begin by putting their own house in order. The High Command, he stated, because the Russians had burnt a few German villages near Memel, issued an order that for every German village or estate burnt down three Russian villages were to be destroyed. Ledebour's accusation was accompanied by shouts of 'quite right!' from the right-wing parties and the Centre, while Liebknecht shouted 'Barbarism!'. Ledebour's defence was that he merely stated a fact, but he was interrupted by new shouts from the right, 'This is treason!', 'Unheard-of treason!', and the president declared that during the war the actions of the High Command must not be criticized. But even during the war it was possible to publish Ledebour's speech with all the interruptions as a pamphlet because parliamentary debates were not subject to the official censorship.[31]

The authorities were, of course, well aware of the different currents within the SPD. In August 1915 the Prussian Ministry of War informed the subordinate military authorities that the SPD loyally adhered to a forceful, unconditional prosecution of the war, for its leaders had to take account of 'the elementary awakening of the love of the fatherland which so long had been artificially suppressed'; but with the long duration of the war 'the radical, unteachable group around Liebknecht and comrades' was once more raising its head, was promoting war weariness and the longing for peace as well as 'tendentious discussions about war aims'. There were, however, considerable objections to any legal intervention, for any sharp, violent measures against individuals or newspapers would only create martyrs, and the impression must be avoided that such measures were aimed at the party as such; only manifest and provable offences, such as treason, must be ruthlessly dealt with, and in general the authorities must act 'with a certain amount of caution'. In October the Prussian Minister of the Interior accused the SPD in general of not furthering the national consensus: in nearly all its meetings the speakers criticized the difficulties caused by the food shortages and used them to create disaffection and discordance. Yet the minister had to admit that the embitterment against the agrarian producers was no longer confined to socialist circles but affected political parties and organizations friendly to the agrarian interests and wide circles of the general population. Indeed, in Munich and other cities the SPD used the constant increases in the price of milk, bread, meat and beer to organize large protest meetings. Already at the beginning of 1915 the SPD leaders warned the government that they could not preserve the political truce if food prices continued their unchecked rise.[32]

If the authorities still hesitated to take rigorous measures against the left-wing opposition the same did not apply to the German pacifists although their numbers were very small and their propaganda was very subdued, and although the authorities were well aware how small their influence was. In Munich, for example, where Dr Quidde lived, the meetings of the 'Peace Association' in the winter of 1915 were regularly attended by no more than 35 to 55 people, half of them 'ladies'. The speakers, above all Quidde, opposed any policy of annexation, in particular that of Belgium. But he also stated that Russia must be weakened in the peace settlement and that Germany had a duty to protect the Germans of Courland and the Baltic area; in the west, peace should be made under conditions that permitted the peoples to live together.[33] In July Quidde wrote a paper 'Shall we annex?' which was sent to influential people, members of the government and of parliament, but immediately confiscated by order of the military. A longer memorandum, 'Real guarantees of a lasting peace', was printed in 32,000 copies but also confiscated. At the end of 1915 the Berlin branch of the Peace Association was forbidden not only to hold public meetings but even private ones of the members, so that they could only meet socially in a café. Yet even there the police intervened and prevented Quidde from speaking. In November the organ of the association, *Der Völkerfriede*, was banned. In the same month the association held its annual general meeting in Leipzig where only 13 branches were represented, and the annual revenue was given as 15,160 marks, a rather modest sum. There Quidde stated that, as the Pan-Germans and others were clamouring for annexations and distributing their demands *en masse*, the Peace Association could not remain silent. The resolution passed by the meeting once more condemned all annexations, but only 'inside Europe' and if they violated the wishes of the population, and at the same time demanded a peace that guaranteed 'the political, economic and national interests of the German people': terms that could be interpreted in different ways. Soon after the authorities forbade the circulation of any communications to the members of the association and forced it to hand over its membership lists, with the result that the number of its branches and members fell by about half.[34]

The Bund Neues Vaterland, founded in 1914, was subject to even harsher persecution, although it had only about a hundred members but many more influential sympathizers. First it was forbidden to send its publications to non-members and in October 1915 to circulate them to its members, and even to inform them of this prohibition! A few days later its offices were searched and its manager was called up. The manageress was arrested under the provisions of the law on 'protective custody' and only released when she promised to stop all activity. In February 1916 any action to promote the aims of the Bund was forbidden for the duration of the war, as was the circulation of its pamphlets and communications. As Quidde stated in 1917, by these military prohibitions the Bund was 'completely paralyzed'.[35] As this kind of organization was unable to continue in an underground form, it disappeared from the scene until the autumn of 1918. The Prussian authorities were convinced that the activity of these tiny pacifist groups 'often borders on treason because it serves to strengthen the will of resistance of our enemies at the expense of our own' and it 'may finally diminish the firm, unwavering determination to hold out':[36] hence stringent measures must be taken against the peace movement and its leading representatives.

In Britain, 'the cry for peace' was taken up by *The Herald* at the beginning of 1915. The paper confirmed its faith 'in the common people, the common soldier', for on Christmas Day a truce was observed across the trenches and British and German soldiers had fraternized. 'It is our earnest prayer and hope that the Christmas Day spirit will reappear, and in such strength as to end in the speediest way this conflict, which is a disgrace to everything that is good and beautiful in mankind.' In January too, the National Administrative Council of the ILP reported that altogether 124 branches or divisional councils had endorsed its attitude to the war, while only 11 branches expressly dissented. A Scottish Divisional Conference unanimously endorsed the war policy of the party. At a Divisional Conference of London and the southern counties held in the same month 'the pro-war party made a very poor show' and mustered only two votes against a resolution put forward by the City of London branch which severely attacked the participation of the Labour Party in the national recruiting campaign. A motion put forward by the Chiswick branch which justified British intervention in the war on account of the German invasion of Belgium was rejected against only four votes. 'So London and the South appears to be quite "sound"'. In February the annual report of the City of London branch stated: 'It may be taken as a good augury for the future of anti-militarist and democratic ideals that the Branch has never been as prosperous as since it took up an attitude of open hostility to the foreign and military policy of the Government and to the hysterical panic and misrepresentation masquerading as patriotism which seemed to hold undivided sway of the public mind...' Among the new members admitted to the branch in March were H.N. Brailsford and G.D.H. Cole.[37]

At the annual conference of the ILP held at Norwich in April 1915 the party's attitude to the war was discussed on a motion put forward by C.H. Norman of the City of London branch which throughout took a determined stand on the war issue. The motion expressed 'strong disapproval of the action of the Labour Party in taking part in a recruiting campaign, and of ILP members of Parliament speaking from platforms on which attempts were made to justify the war and the foreign policy of the Liberal Government which led to the war'. Norman declared that prominent members of the Labour Party had persuaded 'uninformed audiences that it was their duty to lay down their lives, and this was advice which men who were not themselves fighting ought not to give to other men'. On a card vote the resolution was carried by 243 to nine votes. This was a small minority, but there were differences of opinion among the ILP leaders. At the same conference MacDonald stated: 'Well, the war has got to be finished. It was no use at the present moment talking about a mere "Stop-the-war" movement. They had got first of all to lay down under what conditions the war had to be stopped...' And a few months later he again expressed his scepticism in a private letter: 'We have to peg away quietly... To announce suddenly that there is a party in favour of negotiation now would only have a hardening effect upon public opinion.' In his view and in that of the National Administrative Council, the most effective way was 'to demand that the Allied Governments should say specifically and definitely upon what conditions they are willing to consider peace... Our view is that, if the peoples could get together they would very soon settle the conditions of peace. We do not believe that the German people wish to keep Belgium...'[38] But he did not say how this was to be achieved, how 'the peoples could get together'. In the conditions of 1915 his hope seemed very unrealistic.

Among the rank and file of the ILP more radical opinions were held. At the annual conference a resolution was passed unanimously 'that the ILP should at once take action with the Socialists of other countries to bring the war to a close and to establish the International on a broad, lasting basis'. What was meant by that was explained by Herbert Morrison: to get in touch with German and Austrian Socialists and to 'bring pressure to bear upon the British Government'. As *The Herald* commented, it became obvious that certain leaders of the ILP and its members of parliament 'are not prepared to take their stand either with the Socialist members of the Duma or with Karl Liebknecht and his handful of comrades'; this should have been said clearly, 'for it is well known that J.R. MacDonald has stated more than once that the war must be seen through'. But, the paper claimed, among the delegates at Norwich opinions differed very little: 'they almost to a man are Internationalists pure and simple,' united 'in their determination to end this war as soon as possible'.[39]

During the following weeks these opinions were forcefully expressed in *The Labour Leader* which, under the editorship of the young Fenner Brockway, took a determined stand against the war. There Clifford Allen wrote: 'We cannot and must not be content merely with preparing for a good peace in the dim future. Our business is to make the public realize that an immediate peace is not only important in the interests of humanity, but vital if those very peace terms we favour are to be accepted... It should be the urgent business of the ILP to make its call one for immediate peace... A campaign of a national character should be announced by the NAC; it should not (as now) resolve itself into a haphazard series of branch meetings'. He desired cooperation with other organizations which were opposed to the war and the start of 'one peace campaign'. If Allen's remark about a 'good peace in the dim future' was by implication directed at the Union of Democratic Control, the young Ellen Wilkinson attacked it quite directly: 'To the ardent pacifist it is a tragedy that the advocacy of the cause of peace should be largely represented in Britain by as cautious a body as the UDC. Its "four points" are so admirably moderate and remote that no intelligent person, not quite blinded by party, could honestly disagree with them. Its advocacy of the programme is equally cautious... Many ILPers have felt sadly that it was not thus that the great battles of the workers have been won... Clearly it is time that the ILP took the field again with a bold policy. It cannot surely much longer leave its followers nothing to do but apologize for Arthur Henderson [who had joined the government], or assist at the mild functions of the UDC. It cannot leave the great demand that this mad war should cease, to be made by a handful of well-meaning people without a party to back them...'[40]

For the Union of Democratic Control, Charles Trevelyan addressed the ILP conference on the Union's aims and objects, while MacDonald from the chair gave his support to the campaign against secret diplomacy. But there was criticism from the floor when Trevelyan admitted that UDC speakers were advised not to attack the government and to concentrate on the future and the terms of the eventual peace. Yet he achieved his aim and the ILP became pledged to cooperate with the UDC; many ILP branches supported it locally, and UDC speakers often addressed ILP branches, so that in this way the UDC acquired a comparatively large working-class audience. But it is also recorded that at Cambridge the historians Lowes Dickinson and Eileen Power, president and treasurer respectively of the UDC branch, threatened to resign if the ILP were allowed to affiliate to the UDC. According to Fenner Brockway, its members were 'very much the élite', and their 'little contact with the working class through the ILP' did not make much of an impression on them.[41] It should also be remembered that the majority of the UDC leaders were not socialists, but liberals or radicals, and for that reason alone suspected by many ILP members.

The strongest voices in favour of a more radical policy came from Scotland, where James Maxton and others provided energetic and vigorous leadership. In June 1915 the Scottish Divisional Council of the ILP passed a unanimous resolution that, in joining the coalition government, the Labour Party had violated the principles of independence on which it was founded, that the conditions of the war provided no justification for this step as the class struggle had 'in no way been lessened or mitigated'. The meeting repudiated the action of the Labour Party and then requested the ILP members of parliament to separate from it and to form an opposition party. In Glasgow, in particular, opposition to the war was growing. Every Sunday various socialist organizations held meetings in favour of peace. In October George Lansbury addressed a large meeting where he declared that he was 'a pacifist because war was damnably horrible' and that 'the best way to defeat conscription is for the workers to stand still'. 'There was passionate applause.'[42] Open air meetings were also held in Wigan in the north where it was said 'that the war is simply being waged for the sake of armament rings'. On one occasion a debate was held between the ILP and the Conservatives in which the latter defended the war, but in which the ILP received 'considerable support'. At a May Day meeting in Hyde Park a resolution was adopted 'that the workers of Europe have no quarrel with one another' and 'that the real enemy of the proletariat is the Capitalist Class'. Therefore 'this war shall be brought to a speedy conclusion on such terms of peace as will prevent the repetition of so disastrous a crime against humanity'; a United States of Europe should be established on democratic lines to put an end to 'the present ruinous form of militarism'.[43]

Every week *The Labour Leader* published articles against the war and against conscription. Its circulation increased considerably, amounting to 27,250 at the beginning of 1915. By October it had doubled its pre-war circulation and sold over 40,000 copies, and considerably more during the later years of the war. In August 1915 a strong police force descended on the offices of *The Labour Leader* and the ILP, searched them and confiscated two issues as well as the ILP pamphlets on 'British Militarism' and 'The Causes of the War'. The seized issues became the subject of a police prosecution in Manchester, but the stipendiary magistrate who heard the case dismissed it and ordered the confiscated copies to be returned. Some of the seized pamphlets were also returned but others were ordered to be destroyed. *The Labour Leader* published the result under the heading 'Victory'. Henceforth it was permitted to appear without interference by the authorities. Earlier, the Chief Constable of Norwich had enquired what measures he should take with regard to the annual conference of the ILP in that city. The Home Office replied that he 'should take such precautionary measures as may be necessary for dealing with disorder', otherwise 'as little notice as possible should be taken of the meeting', which was 'not likely to do any great harm'. If, however, attempts were made to suppress it 'the result may be to encourage the enemy'.[44] Although the latter was not very likely, it was certainly a wise course.

When one of the more radical ILP leaders, C.H. Norman, founded a Stop-the-war Committee because the party did so little to terminate the conflict, the authorities decided to check the Committee's mail, but the yield proved rather meagre. They found that the letters addressed to the Committee were very few, mainly expressing approval of its aims and sending small donations, from 5 to 10s. None of the intercepted letters seemed 'to indicate that the writer has anti-British sentiments or that the Committee is in any way inspired or assisted from enemy sources'. Moreover, during the period of the 'check', in July 1915, the number of incoming letters decreased markedly, and the conclusion reached by those responsible for it was 'that the members of the Committee are obtaining very small results for their propaganda and the harm they are causing at the present time is practically negligable' (sic). But there was other interference with ILP meetings in favour of peace. When Norman and another speaker addressed an open air meeting on Hampstead Heath on a Sunday in July, the platform was rushed by the organized opposition. The attackers tried to throw the speakers into the Whitestone Pond, but apparently did not succeed. Thus the Hampstead branches of the ILP and the BSP asked their comrades in other parts of London to assist them on the following Sundays.[45] But it is not recorded how effective that help was. In any case, the attitude taken by the authorities strongly contrasted with that of the German military authorities which were responsible for the censorship of all publications and effectively curtailed the rights of free speech and free association during the war, and in particular that of the pacifist organizations which were suppressed by them.

If the ILP leaders were reluctant to mount an anti-war campaign, on one issue they, and the whole of the British Left, were united – that of conscription. In 1915 the party published a pamphlet, 'The peril of conscription', which clearly stated its case: 'Conscription would degrade the nation, imperil the civic basis of its liberty, and profoundly affect the character and progress of our national life'. It would also completely change the character of the British army which 'has been the least despotic on the part of its officers and the least servile on the part of its ranks of any army in the world... Its voluntary principle has been its saving grace. It has preserved it from the baser forms of corruption and the more brutal tyrannies of the conscript armies abroad.' Conscription, the party feared, would spread militarism to the British shores: this was a war against Prussian militarism, 'and millions of our sons and brothers have volunteered their lives in defence of our land and liberty. Let us not by our feebleness render their sacrifice in vain. Let us see to it that, while they are gone forth to beat back Prussian Militarism from our shores, we do not allow a kindred breed of militarism (for, indeed, all spring from one stock) to lay hold upon our country...' It followed that the writer – and by implication the ILP as such – was willing to support the war against 'Prussian Militarism' as long as militarism and conscription were kept at bay in Britain, as long as 'the civic basis of its liberty' was preserved. Other politicians expressed similar fears. Thus Charles Edward Hobhouse, a Liberal MP stated in a letter to *The Times* in July 1915: 'To alter the fundamental traditions of the country by forcing the conscription system upon it, would be... not only an error, but a crime.'[46] On this issue the ILP could reckon with fairly strong support from different sides, above all from the Labour Party and some trade unions.

In July 1915 the National Administrative Council of the ILP declared 'its unabated opposition to any form of compulsory military service'; its imposition would provide 'a powerful reactionary weapon which would continually menace the future industrial and political developments of democratic institutions. It would also enable the governing class to pursue a foreign policy that would inevitably lead to further wars.' The NAC further declared 'that such compulsory service would gravely imperil the foundations of British civic and political liberty which constitutes the main difference between the British and Continental nations.' The NAC therefore called upon the party members 'to resist to the utmost every attempt to impose Conscription. If, in spite of our efforts, the system is imposed, the members of the NAC pledge themselves to resist its operations...' The NAC also undertook to defend those members who would refuse to do compulsory military service. The declaration was sent to all ILP branches which were instructed to organize public meetings against conscription.[47]

The branches certainly responded with enthusiasm. In July a conference of the Yorkshire branches put on record its 'strongest opposition to compulsory military service' which 'would constitute a grave menace to the progress of the nation' and 'impose upon the British people a yoke which is one of the chief curses of Prussian militarism'. In November the City of London branch organized a public meeting against the 'curse of conscription'. 'It is said', the leaflet stated, 'that Conscription is necessary to avoid defeat: our reply is that Conscription means defeat. It represents a victory for the very institution which we are supposed to be fighting'. The meeting duly condemned conscription 'root and branch'. The Scottish Advisory Council of the Labour Party went further and called for a general strike 'in the event of the Government giving way to the present unscrupulous and unnecessary agitation'. When the opposition proved ineffective and the Military Service Bill was put before parliament early in 1916, *The Herald* pronounced it an 'outrage': 'if it does come, the important thing to note is that it will have no moral or democratic sanction whatever. It will be an act of tyranny as open and shameless as the German invasion of Belgium. The men in Parliament have no mandate to pass or even to consider conscription. They were all elected on quite different issues. If they allow the Cabinet to bully them into what they have no right to do, they will not be representatives of the public but slaves of an oligarchy...'[48]

During January 1916 the campaign against conscription gathered momentum. A delegate conference of the South Wales miners' federation decided by a large majority to call a strike if the bill became law. On the Clyde thousands left their places of work as a sign of protest. The conference of the Labour Party at Bristol declared its opposition to conscription in any form by 1,796,000 to 219,000 votes and passed a resolution against the Military Service Bill by 1,716,000 to 360,000 votes. But a further resolution to pledge the Labour movement to work for its repeal was lost by a small majority, and a large majority approved the party's decision to join the government.[49] In spite of all the opposition, the Military Service Act was passed in February 1916, only 36 MPs voting against it. All unmarried men between the ages of 18 and 41 became liable to military service. Henderson and two other Labour ministers tendered their resignation from the government, but withdrew it when the Prime Minister, Asquith, promised that conscription would not be extended to married men. Their exemption, however, did not last long and was withdrawn as early as April. Yet the threat of large strikes did not materialize. The large majority of the nation as willingly accepted conscription as it accepted the other sacrifices which the war demanded.

But there was industrial action, although of a different kind, and it did not take place in England. The centre of industrial unrest was the Clyde which had a long tradition of labour militancy. As in Germany, food prices were rising swiftly – by the end of March 1916 *The Economist's* Index stood 39 per cent, and, by the end of the year, 47 per cent above the pre-war level (roughly the same as in Germany). But wages failed to rise in proportion, and some of the employers demanded that in the munition factories all trade-union rules should be waved. The employment of women on a large scale created another problem, that of dilution of labour. Few women joined the trade unions, and the skilled craftsmen felt their position threatened by the new arrivals, their privileges undermined by the unskilled. As the union officials supported dilution of labour and were pledged not to take any strike action during the war, power in the workshops on the Clyde almost automatically passed to the shop stewards who were much closer to the men and stood up for them.[50] The most remarkable among them was David Kirkwood, an ILP member, who since 1913 was employed as a toolfitter at Parkhead Forge; previously he had been blacklisted there for his part in the engineers' strike of 1897. After his return, he demanded that only trade unionists should be employed at Parkhead and – after lengthy negotiations with the firm in which he was the workers' chief spokesman – he won his point: an early example of the 'closed shop'. Then he gained an increase in wages of ½d an hour above the local rate for the skilled men in all departments and also took up the cause of the semi-skilled workers. 'Men of his stamp, working in the shops and securing tangible results by direct action, naturally acquired an ascendancy over their fellow workers which the officials of the Trade Union could hardly rival.'[51]

In the autum of 1914 the trained engineers on the Clyde demanded a wage increase of 2d an hour which would have increased their weekly wages to 47s 7d. This demand was turned down by the employers who offered only ½d an hour, in spite of their vast profits on war production. In December Weir's of Glasgow brought over American engineers who received the higher rate plus a considerable bonus. In February 1915 the shop stewards of Weir's called a meeting which decided on an immediate strike. Within a few days the strike was joined by all engineers on the Clyde, some 9,000 men. The Executive of the Amalgamated Society of Engineers in London ordered the men back to work. At a meeting of the shop stewards of the Clyde, Kirkwood challenged the representative of the union who declared the workers' demand ridiculous and urged them to resume work, but the vast majority sided with Kirkwood. This was not a political strike. It lasted two weeks during which the men received no strike pay. As George Lansbury put it, 'there is not a single man of all those refusing to work who would not willingly sacrifice time and labour for the good of the country, and in order to defend the lives of his fellow-countrymen at home and abroad, but they refuse absolutely to allow themselves to be made the tools whereby huge profits may be piled up by profiteers, and their unanimous demand is for the Government itself to take over these armament and shipbuilding yards and control them in the interests of the whole nation...'[52] The strike was settled by a compromise by which the men accepted a wage increase of 1d an hour.

During the strike a committee was elected in each factory consisting of representatives from each department. The central strike committee became a Labour Withholding Committee to escape the penalties of the Defence of the Realm Act which was passed in March 1915 and severely restricted the right to strike. It became known as the Clyde Workers' Committee; most of the members were shop stewards or delegates from the shipbuilding and engineering works. After the end of the strike the committee was kept in being to preserve closer cooperation and to exercise pressure on the union officials. The majority of the leading members, except Kirkwood and Gallacher, belonged to the Socialist Labour Party, a very small local party of politically well educated workers with syndicalist tendencies. Already during the strike a vigorous campaign was waged in Glasgow against increased rents. Every method of propaganda was used to influence the women. In one street after another notices were displayed: 'We are not paying increased rents', and the rents could not be collected. When the owners applied for eviction warrants and the sheriffs were sent to carry out the order, they were met by an army of enraged women who forced them to beat a hasty retreat. Finally, 18 workers were summoned before the Small Debt Court for refusing to pay increased rents. But a mass meeting resolved to call a general strike unless the government restored rents to their pre-war level. In November many thousands congregated in front of the court, and the sheriff adjourned the cases which in the end were dropped. When the government passed the Rent Restriction Act the Clyde workers won a significant victory.[53]

In October 1915 there was another clash with the authorities. Two shipwrights were dismissed by Fairfield's because they stood by while waiting for work, and the workers struck in their support. Under the terms of the Munitions of War Act of July 1915, which forbade munition workers to leave their work places, 17 of them were then brought before a tribunal and each fined £10, or one month in prison if they did not pay. Three of them refused to do so and rather went to prison. But there was strong action in their support. A delegate conference of the unions' district committees represented in the shipbuilding and engineering industry sent an ultimatum to the government that, unless the sentences were remitted, they would go on strike; 'the unrest can only be allayed by immediate action on the part of the Minister of Munitions'. Lloyd George, the minister, thereupon suggested to the unions that they should pay the fines; this was done and the shipwrights were released from prison. The Clyde Workers' Committee had taken action on their behalf, and henceforth it held regular weekly meetings. The success of its actions created a sense of power among its members. Their objects were: to obtain control of the workshop conditions and terms of employment and, in addition, 'to maintain the class struggle until the overthrow of the wages system, the freedom of the workers and the establishment of industrial democracy have been obtained'. There clearly was a strong syndicalist component in this programme, due above all to the direct election of the factory committees by the workers and the working conditions in the few large enterprises on the Clyde. The committee also aimed at workers' control; as it stated at the beginning of 1916, 'all industries and national resources [should] be taken over by the government, not merely "controlled" but taken over completely, and that organized labour should be vested with the right to take part directly and equally with the present managers in the management and administration in every department of industry... It is our fixed determination to force the matter to an issue...'[54]

At Christmas 1915 Lloyd George decided to address the Clyde workers, clearly hoping to sway them by his oratory. The meeting in St Andrew's Hall was chaired by Kirkwood and attended by about 3,000 shop stewards and other delegates. Kirkwood introduced the minister as 'the enemy of the workers' and there were shouts from the hall 'get your hair cut'. The choir singing patriotic songs was drowned by the strains of the Red Flag. Although the committee tried to maintain order the meeting became rather rowdy and, according to Kirkwood, 'ended as a fiasco'. During the last days of the year there was another strike, this time at Beardmore's at Dalmuir when the convener of the shop stewards was dismissed for using improper language to the managers. But the men – probably correctly – assumed that it was due to his activity on their behalf, staged a 'sit-in' strike and demanded his reinstatement. Their leaders too were hauled before a tribunal, found guilty and each fined £5 by the sheriff. But the fines were never paid because the Ministry of Munitions first postponed taking action, and finally dropped the cases altogether.[55]

One of the arbitrators under the Munitions of War Act ascribed the unrest not unnaturally to agitation 'by two or three local Trade Union officials who deliberately and for their own purposes circulated, only too effectively, untrue statements as to the origin of the Act, and garbled and misleading versions of its effect... They came forward as champions of Trade Unionism to oppose the Act, their Union's Executives and General Secretaries having sold they said "the Citadel"...' They feared that the Munitions Act would 'furnish the Employers with a machine that would shatter to its foundations the whole fabric of trade-union liberties and customs'.[56] This was a biased account, but it showed clearly the motives of the leaders of the Clyde Workers' Committee: they felt betrayed by their leaders and thus decided to take action to safeguard their rights. We will find a very similar attitude among the leaders of the Revolutionary Shop Stewards of Berlin in the later years of the war. It was the inevitable outcome of the decision of the trade union leaders to abandon the strike weapon and any other militant action while the war lasted.

There was only one other large strike in 1915, in South Wales, and that too was directed against the Munitions Act. In July 200,000 workers came out because of the large increase in food prices since the beginning of the war, and demanded wage increases of 20 per cent which the employers refused to concede The government issued a proclamation which threatened the strikers with fines not exceeding £5 for every day of the strike, but the strikers defied the Munitions Act. They strongly suspected the employers of 'exploiting the national crisis for personal gain' and, with the support of their union, they were largely successful. Most of their demands were met by the government which induced the employers to accept them. The strike had no political motive. The South Wales miners 'are strongly loyal and patriotic', it was stated by a Commission of Enquiry into Industrial Unrest, and they proved this loyalty by 'the heavy recruiting that took place from their ranks during the early months of the War'.[57] Thus, in Britain as well as in Germany, an earlier and tighter control of food prices and war profits would have eliminated the principal causes of industrial unrest and would have deprived the small groups of the political opposition of their most effective means to make anti-war propaganda. This, however, was a lesson that was learned only very tardily in both countries.

The fight against conscription
in Britain

The passing of the Military Service Acts in the early months of 1916 did not bring to an end the fight against conscription carried on by the ILP and other left-wing organizations. At the annual Easter conference of the ILP a resolution was carried unanimously demanding 'the immediate repeal of the Military Service Act' and declaring 'determined opposition to Conscription in any form'. Another resolution urged that members of parliament should bring greater pressure to bear upon the government in favour of a negotiated peace. Yet the party was divided on the question whether its members should be advised to resist the Act and whether they should be assisted in doing so. One speaker urged that this should be done and that the National Administrative Council should publicly declare its support for those resisting the Act, for 'it was better that the ILP ship should sink in the storm with its flag at full mast rather than that it should keep afloat with its flag at half-mast.' But another speaker stated that this was not the duty of the NAC, but 'a matter for the conscience of the individual'. 'The magnificent machinery of the party' must not be put to risk: an argument closely resembling that of the SPD leaders in August 1914 who wanted to save the imposing edifice of the party with its many newspapers and publishing houses from destruction. In the *Socialist Review* a leading member of the ILP wrote: 'Compulsory military service stands in a category of tyranny by itself and calls for our utmost moral and political resistance.' But a writer in *The Herald* clearly pointed out the dilemma which faced the opponents of the war: 'At least three out of every four men in the fighting line are members of the working class. If Labour... uses its great weapon – the strike – it injures the men of its own class in the trenches; if it does not use its weapon, then it has to give way.'[1]

In these circumstances, the ILP was unable to do more than to organize meetings against conscription and in favour of a 'cessation of hostilities', as the City of London branch did. It also refused to accept members who had participated in the recruiting campaign.[2] In December 1916 R.L. Outhwaite, MP, declared at a meeting in the Caxton Hall that the war was reaching into every household and stretching out in every direction: 'Then I hope that the people in this country will rise up and say, we have had enough of war (great applause), we have had enough of war at any price, we will have peace at any price, we demand that reason shall prevail...' In the same month, the Herald League held an open air meeting at Finsbury Park where the speaker went considerably further. He averred that the war would bring forth 'that great movement of the proletariat which will abolish war and all the misery that war entails, because it will destroy the root of war which is capitalism. So long as you have capitalism you will have war. If there is murder on the battlefield there is also murder on the industrial field... When our masters want blood we will tell them to cut their own throats (Hear, hear). If they want plunder they can go and get it themselves; if they want to fight, let the Kings, Emperors, Presidents, Tsars, Financiers and Manufacturers, let them fight it out among themselves. The workers have no cause to quarrel, the workers of all countries are brothers, our brothers in poverty (great cheers) and in subjection. They have one enemy only, that enemy is the parasite, scoundrelly capitalist gang who use them to further their own base and dishonourable ends...' But there was not only applause at Finsbury Park. According to the police one Sunday morning in January 'the Herald platform was overturned and smashed and the speakers and supporters of the League hounded out of the Park by a large crowd of patriots'. According to the report, the opposition to 'the meetings of the "Peace Cranks" in Finsbury Park' had been aroused by prominent hints in the nationalist press.[3] Yet the meetings continued in spite of the opposition they had mobilized.

How unspontaneous the opposition was also emerged when the National Council for Civil Liberties in November 1916 organized a peace conference at Cardiff, which was attended by several hundred delegates, among them many miners and railwaymen. The 'patriots' first tried to get the conference prohibited, and when this failed they organized counter-demonstrations. When the conference opened nevertheless they forced their way into the hall by smashing the doors and overpowering the stewards. The speakers and chairman were forced off the platform which was occupied by the invaders who carried the

Union Jack and Allied flags. There was 'a very nasty scene wherein many received blows that had brawny fists behind them', and pandemonium reigned. The leaders of the invading gang then spoke briefly, and a resolution was adopted 'pledging the meeting to assist the government to wage war to the bitter end'. The local press could report triumphantly that the 'Peace Cranks' had been routed. At another meeting in Wales Philip Snowden, an ILP member of parliament, was asked why he had not voted against the war credits. He replied that in the House of Commons it took more than one member to force a division against a motion and that a vote of only one or two against the war credits might do more harm than good. But he promised that, if an opportunity arose in future, he would vote against the war credits.[4]

The small British Socialist party too, at its annual conference in April 1916, affirmed its opposition to the war which 'has demonstrated the inability of capitalism to preserve peace among the nations' and its 'unshakeable faith in the international solidarity of the working class'. Hence the party sent fraternal greetings to the workers of the world, and in particular to 'the Socialist minorities of France and Germany who have remained true to the teachings of International Socialism'. It promised to use 'the whole influence of the Party in this country' to bring about the end of 'the present fratricidal struggle'; yet this influence was but small and the resolutions expressing these sentiments were carried against considerable minorities of 12 and 17 votes respectively, with 60 odd voting in favour. True to the spirit of international solidarity, the party welcomed 'the magnificent manifesto' issued by the Zimmerwald Conference and expressed its support for the committee appointed at Zimmerwald which aimed at restoring close relations between the left-wing socialists of the belligerent countries: a pledge that it renewed in 1917. In its active support for the Zimmerwald movement the BSP thus went considerably further than the ILP which still hoped to revive the moribund Socialist International. But the support was somewhat academic because the British government refused to grant a passport to any delegate who wanted to attend an international left-wing conference. Even before the outbreak of the Russian revolution the BSP demanded a peace without any annexations and indemnities, on the basis of the right of national self-determination.[5]

By far the most important and most vigorous organization to oppose conscription and the war was the No-Conscription Fellowship which consisted of young men of military age, to a large extent drawn from the ranks of the ILP, but also of those who refused to do military service on religious grounds, especially the Quakers. By 1915 its membership had grown so much that the Fellowship was able to open an office in London. At the height of its influence it had, according to its former secretary, something like 12,000 members about half of whom were serving sentences of imprisonment. The Military Service Act of 1916 established tribunals which had power to decide upon the claims of the conscientious objectors, to exempt them from combatant service unconditionally or only conditionally, in which case they would have to undertake work 'of national importance'. But the so-called 'absolutists' among the objectors refused to do any work which helped the war effort or released other men for military duty, hence they had to serve long sentences of imprisonment. In many cases the tribunals, only too often composed of men totally unsympathetic to the cause of the applicant, refused to grant any exemption so that he found himself forcibly enlisted and liable to be court-martialled, not only once but repeatedly if he persisted in his refusal. In 1916 the leaders of the Fellowship informed the government that they would not accept service in the proposed Non-Combatant Corps because it was a 'part of the military machine' and they were unable to distinguish between combatant and non-combatant service.[6]

At the first national convention of the No-Conscription Fellowship in November 1915 its president, Clifford Allen, declared that, if the Military Service Bill was passed by parliament, the members would 'resist the operation of that Act', that their National Committee was 'considering the most vigorous possible forms of opposition', that they were willing to suffer 'the penalties that the State may inflict – yes, even death itself – rather than go back upon our conviction'. A few months later Allen's claim to absolute exemption was refused by the local tribunal and he went to prison. Before he was handed over to the military authorities he wrote to a friend: 'This I hope will be the proudest experience of my life. I am glad we Socialists have been involved in this business; it has given the Socialist Movement its great chance. I am confident war will never be made impossible by mere "objecting" on the part of pacifists. We must be positive in this struggle. We have got to make the task of building a new social order so enthralling that the glamour of war will cease to attract...'[7] Many years later, his closest collaborator, who then was the secretary of the Fellowship, Fenner Brockway, said that Allen 'had the most magnetic personality I have ever known'. Allen studied history at Cambridge and there, like so many other students after him, he was converted to socialism. He then founded the University Socialist Federation and became the secretary of the first British Labour daily paper, *The Daily Citizen*, but left the paper in 1914 because of its pro-war attitude.[8] It was the young idealists like Allen and Brockway, both active ILPers, who shaped and dominated the No-Conscription Fellowship and made it a force to be reckoned with.

The No-Conscription Fellowship published its own journal, significantly called *The Tribunal*, which was first printed in London and later, for reasons of security, on a private estate at the foot of Box Hill in Surrey. In June 1916 the offices of the Fellowship were raided by the police who carried away all the 20 to 30,000 copies of the last issue of *The Tribunal*, all pamphlets, circular letters and index cards, the lists of the branches and addresses, records of the members arrested by the military authorities, together with the account books and the money found on the premises. Yet the work of the Fellowship was not interrupted and *The Tribunal* continued to appear. There Fenner Brockway wrote: 'Our opponents may say that it is better to live under home-made militarism than German. We reply that to us, militarism is the enemy, not a particular brand of it.' The Fellowship identified militarism with conscription. As it declared in a leaflet from the same period: 'Conscription means to us the climax of that militarism against which our consciences rebel. It means the subordination of civil life and liberty to military authority. To that, as British citizens, we can never consent...'[9]

In another leaflet the 'absolutists' among the conscientious objectors gave their reasons why they could not accept non-combatant duties or undertake work of national importance instead of military service. 'We cannot distinguish', they declared, 'between fighting and assisting those who fight with duties such as organizing supplies, carrying despatches, clerical military work, etc., for all these are designed to make the work of killing more efficient... We cannot undertake such duties under a military oath which necessitates obedience to all orders and makes us part of the military machine... We have always desired to serve our fellow men, but we cannot allow the Government under a Military Service Act to change our occupation, since there can only be one purpose in this, viz., to make the organization of the nation more efficient for the carrying on of war...' The absolutists, however, were only a minority among the conscientious objectors, numbering perhaps 1500, who had to spend the war years in prison. In March 1919 a leaflet of the Friends' Service Committee stated that 5,600 objectors had been court-martialled. Of the majority, about 3,300 accepted non-combatant service, about 3,000 were engaged in medical or similar work, and about 4,000 in other work considered of national importance.[10]

The principal activity of the branches of the No-Conscription Fellowship was concerned with the cases coming before the tribunals, supporting those who were to appear before them, advising them how to present their case, keeping track of those who were arrested, looking after their dependants, keeping watch at railway stations to see that no objectors were shipped abroad, organizing meetings in support of the cause.[11] Bertrand Russell has described how he spent three weeks in the mining districts of Wales addressing small meetings, where he found the majority of the audience in industrial areas sympathetic and did not suffer any organized interruption, as happened only too often in London. From the central office in London instructions were sent quickly to the branches, and in case of arrest substitutes were available to take over. When all the members of the original committee of the Fellowship had gone to prison a new committee was formed with Russell as the chairman. A special section kept in touch with members of parliament who were opposed to conscription and were willing to assist the Fellowship and the victims of the tribunals. Snowden in particular gave them 'magnificent support', but MacDonald's attitude was more cautious because the Fellowship was breaking the law. Thanks to this help, the Fellowship achieved that the death sentences passed on 34 conscientious objectors who had been shipped to France and persisted there in their refusal of military service, were not carried out.[12] In spite of the open hostility of the military and intermittent police harassment, the Fellowship was never actually suppressed – a small sign of British tolerance in spite of the war and the passion unleashed by it.

When put forcibly into uniform or under detention in military barracks, the conscientious objectors used the opportunity to make propaganda for their views among the soldiers, and often found them surprisingly open-minded. Thus one of the objectors reported in 1916: 'I have preached the gospel of Brotherhood and Internationalism from the workers' point [of view] to them whenever possible. On every occasion they have listened attentively to me, have asked me many questions which troubled them, and at the conclusion almost invariably have said: "You are quite right, it would be a happier world if it could come about."...' Another wrote that the soldiers were all friendly and 'have no illusions about war'. At Winchester barracks the conscientious objectors formed a kind of propaganda team which seems to have been remarkably successful: 'We spent most of our time expounding our view to the soldiers, the only thing we lack is leaflets for distribution, they are all fed up with the army and all wish they were COs, some of them tell me not to put on khaki at all costs...' [13] From the point of view of the military, it might have been better to keep these men outside army barracks, but this result of their action against the members of the Fellowship had probably not occurred to them. Nor had they reckoned with the fact that they would not be able to break the spirit of these determined opponents of war.

On the Clyde, no strike took place when the Military Service Act was passed early in 1916, in spite of repeated threats to that effect. But industrial unrest continued. At the beginning of the year the Glasgow socialist paper *Forward* was suppressed by the authorities. Thereupon the Clyde Workers' Committee issued its own paper, *The Worker*. This too was suppressed after the fourth issue because of an article 'Should the workers arm?' A minute search of the premises was carried out and all documents and correspondence were carried away by the police. The chairman of the Workers' Committee, the editor and the publisher of the paper were imprisoned for 'attempts to cause mutiny, sedition or disaffection among the civilian population, and to impede, delay and restrict the production of war material'. At first bail was refused, but after many thousands had come out on strike they were released on bail. More arrests followed, in particular among the shop stewards of the factories where strikes had occurred in favour of those arrested.[14]

In March a new strike broke out at Beardmore's when the firm refused to concede a claim of the convener of the shop stewards, David Kirkwood, that he should be entitled at any time to leave his job and to visit other parts of the works to see what happened with regard to dilution of labour and to discuss the issue with his colleagues. Men at other works on the Clyde came out in sympathy with the strikers who were refused support by their union. Soon after Kirkwood and five other leaders were arrested and informed that they had been sentenced to deportation under the terms of the Defence of the Realm Act. They were told that they could live wherever they liked as long as they remained five miles outside the Clyde area. On the Clyde the deportation caused deep resentment and new strikes broke out in protest. The reply of the authorities was more arrests and deportations of the leading shop stewards. But the strikes soon collapsed; by the beginning of April fewer than a hundred men were still out. The small number refusing to give in were brought before a General Munitions Tribunal and fined a few pounds each, but two shop stewards who declared their conduct justified, £25 each.[15] Nor was there any militant action when John Maclean was tried in April for sedition and sentenced to three years of penal servitude. Soon after six of the leading shop stewards from Beardmore's and Weir's received sentences of up to 12 months of imprisonment. These sentences and the deportations brought to an end the 'revolt on the Clyde' for the time being. The leadership of the Clyde Workers' Committee passed into the hands of a group of industrial unionists who adhered to the American Industrial Workers of the World and opposed all political action, so that the Clyde Workers' Committee became passive.[16]

At its Easter conference in 1916 the ILP unanimously carried a resolution indignantly protesting against the sentences and deportations and demanding an immediate return of the men thus treated; it was claimed that the deportees were refused jobs everywhere and did not even receive unemployment benefits from their union. But the government demanded from them a written undertaking that they would 'take no part, directly or indirectly, in any stoppage of work or in any action designed to secure a stoppage, or in any other action which is likely in any way to delay or interfere with the manufacture or supply of munitions, or any other work required for the successful prosecution of the war', and that they would ventilate their grievances through the recognized trade union channels. A few of the deportees signed as requested, but the others refused. Kirkwood and three other leaders, however, were, 'in view of their conduct subsequent to deportation and their general character', not even given this opportunity. In February 1917 the Glasgow Trades Council once more protested 'against the continued persecution of David Kirkwood and the other workmen deported' and demanded their unconditional return. It may have been the fear of new labour unrest which led the authorities to relent and to permit the deportees to return, at the end of May 1917. By that time too, the large majority of those sentenced to imprisonment had been released, except Maclean who was released at the end of June.[17]

The 'revolt on the Clyde' remained an isolated affair which found no echo in other parts of the country. No doubt the motives of the movement's leaders were to a large extent political, but it seems very doubtful whether the same was true of the masses of the participants. In any case, strong action by the authorities which deprived the movement of its leaders was sufficient to quell the strikes, at least for the time being.

The same proved to be the case in other parts of the country. In April 1916 30,000 men and women jute workers went on strike at Dundee demanding wage increases of fifteen per cent on account of the rise in the cost of living. The military representatives tried to persuade the strikers to resume work without any conditions, but they declined unless their claim went to an impartial arbitrator who was to take into account the rise in prices and the large profits made by the industry. After five weeks the strikers were 'called up' under the terms of the Military Service Act and thus the strike was broken. In June 5,500 engineers and tradesmen employed by Vickers at Barrow went on strike in protest against dilution of labour – the use of unskilled workers for skilled work. The strike was repudiated by the Amalgamated Society of Engineers. After a few days the men were given an ultimatum that, unless they started work on 1 July, proceedings would be taken against them under the Defence of the Realm and Munitions of War Acts; all public houses were closed and picketing was prohibited. These steps were sufficient to terminate the strike and work was resumed as demanded.[18]

In the summer of 1916 members of the Amalgamated Society of Engineers took the initiative in forming the Sheffield Engineering Shop Stewards' Committee: as their union remained passive, the shop stewards, exactly as on the Clyde, emerged as the workers' leaders. But the movement also had syndicalist aims and aimed at the control of industry by the workers. When a member of the union, Leonard Hargreaves, was conscripted into the army the Shop Stewards' Committee called a mass meeting which decided to strike unless Hargreaves was released within six days. By 15 November 10,000 men were out on strike, and the movement spread to Barrow. It was in effect directed against the enlistment of skilled men in general and was again unsupported by the union. In spite of this, the government was forced to give way. Hargreaves was released and appeared in a mass meeting of the strikers. On the next day the men voted to call off the strike. An agreement was concluded according to which the government introduced a trade cards scheme and the Amalgamated Society of Engineers became entitled to issue certificates to its members exempting them from military service. The shop stewards of Sheffield had challenged the government and won a victory which encouraged them to pursue their aims with greater vigour. Yet it was economic rather than political motives which drove them to take action. The workers' standard of living was declining on account of rising prices, while the industrialists were making large profits out of the war. As the union leaders cooperated with the government and refused to sanction any strike, the initiative passed to new leaders who were trusted by the workers. In 1916 the number of days lost through strikes amounted to four million.[19]

The most militant movement that emerged as a force in 1916 was the No-Conscription Fellowship, the leaders of which belonged to the ILP and which was to a large extent supported by the ILP. This organization had no parallel in any other belligerent country, as the continental countries had known general conscription for many decades. No movement to oppose conscription arose in Germany, and conscientious objection to military service was not recognized there. Those few who refused to obey the call-up were classified as deserters. Even extreme left-wingers, such as Liebknecht or the leaders of the Bremen radicals, became soldiers without offering any resistance and apparently without any scruples of conscience. In Prussia general conscription was introduced during the wars of liberation against the French at the beginning of the nineteenth century – when it was welcomed as an advance over the older system which exempted large sections of the population. This system was never seriously challenged, not even by the leaders of the Left. In Britain, the entire military tradition was completely different and thus opposition to conscription found a comparatively large echo, especially in liberal, radical and non-conformist circles. On this basis the No-Conscription Fellowship could develop and challenge the authority of the government. Its members formed a small, dedicated minority, surrounded by a hostile sea of jingoism, but they stood firm. While unable to start a mass movement against the war, they remained loyal to their ideals.

IV

The split in the German labour movement

In the third year of the war the German people experienced growing shortages of the most essential foods, sharply rising prices and declining real wages; these factors and the mounting casualties of bitter warfare for the first time caused a real change in the mood of the public which had been fed on the hope of swift victory. It has been calculated that, by September 1916, the real wages of the male workers employed in the war industries had dropped by 21.6 per cent; those working in civilian industries had lost as much as 42.1 per cent, while the loss was somewhat smaller for women workers. Although the workers earned more, in particular the women working in war industries, prices rose much faster, as the left-wing deputy Wilhelm Dittmann was not slow to point out in parliament early in 1916.[1] Women received considerably lower wages than men, and even the military authorities at Hanover expressed their concern that women working in the flax and jute factories of Wolfenbüttel earned only about 20 pfennigs an hour so that their weekly wages came to no more than 10 to 11 marks. The military feared that this might cause strikes or that the women might be driven to prostitution – with bad effects for the health of the garrisons of Brunswick and Wolfenbüttel. Yet in his reply the Brunswick director of police ascribed the complaints to the machinations of the textile workers' union the local leader of which was 'a dangerous agitator and follower of the radicals'.[2]

Food prices, especially of all 'luxury items', were rising quickly and this caused deep resentment. At Magdeburg the union leaders told the military in the summer of 1916 that the constantly rising prices had brought about a 'deep disenchantment of the working population'; the workers declared that they were unable to continue work with the small quantities of food available, that they were physically at the end of their strength and threatened to go on strike; the workers' wives were particularly militant, and the union leaders were losing control. The press department of the navy reported that the people were up in arms about the excessive prices demanded by the agrarians and the wholesale traders and could not understand why the authorities did not intervene; that poultry and game remained unrationed caused great indignation and was considered 'an obvious preferment of the well-to-do classes'. The Social Democratic deputy David noted that meat and cheese had disappeared from the shops in Berlin, while fish and poultry cost 'unheard-of' sums; potatoes were in short supply and vegetables too expensive: and that was in September. In December the military authorities reported from Magdeburg that the prices of fish and smoked fish had risen by up to 800 per cent since the beginning of the war and that the prices of vegetables, fruit and oil were 'giddily high'. The fixing of maximum prices for vegetables had come much too late, and in the case of apples it had driven up the price.[3]

The result of the growing food shortage was endless queuing which often started in the early hours of the morning; and even long queuing was not always successful. From Hanover the police reported in May 1916 that the better-to-do were able to get meat as they were old customers, while the poorer people often went home without any in spite of many hours of queuing in bad weather. They were told by the butcher that there was no more meat but could observe that the delivery boy went out with large roasts and whole legs to deliver them to favoured customers. It was only in October that a ration card for meat was introduced which provided for 250 grams of meat, inclusive of bones, per week for adults and half that amount for children.[4] But the poor were hit even more by the terrible potato shortage which was caused by the failure of the harvest in 1916; it amounted to only 23 million tons, less than half that of 1915. As early as June it was reported from Hamburg that hardly any potatoes were available. The small quantities delivered were therefore distributed by the trade unions and none reached the shops. 'War kitchens' were to feed the poorer sections of the population. In July the situation improved and there was even a surplus, but by August the potato shortage returned, and the people were equally embittered about the small fat ration of 90 grams per week. By December the deliveries of potatoes were reduced to such an extent that it was impossible to meet the ration of a pound and a half per day, which was finally reduced to a quarter of a pound, while fish – very important for the diet of Hamburg – was virtually unobtainable.[5]

In Frankfurt the stores of potatoes were almost exhausted by the end of June so that the ration had to be halved, and even this was difficult to get because the shops were empty. The food office organized the distribution from the Main quay where many thousands assembled every day, and even there the supply ran out in July. The unions protested strongly against the 'unjust and badly organized distribution of food, especially of meat', through which the poorer sections often obtained nothing in spite of hours of queuing and which caused 'vast embitterment'. At Kiel because of the potato shortage large demonstrations took place in June which were joined by the dock workers. Even in the Palatinate which produced large quantities of potatoes the towns received such small deliveries that the municipalities did not know what to do; the peasants held back in the hope of higher prices and disregarded the threats of the authorities. In the industrial area around Düsseldorf the mood became so threatening that the authorities feared rioting if the supplies of potatoes for the winter did not arrive before the frost started.[6]

Food riots did occur in many towns. In May 1916 many food shops were plundered in Leipzig during three days of riots; as the police were unable to cope and the crowd vented its wrath on the trams and street lights, infantry and cavalry units were brought into the town and a 'severe state of siege' was proclaimed. At Offenbach women and children demonstrated among shouts of 'We are hungry and demand bread'. At Worms two food shops were looted completely and damage inflicted on others and the town hall. In August thousands of women for several days congregated in front of the town hall of Hamborn; a potato cart was stopped and the police were pelted with stones and potatoes; food shops and vegetable barrows were plundered and shop windows smashed. Food riots in Hamburg during the same month lasted for three days and took a political turn. Large crowds shouted for peace and sang the 'Internationale'. To calm the crowds the authorities distributed bread coupons and fats, many rioters were arrested, and order was re-established with the help of the military.[7] Similar riots occurred in smaller towns in which the bakers' shops were the principal target of infuriated mobs which helped themselves to bread off the ration.

The German people became divided into the hungry and those who had enough to eat. The authorities responsible for food delivieries and rationing were unable to cope with the vested interests of the agrarians and of the federal states which tended to look after the needs of their own population. In parliament the socialist deputy Emanuel Wurm exclaimed: 'Either the interests of powerful agrarian circles or the interests of the community! No compromise is possible between the two.' But the peasants too were infuriated by the visits of the cattle and milk controllers, by the commissions which enforced delivery of grain, milk and cattle, by the bureaucratic regulations which forbade them to kill their own pigs and other animals, by the whole elaborate machinery of the war economy. The fierce attacks of some of the Bavarian peasant leaders on this machinery met with increasing applause; the demands for an early end to the war and the enforced deliveries were well received by peasants who felt that they were no longer the masters on their own farms.[8] The maximum prices and delivery quotas which the authorities imposed caused large quantities of food to be diverted to the black market.

Compared with the vast national enthusiasm of 1914, the political mood changed drastically for the worse. From Speyer the bishop, Michael von Faulhaber, wrote in April 1916 to the Bavarian Minister of Education that, because large sections of the people were tired of the war, he would use his journeys round the diocese to administer the sacrament to preach and to tell the clergy that it was their most urgent duty, from the national as well as the religious point of view, to combat disaffection and the distrust of the peasants in the measures of the political authorities. The police, he added, would have to deal with those who created the distrust and discontent, especially in the large towns where the agitators could not be reached by pastoral means. In the autumn several Bavarian districts reported that the people were tired of the war on account of its long duration and the heavy losses, the dearth and the fear that their investments in war loan would be lost. The strongest expression of these feelings came from the leader of one of the most important agrarian institutions of Bavaria, Dr Georg Heim. In February he informed the military authorities that, according to confirmation from all his sources, the mood among the peasants was deteriorating from day to day; he received 'embittered letters' from those serving in the army, in particular about the maximum prices dictated by the government; a soldier on leave who was returning to the front declared in a train 'Liebknecht is absolutely right', and the other travellers including soldiers agreed with him; the general mood could not be worse. The Bavarian Minister of the Interior told one of his colleagues that large circles did not see why the war must go on; the Balkans, Baghdad and Suez were so far removed from people's vision that they could not fathom the connection between these theatres of war and their economic welfare and that of later generations. In a discussion held in November by the members of the Food Council attached to the Bavarian Ministry of the Interior it was emphasized how urgent it was to counter the widespread opinion that the war was continued 'only in the interest of big capital'.[9]

There were similar reports from other parts of Germany. From Landau in the Palatinate it was reported that the population was very reluctant to subscribe to the new war loan because people feared this would only prolong the war. In Cassel it was noted that the mood was beginning to deteriorate; the peasants in particular were hoarding gold and silver coins and were taking their deposits out of the saving banks because they feared confiscation by the government; soldiers on leave were advising the people not to subscribe to the war loan because then the war would soon be terminated. At Düsseldorf the authorities noticed growing discontent and embitterment 'among the entire population'; the women who had to queue for many hours were painting conditions 'black on black' and recounting the deprivations they and their children had to suffer; only working-class women were to be seen in the queues, but not those wearing good clothes. From Hamburg strong dissatisfaction with the long hours of queuing for goods and official permits was reported.[10]

It was also mentioned frequently that soldiers on leave or in their letters from the front were responsible for this change of mood among the population. They urged their families not to subscribe to the war loans, not to sell cattle for the benefit of the army, or to render some other form of passive resistance, for then the government would have to make peace. Many letters from the front complained about unequal and unjust treatment, about bad and insufficient food, about enormous losses. In February the Bavarian Ministry of War stated that such reports 'about real or alleged injustices...were poisoning the mood of whole localities'.[11] Most of the reports about the bad influence of soldiers come from Bavaria or the Palatinate; but this may only be so because of the vast quantities of reports available in the Bavarian archives on the changing mood of the people, and there are similar reports from other areas of Germany. It was, after all, only natural that the soldiers should exercise a strong influence on their families at home. In October 1916 the Prussian Ministry of War, in its summary of the monthly reports of the district commands, stated that they nearly all noticed a considerable reluctance to subscribe to the new war loan, that this refusal was often seen as a means of shortening the war, and that in some places people even hoped the loan would fail.[12]

The longing for peace soon influenced the German labour movement, and within it led to growing polarization, and eventually to a split in its ranks. In August the executive of the SPD drafted a mass petition to the chancellor the signatories of which demanded an early end to the war 'which for more than two years has devastated Europe and imposed upon all participant countries vast sacrifices of blood and goods'. The government was asked to declare its willingness to conclude a peace renouncing all plans of conquest, on the basis of Germany's political independence, territorial integrity and free economic development. Soon signatures for the petition were collected from house to house; but the military authorities intervened, stopped the collection and confiscated the accompanying leaflets which they considered inflammatory. In Dresden, the SPD organized a peace demonstration in which many workmen, women and children took part. They demanded that the government of Saxony should urge the authorities in Berlin to conclude peace soon, and the demonstration ended with three cheers 'for an early peace'. On May Day leaflets were distributed there with the slogans: 'Finish the war! We demand peace! Long live Socialism! Long live the Workers' International!'[13]

In Stuttgart too, demonstrations against the war took place on May Day 1916. But then the government acted. The leaders of the left radicals were arrested and proceedings started against them for causing a riot. Several of them were conscripted into the army. The socialist youth organization was dissolved. But there were new peace demonstrations in June. During the same month a strike broke out at Brunswick, and the strikers adopted a resolution protesting against 'the pointless prolongation of the war in which the whole community is sacrificed to capitalist interests. An immediate peace is possible if the government renounces all annexations and announces its will to make peace without any reservations. The workers of Brunswick urge the government to do everything to end the war and to promote peace.' A leaflet issued by the Group Internationale – the followers of Liebknecht – headed '*Hunger*' accused the government that its only reply to the hunger riots was the state of siege, the police sabre and the use of the army; the government had started the war in a criminal fashion and now it did nothing to counter starvation, while the capitalists, the Junkers, the food speculators were waxing rich; the Germans had been told that the U-boats would cut off the British supplies and force Britain to sue for peace

– fairy tales for children, for the U-boat war had only increased the number of Germany's enemies; now the people were told that the coming harvest would end the famine – another lie, for in 22 months of war all the reserves and everything 'requisitioned' in the occupied countries was eaten up and nothing more could be expected from that source; the proletarians must refuse to serve this government and these ruling classes: '*Down with the war!*' Another leaflet coming from the same group asserted that the real barrier to peace was the lust for conquests of the governments on both sides of the divide; as the German frontiers were well protected and Germany held many thousands of square miles of enemy territory, was it not for Germany to offer the hand of peace? But no peace was possible as long as the ruling classes intended to retain parts of the conquered lands and to exploit them: 'Down with the policy of annexation and conquest! Immediate peace!'[14] A very different leaflet circulated in the trenches of the western front occupied by a Bavarian regiment. Under the heading 'What cannot be found in the German papers' it claimed that the 'great victory' of the Skagerrak (battle of Jutland) was in reality a British victory, that the German high seas fleet had fled and was bottled up in the ports, that Britain still ruled the seas, while the Russians too had gained notable successes.[15]

If the distributors of underground leaflets were caught they were sentenced to short terms of imprisonment by the courts. If set free at the end of their sentence the military authorities had the power to arrest them anew and to impose sentences of 'protective custody'. The same was the fate of the left-wing journalist Sepp Oerter of Brunswick and of the old socialist historian Mehring because he had expressed himself in an intercepted letter in favour of organizing a peace demonstration in the centre of Berlin. More than 50 left-wing socialists in the Rhineland received a letter from the military warning them not to speak in any public or private meeting and threatening them with arrest and imprisonment if they disregarded the prohibition.[16] Yet these measures failed to stem the left-wing trend in the labour movement; nor do they seem to have impeded the circulation of antiwar leaflets and pamphlets which continued to appear in growing numbers all over the country.

The conflicts within the SPD continued to be dominated by the attitude towards the war and the voting of the war credits. This, however, was not an issue of right versus left, for old 'revisionists', such as Eduard Bernstein and Kurt Eisner, sided with the opponents of the war. As the deputy Heinrich Ströbel pointed out in a private letter, this 'is no accident, for it is the revolt of the spirit against indolent, stupid matter'. At the beginning of 1916 it was reported that, among others, the majority of the SPD functionaries of Greater Berlin, Leipzig and the lower Rhine had passed resolutions criticizing the vote for the war credits by the majority of the parliamentary party. In March Haase sharply attacked those whose war aim was 'the conquest of world power and who for this purpose pursued the most extravagant plans of conquest'. His speech caused furious protests and interruptions from other deputies, not least from the right-wing Social Democrats. The majority of the SPD parliamentary party declared that Haase had committed 'a breach of discipline and of faith'; but 15 other deputies affirmed their solidarity with him and formed the Social Democratic Working Group, with Haase and Ledebour as the chairmen and Dittmann as the secretary. Eighteen deputies voted against the budget and were expelled from the SPD parliamentary party.[17] The split of the parliamentary party was bound to lead to a split of the party itself, for it was supported by several strong local party organizations and some of these decided to stop the transfer of their party dues to the central party funds – thus following the example set by Stuttgart in 1914.

The conflicts were particularly acrimonious in the SPD organizations of Greater Berlin where the local functionaries were adherents of the opposition but the leading officers, many of whom were full-time party or trade union officials, supported the official party policy. Hence the local functionaries aimed at replacing the leading officers by members of the opposition. In this they were successful in July, but an attempt by Rosa Luxemburg to conquer the Berlin party for the extreme Left was defeated. Only a declaration of sympathy with Liebknecht was adopted and some local associations which had stopped paying their party dues to the executive were readmitted. The party organization in the working-class quarter of Neukölln, for example, had stopped any such transfer on the grounds that the leadership 'with its nationalist policy has removed itself from the party'. The same decision was taken by the party organizations of Bremen, of Duisburg because the party executive dismissed two left-wing journalists employed by the party paper, and of Brunswick because the leaders themselves had forfeited their membership by violating 'the principles of the party programme'. The Social Democrats of Brunswick expected from the Social Democratic Working Group that they would vote against all war credits regardless of the military situation and would refuse all taxes to 'the government of the state of siege and the world war', thus indicating their distrust of Haase and the group's moderate leaders. By the end of 1916 the important party organization of Leipzig also withheld its contributions to the central party funds. But its leaders were loyal to the Social Democratic Working Group, and so were other party groups which declared their support for its policy. At Frankfurt, the policy of the party executive was sharply attacked by the opposition and, as its influence increased, the local SPD leaders more and more curtailed all discussions. Therefore the opponents of the war founded a local branch of the Proletarian Freethinkers to be able to meet and to coordinate their activities unobserved.[18]

The adherents of the Left more and more argued among themselves whether it was possible, or even desirable, to preserve the unity of the party – a party which in their opinion had betrayed its principles and with which they had little in common. At the beginning of 1916 Rühle, who with Liebknecht had early on voted against the war credits, wrote that he would not promote a party split but would sigh with relief when it happened, for only then would a clear, decisive struggle for socialist aims become possible; he must reject the 'bog' and 'pulp' of a united party which was a 'bog' without any principles and any backbone. The radical socialist paper of Duisburg declared that it would be 'dishonest and pointless' to remain in the same party with the National Social party leaders: that would inflict the most severe damage on the socialist movement. Kautsky informed Adler that it was only the Social Democratic Working Group which still held the party together; without its foundation, Berlin would have been conquered by Liebknecht's followers; as all reports from the front confirmed, he was today 'the most popular man in the trenches'; his followers believed that the growth of the opposition inside the SPD was too slow and thus they wanted to quit, a move more than welcome to the leaders of the party and of the unions.[19] It was thus only a question of time until the split of the party would be carried through on the national level, for Kautsky's plan of conquering it from inside was quite unrealistic in the conditions of the state of siege and the war.

In the course of 1916 the name of Liebknecht indeed became the symbol of resistance to the war. At the beginning of the year he declared in a meeting of the parliamentary party that the 'real sin' of the majority was not the voting of the war credits, but the preservation of the political truce; this violated 'the most elementary principles of Social Democracy', and he felt obliged to conduct on his own initiative a policy as it was demanded by socialist principles. This he proceeded to do. For the evening of May Day 1916 his followers called an anti-war demonstration for 'bread, freedom, peace!' to a square in the centre of Berlin. Several thousand assembled, but so did the police in full force. When they tried to disperse the crowd Liebknecht shouted 'Down with the war! Down with the government!' and was immediately arrested; whereupon there were new shouts 'Long live Liebknecht!' which were followed by more arrests. The demonstrators continued to shout 'Down with the war!' 'Long live the International!' and 'Peace!' until the police finally succeeded in dispersing them. At the end of June Liebknecht was tried for treason and sentenced to two and a half years of penal servitude. As he had been called up for military service, the trial took place before a military court. On an appeal by the prosecution a higher military court increased the sentence to four years and one month. In court Liebknecht declared that it was his aim to work for the defeat of all the imperialist governments and ruling classes by the masses of the people. 'I stand here to accuse, not – to defend myself. Not political truce, but war is my slogan. Down with the war! Down with the government!'[20]

The trial of Liebknecht brought about the first political strike of the war, but it was not led by the Group Internationale. On the day before the trial, the local leaders of the Berlin metal workers' union who were strong left-wingers called reliable shop stewards to a large meeting. From this they selected a small number who were informed by Richard Müller, the leader of the turners' branch, that action was to be taken on the following day: the workers should demonstrate in front of the military court. In about 40 armament works 55,000 men came out on strike, led by the turners and other skilled workmen. Among shouts of 'Long live Liebknecht!' and 'Long live peace!' they marched through the streets of Berlin in perfect discipline. The Bavarian Minister of War was even informed that many streets of the working-class quarters were completely blocked and the police were powerless: 'these were harbingers of revolution'. Although calls for a strike were posted up in many towns of Germany the strike was limited to Berlin and Brunswick. There Liebknecht's followers called a 'general strike', a call that was obeyed by about 60 per cent of the workers in 65 factories. The strikers declared their solidarity with Liebknecht and protested against the lack of freedom under the state of siege, the dearth of food and the preliminary censorship imposed upon their paper, the *Volksfreund*. Their strike lasted only one day, that in Berlin two days.[21]

Demonstrations in honour of Liebknecht and in protest against the verdict also occurred in other towns. Those at Bremen continued for

several days; the crowds marched to the city centre among shouts of
'Down with the government!' 'Down with the war!' The workers
dominated the principal streets until driven off by the police. Other
demonstrations took place at Essen, Hamburg and Stuttgart. But the
crowds demonstrating for peace numbered hundreds rather than
thousands, and the demonstrations remained limited to a few large
towns, principally the old centres of the Left. A socialist deputy who
knew Liebknecht well summed up his opinion a few days after the
arrest: 'Whether L. has acted intelligently or stupidly only history will
tell. I would have been more cautious... It is possible that L. emerges
triumphantly from the affair, possible too that he will be crushed by
force and leave prison a broken man... Among the working masses L. is
by far the most popular man, and that includes the soldiers; and he has
honestly earned this popularity by his consistency and his bravery...'[22]

Some years later one of the founder members of the Group
Internationale described its beginnings: 'A small propaganda group, led
by the head of Rosa Luxemburg, held together by the will of Leo
Jogiches, with no other mouthpiece than a little paper...' (strangely
enough omitting the vital role of Karl Liebknecht). Jogiches was the life-
long friend and mentor of Rosa Luxemburg and came from the same
Polish-Jewish background; like her, he made his home in Germany. The
'little paper' was called *Spartacus*, first published illegally in September
1916 and then at irregular intervals during the war years. The editors
deliberately chose the name of the leader of the revolt of the Roman
slaves of the first century BC as their symbol, and the name of the paper
became that of the group which became known as the Spartacus Group.
With Liebknecht and Luxemburg in prison, Jogiches, Ernst Meyer,
Franz Mehring, Paul Levi and others became the leaders of the group
which remained small and to a large extent consisted of intellectuals.
According to different estimates it had a few hundred or a few thousand
members, and the second figure may well be an overstatement. In
Charlottenburg and Moabit, working-class districts of Berlin, the local
Spartacus Group consisted of seven activists, and one of their functions
was to copy by hand (!) articles from *Spartacus* because its edition was so
small that they never got enough copies. At a conference for the districts
of Hesse and Hesse-Nassau in October 1916 about 40 people were
present, most of them from Frankfurt and Hanau.[23] Many of the
members came from the socialist youth organizations. Active groups
existed above all in old left-wing strongholds such as Berlin, Brunswick
and Stuttgart.

A Spartacus conference held early in 1916 adopted a set of 'guidelines' which were drafted by Rosa Luxemburg. They boldly declared that 'the Second International has been shattered by the war', for it had been unable to build an effective dam against national fragmentation, nor had it adopted common tactics and actions (against the war): hence a new workers' International must be created to coordinate the revolutionary struggle against imperialism and to issue directives to the member parties. A second conference took place in March; it was attended by 34 'delegates', half of them from Berlin and the others representing about a dozen German towns. A few more expressed their agreement in writing. The conference showed how weak was the organizational basis of the Spartacus Group. It nevertheless called for starting 'revolutionary mass actions on a large scale' which should have political content and aim and be fashioned 'into conscious attacks against the war and capitalist class rule'; 'the attack must be undertaken all along the line.' It was announced at the conference that in Berlin the opposition had already split, and discontent was expressed 'with the passivity of the parliamentary " opposition" (in the Reichstag)'.[24]

The differences within the opposition in Berlin centred around several points. The 'moderates', such as the deputies Ledebour and Hoffmann, opposed the 'guidelines' of Rosa Luxemburg which called for the foundation of a new International. They aimed at winning the majority within the SPD through the delegates at a party conference: until then all differences within the opposition should be toned down. The Spartacists, on the other hand, insisted on 'clarity first' and on sharply criticizing the meekness of the 'moderates'; in their opinion, such criticism would serve to strengthen the whole movement. In letters to leading oppositionists Franz Mehring wrote that their views had not approximated but developed more and more apart, therefore separation became not only necessary but a positive gain. In 1915 there had been cooperation between the two wings of the opposition, and members of the Group Internationale wrote leaflets and articles for the 'moderates'; but they had the sad experience that the latter's course swerved further and further to the right, with the aim of winning over waverers such as Haase. Mehring had then made another attempt at bringing about unity and a joint meeting took place, but the 'moderates' insisted on concessions he was unable to make: 'for the time being unity is impossible'. He admitted, however, that the polemics against the Social Democratic Working Group had at times gone too far, and that in this respect Liebknecht – before his arrest – was the main culprit.[25]

At the international socialist conference at Kiental in Switzerland in April 1916 Adolph Hoffmann declared in clear opposition to Rosa Luxemburg's 'guidelines': 'We are not the Third International, we are nothing but a rump parliament. We need not be afraid of a meeting of the International Socialist Bureau. Don't make Scheidemann bigger than he is. Do you really believe that he is an agent of the German government? No, such stupid people who themselves offer their services get a kick in the pants when they cease to be useful...' Hoffmann's view was sharply attacked by Lenin who declared that the split in the sections of the old International was a fact; the people with whom the moderates wanted to resurrect the International 'have died, they are no longer alive, not literally but politically'. The manifesto issued by the conference on May Day 1916 demanded an immediate peace, without any annexations, and called on all socialist deputies to vote in future against the war credits. 'The governments are to know that in all countries the hatred of war and the will to social vengeance are growing, and then the hour of peace among the nations will approach. Down with the war!' The participants were convinced that peace could only be obtained by revolutionary means; mass movements must be organized against high prices and the policies of the reactionary governments. The mood at Kiental was considerably more radical than it had been at the Zimmerwald conference.[26] Yet Hoffmann was surely right that the foundation of the Third International was totally premature, for all over Europe the left opposition was still weak and fragmented, and there was no real unity among its various components. The same was still the case when the new International was finally founded in Moscow three years later, in March 1919, but this fact guaranteed its domination by the one victorious party of the extreme Left, the Russian Bolsheviks.

In September 1916 Jogiches sent a circular to the Spartacus groups which stressed the 'sharp differences' separating them from the Social Democratic Working Group, such as the role of mass actions, the question of the war credits which the Working Group wanted to raise through direct taxes, the issue of the defence of the country, and that of the rights and duties of the International towards the member parties. These differences also emerged at Kiental. There Hoffmann stated that a common front of the opponents of the war was urgently required, but that in the Spartacists' opinion the other oppositionists must be defeated first: they treated them as worse enemies than the SPD leaders. It was essential, he added, to win the masses for the fight against the war;

but the demonstrations which had taken place before the split in the ranks of the opposition were far more successful than the later ones. Paul Frölich from Bremen emphasized the differences in the question of defence on which the extreme Left demanded a clear and sharp definition, while the 'moderates' took a pacifist line, only voted against the war credits 'because today the frontiers of Germany are secure' and thus misled the workers. Naturally, the SPD executive rejoiced about these conflicts in the camp of the opposition, and in particular about the Spartacus attacks on the 'soft animals' of the Social Democratic Working Group. In general they pilloried the Spartacist anti-war propaganda as being grist to the mill of Germany's enemies; the German workers in the trenches would have to pay with blood for 'these unheard-of allegations of so-called Social Democrats'.[27] The Spartacists were a tiny minority, but they were the most determined opponents of the war, and their propaganda influenced larger circles.

Smaller still was another group which had its centre at Bremen and stood to the left of the Spartacists. Its members called themselves the International Socialists of Germany, but more usually they were called the Left Radicals or the Bremen Left. Their leader was Johann Knief, a radical journalist, who was in close contact with Karl Radek in Switzerland and through him with the exiled Bolshevik leaders. Making a virtue out of necessity Knief held that, although the proletarian movement was a mass movement, the initiative to the mass actions of the future could come from small, and even from minute groups. At the meeting of extreme-left delegates in Berlin at the beginning of 1916 he criticized the Spartacists for their lack of a firm aim: the aim must be to break not only with the SPD leaders, but also with the 'moderate' oppositionists and to prepare for 'the creation of a revolutionary party'. In the *Bremer Bürger-Zeitung* he stated curtly in May: 'The split will and must come.' When the left-wing Bremen deputy Henke replied that it was most important to achieve 'unity on the Left', Knief's reply was that unity with 'social imperialists' was out of the question. At a meeting of the Bremen party organization Henke was sharply attacked for his ambivalent attitude, for his cooperation with the 'moderates' around Haase who offered no guarantee that they would ever conduct a real working-class policy: it was necessary to break with them. But the leaders of the 'Bremen Left' also criticized the Spartacists for not following a clear line on the issue of Germany's defence and for being uncritical of the British ILP and the Russian Mensheviks. In their opinion, the SPD had collapsed in August 1914 and the most important task was to achieve 'clarity' and to draw sharp lines of demarcation.[28]

As the Left Radicals were no longer able to air their views in the columns of the *Bremer Bürger-Zeitung*, they issued, in the summer of 1916, their own journal, *Arbeiterpolitik*, which continued to be published legally during the war years. One of its most regular contributors was Radek who sent his weekly articles from his Swiss exile, in spite of the censorship, by simply writing on the envelope in large letters 'Please don't delay, manuscript, subject to local press censorship'. According to Knief's judgement, without Radek the *Arbeiterpolitik* would never have become what it was in the eyes of its supporters; without his weekly articles it could have 'packed up'. There Radek time and again preached the necessity of a split. It was an 'historical necessity' and also directly useful to the workers' cause; a reconstruction of the International would only be possible after the separation from the 'social imperialists'. Radek stated that the German working-class movement was divided into three parts: the 'social imperialists', the 'centre', and the 'left radicals', thus completely ignoring the Spartacists or simply lumping them together with the 'centre'; if the latter constituted themselves as an independent party they would sooner or later be ground to pieces between the upper and the nether millstones of the Right and the Left.[29] No wonder that the Spartacists declined to collaborate with the new journal: the old enmity between Radek and Rosa Luxemburg revived. A Spartacist from Saxony withdrew his cooperation when Paul Frölich, one of the Bremen leaders, published an article demanding a breach with the reformist trade unions, which in the eyes of the other left-wingers were particularly important in wartime.

At the international socialist conference at Kiental in April 1916 Frölich, amidst great hilarity, attacked the views of the Spartacists and Rosa Luxemburg. But he earned the approval of Lenin who stated that only the 'Left Radicals' had a clear and precise point of view. Lenin, too, found fault with the *Junius* pamphlet of Rosa Luxemburg – written in prison and published illegally under that pseudonym – because it did not draw a clear dividing line against the 'centre' the members of which were, in his opinion, afraid to issue revolutionary slogans. To Lenin, 'the largest defect of revolutionary Marxism in Germany' was the lack of 'a firm illegal organization systematically pursuing its way': in other words, there were no German Bolsheviks.[30] This assessment was certainly correct. There were the old differences between Lenin and Luxemburg on the principles of the organization of the revolutionary party which had come to the fore as early as 1905, and the *Junius* pamphlet said nothing about organizational issues, a topic always of paramount importance to Lenin. It sharply analyzed 'The Crisis of Social Democracy' (its correct title), but it put forward no recipe for revolutionary organization or action. Throughout, the principal activity of the Spartacus Group was to make propaganda against the war and against the Imperial government, but not to organize a revolution.

During 1916 there were many strikes, but the majority were for higher wages and had no political purpose. Their main cause was the shortage of the most essential foodstuffs. Although the number of strikes rose by only 70 per cent, the number of strikers increased tenfold compared with 1915 and reached 124,000. Strikes were particularly noticeable among the dockyard workers of the large ports and among the miners of the Ruhr. In June the workers of the Germania and other yards at Kiel came out on account of the potato shortage, but they resumed work when additional rations were provided from naval stores, after a few bakers' shops had been looted. In July a large strike occurred at Bremen in which about half the workers of the Weser dockyards took part. As the Bremen police reported, the strike took place against the wishes of the union leaders who lost control of their members. In October it was the turn of the dockyard workers of Hamburg who demanded higher wages. They remained inside the docks without doing any work and thus forced the management to make concessions. Work was resumed by them on the second day.[31]

In August there were the first larger stoppages in the mines of the districts of Düsseldorf, Arnsberg and Münster, caused by severe food shortages, especially of fat without which, the miners declared, they were unable to work. They complained that their wages had not risen in comparison with the prices and that the authorities did too little to curb inflation. The management promised to provide, if possible, one pound of bacon a week for every miner, and this was sufficient to end the strike. But in October new strikes broke out on account of the potato and fat shortages. In November munition workers in the district of Düsseldorf demanded a wage increase of 100 per cent but were eventually satisfied with 50 per cent for Sunday work and some other concessions. About 20 'radical socialist agitators' were called up and some other ringleaders dismissed. The most remarkable strike, however, was organized by the young workers of Brunswick against a decree issued by the commanding general of the Tenth Army Corps which prescribed that minors were to receive only 16 marks of their weekly wages; any higher wages were to be paid by the employers into a savings account in the name of the minor in question who would only be entitled to use it on reaching the age of 21 or at the end of the war. Thereupon the young workers of Brunswick decided to stop work on May Day and demonstrated in the streets, supported by many women. Windows were smashed and two shops looted. During the following days the strike spread, many young women participated, and the military authorities promised that the savings decree would be mitigated. But the young strikers rejected any compromise solution. Serious clashes occurred with the police, which was then replaced by military units including cavalry. After a heated discussion the trade unions decided to support the strike unless the decree was rescinded, and this was done on 6 May. The commanding general resigned, and many of the young strikers were conscripted.[32] They had won a success but at considerable cost. Brunswick was one of the very few industrial centres where the Spartacists had strong influence, especially too among the socialist youth movement. It clearly was an exceptional case.

Meanwhile the military authorities continued their campaign against the German pacifists. The bookshop of the Peace Society at Stuttgart was closed and any activity in support of its aims prohibited; its journal was suppressed. In Berlin several women were put on trial and fined because they had distributed a message from the Archbishop of Canterbury which condemned wars and power politics and urged reconciliation. In the summer of 1916 several prominent pacifists, such as Quidde, Eduard Bernstein, Gustav Landauer, Helene Stöcker and the well-known historian Max Lehmann, founded a new organization, the Zentralstelle Völkerrecht. It was opposed to a peace of annexations and force as well as to a war to the bitter end; the aim should be a 'peaceful organization of Europe and the rest of the civilized world, excluding antagonistic power alliances' and the oppression of one nation by another; Belgium should be restored, foreign policy be controlled by parliament and disarmament be carried out on an international basis. In this sense the new society petitioned parliament, but its efforts produced no effect.[33] In contrast with the Peace Society, the Zentralstelle Völkerrecht was permitted to continue its activities on a modest scale. It was hardly dangerous from the point of view of the authorities and never acquired a large membership.

The number of activists on the extreme Left also remained very small, and its growth was held back by internal bickering and infighting, rather than by the ponderous measures of the authorities. In 1916, there existed – apart from the SPD to which the majority of the workers continued to adhere – five different groups on the Left: the moderate oppositionists – people like Haase and Bernstein who were pacifists and not revolutionaries – the left-wingers such as Ledebour and Hoffmann who supported the Zimmerwald movement, the Spartacists, and the Left Radicals of Bremen and some other north German towns. And there were the radical shop stewards of Berlin who were able to bring the workers out on strike for political purposes: a feat which none of the other groups was able to achieve. The foundation of the Social Democratic Working Group was the logical outcome of the dispute over the voting of the war credits, but it did nothing to unite the opposition or to abate the political and personal conflicts between its various components – conflicts that were to bedevil the history of the following years. In 1917, however, the Left was to receive a vital impetus, not only by the continuation of the war, the mounting casualties and food shortages, but above all by the outbreak of the Russian revolution.

V

The impact of the Russian Revolution

The outbreak of the Russian revolution in March 1917 had immediate repercussions in Germany. The overthrow of a mighty empire which had been one of the principal enemies was bound to awake in Germany expectations of an early peace and ultimate victory – hopes that were soon to be disappointed, for the new Russian government continued the war on the side of the Allies. But on the German Left quite different hopes were aroused: after all, might it not be possible to achieve in Germany what had been done in Russia? If the Russian tsar could be humbled what about his German counterpart? If the old order were to crumble could not peace be concluded and the misery of the war be brought to an end? When, soon after the victory of the revolution, the Soviet of Petrograd took up the slogan of 'peace without annexations and indemnities' this slogan found a ready echo among the war-weary and starving masses of central Europe. They had no stake in German imperialist goals and wanted the war to end as quickly as possible.

The reports of the commanders of the military districts clearly showed the effect of the Russian revolution. From Hamburg it was succinctly reported early in April: 'The wind has carried across the seeds of the weeds, and there are many indications that they sprout in many places.' The Württemberg Ministry of War noted that the news of the part played by the Russian workers influenced the German workers who believed that they could strengthen their position considerably in the factories and increase their influence on the government; the employers were often told by the workers when they put forward their demands that they would follow the Russian example; remarks could be heard in the trams and pubs that the munition workers would stop work if their demands were not met and peace was not concluded. But the

Ministry did not consider these utterances dangerous and did not fear any unrest 'in view of the sober...character of the Swabian workers'. The Bavarian military authorities reported at the same time that the miners were influenced by the currents from Russia, that in pubs frequented by Social Democrats people made remarks referring to these events, to an understanding with the Russian and French socialists, to strikes and riots in Germany; the mood in Bavaria, the report added, also deteriorated because of the ever growing shortage of beer.[1]

From other parts of Bavaria – his railway journeys in Franconia, Swabia and Upper Bavaria – a professor reported that middle-aged men with a Munich dialect were starting political talks on the trains and in the waiting rooms along the lines 'Why subscribe to war loan', 'Those on top must go', 'The Russian people, they know better'; such talks dominated whole compartments and anti-monarchical sentiment was 'in the air'. An informant from Upper Bavaria confirmed the propaganda against the war loan: 'The war has brought us the food shortages; as soon as it is over they will come to an end; thus we must force the bigwigs to make peace! They have enough to eat...' The Saxon Minister of the Interior, also in April, noted the 'mounting irritation' of the population on account of the shortages, but equally caused by 'the political changes in the Russian Empire the effects of which on restless spirits outside Russia are unmistakable'. At a meeting of strikers in Leipzig one speaker exclaimed: 'In the East the blazing flame of the revolution shines while the German workers bend under the yoke'; he urged the strikers to form a workers' council so that the people would go to 'the right forge'. In the same month the authorities reported from Magdeburg that the Russian revolution provided 'a powerful impetus' to all those who desired a democratic transformation of the Prussian constitution and administration. And at Danzig the military found that the success of the Russian revolution reinforced the hostility towards the fatherland of all those inclined to revolt: 'hunger is a powerful agitator', as proved by the mass demonstrations in the town.[2]

Similar tendencies were observed in the summer of 1917. In the area of Magdeburg, according to the military authorities, 'the people have become very susceptible to radical socialist influences, and their ultimate aim is the overthrow of all existing institutions, especially of the monarchy' – tendencies inspired by the course of the Russian revolution. In Baden, it was stated, the general mood became 'greatly excited' on account of the revolution, and there was a lot of talk that similar measures ought to be taken in Germany, France and Britain;

'democratic and republican phrases' were much in vogue, even in patriotic circles. In general, the 'Büro für Sozialpolitik' in Berlin noticed that 'the sympathy with the Russian people and its revolution' was expressed time and again; people emphasized how regrettable it would be if the revolution should end 'in blood and dirt'.[3] The Spartacists printed leaflets expressing their solidarity with the Russian revolution: 'The victory of our Russian brothers is our victory, a victory of the international proletariat which even in wartime has remained loyal to the idea of international fraternization... The revolution has triumphed in Russia, in its sign we too will gain victory when our turn comes!' Another Spartacist leaflet praised the Russian workers' and soldiers' council which had issued an appeal for peace without annexations and indemnities, on the basis of free national self-determination; the new Russia would only continue the war until Germany renounced the rape and exploitation of foreign countries.[4] An ingenious way of spreading revolutionary propaganda was found by printing or writing in indelible ink on paper money 'Follow the Russian example, then we will have peace', 'No peace without revolution', or 'Long live the revolution, down with the war', so that the authorities had to withdraw the notes carrying such slogans. In Berlin demonstrations of solidarity with the Russian revolution took place, among shouts of 'Long live the revolution' and 'Down with the war!', and the deputy Ledebour made a speech welcoming the revolution.[5]

From her prison cell Rosa Luxemburg wrote to a friend in April: 'The wonderful events in Russia affect me like an elixir. What comes from there brings for all of us great tidings of joy. I fear that all of you underestimate it, do not realize sufficiently that it is our own cause that is victorious there... I am absolutely certain that a new epoch is starting now and that the war cannot last much longer.' Another prominent Spartacist exclaimed among strong applause: 'If the red flag flutters above the Winter Palace of Petrograd we see in it a symbol in the sign of which we call to the Russian proletarians: we will do the same!' In April too, the mayor of Düsseldorf reported that the success of the Russian revolution was inspiring the large section of the working class which had revolutionary and internationalist convictions so that political discontent was on the increase.[6]

Enthusiasm for the Russian revolution was not limited to the extreme Left. Even the very moderate opposition leader Haase declared at the foundation conference of the Independent Social Democratic Party (USPD) at Easter 1917: 'The storms of March blow through the world.

The dawn of freedom shines across the Russian frontiers into this hall. We are full of admiration for our Russian brothers fighting for peace and freedom.' The parliamentary group which had split from the SPD a few months before sent greetings to the Russian socialists hailing 'the decisive rising of the Russian proletariat' and its victory over despotism which inaugurated 'the liberation not only of Russia, but of all mankind from the blight of the war'. Addressing the chancellor in parliament Haase added that it was dangerous to wait with constitutional reform: did he not notice the rising tide of protest? Did he want to risk 'that the masses in Germany talk Russian?' Another left-wing deputy declared that it was the duty of the German socialists to demonstrate their sympathy with Russia and to follow their example so as to obtain an early peace. The *Leipziger Volkszeitung* wrote as early as March that in Russia, in spite of the war, a revolutionary people had broken the chains of centuries of servitude, while in Germany – the country of the 'best organized working class' – nothing was gained but 'soft murmurs of ministerial reform promises which sound like the responses of the Delphic oracle'.[7]

Approval of the revolutionary events in Russia was not only expressed by the left-wing opposition. The leaders and executive of the official SPD, too, went on record expressing their sympathy. In April the party executive declared: 'We salute with passionate accord the victory of the Russian revolution and the revival due to it of international efforts to bring about peace. We declare our consent to the decision of the congress of the Russian Workers' and Soldiers' Councils to prepare a general peace settlement without annexations and indemnities, on the basis of the free national development of all nations. We consider it therefore the most important duty of the German Social Democratic Party and of the socialists in all countries to oppose the power dreams of an ambitious chauvinism, to urge the government to renounce all policies of conquest and to bring about as soon as possible on this basis decisive peace negotiations...' Even earlier Scheidemann wrote in the central party organ, *Vorwärts*, (in a clear allusion to Germany) that in China the mandarins had forcefully opposed any reform; they wanted an absolute emperor as long as he did what he was asked to do, and thus they undermined the monarchy and laid the foundations of a republic. The article continued: 'The clock shows five minutes to twelve', and the chancellor intended to start reforms in Prussia after the war; for that time various reforms had also been promised in Russia, but for the Russians the war lasted too long and the more they suffered from hunger the more intolerable the delay seemed to them. They were saying: if bread and potatoes cannot be obtained by all, what hinders us to give to everybody at least equal rights? Now was the time to take action. In parliament too, the Social Democrats urged the government to do everything to bring the war to a speedy end and 'to accept the peace formula of the Russian provisional government, no annexations and no indemnities, in its essential parts'.[8]

Curiously enough, the attitude of the SPD leaders did not even change after the Bolshevik revolution. A few days later *Vorwärts* commented that the new Russian government suggested an immediate armistice on all fronts: 'We German Social Democrats do not see in the Russian Bolsheviks men whose theories are right in every detail and whose methods can be applied to every country; but we see in them socialists and comrades, and therefore we gladly recognize that their first deed after seizing power is positively worthy of socialism.' Even the extremely moderate party leader Ebert stated in large public meetings amidst thunderous applause that the victory of the Russian Soviets was a victory for peace; the German workers would consider it 'their honourable duty to support the struggle of the Russian revolution and to strengthen the success of democracy (*sic*) with all their power'. Elsewhere Ebert emphasized that the German Social Democrats had established close contact with their Russian comrades and that the latter were overjoyed 'that we in Germany help them with such mass demonstrations'. It was the duty of the SPD, he continued, 'to do everything to ease the struggle of the Russian revolution and of Russian democracy, to strengthen it in its fight for peace and to support it...' Again Ebert's words met with the strong approval of the thousands of people assembled in the hall.[9] In retrospect these sentences may seem strange, but they can perhaps be explained by the powerful longing for peace and by the hope that the Bolshevik revolution would bring peace at least with Russia, and perhaps also by the presence of many radical young socialists in the audience who, according to the police, had come 'to create a scandal'.

That the slogan of 'peace without annexations and indemnities' which was issued by the Soviet of Petrograd found such a strong echo in Germany was due to the great longing for peace which permeated the whole country and was not limited to any social class. The syndic of the University of Munich, who on his daily railway journeys into town had ample occasion to listen to the ordinary people, heard them express the general opinion that 'annexations and indemnities are nonsense', that only Social Democracy could bring peace; the people were putting their 'devout hope' in the international socialist conference which was to meet in Stockholm on the initiative of the Russian Soviet; they believed that the war was caused by big 'capital' against which the nations must finally make front. He added that the people who talked in this way were not Social Democrats, but simple folk from small places, the descendants of peasants and living among peasants.[10] From Bayreuth the senior military officer confirmed that the peasants of the area desired peace at any price and were, contrary to their former attitude, accessible to socialist propaganda. In the Reichstag these sentiments were voiced by Haase: in Russia half-a-million workers had demonstrated for peace; on one of the flags carried by the demonstrators a Russian worker was pictured holding out his hand to a German worker with the words 'Comrade, make haste!' 'That is the call which goes out from Russia to the masses in Germany and Austria, to the masses in France, Britain and Italy, and only if the masses make haste will we be able to reach the goal of our longing – the end of this frightful war. ... The governments do not bring peace, only the people can do so.'[11]

At its foundation conference in 1917 the Independent Social Democratic Party issued a manifesto which once more expressed admiration for the Russian workers 'to whom we owe it that the stronger bulwark of reaction, tsarism, has collapsed... The Russian proletarians have fought for democracy, for the opening of the road to socialism, and also for peace, for the early end of this most terrible of all wars... We demand a peace through an understanding between the nations, without direct or hidden annexations, on the basis of the self-determination of the nations, with an international limitation of armaments and obligatory courts of arbitration...' The executive of the SPD, too, declared that the Russian revolution offered a possibility to establish contact which must not be ignored, that the slogan of peace without annexations and indemnities should be accepted by the German government as the basis of a general peace, otherwise Russia would continue to fight on the side of the Entente. That the slogan was not only taken up by the executives of the Social Democratic parties but had penetrated to the ordinary workers, is shown by its repetition by the striking workers of a large munition works in Berlin-Lichtenberg in April 1917; and they elected a workers' council which alone was to be entitled to negotiate. When the senior officer of Stettin in the same month received a workers' deputation from the dockyards he was horrified to find them strongly defending a peace without annexations and indemnities. When he countered by pointing out to them that without an indemnity Germany was bound to collapse, they replied that the other nations were in the same boat, and even more so if they were forced to pay an indemnity to a victorious Germany.[12]

The initiative for the calling of an international socialist conference to Stockholm came to a large extent from the Russian Soviets, especially those of Petrograd. Their aim was 'to unite all forces of the international proletariat to obtain a peace without annexations and indemnities, on the basis of the right of self-determination'. In contrast with the Zimmerwald movement, Stockholm was to bring together not only socialists opposed to the war, but also those who hitherto had supported their governments in war-time – provided that they accepted the Russian formula and agreed to abide by the decisions of the conference and to support them in their own country. The German government permitted not only the leaders of the SPD to go to Stockholm – among them Ebert, Scheidemann and the trade union leader Legien – but also a delegation of the newly founded USPD, among them Haase, Bernstein and Kautsky. One Social Democratic journal commented that, of the nine-man delegation of the SPD, eight were of working-class origin, but considered it strange that the USPD sent four delegates who were Jewish academics and a fifth (Kautsky) who was of German-Czech origin: for tactical reasons and because of the likely effect in Germany, the journal stated, it would have been better if the USPD had sent a less one-sidedly composed delegation.[13]

Yet the planned international conference did not materialize because the French and British delegates failed to reach Stockholm, partly because their governments refused to grant them passports, partly because they were unable to secure a passage. The British War Cabinet decided, instead of allowing representatives of the ILP to go to Stockholm, to send a reliable Labour Party delegation 'who would represent our national aims in this war in their right light'; but the president of the seamen's union refused to permit any delegates to travel there on ships manned by members of his union. The absence of delegations from the Allied countries made the conference abortive. Even before this became clear Haase was far from optimistic. At best, he thought, the conference would provide 'a broad basis for the Social Democrats of all varieties and shades who are unable to do anything effective for peace and will divide once more at the first opportunity'. In his opinion, the followers of Scheidemann had learnt nothing from the developments in Russia; they acted as the apologists of the German government and as if they were carrying out its instructions; thus they 'unveil our whole political misery; but how can the peace movement be advanced by that?' Bernstein, on the other hand, who used the opportunity of his journey to Stockholm to write to MacDonald, thought that the cause of peace could not be promoted by anti-war minorities and socialists from neutral countries, but only through 'an understanding of the mass of socialists in all countries. Had the Stockholm conference come to pass we should, I am sure [have] achieved a good step in this direction.'[14]

In Stockholm the SPD leaders were asked a number of very precise questions and their answers revealed to what extent they still defended the policy of the German government. It is true that they declared themselves as requested against all annexations and indemnities and for the restitution of an independent Belgium. But they also demanded the return of the colonies 'torn' from Germany, and they were only willing to recognize the right of self-determination for parts of the former Russian Empire, such as Congress Poland and Finland – thus not for the Polish provinces of Prussia – and not for Alsace and Lorraine, to which France in their opinion had no 'historical right' and which by the peace of 1871 had regained their 'original political status', so that the return of the two provinces to France would be 'nothing but an annexation'. In Stockholm, the Zimmerwald movement – in view of the failure of the planned general conference – held its own third international meeting which was only attended by the delegates of the left-wing minorities, among them the USPD. The manifesto issued by it repudiated isolated strikes in individual countries and called for 'mass actions of the international proletariat, in every factory... and every hut'. One of the few who opposed the call for mass strikes was Haase because he feared to make a promise that he would not be able to keep.[15] As far as international socialist action was concerned he was proved right by events, but for Germany his fears were unjustified as the great strike movement of January 1918 was to prove; but this had no repercussion in an Allied country.

After the victory of the Bolshevik revolution the USPD hailed it as 'an event of world-historical importance'. The party hoped that another winter campaign would be unnecessary, but this hope would not be fulfilled if the German workers remained the passive spectators of events in Russia: the German plans of annexation formed an obstacle to peace and therefore mass demonstrations for a peace without annexations must be organized everywhere. Yet the announced meetings in honour of the Russian revolution and the Soviet peace initiative were prohibited in Berlin, as were demonstrations in other towns. In spite of the prohibition demonstrations took place in Berlin and elsewhere among shouts of 'Down with the war' and 'Long live Liebknecht'; they were forcibly dissolved by the police. The SPD organ *Vorwärts* commented: as the whole nation agreed with the demonstrators that peace should be concluded, there was no reason to classify such manifestations as 'dangerous'; they were merely the reflection of great events; if similar demonstrations occurred in Paris or London, if the general desire for peace exercised an equal influence there, 'then it will not be long until we have Peace!' At Dresden a mass meeting organized by the SPD adopted a resolution hailing 'the achievements of the workers in the Russian revolution', wishing them further success in their difficult task, assuring them of German solidarity and demanding 'an immediate armistice for the preparation of a democratic peace'.[16]

It was in vain that Lenin and Trotsky appealed to the German 'soldiers and brothers' to assist them 'in the struggle for an immediate peace and socialism'; in vain did they quote the 'great example' of Karl Liebknecht and call for an 'international socialist revolution'. The German army advanced further and further into Russia, and the German government insisted on separating the Ukraine from Russia and on concluding a separate peace with an 'independent' Ukrainian government. This policy Ebert at the beginning of 1918 called 'a great illusion' of the Imperial government. He believed that it was essential to continue the negotiations with the Bolsheviks – which had broken down at Brest-Litovsk – for it would be impossible to reach the peace desired by the German government with the Ukrainians. But if peace in the East failed to materialize that would give to the Entente powers ample opportunities for propaganda, especially in the neutral countries.[17] Peace was finally concluded at Brest-Litovsk, but it was a dictated peace, a peace of the victors. Yet when the peace treaty with Soviet Russia was voted on in the Reichstag, only the small group of the USPD voted against it, while the SPD – in spite of all its earlier protestations about annexations – only abstained, on the flimsy grounds that the treaty was bringing peace in the East. This was a very dubious argument, for severe fighting between red and white Russian armies continued, and soon the German army of occupation was heavily involved in it.

During the early months of 1918 there were some more declarations of sympathy with the Bolsheviks, but they were few in number and they came from left-wing members of the USPD, where such sympathies might be expected. Thus the deputy Henke called the Bolsheviks his model and 'fighters for peace'; he had always held that during a transitional period the proletariat must exercise a dictatorship; the dictated peace of Brest-Litovsk would convince the workers that in such questions there existed only an 'either or'; the 'preconditions for a social revolution' were much better in Germany than in Russia, and there it would triumph too. In Munich another USPD functionary declared that at Brest-Litovsk Lenin and Trotsky had succeeded in hoodwinking Germany and had been able to demonstrate their aims to the whole world. The USPD leaders once more emphasized that the class-conscious workers of Germany would support the Bolsheviks in their efforts to realize socialism and would oppose any hostile intervention by capitalist governments with all the means at their disposal.[18] At the beginning of 1918 the *Spartacus Letters* stated that the precondition of success for the Russian revolution was the rising of the proletariat in Britain, France, Italy, and above all in Germany, and then a general peace would have followed; but if the revolution remained limited to one country, while in the other countries the workers followed a bourgeois course, the action of the revolutionary *avant-garde* would be turned upside down; therefore the international effect of the Russian revolution was an 'immense strengthening of the power of German imperialism', and for that the German proletariat must be held responsible.[19]

In assessing the effect of the Russian revolution the Prussian Minister of the Interior stated early in 1918 that in all countries the radical parties had become conscious of their greater power; in Germany, the right-wing and the left-wing Social Democrats reacted to the events 'with a greatly increased sense of their own power': not that they became more inclined to use political force, but the conviction grew stronger than ever that democratic demands would carry the day, that they would be fulfilled as a matter of course; even in wide bourgeois circles it was recognized that, in view of the developments in Russia, a democratic change had become inevitable in Germany. In the opinion of the minister, this applied above all to the introduction of the equal franchise in Prussia, 'the demand that links the Social Democratic leaders most intimately to the masses,... the banner under which Social Democracy has fought the elections for decades. The equal franchise is wanted by every Social Democrat, every worker...'[20] This was a very shrewd observation as far as the two Social Democratic parties were concerned. It was only on the extreme Left that the Russian revolution caused a desire to emulate the Russian example, and for the time being the extreme Left was powerless.

In Britain, too, the outbreak of the Russian revolution was enthusiastically hailed by the political Left. The tone was set by Bertrand Russell in March 1917 in the *Tribunal*, the organ of the No-Conscription Fellowship: 'All lovers of liberty should rejoice in the overthrow of an ancient, corrupt and cruel tyranny. The fear of Tsardom has been one of the main incentives to militarism in Germany, and the disappearance of Tsardom is certain, in the long run, to promote German Liberalism and Socialism at the expense of the Junker. There is hope at last of a better Europe; a beginning has been made in the East; it is for us in the West to claim the same rights as are being won by our brave comrades in Russia.' A few days later *The Labour Leader* too mentioned the likely effect of the revolution on Germany, for in the German parliament 'our comrade Herr Ledebour' had rejoiced in the overthrow of tsarism and stressed that the great events in Russia made it all the more urgent for the Germans to fight 'their own bureaucratic absolutism'. In *The Herald* George Lansbury classified the revolution as 'the biggest event of the war': 'if our comrades succeed in establishing a Social Democratic Republic, it will be the most momentous event in the history of our time.' He called on socialists of all countries to unite 'to put an end to all this misery' and to secure the calling of a real international conference which would, 'by mutual consideration and concession', end the war and establish 'the law and spirit of comradeship and love'. And he quoted the concluding words of the *Communist Manifesto*: 'Workers of all countries, unite. You have nothing to lose but your chains. You have a world to gain.' At the beginning of April the National Council of the ILP and its members of parliament sent to Russia their congratulations 'on the magnificent achievement of the Russian people in the long struggle against serfdom, official tyranny and persecution'. They were convinced, they declared, that the Russian revolution 'will everywhere help forward the cause of the people and of socialism and of international solidarity, and will hasten the coming of peace, based not on the dominance of militarists and of diplomats, but on democracy and justice.'[21] The British Left had always been uneasy about the alliance with a reactionary government. The Russian revolution removed this obstacle and seemed at the same time to open the road to peace.

But enthusiasm for the Russian revolution went considerably further. In early April a mass meeting to welcome the revolution was organized at the Albert Hall and there Lansbury, among prolonged applause, exclaimed that in Petrograd for the first time in modern history 'soldiers, working-class soldiers, have refused to fire on the workers'; in Russia, they had learnt the lesson, 'the greatest lesson of all,... and it is for us to learn it now – because we can understand that when the working classes of all nations refuse to shoot down the working classes of other countries, Governments won't be able to make wars any more. (Tremendous applause.)' Another speaker, A. Bellamy, declared that the meeting not only hailed the Russian revolution, but the beginning of revolution in Britain. There was more enthusiasm when an ILP member of parliament, W.C. Anderson, stated that the revolution was going to spread rapidly, 'the effect is going to be felt in every country'. But the strange irony was, he continued, that while freedom was forging ahead in Russia, it became more and more restricted at home: 'all freedom of the subject, freedom of conscience, of thought' had suffered during the war; 'you have got to ask for the government of the nation *for* the people *by* the people.' The secretary of the Transport Workers' Federation, Robert Williams, stressed that in Britain, Germany and the whole world an honourable and lasting peace could be gained if other countries followed the example of Russia. One member of the audience later described the meeting: 'It was like the dawn. It was a marvellous feeling... It was more like a revivalist meeting in some ways... This probably meant the beginning of the end of the war.' A serving soldier who was also present in the Albert Hall felt that 'the fiery speeches' impressed upon them 'that the Russian revolution was not going to stop at the Russian frontier', that it was going 'to find an echo in the hearts of the German, French and British proletariat'. He noticed the same enthusiasm some weeks later at the May Day demonstration in London: 'it found its motto in the "bloodred banner" that we all saw, inscribed with the international device "Workers of all countries, unite!"; it found the approval of the people in the cheers for Russia, for Liebknecht, for the German Social Democratic Minority, for Peace.'[22]

From its annual Easter conference the ILP once more sent to Russia 'its enthusiastic congratulations on the establishment after long, sustained and courageous struggle, of a politically free nation and the overthrow of the evil reactionary forces that centred round Tsarism;... it records its conviction that such a revolution cannot fail to change the whole face of Europe and hasten the coming of democracy and the growth of wider freedom in every land...' The seconder of the motion stated that in Britain 'the oppression they had to strive against was the capitalist', and not oppression by the monarchy; if Britain 'was to be a worthy companion of a free Russia', any such imposition must be destroyed. In parliament MacDonald pleaded that the Russian revolution should be supported by Britain. Yet when he wrote to the Petrograd Soviet in June his letter was rather cool and he had very little to say about the Russian revolution. With regard to the Soviet formula of no annexations and no indemnities, he observed that the Russians would 'have to go further and consider in detail some of the more outstanding problems which the war has compelled Europe to face'; the claims of the nations which wished to become independent should be established and supported; for the meeting of the Socialist International the basis of an agreement should be drawn up 'which free men of good will' could accept and defend. The ILP intended to send MacDonald and Jowett as delegates to Russia, and for this purpose (but not for the Stockholm conference) the British government was willing to give them passports. Yet the two delegates were prevented from sailing by the veto of the seamen's union which objected to the Russian formula of 'no indemnities' because it demanded compensation for the dependents of victims of German naval actions, and MacDonald had to send a letter of apology to Petrograd.[23]

The annual conference of the British Socialist Party in April also recorded 'its profound admiration for the revolutionary initiative and energy with which the Russian working classes... have affected a stupendous political transformation of their country'. In its opinion, the revolution heralded 'the rebirth of the International and its revolt against the unending slaughter brought about by the Imperialist rivalries of the ruling cliques'. The BSP pledged itself 'to act in the spirit of the Russian Revolution' and to fight 'the despotism and militarism which are growing up in this country'. The party chairman, Sam Farrow, in his opening address went further and asserted that 'the evil spell cast upon the world by the war' was broken and that imperialism had received 'a mortal blow'. But even he had to admit that the German working class 'is still paralyzed by fear' – although in his opinion the spell was rapidly disappearing. The National Peace Council was considerably more cautious and only recorded 'its gratification of the recent political changes in Russia and its cordial welcome of that great nation to the ranks of free and democratic countries'. The Council also welcomed the declarations of the Russian provisional government and of President Wilson that the United States had no quarrel with the German people: on the basis of these two declarations an early effort ought to be made to achieve peace through negotiation.[24]

As in Germany, it was the slogan of peace without annexations and indemnities which caught the imagination of many ardent socialists, and not only theirs. The Scottish Advisory Council of the Labour Party adopted it with a large majority at its annual conference, and at the same time demanded that the party's representatives should leave the coalition government. In Glasgow and other Scottish towns great demonstrations took place under the slogans 'Down with the war', 'Immediate peace' and 'Long live Free Russia'. With a very small majority the annual conference of the Labour Party decided to send a delegation to the Stockholm peace conference, but at the same time voted not to allow any separate delegations to the ILP and the BSP (which were both affiliated to the Labour Party), thus attempting to exclude the Left from participation. Williams of the Transport Workers' Federation claimed that the voice of the workers would be increasingly heard in favour of peace: 'Those who caused the war cannot bring about peace... We desire the help of the German and Austrian Socialists just as they need ours...' At a public meeting at Woolwich in July 1917 Snowden, referring to the Stockholm conference, declared that, if the government should refuse to take notice of the peace terms formulated there, the Russian example must be followed – a remark which caused such enthusiasm that he was unable to continue for three or four minutes. According to Snowden, the ILP had always favoured the policy of no annexations and no indemnities; the revolution would come to England 'as sure as the sun sets', and the workers must redouble their efforts to achieve that goal; there was 'complete sympathy' between the ILP and the ideas of the Russian revolution.[25]

Some months later Lansbury spoke at Leicester in a very similar vein. He urged his audience to act in the spirit of the Commune of Paris of 1871; the failure of the Russian revolution to bring about general peace was principally due to the lack of help it received from British democrats: the only way to gain peace was for the common people to demand it, and Britain must lead the way towards it. The question seems to have been raised whether his speech gave any grounds for persecution, for a minute was added to the file: 'Sympathetic references to the Paris Commune of 1871 & the Russian revolution would not of course be in themselves illegal. Unless measures are to be taken for suppressing Pacifist propaganda of the ILP type...' Apparently, no such measures were contemplated. At a meeting in the town hall of Birmingham in September 1917 the leader of the Transport Workers' Federation, Tom Mann, exclaimed: 'I have been an advocate for a revolution for this country for the last 30 years; Russia is doing it, how much longer are we going to wait?' And at an ILP meeting in the same city a soldier on leave, according to the police, went further: 'Why don't you people start the revolution? You are too peaceful, look at Russia. You do not care what life you sacrifice, all the manhood is gone.' Yet few actions followed all these revolutionary declarations, and one of Lansbury's correspondents quite rightly wrote to him that it was time 'for the leaders of British Labour to tell us how to act'.[26]

Yet there was some action, but it took a rather curious form. In August 1916 the ILP and the BSP, which was a much smaller but avowedly Marxist party, set up a United Socialist Council, and in June 1917 this Council organized the Leeds Convention in honour of the Russian revolution. It was attended by many prominent pacifist and socialist leaders and altogether by 1150 delegates, among them nearly 300 from the ILP and almost 90 from the BSP, and also 580 sent by trade unions and trade councils, among the latter those of Glasgow, Leeds and Sheffield. At Leeds MacDonald declared: 'Today we congratulated the Russians without any reservations whatever. We do it not because the Revolution has happened, but because for years we wanted it to happen... Now the Russian Revolution has given you the chance to take the initiative yourselves. Let us lay down our terms, make our own proclamations, establish our own diplomacy, see to it that we have our own international meetings...' The Convention received fraternal greetings from the Executive Committee of the Russian Soviets who wired that they hoped to meet the representatives sent from Britain in July: a telegram received with great enthusiasm. On foreign policy a resolution was adopted which pledged the delegates to work 'for the reestablishment of a general peace which shall not tend towards either domination by or over any nation, or the seizure of their national possessions, or the violent usurpation of their territories – a peace without annexations or indemnities and based on the rights of nations to decide their own affairs'. The British government was urged to announce its agreement with the war aims of the Russian provisional government. Snowden emphasized that it was time to tell the government 'what are *our* conditions of peace'.[27]

If the Leeds Convention meant to moderates like MacDonald and Snowden a step towards a negotiated peace, others were prepared to speak in much more radical terms. Amid great applause Robert Williams exclaimed that parliament had done nothing for the people during the war and would not do anything for them; if the Russian revolutionaries had respected the constitution of Holy Russia, the Romanovs would still sit on their throne; if they were really sincere with their greetings sent to Russia they must take action like the Russians and establish the dictatorship of the proletariat: 'We want to assert our right to the ownership and control of the country... We are competent to speak in the name of our own class, and damn the Constitution. (Loud cheers.)' An ILP member of parliament, W.C. Anderson, moved a resolution: 'This Conference calls upon the constituent bodies at once to establish in every town, urban and rural district, Councils of Workmens' and Soldiers' Delegates for initiating and co-ordinating working-class activity... and to work strenuously for a peace made by the peoples of the various countries, and for the complete political and economic emancipation of international labour.' Anderson added: 'If a revolution be the conquest of power by an hitherto disinherited class, if revolution be that we are not going to put up in the future with what we have put up with in the past, we are not going to have the shams and the poverty of the past, then the sooner we have a revolution in this country the better.' The tasks of these British 'Soviets' enumerated in the resolution were: to note and 'resist every encroachment upon industrial and civil liberty', to support trade union work and to safeguard the position of women workers, to take steps to stop the racketeering in food and other necessities, to take up questions such as the pensions of disabled soldiers, their training for civilian occupations, and the maintenance grants paid to dependants of serving soldiers. All these, however, were social rather than political tasks, and they had nothing to do with an intended take-over of power. A provisional committee consisting of the conveners of the conference was appointed to promote the formation of local workers' and soldiers' councils. But nothing was done to enrol soldiers in them, or to carry the campaign for their formation into the army. As Snowden, one of the members of the committee, wrote later: 'When the committee which had organized the conference met afterwards, we considered it unnecessary to carry out the proposal.'[28] It was a very strange 'Soviet' campaign.

In truth, the political situation in Britain was so entirely different from the turmoil prevailing in Russia and the chaos engulfing a defeated country that the envisaged workers' and soldiers' councils, even if they had been established locally, could not possibly pose a challenge to the authority of the government or aim at establishing 'dual control'. Nor was there any spontaneous revolutionary movement from below which – as happened in Russia in 1917 and in Germany in 1918 – caused such councils to be formed in town and country alike and to curtail the powers of the authorities, at least for the time being. When the National Administrative Council of the ILP met a few weeks after the Leeds Convention Snowden reported on the progress of the movement and the activity of the workers' and soldiers' council. Those present agreed that 'it must not interfere with or limit the work of any existing organization', that it must only be an advisory body, and that 'it must not be allowed to dissipate the energy of members of the Party'. The leaders of the ILP, although they dominated the provisional committee, clearly feared that a rival and more dynamic organization might develop and therefore decided to limit its functions and influence from the outset. But these fears were unjustified. In October MacDonald was able to report to the ILP that the national workers' and soldiers' council 'was greatly hampered by lack of funds' and that there was 'not much prospect of activity' by it.[29] It was in vain that Lansbury in *The Herald* appealed to all 'to join in this great effort to revolutionize the conditions of life in this country'. In London, a meeting to form a local council was held at Islington in a church the clergyman of which was a pacifist. But a mob led by army officers besieged the church and succeeded in bursting into the hall, armed with wooden boards from which long rusty nails protruded. Mrs Snowden, however, refused to leave the hall unless the men present were permitted to leave together with the women, and the officers hesitated to assault women. But then pandemonium broke out, everybody tried to escape from the hall as best they could, while the police did nothing to protect those present. Similar scenes occurred elsewhere, the nationalist mobs being goaded to fury by the right-wing papers. At Newcastle, the only woman member of the provisional committee, Charlotte Despard (the sister of Sir John French, at that time commander-in-chief home forces), attempted to found a local 'Soviet'; but soldiers invaded the hall, free fights broke out, and the platform was rushed; and thus the only meeting of the Newcastle 'Soviet' came to an inglorious end.[30]

When the provisional committee in August called a meeting to Glasgow, where the council movement might have struck root and where sympathy with the Russian Soviets was running strong, the Secretary for Scotland stepped in and prohibited the meeting which, he feared, 'will give rise to grave disorder'. The Scottish Advisory Council of the Labour Party, the Govan Trades Council, the District Council of the National Union of Railwaymen and many others protested in vain against this infringement of the right of free speech and meeting, or against 'a form of Prussianism that is dear to the hearts of the British Kaisers, in denying the right of accredited delegates to hold a private conference'. At Larkhall, however, not far from Glasgow, an open air meeting was held; there the speakers who would have addressed the prohibited conference spoke in the presence of the delegates elected to it, and it passed without a disturbance of any kind. In London, the provisional committee organized a district conference which also passed peacefully. It pledged itself to work for a peace made by the peoples and 'for the complete political and economic emancipation of international labour', as well as for the programme of the Leeds Convention. It also demanded 'the right of association' for all serving soldiers, but that was a demand the government had no intention of granting.[31] The whole 'Soviet' movement petered out before the Bolshevik seizure of power and it never revived.

The attitude of the ILP towards the victorious Bolsheviks varied considerably. At first *The Labour Leader* rightly pointed out that Russia was now definitely out of the war and that the Allies had themselves to blame for this: if they had shown sympathy with the aims of the Russian revolution and helped the Russians to consolidate its achievements, the course of events would have been very different. After the elections to the Constituent Assembly in December, the paper expressed the hope that the Bolsheviks would 'form a responsible and representative government' together with the Social Revolutionary Party, and then the foreign governments would have to recognize the new Russian government. But the paper was misinformed when it stated that the Bolsheviks were 'by far the strongest single party' in the Constituent Assembly, for the Social Revolutionaries were more than twice as strong. As Lenin was determined to retain power, no 'democratically and constitutionally elected government' could be established in Russia and the Constituent Assembly was dissolved by force. Thus by March 1918 Alfred Salter was able to state in *The Labour Leader*: the Bolsheviks 'have destroyed an assembly freshly elected by universal suffrage, they have respected the right of national self-determination neither in the Ukraine nor in Finland, ... and they have rigorously suppressed and gaoled many of their opponents, both socialists and reactionaries. They have appealed from principles to force.'[32] At an ILP meeting in Wales, on the other hand, the speakers declared that the ILP was using the 'wrong tools': the socialist revolution could not be brought about through parliament as Keir Hardie had believed; the workers must make the leaders change their tactics, they had 'much to learn from our Russian comrades', and the ILP must commit itself to Bolshevism. At Manchester, a prominent ILP leader spoke out against the use of violence, but added that the workers might have to use force against a counter-revolution, 'and then we must do as Lenin and Trotsky have done in Russia' – a remark which was followed by applause. At about the same time Clifford Allen expressed his doubts as to whether the Bolsheviks were justified in denying 'any political right to the bourgeois'. He conceded that it might be necessary for the party in power to deny political rights to those who refused to accept 'the new social outlook of the great majority of the nation', the working class, and this would certainly be the case in a country with the bitterness of the Russian past. But he also hoped that the Soviet government would relax the restrictions imposed as speedily as possible.[33]

Meanwhile Macdonald and Snowden were content to urge, in and out of parliament, that the Soviet state should be granted diplomatic recognition and that any military intervention in Russia must be opposed. The last theme was also taken up by the BSP at its annual conference in April 1918. But it went considerably further and recorded its 'whole hearted admiration for, and complete agreement with, the courageous efforts of the Bolshevik Government of Russia in its struggle against international capitalism on behalf of the world's workers for peace'. There John Maclean exclaimed that 'we were in the rapids of revolution. We must stand by our Russian comrades and be prepared to risk our lives on behalf of our class'. Another speaker declared that the Bolshevik revolution was 'absolutely and completely in line with the BSP', that the ILP did not support the Bolsheviks, and only the BSP was doing so. The BSP viewed the Bolshevik revolution as the natural culmination of that of February and continuously praised the achievements of the Bolshevik government.[34]

Thus the Russian February revolution made a great impact in Britain as well as in Germany, but that was above all because large numbers of working men and women were longing for peace and passionately took up the slogan of 'peace without annexations and indemnities'. The Bolshevik seizure of power eight months later aroused a much more limited echo because – in spite of the war – in both countries the number of determined socialist revolutionaries remained very small. While the war lasted no barricades went up in Berlin or London, and when the old order finally collapsed in Germany it was because the country was defeated and had to sue for an armistice, and not because it was overthrown by any revolutionary party. Until that moment was reached, the forces of the *ancien régime* proved considerably stronger than its adversaries, and all revolutionary propaganda had a rather limited effect. It seems that the mood of nationalism which prevailed all over Europe made the majority of the population, and even of the working class, unresponsive to the propaganda of the anti-war groups and parties.

VI

A *naval mutiny*

The call from Petrograd for the meeting of a socialist peace conference in Stockholm had a sequel in the German navy which turned into tragedy for the leading participants. During the whole war, the German High Seas fleet saw only one major encounter with the enemy, the battle of Jutland in May 1916, at the end of which it was forced to return to port by the highly superior British navy on which it had inflicted serious losses; and in port the German navy remained during the later years of the war. Thus the sailors on board the battleships and cruisers saw no more fighting and had little to do; but their officers – often the juniors of the men by many years – tried to make up for this by maintaining a stringent discipline, by hours of punitive drill or days of detention for minute lapses, the most detailed kit inspections, and a variety of petty rules and restrictions. All this caused deep resentment among the sailors many of whom were skilled workers recalled to military duty during the war. As early as June 1915 one sailor wrote in his diary that treatment of this kind caused a 'gulf' between officer and man, in particular in wartime. Another cause of friction was that the rations of the sailors were cut on account of the deteriorating food situation – their bread ration was halved already in 1915 – while six or seven courses were still served in the officers' mess. In November 1915 the men's bread ration was cut once more so that many went hungry, while the officers at large dinners still consumed several meat courses. By the beginning of 1917 potatoes were served to the men only once a week, and swede and cabbage now formed the main ingredients of their meals. As a sailor wrote, the cardinal question of the day always was: what do we get to eat today? And a stoker exclaimed: 'We eat swedes, dried swedes, and again dried swedes, while the officers still eat and drink in a way not all that different from peace time.' He claimed that as the result of lack of food the men 'collapsed like flies'.[1]

Sailors who complained about bad or insufficient food received short shrift from the officers. One captain indeed declared that the food was much too good; bread and water would also do. On another ship the men refused to eat the dried vegetables so that they were thrown away, but no other food was issued. When the men complained the first officer told them that they had acted 'unpatriotically'. Soon after they again rejected the dried swedes and were given dried cabbage instead, which was eaten. On another ship the sailors during a night exercise ate their bread ration for the following day and then declared they were hungry when ordered to appear on deck the next morning, but finally they obeyed the order. Other sailors complained that the food issued was uneatable and were curtly told by their captain that what happened to them was of no importance because he could get as many men as he liked: the only thing that mattered was whether the ship was ready for action. When a tun of beer 'disappeared' on board and the sailors refused to name the 'thief', they were condemned to do two hours of rifle drill a day in their off-duty period for four weeks, often in the boiling sun. But in another case the sailors won. When they refused to fetch their dinner of dried swedes they were severely reprimanded by their officer and told that the officers too had to eat swedes. But they replied that they would like to eat swedes in that form, namely a lot of meat with a spoonful of swedes, and demanded bread and bacon and a proper dinner which they were given. At Kiel, sailors on another ship refused to appear on deck in the morning because they had not been issued any bread at breakfast and remained below. A deck officer commanded each man to obey orders but the men took no notice. In the end, they were given food and then they returned to duty.[2]

That the complaints about bad and insufficient food were justified was admitted by the naval authorities: what they did not want to recognize was that one of the main causes of dissatisfaction was the much better food served to the officers – a fact that could be easily observed every day under the conditions of life on board a battleship. In an attempt to find an outlet for the complaints the Admiralty in Berlin in June 1917 decreed that sailors' food committees were to be appointed on each ship to make suggestions for an improvement of the food and to be consulted in case of need. It was hoped that their members would help to enlighten the crews about measures that were economically necessary, would exercise a good influence on the men, or could even be entrusted with certain minor duties. On some of the big ships the food committees soon developed considerable activity. In one case it was established that 25 pounds of butter had been diverted from the men's kitchen to that of the officers, as the latter explained in 'exchange' for margarine. In other instances, the food of the men improved considerably thanks to the efforts of the food committees. Some of them became more active and energetic. They demanded to see the purser's food accounts, or they established cases of fraud or misuse of food stores. Soon members of the committees began to visit other ships to see how their affairs were managed there, or to exchange information and ask for advice. As the men were restless and disgruntled, new demands soon arose, above all that the food committees should not be appointed but elected, and some captains conceded this demand. On ships where so far no food committee existed the men demanded that it be established. Some food committees developed into centres where the men's complaints were aired, not only relating to food, but also to leave and conditions of service. In the different sections of the ship trusties were elected to hear and investigate complaints and to take them to the food committee. At Wilhelmshaven, links from ship to ship were established to air the grievances. A loose network developed through which the sailors kept in touch with each other.[3]

Meetings were also held on land, usually in public houses in the harbour. There the sailors of different ships met and naturally they discussed their complaints about food and other issues. As many of them were reservists with a solid background of trade union and political activity, the discussions also included political topics; and by 1917 no topic was more burning than that of peace. Some sailors had old friends on board other ships and thus close links could quickly be established. Apparently the stokers were specially interested in politics. Many of them read the most prominent opposition paper, the *Leipziger Volkszeitung*, and discussed its articles when they met on land. From this it was only a short step for those who were well versed politically to give talks on subjects such as the Anti-Socialist Law of Bismarck, the Balkan wars, or the causes of the world war. It so happened that a journalist on the staff of the *Leipziger Volkszeitung* was called up in 1917 and served at Wilhelmshaven, and he too talked on political topics, such as the origins of the war.[4]

By no means all the sailors sympathized with Social Democracy. Stumpf, the author of the diary which is one of the most interesting sources for these events, stressed repeatedly that he was 'patriotic', and he and many others rejoiced at every German victory. But they wanted peace and they hated their officers who were martinets and 'guzzled' while the men went hungry. As early as 1915 Stumpf wrote: 'We all wish that the "Heligoland" would strike a mine and tear the whole officer quarter to shreds' (*sic*). Later he mentioned 'the *idée fixe* that the war is only conducted and prolonged in the interest of the officers'. Even those sailors whose heart was on the Left had very hazy political ideas. When Stumpf once asked them what they would do if they were all-powerful, the answer was: 'Dissolve army and navy and discharge them! Scheidemann for chancellor and Liebknecht as minister of war!' That Scheidemann and Liebknecht were bitter political enemies and differed diametrically on the issue of the war seems to have escaped them. Stumpf also hated the non-commissioned officers who treated the ordinary sailors like dirt and succeeded in destroying in his heart 'the ideals of love of the fatherland and of justice', and he added significantly: 'What no book, no paper and no socialist has been able to do, that the military system has accomplished. I have learnt to hate and despise this embodiment of authority like nothing else in the world.' As to the officers, they should 'go to hell and not involve us in any more wars. They should learn an honest trade or perish!'[5] That a 'patriotic' sailor did write in such terms explains a good deal about the events in the navy in 1917 and 1918.

A minority among the sailors, however, had left-wing views, or had been organized Social Democrats before their call-up. One stoker wrote in March 1917 that the Russian revolution must serve as an example not only for socialists, but for every thinking worker; if the unorganized Russian masses could accomplish such deeds should that not make the well-educated SPD leaders blush? From his reading he noticed with approval that the radicalization and democratization of the trade unions was progressing fast, for they were plagued by the disease of bureaucracy. Early in the same year another stoker wrote on a blackboard in the engine room: 'When will the war end? A life of famine!' to which another added: 'Same pay, same food, and the war would long be forgotten!' Others wrote: 'Down with the war!' and 'What are German soldiers? White slaves! Down with the aristocrats!' The writers were each sentenced to nine months of imprisonment for causing dissatisfaction. But even the leaders of the sailors were badly informed. As a witness one of them said later that, when they heard the news of the Russian revolution, they felt: now the opportunity has come to take up the struggle for peace; but they did not know how to conduct the struggle; of the Zimmerwald conference and the stand taken by Liebknecht they heard only very late; in 1917 they received the first copy of a *Spartacus Letter*.[6] None of the sailors seems to have had any contact with the Bremen Left in spite of the short distance from Bremen to Wilhelmshaven, nor with the Spartacists whose leaders were in prison and whose small underground groups the sailors could not contact.[7]

Several sailors, however, while on leave in Berlin went to see deputies of the USPD in the Reichstag where the party had its offices. As the sailors wanted peace above all, it was natural for them to contact the only legal party which stood out for an early peace. They even thought of contacting the two Social Democratic parties because the SPD, too, was in favour of peace, but in the end opted for the USPD as the more radical party. In June 1917 Max Reichpietsch, one of the most active radical sailors, saw the deputy Dittmann and told him that the USPD had many followers among his comrades, that from time to time they met on land to discuss their affairs and to listen to political talks, and that they lacked propaganda material to spread their ideas. Dittmann asked Reichpietsch to put the complaints about bad food and harsh treatment in writing and introduced him to the party secretary, Luise Zietz. She expressed satisfaction that the ideas of the party were gaining ground in the navy: the same happened in the country at large where whole local party groups went over from the SPD to the USPD. The party chairman, Haase, saw Reichpietsch later and warned him to be cautious with their meetings because he feared that one or the other might be induced by inexperience or temperament to make rash remarks which could be used against him. Reichpietsch took away copies of parliamentary speeches by Haase and Dittmann which were legally published, and after his return to Wilhelmshaven wrote that the pamphlets had been enthusiastically received on board and asked for more copies. Some other sailors on leave also contacted deputies of the USPD and were asked to report back if any difficulties should arise on board the fleet.[8]

At Wilhelmshaven, Reichpietsch, who saw himself as the movement's leader, seems to have considerably exaggerated what had been said to him in Berlin and the importance of his contacts there. The sailors were eager to show their mettle and to support the cause of peace. Many wanted to join the party which promoted the good cause. From Reichpietsch's ship, *Friedrich der Grosse*, a list of about 60 names of those who wanted to become members was sent to Berlin, from another ship over 100, and from a third about 400 names. This was done quite openly as the USPD was a legal party which soldiers could join. From their reading of the *Leipziger Volkszeitung* or in Berlin the sailors heard of the impending meeting of the socialist peace conference in Stockholm, and the idea gained ground among them to compile such lists so that the USPD delegates could prove there that a large section of the sailors supported a peace without annexations and indemnities: they must know how many stood behind them. One sailor said on his return from Berlin that, if the deputies could not bring peace, the people would have to do it. He also suggested that the sailors should elect trusties to promote the good cause. On *Prinzregent Luitpold* a leaflet circulated referring to the Stockholm conference: 'It is clear to everybody that our representatives at this conference...can only operate with figures, proving so and so many thousands of soldiers as party members. To enable them to do so it is necessary that everybody joins the party who sees in the past activity of the opposition party the best guarantee to serve his and the people's interests and to further the general cause of peace... Therefore, comrades, become members of the opposition party so that it can press the government even more energetically than in the past to bring about peace negotiations.' A more straightforward leaflet calling for support was found on *König Albert*. One sailor declared that the signatures were to prove to the deputies that the sailors were opposed to a war of conquest and to the ideas of the Pan-Germans, for even the Emperor had repudiated a war undertaken to conquer foreign lands.[9]

When these matters came to light and arrests were made among the crews of the affected ships in August 1917, the naval authorities at first stated that the agitation was in favour of an immediate peace, that money had been collected to bring this about, that members of the food committees looked at themselves as a kind of 'soldiers' council' formed with the consent of the officers, and that two groups were particularly susceptible to this kind of propaganda – the Alsatians and 'of course all metal workers'. Soon, however, there were much more serious allegations, aimed in the first instance at the USPD, above all Dittmann and Luise Zietz. The party's aim, it was claimed, was 'to incite the crews so as to diminish or totally destroy the battle readiness of the fleet by large-scale refusals to obey orders and demonstrations'. By October it was claimed that a stoker on *Friedrich der Grosse* had established a 'centre for the whole fleet', that trusties and sub-trusties were to be elected on each ship with the task of enlightening the crews (an allegation indicating the formation of soldiers' councils). Several instances of refusals to obey orders were quoted – but they were all non-political, concerned with the issues of food, leave, absence without leave, etc. It was further stated that, in spite of the arrests of the leaders, their followers pursued the idea 'with almost fanatical tenacity', that new trusties took the place of those arrested and contacted their comrades on shore, and that more arrests had been carried out. Another claim was that an underground revolutionary organization, a Soldiers' League, existed on several ships and that its emissaries visited yet other ships to explain the League's aims.[10]

Claims such as these have been repeated in the literature on the subject,[11] but the evidence in their support is rather thin. It comes from the interrogations of arrested sailors some of whom apparently exaggerated their own role or put the blame on others. Even the *Oberreichsanwalt* (chief prosecutor) had to admit that Reichpietsch, in talking about an 'organization', only meant the food committees and the election of some of them. But other accused – according to the notes of their interrogations – talked about the plan of a general strike if the government should decline to start negotiations for an immediate peace, a strike in which the navy was to participate. Another mentioned the use of force in such a case which Reichpietsch had allegedly encouraged by the words 'Break the chains!' Yet another sailor referred to a naval strike if no peace were concluded within a given time and to conversations about a refusal to shoot down striking workers; the organization in the fleet should be built up so that, if a general strike was proclaimed, it would be able to support the USPD and enforce the conclusion of peace.[12] Yet it has to be borne in mind that the accused made their depositions under acute stress and that the notes were written down by men who certainly were not sympathetic to them; they are not verbatim accounts, but only summaries of what the sailors said during the interrogations. Perhaps some of them planned a naval strike to support a general strike in favour of peace, but we cannot be certain. The evidence of a Soldiers' League is even flimsier; later one of the participants expressly stated he had never heard that expression.[13]

In any case, the events which led to the arrests and the discovery of the links to the USPD were non-political and connected with ordinary infractions of military discipline. On 1 August it was announced on *Prinzregent Luitpold* that a film would be shown in the morning, but when the weather improved this was changed to a military march on shore. This the stokers of the third watch considered a grave injustice because they thought themselves entitled to a film show or an excursion.

Therefore 49 of them left the ship, formed a column outside the docks, marched to a dike and stayed there for several hours, but then they returned aboard where 11 of them were punished. In protest against this arbitrary punishment the men decided to repeat the outing on the next day so as to force the captain to revoke the punishment, and this time about 400 participated. But again they returned peacefully after a few hours. During the outing the stoker Albin Köbis allegedly made seditious speeches in which he pointed out the purpose of the action and shouted 'Down with the war!' Similar breaches of discipline occurred on other ships; some sailors started a collective action to obtain leave. It was the investigation of these incidents which led to the discovery of the political background and the arrest of the leaders. On 2 August too, the police discovered a 'secret' sailors' meeting in a pub ashore and arrested six participants, while the others had already left. In another pub more than 20 sailors listening to a talk on the origins of the war were arrested by a detachment of marines who appeared with loaded rifles.[14] But there was no resistance.

The naval authorities were severely perturbed by what they saw as a collapse of military discipline in the high seas fleet, and they suspected behind it a plot led by the leaders of the USPD; but it proved impossible to bring a case against them. The military courts meted out draconic punishments to the sailors. As early as August 1917 one sailor from *Prinzregent Luitpold* was sentenced to death for mutiny and ten others to terms of imprisonment. Two sailors who, according to the police, were the 'speakers' at a clandestine meeting were each sentenced to ten years of penal servitude. During their trial the presiding judge declared it unnecessary to hear certain witnesses because they had nothing incriminating to say. In another trial of 13 men, four were sentenced to death and all the others to long terms of penal servitude, although only one witness incriminated them and he was classified as an adventurer even by the officers. In yet another trial of the alleged ringleaders five death sentences were passed and four others sentenced to between ten and 15 years' penal servitude. Men of such different political persuasions as Scheidemann and Stresemann intervened on behalf of those under sentence of death by writing to the State Secretary for the Navy, and most of the death sentences were commuted to penal servitude. But the sentences against Reichpietsch and Köbis were carried out and 75 other sailors were imprisoned, most of them for a considerable time.[15] The severe sentences achieved their object for the moment: there was no further unrest in the navy until October 1918. As early as January 1918 an underground leaflet was distributed in Berlin in honour of 'the revolutionary sailors of Wilhelmshaven' which promised that the German working class would one day liberate those condemned to penal servitude, the 'true heroes' of the war.[16] It looks like poetic justice that today two streets in West Berlin, where the naval headquarters once stood, are called after Reichpietsch and Köbis.

In 1917 no comparable events occurred in the Germany army – it has often been said that this was because the army was fighting while the navy saw no action of any importance. Another reason for the absence of serious unrest from the units of the army until the summer of 1918 is that, at least in the trenches, a close personal relationship existed between officers and men, that officers did not enjoy the privileges with regard to food and quarters which they enjoyed in the navy. But the army kept large numbers of men in the rear and in home garrisons and reserve battalions, and there the officers certainly had the same privileges. Nor did the treatment of the soldiers change for the better. In parliament the Social Democrats often complained that the men were still treated in the notorious style of the Prussian army, that no account was taken of the fact that the war-time recruits often were middle-aged men with grey hair, that there was too much drill and too many parades and inspections of no military value, that in the rear and in the garrisons there was far too much insistence on saluting in style. Another complaint concerned the ancient punishment of tying delinquent soldiers to a tree or cannon which was still in use, and sometimes it was forgotten to untie the culprit: a punishment which aroused the soldiers' wrath. The SPD also complained that those who subscribed sufficiently large sums to the war loan were given preferential leave, that soldiers were not allowed to subscribe to Social Democratic papers or received them only in a censored form, that there was still discrimination against Social Democrats on account of their political conviction, although the Emperor himself had declared that he knew no longer any parties. In many cases, it was claimed, it was refused to grant commissions to agnostics, Jews and Social Democrats.[17]

There can be no doubt that factors such as these caused dissatisfaction which expressed itself in the soldiers' letters, but it went no further. There can also be no doubt that – like the sailors – most soldiers wanted peace, an early peace through negotiation. When the Social Democratic *Münchener Post* in May 1917 demanded an immediate peace and encouraged its readers to write in and to declare their consent, large numbers of soldiers of the First Bavarian Infantry Regiment which held positions in the Vosges mountains west of the Rhine did so. According to their officers, many of them believed that the government delayed peace negotiations because it did not have the courage to admit that Germany was defeated. Other Bavarian soldiers wrote to the paper that in their company 99 per cent would sign if they were given the chance; or that they did not know a single soldier in their battalion who would not agree, that the longing for peace filled everyone, whatever his occupation was, that only the professional soldiers were still enthusiastic for a 'Hindenburg peace'. The only point they regretted was that they could not ask every soldier to sign. But in some units the officers started searching enquiries and announced that the collection of signatures was a punishable offence. When Scheidemann visited the eastern front in the winter of 1917 to 1918 and talked to the troops entrenched in a wood far inside Russia, they told him in no uncertain terms that they approved of the peace resolution passed by the Reichstag and then shouted: 'Finish it! Peace! We want to go home! End it!'[18] (In July 1917 the majority parties of the Reichstag had passed a resolution in favour of a peace of understanding and permanent reconciliation which would be incompatible with any territorial annexation and with political or economic oppression.)

According to the Bavarian military authorities, in the garrison units the mood was worst at the end of 1917 among soldiers who were independent craftsmen or shop keepers by trade, less so among the peasants or workers. A Prussian officer wrote from the eastern front in July that there was 'a sultry, revolutionary mood' among the men, especially in the Prussian units; they talked openly about deserting to the Russians, 'where it could not be worse and where they would get enough to eat'; they blindly believed in a peace without annexations and indemnities, and their whole fury was directed at the Pan-Germans who wanted to prolong the war; they were threatening to shoot their officers and considered all members of the upper classes 'swindlers and exploiters of the lower orders'.[19] This letter came from the Russian front where some units were clearly affected by revolutionary propaganda, but its very sombre colours are not confirmed by other sources. We know that there was fraternization between Russian and German soldiers, but it is difficult to estimate its extent and effect. At the western front, nothing like it occurred; there in general German morale was more or less preserved until the tide of war turned in 1918, and there was no mutiny of any size. But there was a growing amount of desertion. In October 1917 the chief of staff of the home forces issued a memorandum that conscripts were secretly leaving Germany 'in droves' and that these flights had reached 'an incredible extent', as had those of prisoners of war and civilian internees. The German deserters, the memorandum continued, were then interrogated by the enemy intelligence services about the recent news from the front, from their garrison service or from the navy: to the enemy, they were 'a symbol of the military and economic decline of Germany'. This was a remarkably frank admission and proves that desertion had become a major factor for the army. At Brunswick, the Spartacists were active in providing deserters with false papers and money which they collected among local members of the USPD; the papers were those of fallen soldiers, which were suitably doctored, and food coupons were contributed from those sent to the food offices which 'failed' to arrive there.[20] Then the deserters were sent on to Berlin where they could more easily find shelter. Many escaped across the frontier to Holland or another neutral country.

In the British army in France, however, a sizeable mutiny occurred, but it was entirely non-political and directed above all against the military police whose members had not served at the front and tried to impose a strict discipline in the camps of the rear. Discontent was ripe at the 'Bull Ring' at Étaples where men with long front-line experience or just back from a military hospital were put through a two weeks' rigorous training course in gas warfare and marching. One soldier later declared that the course was 'like passing through hell for two weeks'. It was difficult for the soldiers to obtain a pass into Étaples, and their food and accommodation was of poor quality. They thus had legitimate grievances. On 9 September 1917 the military police arrested a New Zealand gunner at the railway bridge where soldiers off-duty used to collect, but he had committed no offence and was soon released. In the afternoon a large crowd assembled at the bridge. The military police found it difficult to preserve order and to move the men away from the bridge. Soon there were angry disputes and scuffles. One policeman lost his head, pulled out his gun and fired several shots. Some soldiers were wounded, one passing corporal was shot in the head and died later in hospital. The infuriated men stoned the huts of the military police and marched into Étaples. In the evening some of them tried to break into a café where two military policemen had sought refuge. The camp commandant and about a dozen other officers were thrown into a nearby river; but the main anger of the men was directed at the hated 'redcaps'. By night all were back in camp and on the following morning they returned to training. But in the afternoon large crowds again gathered at the railway bridge and broke through a cordon which tried to prevent them from marching into town. As on the previous evening, eventually the men went peacefully back to camp. On the 11th and 12th new demonstrations took place, large numbers of soldiers broke out of camp and went to Étaples but returned later.

Meanwhile the commandant of the base urgently demanded the sending of reinforcements which arrived on the 12th, and a cavalry brigade was held in readiness. Then the trouble subsided; the authorities made concessions and introduced improvements in the training programme. The old system was more or less abandoned and the leading officers of the 'Bull Ring' were replaced. By a show of force and some concessions the mutiny was quickly brought under control – without resort to heavy punishments or arrests on any scale.[21] But it was not a political mutiny, and army discipline was not seriously endangered by it. It was only after the end of the war, when demobilization was delayed and British soldiers were sent to Archangel to help the Whites in the Russian civil war, that more serious mutinies occurred in the army. The largest mutiny of the war took place in the spring of 1917 in the French army; it was suppressed and many of the mutineers were shot. The causes of the mutiny were the failure of a great French offensive at Chemin des Dames, and general war-weariness at a time when there seemed to be no prospect of winning the war. The causes were not political. The blood-letting of the German army at Verdun in the previous year had been much heavier, and yet there was no sign of resistance. Was it the famed Prussian discipline which prevailed, or was it a conviction that German arms would nevertheless triumph in the end? Perhaps it was a mixture of discipline and patriotism which prevented a mutiny or a breakdown of military discipline in spite of the terrible losses which the German army suffered at Verdun and in many other battles.

VII

Political strikes in Germany

The first clearly political strike in Germany occurred in June 1916, on the day when Liebknecht was tried by a military court; but it was on a small scale and it only affected two towns, Berlin and Brunswick. There were 240 strikes in 1916, affecting 124,000 workers. But in 1917 the number of strikes more than doubled, to 562, and the number of strikers more than quintupled, to 651,000. Yet the large majority of these strikes were non-political, caused by demands for higher wages or more food. Indeed, in the official reports the hunger of the working masses is very frequently given as the cause of the strikes. The motive for the great strikes of April 1917 was a similar one. It was announced in March that from 15 April the bread ration would be cut by one quarter, from 1800 grams a week to 1350, with similar cuts in the additional rations for those doing heavy and very heavy work. At the same time it was promised that the potato ration fixed at three pounds a week, but often unobtainable, would in future be distributed regularly, and that the meat ration would be increased.[1] The strike movement which began in Berlin and quickly spread to other industrial centres started in protest against this announcement, but it did not remain non-political, for political demands were quickly put forward.

In April a leaflet was distributed in armament works in Berlin that the working people were condemned to hunger and would perish from exhaustion: 'Our brothers, the Russian proletarians, four weeks ago were in the same boat. We know what happened in Russia: there the working people have risen and enforced not only the regulation of the food question. At the same time – what is far more important – they have conquered freedoms of which the German worker does not dare to dream. The Russian workers have smashed tsarism and gained the democratic republic, the appointment of a people's government! *And we?*... Leave the working places and factories! Stop work!... Down with the war! Down with the government! Peace! Freedom! Bread!' A Spartacist leaflet demanded freedom for all political prisoners, the stopping of all political trials, the ending of the state of siege, the rights of free association and meeting, and a free press; the working class must organize itself to enforce peace and to gain political liberty.[2]

On 15 April a general meeting of the Berlin metal workers' union took place at which all factories were represented and the decision was taken to call a strike. This had been well prepared by the union's shop stewards, but two days before their leader, Richard Müller, was called up and taken to an army camp. The meeting demanded his release and announced that the strike would continue until this was achieved. The leaders of the SPD and the Free trade unions discussed whether to issue a joint appeal against the strike. When the secretary of the Berlin metal workers stated that any such admonition would be totally useless, Scheidemann replied that to declare against the strike would therefore be 'a vast political stupidity', and the suggestion was dropped. On 16 April more than 300 armament works in Berlin were on strike. According to the police, the strikers numbered almost 150,000; according to the metal workers' union, 210,000 strikers registered. With the strikers belonging to other unions their number may have reached about 300,000. Most of them, however, returned to work on the 18th, and only a small minority continued the strike for a few more days.[3]

From the outset the strikers' demands took on a political colour. At a mass meeting in a Berlin park they demanded peace, and two soldiers present tore off their insignia of rank. At a strike meeting in Pankow a speaker urged the strikers to be united and to turn against the propertied classes; a sharp wind was blowing from the east; he hoped it would soon be stronger than the wind blowing from the west at the time of the French revolution. Haase, Dittmann, Ledebour and other USPD deputies addressed strike meetings. Adolph Hoffmann spoke to the workers of the Knorrbremse factory: now the socialists had the duty to stop the war against revolutionary Russia; they must demand freedom of the press, the equal franchise and other basic rights: 'you have the weapons in your hands to gain all these rights.' At the German armament and munition works the strikers elected a workers' council to submit their demands to the chancellor. At the Knorrbremse too, a workers' council was elected for the same purpose; it was to demand the release of Liebknecht and other political prisoners, the raising of the state of siege, complete political freedom, provision of sufficient food, and an end to the war without conquests and indemnities. A trade union official who advised the workers of the German armament and munition works to return to work was shouted down, and very much the same programme was adopted there, including freedom of political meetings and an immediate change in the Prussian three-class franchise. Similar demands were put forward in mass meetings of the strikers which were addressed by deputies of the USPD.[4]

In Saxony, the authorities noticed unrest in the factories on account of the bread shortage already before 15 April. On the 14th leaflets were distributed calling for bread and peace. In mass meetings of the strikers at Leipzig at first only the food problems were discussed. But then the USPD leaders raised political issues, and the union leaders lost control when the former pointed to the shining example of the Russian workers; they also called for the formation of workers' councils. The principal demands of the Leipzig strikers were: a declaration by the government that it was ready to conclude peace renouncing all open or hidden annexations, abolition of the censorship and the state of siege, complete civil liberty, general, equal, secret and direct franchise for all public institutions on the local, state and national levels, liberation of all political prisoners and stopping of all political investigations. All trades and occupational groups were urged to elect representatives who were to form the Leipzig workers' council together with the delegates of the metal workers and the USPD. (As the SPD had no influence left in Leipzig it was omitted.) A workers'deputation was to submit the demands to the chancellor and work was not to be resumed unless the government made 'satisfactory concessions'. Deputies of the USPD distributed the Leipzig programme among the strikers and their delegates in Berlin, but they could not prevent that it was decided to restart work on the 18th.[5]

At Brunswick the ducal authorities early in April discussed the forthcoming cut in the bread ration with workers' representatives. These reported general indignation about the system of food distribution and advised the establishment of general people's kitchens to pacify the workers: the people were 'absolutely unable to carry the burden any longer' and peace must be made. The local secretary of the metal workers' union asked the government to make far-reaching concessions, for only a spark was needed to cause a conflagration. Here the April strike was only partial, and a workers' delegation raised, above all, social demands, such as a more equal distribution of food and the establishment of people's kitchens. The ducal government adopted a cooperative attitude and made some concessions, but declared itself powerless to do anything about the food shortage. Therefore, the workers declared, peace was the only way out.[6] Partial strikes also took place at Halle and at Magdeburg. The Prussian authorities in Berlin, however, proved less cooperative. The State Commissar for Food, Michaelis (the later chancellor), received a workers' delegation and conceded that they could form a committee to assist the mayor in questions of food distribution. With regard to the arrest and conscription of Richard Müller – in the eyes of the delegation a punitive measure as he was unfit for military service – Michaelis only offered to talk to the competent military authority: if the workers were right their wish would probably be fulfilled. The military finally agreed to release Müller if it could be proved that he was called up for non-military reasons and was claimed by his factory. The workers' delegates were naturally dissatisfied with these vague promises but nevertheless decided by a majority vote to resume work.[7]

What irritated the military authorities most was that the strike, which had started spontaneously, developed into a political demonstration. When the head of the *Kriegsamt*, General Groener, addressed the parliamentary committee in April he ascribed the strikes to a 'depression' among the workers when the ration cuts were announced; they wanted to show the government that it had neglected to take precautions in good time; the idea of a strike had spread like wildfire through the factories; then the trade unions assumed the leadership and it was decided to restart work. With the Leipzig programme and the 'impertinent telegram to the chancellor', however, things took a radical political turn: here Groener indicated the 'appointment of a workers' council after the Russian pattern' and the demand that the chancellor was to receive a deputation: 'that was crazy, more than crazy!' These political motives were transmitted to Berlin and carried into the factories. 'I demand that the strikes must stop.' Groener threatened the sharpest measures against the 'wire-pullers'; 'these political traitors' would be hit with the full force of the law, and the workers must air their grievances and all wage issues through legitimate channels (meaning the unions). Groener ordered all armament works to display a poster: 'A cur who strikes while our armies are confronting the enemy!... The worst enemies are among us – the pusillanimous and the far worse who foment strikes. These traitors to fatherland and army must be branded in front of the whole nation. A coward who listens to their words!'[8]

127

On 20 April the SPD leaders were received by the chancellor to discuss what should be done about the strike which was still continuing in a few places. They strongly advised against strong measures: the movement was declining and things should take their natural course. To their surprise they were informed that the meeting to be held that day was forbidden and that the Berlin factories where the workers had not yet returned were 'militarized'. Bethmann Hollweg and Groener told them that it was impossible to wait any longer because the workers were mocking the authorities that they had no power left, that the strikers had conquered the streets. The 'militarization' of a factory meant that an officer took over the management, that any strike was forbidden and that those who resisted orders and were of military age became liable to military punishments. The alleged ringleaders were arrested or called up. By these methods the remaining strikers were forced back to work. The military authorities were able to claim that their tough methods had achieved success and that, contrary to all rumours, no strikes had occurred on May Day. Their wrath was aroused by the part played during the strike by the deputies of the USPD. According to Groener, they had remained in the background 'with considerable skill' and come very close to violating certain provisions of the criminal code.[9] That they put themselves at the disposal of the strike movement and were radicalized by it, has also been acknowledged, a little grudgingly, by East German historians. The Spartacists, in spite of all their criticisms, praised the USPD leaders for doing their duty 'fully and completely'. According to Müller, whose call-up had been a factor in the strike, the workers did not feel that they had been defeated but 'saw in the defeat a victory': for the first time, they realized 'the colossal power which they possessed in the political mass strike'.[10]

In any case, during the later months of 1917 there were more political strikes, although none of them spread very far. In August yet another strike occurred at Brunswick where Spartacist influence was strong. The strike affected all larger enterprises of the town and lasted four days; according to the police, 6,400 workers took part. The strikers put forward eight, mainly political, demands, such as abolition of the state of siege and of all political restrictions, liberation of all political prisoners and of all those sentenced because of food riots, the general, equal, direct and secret franchise for men and women (in a state where the franchise was notoriously antiquated), a promise of no victimization of the strikers, and an undertaking by the ducal government to press for peace on the basis of national self-determination and without annexations and indemnities. At a strike meeting a turner called on the workers to persevere and to look to the east where the workers had achieved something. But the military authorities in Hanover issued a decree which threatened severe punishments and 'militarized' the principal factories, and the strike collapsed. Special military courts sentenced 126 people to fines or to imprisonment varying from three days to 12 months. Simultaneously unrest broke out in Halle and the nearby Leuna chemical plant, where more than 12,000 men came out on strike. They demonstrated and demanded more food, shorter working hours and an immediate peace, but resumed work on the following day.[11]

In December a strike broke out at the Daimler works in a suburb of Berlin where the workers adopted tactics of passive resistance. The metal workers of Berlin declared their solidarity with the strikers in many meetings and threatened to join the strike if military measures were taken against the Daimler workers. In spite of the threats the Daimler works were put under military management and – as the governor of Berlin proudly reported to the Emperor – the metal workers did not come out on strike. The Daimler workers had no option but to return, and the works' committee 'very modestly' asked for the militarization to be rescinded.[12] No wonder that after these successes the military began to see the solution of the problem of labour unrest in the militarization of the factories where strikes broke out; if the workers, most of whom had served in the Prussian army, were put under military orders they would obey, and that would be the end of the trouble. Early in 1918, however, there was more trouble, and on an unprecedented scale. Hitherto the political strikes had been confined to a few industrial centres – Berlin, Brunswick and Leipzig where the Left was particularly strong. The unrest of 1918 started in Austria, and from there it quickly was transmitted to Germany.

In Austria, in contrast with Germany, the Bolshevik revolution was almost enthusiastically welcomed by the Social Democrats. As early as 9 November 1917 the *Arbeiter-Zeitung* of Vienna reported that 'the workers and soldiers of Petrograd' had arrested the government of the bourgeoisie and taken over power; 'for the first time since the bloody end of the Paris Commune a European capital is in the hands of the proletariat.' A few days later the paper sent its 'passionate wishes' to Russia: if the Bolsheviks remained victorious 'a new epoch begins in the liberation struggle of the international proletariat.' The Austrian Social Democrats wholeheartedly welcomed the Bolshevik revolution not only for reasons of international solidarity but also because it would bring peace: 'The fate of all nations is being decided in Petrograd. The victory of the bourgeoisie means the prolongation of the war, the victory of the proletariat means peace!'[13] Thus, even more than in Germany, the hopes of the war-weary masses were aroused by the peace negotiations at Brest-Litovsk, and there was widespread despair and indignation when their success was jeopardized by German annexationist demands and the vast appetite of the German military.

The immediate cause of the strikes which broke out spontaneously in Lower Austria in mid-January was not the stalemate at Brest-Litovsk but (as in April 1917) a severe cut in the flour ration due to diminishing deliveries from Hungary and Rumania. On 14 January the workers of the Daimler motor works at Wiener Neustadt came out on strike and were immediately joined by those of several other armament works. The strikers marched to the town hall and demanded the restoration of the old flour ration, but the town council was unable to obtain this concession from the authorities in Vienna. The strike spread like wildfire through the other industrial towns of Lower Austria and to Vienna, and from there to Upper Austria, Styria, Moravia, Bohemia, Galicia and other provinces of the monarchy. On the 18th a general strike was proclaimed in Budapest where more than 200,000 people joined the movement. In Vienna and Lower Austria alone, their number rose to about 266,000. The Austrian Social Democratic Party published a manifesto which demanded a quick ending of the war, without open or hidden annexations, the vote for women, proportional representation, and the rescinding of the militarization of the factories. The party also decided to establish a workers' council for Vienna consisting of the local functionaries of party and trade unions. The strike lasted for about a week and was only broken off after considerable concessions by the government with regard to the distribution of food, the militarization of the factories, and a promise that the peace negotiations would not be allowed to founder on any annexationist aims. It required the whole eloquence of Victor Adler to persuade the Vienna workers' council to accept the compromise after a long and very heated discussion.[14]

Even before these events in Austria, leaflets appeared in Germany calling on the workers to force the government to make peace and to take the solution of the peace issue into their own hands. In Berlin, the movement in favour of a strike grew, and from below the demand was raised that the leaders of the USPD must publicly call a strike. The initiative came again from the group of shop stewards of the metal workers' union which was by then well organized with strong grass roots in the factories: a small group of about 40 which began to call itself the Revolutionary Shop Stewards, led by Richard Müller. It included the leaders of the turners' branch and other well paid and skilled workers, workers indispensable for the running of the factories. In January they met the USPD leaders to discuss what action to take. Haase and the majority of the deputies believed that a mass action for peace was necessary but feared that an appeal for a mass strike would destroy the party (strangely echoing the attitude of the SPD leaders of 4 August 1914 of which they disapproved). After a long discussion it was agreed to publish a manifesto drafted by Haase and signed by the 25 deputies of the USPD: '... On 28 December 1917 the German government has left no doubt in the negotiations at Brest-Litovsk that it intends to separate Poland, Lithuania, Courland and parts of Finland from Russia, that in particular the Lithuanians and Latvians are to be made the vassals of Germany and to be incorporated in the German Empire... Germany intends to annex Russian territories... Our meetings in favour of peace have been forbidden, our press is exposed to the sharpest measures, any criticism is made impossible... Only a peace without annexations, without indemnities, based on the right of self-determination of all nations, can save us. The hour has struck in which you must raise your voice for such a peace. *You now have the word!*' The leaflet was printed in large quantities and distributed all over Germany. But the suggestion of the radical minority that the leaders should call for direct action was not adopted.[15]

The Bavarian authorities feared that the movement would spread from Austria to Germany, and a prominent Catholic politician was consulted by the Ministry of the Interior about the mood in working-class quarters. He did not consider the danger imminent but was told by his informants that working-class and lower middle-class circles demanded peace, peace at any price, and that very little was required to bring about an explosion. Only a few days later Kurt Eisner exclaimed at a meeting of the USPD in Munich, which was attended by about 250 people, that apart from the war profiteers, there was no one in Germany who did not consider it necessary to terminate 'the lunacy of the war'; when news of the negotiations of Brest-Litovsk leaked out it suddenly became clear to the Austrian workers who was responsible for the war and its prolongation, and 'all wheels in Lower Austria stood still'; there was no bargaining about bread or meat, but political demands were raised, above all for freedom of speech and writing, of meetings and association, the liberation of the factories from the military dictatorship; the hour had come when the German nation must exercise its right of self-determination, now its will must be enforced, and the means to that end was the mass strike which would start within a few days; the Berlin workers would come out to gain their demands: the raising of the state of siege, the liberation of the political prisoners, freedom of meetings and association. It was treason, Eisner concluded, not to want peace, it was treason against humanity not to sacrifice everything for a general peace, and for that crime there could be no pardon. In the opinion of the Berlin director of police, the workers had learnt from the Russian revolution that it was possible to seize power, that what was achieved in Russia by force could be gained in Germany in the same way.[16]

In Berlin the strike movement started on 28 January – two weeks after Austria – and throughout Berlin remained its centre. According to the official reports, on the first day about 45,000 workers came out, by the 30th their number had risen to 150-180,000, and then it declined; according to the strike leaders, half-a-million men participated. The Berlin munition workers followed the instructions of their shop stewards and union officials who were influenced by the Revolutionary Shop Stewards. On the 28th the delegates of the strikers met in the trade union house. Richard Müller presided and put forward a programme which contained the usual left-wing demands for a lifting of the state of siege and of the militarization of the factories, the freeing of political prisoners, freedom of speech and the press; the same applied to the speedy conclusion of peace 'according to the provisions formulated by the Russian people's commissars at Brest-Litovsk'. As to the internal development, the strikers demanded the 'thorough democratization of all public institutions in Germany, and in the first instance for the Prussian Diet the introduction of the general, equal, direct and secret franchise for all men and women above the age of 20.' The workers of the other belligerent countries were called upon to start mass strikes, 'for only the international class struggle will bring us finally peace, freedom and bread'. The demands of the strikers had become more concrete, but in reality there was little hope of achieving them before the collapse of the German Empire. It was a programme for peace and democracy which contained no socialist demand: there was nothing about the nationalization of the armament industry, about workers' control, or workers' participation in management. Arthur Rosenberg thought that such demands were 'beyond the horizon' of the Berlin workers; but they were socialists, and their leaders well trained and educated men. They must have deliberately omitted any demand likely to divide the movement at a very critical moment. The shop stewards and the USPD aimed at a 'powerful demonstration for the aims of the movement' and at gaining the maximum of concessions from the government.[17]

The strike had the full support of the USPD leaders who were present at the meeting in the trade union house. The delegates elected 11 members of the Revolutionary Shop Stewards as their strike committee and invited the USPD as well as the SPD to appoint three representatives each to the committee. Thus Haase, Ledebour and Dittmann for the USPD and Ebert, Scheidemann and Braun for the SPD joined it. As the SPD executive explained later, this was done because many party members from the striking factories demanded it and because it was essential 'to keep the movement on an orderly course and to bring it as quickly as possible to a conclusion through negotiations with the government'. That both parties delegated their top leaders indicated the importance they attributed to the strike. The leaders of the Free trade unions, on the other hand, declared their 'neutrality' because it was a political strike. As the Saxon envoy reported to his government from Berlin, the SPD leaders found themselves in a most difficult position; the masses were rapidly moving to the Left and the leaders feared to lose all control over them if they continued to support the government at a moment when it was unable to conclude peace with the Bolsheviks: how then would the government ever be able to achieve a general peace? In addition, it was widely believed that this was the time for the SPD to show that 'it still possessed proletarian power' and thus the split in the working-class movement would be healed.[18]

According to the police and the military authorities, the delegates' meeting in the trade union house amounted to the constitution of a workers' council 'on the Russian pattern' as the delegates were elected by the workers. This opinion was shared by the extreme Left which coined the slogan that in every factory and locality workers' councils must be formed from which the trade union officials and 'the government socialists' (meaning SPD functionaries), 'these voluntary agents of the government', must be excluded: they had 'nothing to seek in the meetings of the strikers!' The Spartacists also tried to organize their followers among the delegates into a 'left-wing' faction; but they were only a small minority, were 'disunited, had no plan of action and disappeared in the large crowd'. As the police soon closed the trade union house and prevented a second meeting of the delegates, the masses of the strikers were badly informed about the course of events, and very few information centres were established in the localities. Central direction was lacking and the strike committee found itself isolated. The strikers, however, were in a fighting mood, many clashes with the police occurred and some acts of violence. As the tramway personnel refused to join the strike there was sabotage of the tramway lines. After the collisions with the police shouts could be heard: 'Comrades, tomorrow we will come armed.'[19]

The authorities prohibited all meetings of strikers and the formation of local strike committees. The SPD paper *Vorwärts* was banned because it had allegedly given too high a figure for the participants in the strike. The central strike committee, reinforced by the SPD and USPD leaders, tried to negotiate with the government; but the State Secretary of the Interior refused to see any workers' representatives and would only receive the party leaders who were parliamentary deputies. The military authorities then forbade any further meeting of the strike committee and any activity of its members in directing the strike. The enlarged executive of the SPD met and declared that the movement was not opposed to the defence of the country, nor did it aim at furthering any hostile imperialism; it was caused by shortages of food and the pressure of the state of siege; it could have been ended quickly if the government had not used force and fulfilled the demands which were considered justified by the vast majority. Instead, the declaration continued, the government refused to negotiate with the workers' representatives and used repression – with the result that the strike spread to ever new groups and places, without any direction or control: the responsibility for this development rested with those who refused to listen to the voice of reason and pursued a policy of power and force against their own people. At the end the resolution repeated the demands for peace, for the lifting of the state of siege, of all restrictions of civic liberties, and of the 'militarization' of the factories. Coming from the party which throughout the war had 'stood out without any reservation for the defence of the country' these were very strong words. By now the SPD leaders were convinced that the interests of the country were endangered by 'the absence of political wisdom on the side of those who prolonged the war for aims of which the people disapproved'. The pressure from below was driving the SPD leaders to the Left. In spite of their declared 'neutrality', the leaders of the Free trade unions also protested against the 'measures of force' and 'threats of force' of the military. In their opinion, the prohibition of all strike meetings made it impossible to achieve an 'orderly resumption of work' and only further increased the bitterness of the strikers.[20]

On 31 January the military authorities proclaimed the 'severe state of siege' for Berlin; extraordinary military courts were to try all cases of treason, riot, resistance, sabotage, mutiny and inducement to mutiny. A warning was issued that any attempt to disturb law and order would be dealt with by strong military measures. The police were reinforced by 5,000 NCOs of the army. They tried to clear the streets, but the masses only moved on the other parts. In one of the large parks the SPD leader, Ebert, spoke to the strikers, asked them to remain calm and to avoid all clashes with the forces of order: it was their duty to produce the best weapons for their fathers and brothers at the front and they all desired victory. When he was interrupted by shouts of 'strikebreakers' he declared his solidarity with the strikers' demands, but his speech was considered 'too soft' by his listeners. Police were sent to the park to arrest the speakers and break up the meeting. By that time Ebert had finished and Dittmann taken his place. The appearance of the policemen caused considerable unrest so that Dittmann could not be heard, and he abruptly ended with a shout for 'the general democratic peace'. He was immediately arrested and tried by a military court for attempted treason and resistance to authority; as he was caught *in flagranti* he was not covered by his parliamentary immunity. The prosecutor demanded six years of penal servitude, and Dittmann who did not want to incriminate Ebert was sentenced to five years' detention in a fortress.[21] The man whom the military considered responsible for the unrest in the navy but were unable to indict was silenced.

The chancellor, Count Hertling, declared his willingness to negotiate, but only with 'representatives of organizations', among whom there could also be those of the strikers but they must be the leaders of the recognized trade unions. The strike committee which was dominated by the Revolutionary Shop Stewards rejected the participation of the union leaders because they had declared themselves 'neutral' towards the strike. It also demanded that five of its members should represent the strikers, while the government was only willing to concede three. The union leaders did not expect much from the negotiations and only aimed at bringing the strike to 'a decent end'. The leaders of one union, however, – interestingly enough those of the white-collar workers – objected to the attitude of the other union leaders and moved that, as they clearly no longer possessed the confidence of the masses, they ought to resign so that the workers could elect new leaders 'willing to lead the strike to a victorious conclusion, i.e. an immediate peace abroad and the immediate introduction of the most important internal reforms'. But their motion was rejected by the other union leaders. The government in its turn insisted on the participation of the official union leaders; as this condition was turned down by the strike committee, no negotiations took place. The union leaders thought that this attitude should have caused the leaders of the SPD to draw a sharp dividing line between themselves and the strike committee. But Ebert replied that the question was put to about one hundred factory trusties, all SPD members, and they unanimously advised against it because then the whole odium of betraying the movement would have fallen on the party. Indeed, by dissolving the strike committee and the delegates' conference the authorities themselves precluded the possibility of meaningful negotiations.[22]

As the strikers rejected the union leaders and their mediation, only two possibilities existed in practice: to start an armed uprising as propagated by the Spartacists – and this had no chance of success as long as the armed forces remained loyal – or to call off the strike without any negotiations, which would amount to a defeat of the movement. A Spartacist leaflet urged the workers to meet force by force, not to expect everything from the strike committee and the workers' council: 'The blessing does not come from above. It lies in the masses, in their direct fight. The decision about the outcome of our struggle... will fall *solely and only in the streets*... Try by all means at your disposal to win our brothers in uniform, the army, for the cause of peace. The dictatorship rests on bayonets and is lost as soon as these are wrenched from its hands... We must talk "Russian" with the reaction!'[23] But this and similar appeals to the soldiers produced no response. It took another nine months before the army sided with the strikers, and by then it was clear to everybody that the war was lost.

By the beginning of February it became clear to the strike leaders in Berlin that they could not win, and on the 3rd they decided to break off the strike, which had lasted exactly one week. The decision was probably also taken because meanwhile seven of the most important factories had been put under military orders and the workers were commanded to resume work by the 4th: those not obeying were threatened with the punishments of the law of siege and those of military age with conscription. The number of strikers shrank and the military authorities were confident that the strike would soon reach its end. They also drew the lesson from this 'success' that it was essential 'to use harshness against misled masses in all circumstances... Any attempt to introduce Russian conditions here must be ruthlessly suppressed.' Conditions in Germany, the report to the Emperor continued, were completely different from those in Russia, for the mass of the population was 'perfectly content', discontent was due only to agitation, and any concession would only increase the authority of the agitators and leaders as well as 'the cupidity of the masses', while severity would soon lead them back on to the right path.[24] If such views prevailed in the highest circles it is not surprising that no concessions were made while there was still time – for example on the vital issue of the Prussian franchise – and that the authorities were taken by surprise by the events of November 1918.

In contrast with the earlier strikes the movement quickly spread to all corners of Germany, although in most places work was resumed after a few days, considerably earlier than in Berlin. At Kiel the strike began even earlier than in Berlin. On the second day, 23,000 dockers and shipwrights were on strike, but by the end of January their number was halved. Their demands corresponded to those raised in Berlin, but included the immediate summoning of parliament so that it could take part in the peace negotiations, the dissolution of the Prussian Diet and new elections, so that its deliberations on the change of the franchise would no longer be 'a mockery of the Prussian population'; the workers' trusties should not be conscripted as a punishment for defending the workers' interests. Allegedly the Kiel strikers aimed at creating a central workers' council for the whole of Germany. Workers not obeying the strike call were threatened by the pickets and had to be protected by military patrols.[25]

In Hamburg the strike began on the same day as in Berlin, but only on a small scale. By the following day, however, 28,000 workers, above all from the dockyards were on strike, but only for a few days. The strikers held a mass meeting in the trade union house where at first their economic grievances were aired, but then political demands, especially for a peace without annexations, were put forward. The workers of Blohm & Voss were above all indignant about the system of 'horrendous fines' levied by the firm, the attitude of the foremen and masters and the inedible food, the rotten swedes served in the canteen. One speaker exclaimed that they were not fighting for ten grams of butter, but 'for all who hate the war'. Another speaker who pronounced for 'peace, freedom and right' was stopped by the supervising policeman. At a later meeting satisfaction was expressed that working-

137

class unity was restored by the strike and that in Berlin the SPD, the USPD and the strikers had formed a workers' council; the signal to resume work should come from there; the fratricidal strife must end, for the dockers had enough on their hands fighting the dock owners.[26]

At Bremen the strike started later and was on the whole limited to the dockyards; work was resumed after three days. At the Imperial dockyards in nearby Wilhelmshaven 60 per cent of the workers came out for one day. The chairman and vice-chairman of the works' committee said that they were totally surprised by the movement, and at an open-air meeting the trade union officials succeeded in calming the workers who then turned down a suggestion of a USPD member to proclaim a general strike. Four USPD members were arrested and 58 others whose names were found on a membership list discovered during a search were called up. At Rüstringen close to Wilhelmshaven the strike was equally short and no special political or economic demands were raised. At Emden, the strike lasted two days; at a meeting held on 1 February it was decided against strong opposition of the young and women workers to resume work. At Bremen and Hamburg the striking dock workers were sent call-up notices by the military and were told that they were assigned to work in the docks under military law. But they were paid their old wages with additional piece rates (which included the military pay), so that the 'military order' was not disturbed and unrest subsided.[27]

Apart from the large ports, the Rhine-Ruhr industrial area was strongly affected by the strike movement. On 28 January 35 mines were idle, on the next day 54. But by the end of the month the movement subsided and only one mine at Lünen continued the strike. In contrast with earlier strikes political demands were raised, above all for an immediate peace. While the leaders of the Christian and other unions opposed the strike, those of the Free miners' union refused to sign an appeal not to strike.[28] At Cologne, several thousand workers of the armament works went on strike for two days, here too against the opposition of the Christian unions. In the discussions with the authorities the leaders time and again expressed strong apprehensions that the government would not keep its promises with regard to a peace without conquest and the introduction of the equal franchise in Prussia. At Düsseldorf, the movement started with the quick distribution of the USPD peace manifesto in the working-class streets, at the tram stops and in the trams and factories, but only a minority of the metal workers obeyed the strike call. Their union official adopted the attitude that this was 'a purely political affair' with which he had nothing to do: the majority of his members tended towards the USPD and would refute any pacifying attempt from his side. But according to the police, the USPD members themselves were disunited, the younger ones pressing for strikes and demonstrations, while the more prudent ones believed that political slogans alone would not move the masses and that it was necessary to wait until the food situation became still worse; they were certain the strike would fail because the authorities and the military had ample warning. From the south of the Rhine province the authorities were able to report that no strike at all had occurred because the Christian unions to which the majority of the workers belonged declared against the strike, and their declaration induced even the leader of the Free unions at Saarbrücken to pronounce against any strike in wartime.[29]

In the industrial belt of central Germany, large strikes occurred once more in Halle and Magdeburg in which about 17,000 workers participated for two days. But the strike movement in Leipzig, a stronghold of the USPD, remained very weak, and the authorities gave the total number of strikers in the kingdom of Saxony as a mere 3,500. At Brunswick there was no strike at all, probably because of the defeat of the strike six months earlier. But in Cassel, where the USPD was very weak, more than 12,000 workers came out under the leadership of the Free unions. The strike meeting was presided over by the union secretary, Albert Grzesinski (a Prussian Minister of the Interior some years later), and adopted the political demands put forward in Berlin. Grzesinski explained that the two Social Democratic parties had taken over the direction of the movement; the workers should follow their lead and trust them, and the strike was very brief. In Jena too, the strikers raised the same demands as in Berlin. In Deuben in Saxony the USPD speaker emphasized that the movement was directed against the annexationists but was contradicted by the strikers who told him that the principal attack should be aimed at the government; there, too, SPD and USPD joined hands in supporting the strike.[30] In East Germany, the only strike of any importance took place in Danzig where the dockers and shipwrights stopped work for three days; there too the local leaders of SPD and USPD combined to direct the movement. A strike at Königsberg was only prevented by the end of the strike in Berlin.[31]

In the south and southwest of Germany, there were considerable movements. In Bavaria, where the general mood was hostile to the war, the strike began in the armament works of Nuremberg and Fürth on 28

January – the same day as in Berlin – with over 12,000 participants. At the largest firm concerned, a man in uniform posted himself at the gate with the words: 'Who wants peace stays out, who wants the war to go on goes inside!' Those who went in were spat on and vilified by the strikers. At Nuremberg, they went from factory to factory shouting 'peace' to persuade the remaining workers to join. A vast demonstration took place in which tens of thousands, many youngsters and many soldiers in uniform took part. They carried posters with the slogans 'bread', 'peace' and 'Liebknecht must be freed'. At street corners printed notices were posted up that the workers of all countries were demonstrating for peace, in Berlin alone half a million. At Fürth the demonstrators went to the town hall and submitted demands for 'an immediate Trotsky peace', a pardon for Liebknecht and no victimization. In both towns the local leaders of SPD and the unions actively participated in the strike and the demonstrations, as the authorities thought, in order not to lose any more followers. The strike was conceived as a counter-demonstration to the propaganda of the extreme Right for vast annexations and as a means of exercising pressure on the government. The demonstrations and open air meetings were completely orderly, and the organizers themselves asked the police to be present so that any unruly elements might be handed over to them. But unsuccessful attempts were made to stop the trams. On 29 January about 50,000 men and women were on strike; it was very general, with large and small factories participating; then the leaders decided to end it.[32]

In Munich, where Eisner had prepared the ground, the strike began later, perhaps because he and other USPD members were arrested as a precautionary measure. Although the Christian and the Free unions advised against a strike about 8,000 workers participated. The strikers adopted a resolution sending brotherly greetings to the workers of Belgium, Britain, France, Italy, Russia and the United States: 'We do not want to kill each other. We will call to account our governments which are responsible for the world war. Together we will enforce world peace...' On 3 February a mass meeting of the strikers voted to end the strike and to resume work the next morning, but to maintain their demands and to present them to the Bavarian government. At Schweinfurt, a speaker of the USPD addressed a meeting in the market place. He demanded peace and freedom for all political prisoners: 'We want to show the government that we do not need a Prussian general as our guardian' (meaning at the negotiations of Brest-Litovsk), and he asked his audience to disperse peacefully 'so that the ruling classes see what we can do'; if their demands went unheard, however, different methods might be adopted.[33] Eisner was accused of treason but released a few months later so that he could contest a by-election; he was never tried.

In the south-west, the largest strike occurred in Mannheim, with 15,000 participants according to the military authorities (22,000 according to the strike committee). The first large meeting was directed jointly by the local SPD and USPD leaders; a small and a large committee – composed of members of both parties in equal numbers – was responsible for the conduct of the strike. Its main purpose was to obtain a peace without open or hidden annexations; the demands were the same as those of Berlin, but also for a democratization of the grand-duchy of Baden, such as the abolition of the first chamber, the vote for women and a democratic franchise. On 4 February, when the strike in Berlin was broken off, the Mannheim strikers decided to go back.[34] In Ludwigshafen on the opposite bank of the Rhine, about 7,000 workers joined the strike, with demands identical with those of Berlin, and at Frankenthal about 5,000. Both strikes were short.[35] No strikes at all took place at Stuttgart or Frankfurt although in both towns the Left was strongly represented. The Stuttgart police were able to report that not even leaflets in favour of a strike were distributed there.[36] Perhaps the Left had been intimidated by the earlier arrests and conscription for the army.

In short, there was no general strike 'of all the workers employed for purposes of the war' – the idea promoted by the Zimmerwald movement, but only a very impressive partial strike. In September 1917 Eduard Bernstein, who had joined the USPD, wrote to Ramsay MacDonald from Denmark: 'From what I know of my country I must in all honesty confess that there are there the greatest odds against its feasibility. There is certainly a great amount of discontent, a very restive spirit abroad, and a number of strikes might undoubtedly break out. But with a most strongly organized military government at the helm of the country, the whole middle classes, the majority socialists, the big trade unions as opponents they [the strikes] would have little chance of lasting any length of time... In short, I am an unbeliever in the idea of bringing this solution about on the instigation of the minorities [in the socialist parties] and some neutral countries...'[37] Bernstein's scepticism with regard to Germany – and equally the other belligerent countries – was amply justified by events. The hold of the German military machine and the government was not seriously shaken until the autumn of 1918.

The strike was far from universal and, surprisingly, some of the old strongholds of the Left remained quiet. But it was a great event in the history of the German working class – like the general strike of March 1920 against a reactionary attempt to overthrow the Weimar Republic. This was also emphasized by the USPD a few weeks after the end of the strike. It stated that the movement had fulfilled its purpose: to tell the rulers that the workers were tired of being 'used as the blind tools of their policy of suppression and exploitation, the mere objects of a military dictatorship'. The workers, the declaration continued, did not want to produce the weapons for the subjugation of their Russian brothers, who had laid down their arms and no longer waged war against Germany, and equally opposed any plan of intervention in the Russian civil war.[38] The statement did not mention the role of the SPD and union leaders during the strike; but it is clear that it was most successful where the local leaders of the two parties cooperated, that the USPD alone was simply not strong enough to lead such a vast movement. On the other hand, it is obvious that the SPD from the outset aimed at a limited movement, at bringing it to an end as soon as possible, even if no concessions were made. Thus the strike was bound to fail: it could not possibly bring about the end of the war. Many workers soon complained about this lack of success. And there was a heavy price to pay because the military reacted by calling up tens of thousands of the strikers in Berlin alone, especially the members of the factory committees and of the delegates' conference, 'all alike blown away within one to three days', as a leading Spartacist had to admit soon after. In their military papers the agitators called up were classified with the words 'Berlin 1918'. The most likely result of this policy, however, was that the agitation was carried into the army. Indeed, one of the new recruits has told the story of how he was made welcome at the western front by his unit and had to tell the soldiers time and again about the strike; but what they were most eager to hear from him was whether 'the shit would not end soon'.[39] Clearly, they no longer expected a German victory but were looking to the hinterland to bring about the end of the war.

VIII

The German Left gathers strength

The political strikes of 1917-18 indicated that among the German working class radical, anti-war tendencies were gaining ground, that the mood of political unity which permeated the country at the beginning of the war was rapidly disappearing. These changes, however, not only affected the working class but the whole country. This was above all the case in Bavaria where the critical temper of 1916 became considerably stronger and more diffused. In July 1917 the authorities reported from Augsburg that the mood of the population was worse than ever since the beginning of the war: 'the people seem to despair of a happy end to the war' and their power of resistance was nearing its end. As causes of the despair the report mentioned high taxes, heavy burdens, the seizure of cattle, the melting down of the church bells. A few months later a sergeant wrote from the same town that the German worker had lost interest in the outcome of the war: whether the German or the British capitalist exploited him made hardly any difference; if German industry were taken over by the British the German worker would benefit because for Britain workers were more essential, therefore they would get higher wages. In the district of Ebersberg to the east of Munich the peasants believed that the war was lost; even the priests and teachers were no longer willing to counter this conviction. In another rural area the peasants no longer paid anything into their savings bank so that the latter would not be able to subscribe to the war loan. In the Allgäu too, the taking down of the church bells caused deep despondency and irritation; that, people said, was the last straw, but what would happen when the copper was used up? In July the press section of the Bavarian War Ministry found that even 'the glorious offensive in the East' did not arouse any interest; the mass of the population was apathetic and

143

distrustful of German successes; while in the towns the general characteristic was tiredness, the reports from the country spoke of despair; this was partly due to the failure of the Stockholm conference, partly to the uncertainties of the internal situation, partly to the prospect of yet another war winter, the main responsibility for which was attributed not to the enemy, but to the German government.[1]

Another cause of the growing exasperation was the steep rise in prices and the black market in food and other goods. According to the head of the press section of the War Ministry, very large circles were more and more convinced that the government did not seriously try to fight these evils nor intend to get to the root of the problem; a 'mood of crisis' had arisen among the suffering population. The bitter mood of the people was not only directed against those who used the war to make large profits, but also against those who did not stop it 'with the necessary ruthlessness' and against the state which proved powerless to help them. While the organized workers, thanks to their disciplined unions and high wages, were better able to cope with the tribulations of the war, so the writer stated, the millions of people who were not organized, the small shopkeepers, craftsmen, small officials and people with fixed incomes were sinking down to the level of an 'economic proletariat' on account of the terrible inflation and their economic misery; this 'new proletariat' consisted of absolutely 'loyal elements', but at any moment quite spontaneous irruptions of social discontent might occur. The political consequences of this fundamental change, he believed, would only appear in full force after the end of the war; it would be a mistake to close one's eyes before these facts: the preservation of the value of money at home must be treated as 'a compelling military requirement to which all other considerations have to be subordinated'.[2] Yet the author, a middle-aged officer of the Bavarian War Ministry, did not indicate how this was to be achieved. As the war was financed by the printing of more and more paper money, inflation was the natural result, and in the early 1920s the inflation of the war years was to be followed by inflation on a much vaster scale. But what he wrote about the new proletariat and the likely political consequences of this development was truly prophetic. Their feeling of security, their loyalty towards the established order, were destroyed by the war and its aftermath, and thus they developed radical tendencies of their own, not of the Left, but of the Right. This, however, was not what he expected, for he thought that 'these millions of voters' would move to the Left and finally would opt for 'parliamentarization and democratization', slogans which during the war hardly yet influenced these social groups.[3]

The fundamental social changes which affected Germany were also noticed outside Bavaria. From Frankfurt the military authorities reported that all those living on fixed incomes were losing their former status and approximating the status of people who lived from hand to mouth; the social decline of the officials brought with it a danger to the state that must not be underestimated; the state and the communes must combat the feeling that the officials were exposed to economic developments without getting any protection. At Leipzig it was noticed that the suffering of large groups of the *Mittelstand*, unable to augment their incomes, was increasing from month to month, and with it their irritation against those whose earnings grew (apparently meaning the working class and the war profiteers). The same feeling was expressed by Colonel Bauer (Ludendorff's adjutant) who lamented the destruction of the *Mittelstand*, especially the suffering of the families of officers and officials, small honest merchants, etc. In his opinion, 'the workers have exploited the situation and secured wages which generally are very high and partly enormous'.[4] What he did not see was that by September 1917 the *real* wages of workers in non-war industry amounted to only 52.7 per cent of the pre-war level, and in the war industry – where wages had risen noticeably – to 78.8 per cent, and that only small rather specialized groups were able to preserve or improve their standard of living.[5] The leaders of a large organization of the *Mittelstand* themselves angrily demanded a more equitable distribution of food in war-time; their women and those of the workers had to queue for hours outside the shops, but they never spotted those of the 'upper ten thousand' in rank and file with them; not the British, but the producers and profiteers were starving the people, 'and our state does nothing about it'; they called for 'a Hindenburg' to create order in the economic muddle. Bitterness also reached a high point among the white-collar workers who were in a much weaker position than the blue-collar workers, could not obtain higher wages and feared to lose their privileged social status.[6] Among all these groups of the old and the new *Mittelstand* the fear of proletarization became very real and drove them into opposition.

In 1917 the rapid decline in public morale was noticed by the authorities in many parts of Germany. In Berlin, according to the police, people were convinced that, with more and more enemies, Germany would be defeated in the end; large sections were no longer interested in the war news and did not believe what the papers wrote about hunger riots abroad: why did they not write instead about the hunger riots in

Germany? In Danzig in the east, the military authorities assessed the mood 'as very serious'; the depression was caused by the general conviction that there would be another war winter, that the harvest was only mediocre and that there might be a 'bad peace'; even well meaning, nationally minded people were close to despair. In Mainz, the military reported, popular indignation ran high on account of the long duration of the war, the dearth of food and the high prices; the smallest events, such as the stopping of soldiers for not saluting properly, immediately caused threatening crowds to assemble; everywhere, in the trams, the markets, the people's kitchens, one could hear exasperated talk. At Mannheim, the same mood prevailed; it was considered 'intolerable' that the military could not find ways and means to curtail the vast profits of the army contractors; they were buying up real estate and putting up new houses while the little people were fined for exceeding the maximum prices by a small margin. A sergeant reported from the same town that he overheard many remarks such as: 'We cannot hold out much longer, we will have to pay in any case; the English will not give in until we do, for next year the food will be even more insufficient; whether we give in now or in a few months' time, it's all the same.'[7]

This was not only the mood in the large towns, but it also affected the countryside. The president of the peasant association of Trier wrote that the peasants were indignant about the differences between producer and consumer prices; there was no longer any joy about German military successes, no hope of a better future, no interest in work; the peasants, his informers told him, sharply rejected the arguments for subscribing to the war loan and very little was subscribed. From Limburg on the Lahn it was reported that large subscriptions, people believed, would serve to prolong the war and that the peasants were particularly irritated by the enforced deliveries of their produce. In a Franconian village the peasants decided to boycott the war loan: it was all the same to them, they said, whether they became Russian or French. The *Landrat* of Rüdesheim on the Rhine found that the mood continued to deteriorate, partly on account of the food shortage and the general longing for peace; there were many thefts from the fields and a vast amount of poaching. At Rüdesheim too, many refused to subscribe to the war loan because that would only lengthen the war; in many cases this refusal was instigated by serving members of the forces who said that the war was only conducted in the interest of the money bags and only they derived advantages from it. In the countryside around Stettin in Pomerania the peasants were infuriated by the total lack of working clothes and boots and by the horrendous prices. In the clothes and shoe shops they were bartering goods for butter, eggs and other food, and those who could not offer any were unable to buy anything in the shops. If people from Stettin sought potatoes or butter they had to give the peasants oil or materials in exchange. From Mainz too the military reported a flourishing barter trade in which money no longer played any part; many people acquired goods they did not need themselves and used them for barter 'by several degrees'. In the rural districts around Mannheim the embittered peasants refused to deliver food unless they received quantities of coal; the poorer people were forced to communal cooking by lack of coal and to heat only one common living room, so the military reported.[8]

Above all, it was the terrible food shortage which undermined public morale and caused ever deepening depression among all social groups. At the end of 1917 the official weekly rations in the majority of towns amounted to four pounds of bread, seven pounds of potatoes, about 240 grams of meat and 80 grams of fat. But the rations were often not available. During the winter of 1916-17 large industrial towns of the Rhine-Ruhr area – Düsseldorf, Duisburg, Elberfeld-Barmen, Mülheim, Oberhausen – could not distribute any potatoes for five weeks, and at Essen only the workers employed in heavy industry received any, not the general public. In November the potato crisis repeated itself. In Munich, potatoes as well as beer were in short supply, and the quality of the bread deteriorated sharply. At Wiesbaden, where potatoes had been very short in 1916, none could be distributed in June-July 1917. An urgent appeal to the central potato office to permit a higher ration of flour received no reply, as the town council reported. In Hamburg the potato shortage was equally severe. None were distributed in April, the quality of the swedes which were distributed instead deteriorated with the advancing season and finally had to be stopped. The winter of 1916-17 went down in German history as the 'Swede Winter', when swedes were added to bread, jam and many other foodstuffs. At Hamburg a leaflet was distributed, 'The German Confession of Faith': 'I believe in the swede, the general feeder of the German people, and in the jam, its comradely relation, conceived by the urban distribution centre, through which all my hopes of getting potatoes are dead and buried,...resurrected as fruit, from which it will be made into breadspread for Germany's heroic sons. I believe in the holy war,... the community of hoarders, higher taxes, cuts in the bread ration, and the eternal life of the bread coupon. Amen.'[9]

147

No wonder that many, especially working-class women, took the law into their own hands. At the SPD party conference in October 1917 a tobacco worker from Saxony recounted that innumerable women and children were resorting to theft. In her information centre, a mother of six appeared recently who had taken part in a potato theft and been sentenced to three months' imprisonment; women came to her with medical certificates that their hands and feet were getting numb or that they were unable to bear healthy children; the worst was the fate of women working at home, surrounded by undernourished children. In Elbing, in eastern Prussia, women demonstrated during the same month in front of the food office and were so successful that the authorities distributed herring and cheese which were meant for a later period. At Stade, near Hanover, women and children with their faces blackened pushed into the bakers' shops, put money on the counter and went away with the loaves without leaving any coupons. In the same district, bread carts were stopped by crowds and the bread was quickly seized. In the spring of 1917 half-starved children from Frankfurt swarmed into the near-by villages and begged the peasants for potatoes; those fortunate enough to get any then had to walk back to town because the stations were watched by the police who confiscated all goods obtained 'illegally'. The police also guarded the bridges over the Main to prevent any smuggling of food into Hesse from rural areas where supplies were a little better.[10] With the harvest of 1917 matters improved somewhat, but not for long, especially as the hopes to obtain large supplies from the occupied Ukraine were not fulfilled on account of the chaotic conditions and the continuation of war and civil war.

Food riots broke out in many German towns, above all during the first six months of 1917. In January there was unrest in Hanover and in Harburg near Hamburg. In Hanover, many food shops were looted and bakers forced to sell bread without coupons, after women and children had in vain demanded bread at the town hall to make up for the potatoes which were unobtainable. At Harburg the crowd, mainly women and children, threw stones through the windows of the town hall and the mayor's house; 50 people were arrested. The women workers were particularly indignant that they were denied the additional rations for heavy work. In February new food riots broke out at Harburg. In the Hamburg dockyards leaflets were distributed inciting people to loot the food and bread shops. During two days of rioting bread was stolen from 116 shops in the city, and six companies of infantry were brought in to restore order. In the same month a crowd of many thousands, led by soldiers on leave, assembled in front of the town hall of Barmen in the Rhineland and demanded food. When this was declined stones were thrown. The police and the fire brigade tried to clear the square, but the latter's hoses were cut, the town hall was demolished, bakers' shops were plundered and many shop windows smashed. Here too the army restored order. In April there were riots in Mainz, with windows smashed and shops looted, principally those of Jewish firms. In June severe riots occurred at Düsseldorf and Stettin. At Düsseldorf 50 shops were plundered, mainly for food. As the police were unable to cope, the 'severe state of siege' was proclaimed and an extraordinary military court imposed harsh punishments; 200 people were arrested. At Stettin too, the police had to ask for military aid and were then able to disperse the crowd after considerable looting. In the industrial towns of Upper Silesia the unrest lasted from June to July. In Hindenburg, hundreds of demonstrators demanded food and, when this was refused, stormed the *Landrat* office, battled with the police and plundered shops. There and at Gleiwitz many thousands demonstrated in the streets, officers were beaten up, and order had to be restored by cavalry units. In Upper Silesia and elsewhere the main cause of rioting was the lack of potatoes.[11]

The heavy losses of the war, the uncertainties about its outcome, the lack of food, coal and all necessities, resulted in an overwhelming longing for peace which is stressed in numerous reports from all parts of the country. In May 1917 the military authorities reported from Karlsruhe that broad sections of the population strongly expressed this longing, that the masses no longer believed in a defeat of Germany's enemies and that 'the idea of a compromise peace' found many adherents. A report from Mannheim of the same month went further: the 'timid' would accept not only a peace through negotiation but demanded peace at any price. The town council of Frankfurt noted in December that the quiet was deceiving and that the 'widest circles, especially of the working class', ardently desired the end of the war; even if many appeared to be willing to grit their teeth and to face another war winter, they only did so in the expectation that the war would be over by the spring so that the food situation would improve. From Danzig 'ugly scenes' in the markets and foraging in the countryside by women were reported; the embittered women would stir up the working members of the family who then carried the agitation into the factories, preparing the ground for 'the peace agitators who were active everywhere'. The press section of the Bavarian War Ministry stated in September that the longing for peace was so strong that people were completely apathetic about the fate of the nation, the events at the front, and the question whether the war was won or lost. The peasants around Bayreuth demanded peace at any price although hitherto they had been indifferent to all left-wing propaganda. In Munich posters were put up in July during the night: 'All means are permitted against war or the murder of people! No bread without peace! No peace without revolution!' In certain factories at Düsseldorf and Essen handbills were circulating calling for a general strike 'to enforce peace'.[12]

In parliament, the deputies of the USPD made themselves the spokesmen of this popular longing. There Haase repeatedly demanded a peace without annexations and indemnities, claiming that 'bread, freedom, peace' had become the slogan of the whole world. There Ledebour declared that the idea of a fourth war winter was 'intolerable', that it was necessary to stop 'the self-destruction of humanity', the 'pointless slaughter'. As the vast territorial ambitions of the German ruling class prevented even the conclusion of peace with the defeated Russia, he stated flatly that Germany had no right to annex the Baltic lands because they had once belonged to the Teutonic Knights, that among their three million inhabitants the Germans formed a minority of only 200,000 and that it was by no means certain whether they all wanted to be annexed by Germany. But even if this were the case, could 200,000 decide upon the fate of a country of three million inhabitants? 'That is the most monstrous plan which has ever been put forward in this House.' The SPD too was strongly influenced by this popular pressure. At its party conference in October 1917 the deputy, Gustav Hoch, exclaimed: 'The strength of the people is at an end, not only with us, but in all countries. If peace is not concluded from above within weeks, it will be enforced by revolutionary convulsions which we can notice everywhere... The last discussions in parliament have without doubt caused an enormous bitterness everywhere, not only against the government, but also against a parliament which has put up with this policy and against the parties which have put up with it...' In Hamburg, the Left organized a large popular demonstration 'for peace, freedom, equality and bread' which was dispersed by the police. A mass meeting of the SPD in Frankfurt, attended by more than 20,000 demanded that the government must clearly demonstrate its readiness to make peace without demanding any conquests.[13] It is very difficult to say to what extent this general longing for peace was reinforced by the outbreak of the Russian revolution. It seems likely that it was above all caused by the enormous suffering and the heavy casualties. But there can be little doubt that the lust for annexations revealed during the negotiations of Brest-Litovsk met with considerable popular opposition, because the people feared that these far-reaching demands would prolong the war.

This widespread feeling also caused strong opposition to the new *Vaterlandspartei* – a party expressly founded by Admiral von Tirpitz to promote an annexationist peace and to fight 'the all-devouring tyranny of Anglo-Americanism' for the 'freedom of the European continent'. It was widely believed that the party's agitation for a 'peace of victory' and for large.scale annexations exercised a strong influence on the government and prevented the reaching of an agreement with the Bolsheviks. As the SPD conference of October 1917 put it, the new party and similar Pan-German circles were responsible for 'time and again providing those in the enemy countries who wish to prolong the war with arguments to whip up the war passions among their peoples; and at the same time they are guilty of weakening and endangering the unity of our people'. Among the causes of the January strikes Ebert expressly mentioned the 'wild agitation' (*Hetze*) of the *Vaterlandspartei*, and the same point was made in the speeches made to the striking workers. At Leipzig, Mannheim and Stuttgart meetings organized by the new party were disturbed by left-wingers to such an extent that the police were forced to close them.[14] While the peace propaganda of the Left was constantly hampered by the censorship and the intervention of the authorities, the mass propaganda of the *Vaterlandspartei* was able to proceed unhindered, thanks to the tacit support of Ludendorff and the military. The party could soon boast more than a million members, proving the strength of its appeal to the middle classes, at least in Prussia.

In Bavaria, the mood of the population became also strongly anti-Prussian and even anti-monarchist. In February 1917 the Bavarian War Ministry noted that the anti-Prussian feeling only mirrored the mood in the army, where it was widely believed that the Bavarian regiments were always put into the most difficult and dangerous positions, so that their losses were much heavier than those of the Prussian units. An official report from Augsburg simply stated that the Main frontier (which had once separated the south from Prussia) was reappearing everywhere. At a conference at Cham in the Upper Palatinate the priests declared that it was widely said the king of Bavaria was half Prussian and wanted to extend the war as long as possible on behalf of Prussia; the war was only prolonged for the sake of Prussia. The secretary of a peasant association in Upper Bavaria wrote at the beginning of 1917 of a planned, underground agitation against the king; he had to listen to such opinions

151

of the king expressed by good middle-class people that he must fear for the future of the monarchy; many held the king responsible for the exploitation of Bavaria by Prussia which allegedly caused wide-spread hunger. In the summer of 1917 the Bavarian government was moved to issue leaflets to disprove the view that Bavaria had to 'wage war only for Prussia'. In July the crown-prince of Bavaria considered it necessary to express his worries to the prime minister. The Bavarian government, he wrote, was blamed for putting up with everything coming from Berlin; many members of the *Mittelstand* – which once had been decidedly pro-monarchist – now held the opposite view because they made the government responsible for their misfortunes and the same tendency affected many smaller places. He significantly added that 'in the other German states' the anti-monarchist tendency was if anything stronger, that serious people doubted whether the Hohenzollern dynasty would survive the war. This opinion was indirectly confirmed by the bishop of Limburg on the Lahn who issued a circular that 'paid agents of the enemy' were trying to 'incite' the German people against their princes so as to undermine the national power of resistance: the clergy were urged to oppose these attempts 'with all determination'.[15]

The party which should have benefited greatly from this growth of opposition to the war was the USPD – the only legal party to demand an early peace and to reject all annexations. But this was hardly the case. The party was officially founded at Easter 1917, but already at the beginning of the year the Social Democratic Working Group and the Spartacus Group held a joint conference in Berlin which proved how divided the opposition was in its attitude to the SPD and on other issues. The conference was attended by 157 delegates representing 72 constituencies (about one fifth of the total number); 35 of them belonged to the Spartacus Group. In his opening speech Haase rejected any suggestion that he intended to destroy the SPD: 'We intend to remain in the party because we will with certainty win over the masses [of the members]. We would be fools if we wanted to remain a sect...' The speaker of the majority, Lipinski, submitted a resolution counselling against withholding from the SPD executive its share of the membership dues; these tactics did not weaken it financially but provided it with a good opportunity to expel local organizations and thus to deprive them of any influence on party policy; the party institutions should be used to conquer it. This was opposed by the Spartacist spokesman, Ernst Meyer, who advocated the blocking of the party dues, but only if this was done by entire constituency parties. He did not suggest that the opposition should secede from the SPD: it should remain inside 'as long as we can lead the class struggle against the party executive; the moment that we are hindered in this we will not remain in the party.' The party was to be used only 'as a recruiting ground for the proletarian, anti-militarist class struggle'.[16]

Meyer was seconded by a Spartacist delegate from Duisburg who sharply attacked the Social Democratic Working Group: 'no one will be able to tell me what it really wants for it does not want anything' (angry interruption by Ledebour); the Working Group, he declared, was in a 'state of pulp'. To get it out of it and to give it a 'firm purpose', the Spartacists submitted certain proposals. Among them there figured prominently the withholding of the party dues, by which they intended to demonstrate that they had nothing in common with the policy of the SPD: 'it is the step to separation'. But this step was vigorously opposed by Haase as a 'fetish' and rejected by the conference by 111 to 34 votes, only the Spartacists voting in favour. A resolution submitted by Eisner to mobilize the proletarian masses against the government by means of an independent democratic and socialist propaganda for world peace was adopted unanimously. The conference provided the SPD leaders with the opportunity they had been waiting for. A few days later they announced, not without justification, that it amounted to the founding of 'a separate organization against the party' and that the opposition had removed themselves from it.[17] The split which had begun in the parliamentary party over the issue of the war credits had become final and – in spite of Haase's apprehension – it was necessary to found a new party.

This was done in April 1917 at Gotha where the two wings of the German socialist movement had united 42 years before. Present were 124 delegates, representing 91 constituencies (only a fraction of the total); a full third of them came from Berlin and Saxony, the strongholds of the opposition, while many other parts of Germany were only very weakly represented. In his opening address Haase emphasized that the conference was to open the path to 'a truly socialist policy which is sharply divided from the policy of the government socialists who have made their peace with the bourgeois parties'. He declared that only those should join the new party who were determined to work together: if the groups further to the Left had only come to Gotha because the new party 'would provide a protecting roof during the state of siege', he must vigorously oppose this, for it seemed to him that the Spartacists did not fight so much against the 'government socialists' as against the so-called

Centre of the party. He had to reject the term 'Centre' for in reality they were decidedly to the Left. A Spartacist delegate from Stuttgart denied that his group would secede from the new party as soon as the war was over: they would only do so if its policy was not conducted according to the principles of the Spartacists (which came to about the same thing). He called for actions against the war and claimed that hitherto every action had been called off in mid-stream by the moderates. Another Spartacist, Meyer, admitted that his group was very sceptical with regard to unity with the moderates; they would only opt for it if they were not hampered in making propaganda for their views inside the new party.[18]

Other voices at the conference opposed in principle any cooperation with Haase and the moderates. Rosi Wolffstein from Duisburg declared that she had a binding mandate to vote against any cooperation. Even if the conference accepted the proposals of the Spartacists, the members would have to decide whether to opt for unity or to rally around a new programme as the cornerstone of a new left-radical movement. A delegate from Bremen also rejected any compromise solution and considered the foundation of a new left-radical party necessary. If the moderates united with the Spartacists, he correctly prophesied, the internal struggle would absorb the best part of their energy and the fight against capitalism would suffer; the workers were best served by revolutionary action against the war; they were unable to combine with the moderates because the latter had the same platform as the 'social patriots' – a remark which provoked laughter. Then, however, Dittmann reported that behind the scenes a compromise had been worked out on the organizational issue, the Spartacist proposals having been accepted as the basis of discussion. Haase asserted that therefore independent actions of any group would no longer be feasible in the new party: only local or district organizations were entitled to start actions of their own. But several Spartacists present denied this interpretation and only conceded that the new party would not be held responsible for such actions. Moderate speakers in their turn claimed that this was contrary to the compromise reached in committee, on which the Spartacists had after all been represented; it was essential that the different groups should try to live and work together, and the Spartacists ought to stop the bitter polemics against the so-called Centre which only too often amounted to abuse and vilification.[19]

The 'organizational guidelines' adopted by the conference laid down that the groups of the opposition were to be merged in every place and district, but that each local party organization was to have 'far-reaching independence and freedom of action', that the central leadership was to hear the representatives of the districts before any important political decision was taken, that the stress of political action was to be transferred 'to the masses' and, if possible, a vote of the members was to be taken on issues which determined the party's attitude for any length of time. The party was to have a federal structure with considerable freedom of action for local organizations: that was the basis of the compromise reached with the Spartacists. The USPD lacked a strong central leadership and any clear aims. Even so, the delegate of the Left Radicals from Bremen and Hamburg expressed regret that the Spartacists had decided to join hands with the 'Centre': for them, unity was impossible because there was no 'common intellectual basis'.[20] The foundation conference of the USPD only confirmed that the left-wing opposition was divided into at least three parts two of which were now linked in an uneasy alliance in the new party. This alliance was to last a mere 20 months, for at the end of 1918 the Spartacists decided to found their own party, the KPD; they no longer needed a 'protecting roof'. All the later divisions of the German working-class movement were foreshadowed in the discussions at Gotha in 1917.

It is uncertain how many members the USPD had when it was founded, and how many remained with the SPD. According to its own figures the USPD had 120,000 members by the autumn, while only 170,000 remained loyal to the SPD. But 120,000 almost certainly was an exaggeration, and much less than 100,000 is a more likely figure. In any case, the party failed to win over the majority of the members of the SPD, which throughout remained considerably stronger and at that time still claimed close on 250,000 members. Of the total USPD membership, more than half were concentrated in three areas, Berlin, Leipzig and the Lower Rhine. There the party succeeded in capturing the district organizations of the SPD, as it did in some other places, such as Brunswick, Frankfurt and Halle. But there were large parts of Germany where the USPD had no or very little influence, and this applied even to important industrial centres, such as Cassel, Cologne, Hanover, Magdeburg or Westphalia. In Würzburg, in October, Ebert was able to announce that only 56 constituency parties out of 357, and another 21 small local party groups had left the SPD, in other words that its organizational structure was still more or less intact; only in some places – Berlin, Brunswick, Leipzig – was it seriously weakened. In Leipzig, the SPD had to found its own new party group, but it had only 80 members, and in Brunswick the situation was similar. For either party, much clearly depended on the popularity of the local leaders; but it is difficult to explain the failure of the USPD in 1917-1918 to build up a strong, nation-wide organization. In November 1917 the *Spartacus Letters* stated rightly that the really important issue was not whether the party had 120,000 or even more members, but why the great mass of the German working class including all these party members were quietly suffering 'the fourth war winter, the fourth year of hunger, misery, atrocity and mass murder, without a stir or a murmur.'[21] Action was attempted in January 1918 but it failed.

Police and similar reports from different parts of Germany emphasized this very uneven distribution of party strength. According to the head of the Berlin police nine tenths of the working class supported the Left; nowhere else had the SPD leaders lost so much influence; even the larger unions, such as those of the building, wood and metal workers, pronounced decisively against the SPD policy; but the Spartacists were comparatively weak and not able to muster more than about one seventh of the strength of the moderates among the party's local functionaries, and in Stettin SPD and USPD were about evenly matched; but in Breslau – Bernstein's constituency – the Left was very weak. In November the USPD organized demonstrations for peace in Berlin during which the workers broke through the police cordons and penetrated to the centre among shouts for peace. In Brunswick, the members decided to join the USPD after hearing a report on the Gotha conference; the speaker stressed that the masses must be mobilized for action and that parliamentary work was much less important. A military report from Frankfurt stated that the opposition was making headway in the industrial areas and had conquered the majority in three local constituencies. In Düsseldorf, the large majority of the organized socialists followed the opposition and the same applied to the members of the unions. A meeting of the SPD in November was attended by 2000 people, but among them only a few were loyal to the party, and the speaker was only able to make himself heard by making considerable concessions to the Left. The local left-wing leaders also made it clear to the USPD that they were dissatisfied with the attitude of its deputies and desired a more forceful policy. At Elberfeld too, the USPD was much stronger than the SPD.[22]

In Baden, however, the USPD was very weak, even in Mannheim where it could muster only about 250 people for a peace demonstration in November. In Karlsruhe, only 24 people attended the constituent meeting. The party organizations remained loyal to the SPD. USPD meetings in Munich in July were attended by about 80 people, among them some soldiers in uniform or in civilian clothes. Another meeting, in December, drew only 13 men and three women, but the chairman announced that the local party meanwhile had 300 members. A peace meeting in August was prohibited by the authorities, but several hundred assembled in spite of this and remonstrated against the ban. At the end of 1917 the SPD organization of Hof in northern Bavaria went over to the USPD following its parliamentary deputy. In the military district of Cassel, which comprised large parts of Hesse and Thuringia, there was only one 'black spot', the town of Gotha, which was a stronghold of the USPD. Early in 1918 the new chancellor, Count Hertling, wrote to Hindenburg that the USPD was slowly growing and that the SPD leaders were extremely worried whether the great majority of their voters would still support them. But he advised against strong measures by way of censorship because that would only increase the circulation of secret leaflets, even further than was already the case.[23]

The USPD was not a revolutionary party and did not aim at the violent overthrow of the Imperial régime. The party leader, Haase, was a very honest and sincere man, a lawyer like Liebknecht, but far removed from the latter's revolutionary and anti-militarist ardour. Even General Groener, who was very hostile to the USPD and all it stood for, was convinced that Haase 'was anything but the leader of a revolution'. Under oath at the Munich stab-in-the-back trial in 1925, Groener recounted that, after the April strikes of 1917, he had asked Haase to a private conference during which he explained to him the situation at the front and the need to increase the production of munitions, at a time when a big attack of the Entente was expected. Haase thereupon gave Groener his hand and promised that he would see to it that no strike took place on May Day. One cannot imagine Liebknecht making such a promise. The USPD – like the British ILP with which it had much in common – stood for peace, a peace without annexations, and for the rights of the smaller nationalities, whether inside or outside the German orbit. In its declaration for the Stockholm conference the party came out for 'the complete independence of Belgium' and for the reparation to the Belgian people of all the damages caused by the war. With regard to Poland, the USPD declared it illogical to concede the right to independence only to the Poles in Russia, but to deny them this right in Prussia and Austria: 'we understand the deep longing of the Polish people for national unity' – a very remarkable declaration in the circumstances of 1917 and very different from the attitude taken by the SPD leaders in Stockholm. In the first instance, however, the declaration continued, 'the proletariat of every country must do everything to bring about the end of the world war, to fight for peace.'[24]

Declarations such as these were bound to infuriate the military, as did the actions of the USPD deputies in support of the political strikes. In June 1917 the Prussian Minister of War wrote to the military authorities that this 'dangerous activity' must be countered with determination and the USPD must be deprived of the facility of spreading its views; meetings which were to be addressed by known agitators were not to be allowed, and if any spoke in a meeting without prior notification it was to be dissolved immediately; another reason for a dissolution was any malicious attack 'on the right-wing sections of the working class in the SPD' because this would violate the *Burgfrieden*; the USPD should not be permitted to publish any new papers, and most rigorous measures were to be taken against the distributors of anti-war leaflets and pamphlets; but parliamentary deputies were not to be prevented from speaking in their constituency and were only to be taken into 'protective custody' with the consent of the minister. Even the manifesto in which the USPD announced the foundation of the party and invited people to join was confiscated by the censorship.[25] Yet in spite of the censorship the *Leipziger Volkszeitung* and a few other USPD papers continued to be published and – under the watchful eye of the police – the party was allowed to hold some public or private meetings.

The Spartacists joined the USPD, but only after much soul-searching and against considerable opposition from within their own ranks. Some of their local groups, however, did not accept the decision to join as they distrusted the 'soft' policy of the new party, and others only did so very reluctantly. A few days after the Gotha conference the Spartacus leaders issued a circular that their revolutionary position must 'under no circumstances be sacrificed' to any common action with the USPD members; any local cooperation with them was only permissible if they fully accepted the Spartacists' slogans and demands, including their leaflets; it should be attempted 'to push them on to our point of view'. Even in Berlin, however, the Spartacist following remained small. In a by-election at Potsdam-Spandau the veteran historian Franz Mehring was put up as the left-wing candidate, but he only received 5,000 votes, while the totally unknown SPD candidate was elected with more than three times that number. But the Spartacists consoled themselves by claiming that 5,000 Social Democrats who knew what they wanted had clearly voted against the policy of the 'social patriots', for socialism and against the war, while those who voted for the SPD candidate were a 'general mish-mash', united only by their hatred of socialism. In the spring of 1917 the Spartacists issued several calls for a general strike, 'a strike at the front and at home', but their passionate appeals to follow the Russian example and to overthrow the government met with little response. One such leaflet also called for the abolition of the federal states with their separate Diets and the establishment of a republic, which alone could indemnify the German working class for all the sacrifices of the war. Another appealed to the soldiers not to shoot when ordered to do so, and to the workers to stop all work on armaments and munitions and to reject any activity connected with the war which could only be finished in this way.[26]

This kind of revolutionary rhetoric, however, did not find an echo, and the Spartacists were unable to influence the outbreak and conduct of the political strikes of 1917 and 1918 as their strength in the trade unions was very small. This weakness was reinforced by the fatal tendency of extreme left-wingers to issue the slogan to 'leave the unions' and to found 'unitary' workers' associations from below in the factories. This policy was due to the passivity and 'treason' allegedly committed by the union leaders and their cooperation with the government in wartime. At Düsseldorf, the left-wingers founded a General Workers' Association, but it never gained more than a few hundred members; according to the military authorities, all its members were Spartacists. At Stuttgart, a meeting of the local USPD by a small majority decided in favour of the foundation of 'a new fighting trade union organization' which was to combine political and trade union work. But the move was opposed by the *Leipziger Volkszeitung* which declared that the splitting of the unions would only cause great joy on the side of the employers.[27] Although nothing much came of these attempts during the war, it remained a constant tendency on the German extreme Left in the after-war period during which numerous efforts were made to found 'revolutionary' unions or general workers' associations. They all ended in failure as the workers remained loyal to the established trade unions.

The call to quit the unions which had become 'vehicles of treason' also emanated from *Arbeiterpolitik*, the journal of the Left Radicals who were present at the Gotha conference but refused to join the USPD and continued to attack the Spartacus Group. *Arbeiterpolitik* held the Spartacists at least partly responsible for 'the demise of the Left Radical movement' in Germany, while Ledebour and Dittmann were accused of using 'tactics of political parasitism' and Haase and Hoffmann of being ever ready to break their word. The Left Radicals of Hamburg resolved that there was no difference of principle between the 'social patriots' and the 'social pacifists', i.e. the USPD, that both must be fought as a matter of principle because the latter were 'crippling the fighting power of the working class'. While *Arbeiterpolitik* admitted that differences existed between the USPD and Spartacus, with regard to street demonstrations, mass actions, etc., it claimed that these differences were not 'fundamental'. There Karl Radek argued that a united front 'between us and the Centre' was out of the question and that the idea of forming a joint party with it was 'a dangerous utopia'. In the spring of 1918 a group of the Left Radicals in Hamburg wrote to a local Spartacus group in Berlin that their rejection of all pacifist ideas sharply clashed with the theory and practice of the USPD: a precondition of uniting with the Spartacists therefore was their separation from the USPD – a decision that could not be left to the individual members; 'political Schlemils' could not be used for any political action, and their experience counselled against any cooperation with the USPD.[28]

Compared with the very small membership of the Left Radicals and the Spartacus Group, the USPD was a mass party; it was only in Bremen and Hamburg that the Left Radicals had groups of any size. From Essen one of their members wrote to Bremen in September 1918 – a few weeks before the outbreak of the revolution – that there only a remnant existed which, in 1917, had not joined the USPD; even their links to the Spartacists in Duisburg were cut since their leader was at the same time the chairman of the local USPD. The writer even declined to receive any copies of *Arbeiterpolitik*, for he only wanted to start making propaganda when he had a 'clear field', and so far a general lack of clarity existed 'in our own ranks'. He clearly felt completely isolated – and that in one of Germany's major industrial centres. But, however small the groups of the Left Radicals were in 1917-1918, their sectarian views exercised a strong influence on the German Communist Party when it was founded at the end of 1918 and continued to influence the course of the KPD for many years to come. It may seem strange that the military authorities permitted the publication of *Arbeiterpolitik* throughout the war years. Was it because they welcomed the attacks on the USPD? They argued that its uncensored articles allowed them an 'insight into the plans and organization of the movement' and that the journal facilitated 'the supervision...of the apparently growing Left Radical movement' – a purpose which they achieved by perusing the correspondence of the journal.[29] Thus it was able to publish articles by Lenin, Radek and other leading Bolsheviks as well as long commentaries on the Bolshevik victory and the measures taken by the Bolshevik government. In Germany, this small group was the only one to identify itself completely with the Bolshevik revolution.

That the SPD leaders were worried by the growing radicalization of the working class is confirmed by the report of the Saxon Minister of the Interior about a conversation with two SPD deputies in April 1917. They told him that, in view of the bad food situation, it was extremely difficult for them to keep the population quiet; many strong elements among the workers were pressing them to represent the wishes of their class more forcefully in the Saxon Diet, and they could not disregard this continuous pressure. When the minister enquired what these wishes were they replied: the abolition of the four-class franchise for the second chamber of the Saxon Diet, the reform of the first chamber, and the cancellation of the privileges of the residents in the communes. In Prussia, the SPD for very many years had bitterly attacked the three-class franchise by which the second chamber of the Diet was elected in an indirect form so that the party was unable to win more than half a dozen seats. Under the conditions of the *Burgfrieden* these attacks had stopped for the time being, but they revived strongly in 1917. In March Scheidemann wrote in *Vorwärts* that the government favoured a reform of the franchise only after the end of the war: that had also been the policy of the Russian government, and the result was the outbreak of the revolution. 'Now is the time to act decisively. The difficulties which might arise if the government now asks for the [equal] franchise in Prussia weigh as lightly as a feather compared with those which may arise if no such move is made.' In April the SPD executive demanded the immediate disappearance of all inequalities of civil rights in state and commune and the replacement of government by the bureaucracy by the rule of parliament. In the same month the Emperor addressed his famous 'Easter Message' to the chancellor which promised a reform of the Prussian franchise and the adoption of the direct and secret ballot for the time *after* the war, but did not include the introduction of the equal franchise, a promise that was only added in July. The decisive point, however, was that it was a vague promise and that it postponed the abolition of the three-class franchise to the post-war period; and there was the danger that the first chamber, the 'Herrenhaus', could block any reform.[30]

These hesitations and reservations aroused the indignation of the SPD leaders. At a meeting of the parliamentary party a right-wing deputy said resignedly that while the war lasted, the most important means of exercising pressure, the strike, could not be used, and other methods to achieve a change of the franchise did not exist; if nothing was changed the workers' confidence in the party would be undermined. But in the Prussian Upper House the bearer of one of the most distinguished names in Prussian history, General von Kleist, exclaimed: 'I call to those who intend to undermine the strong structure of the Prussian state which has withstood storms and bad weather, and who want to create a substitute of unproven worth: hands off the old Prussia! And I call to those who honestly...want to make small structural improvements: Let's take our time, or as one says in Berlin: always gingerly with young horses!' Thus, when the SPD conference assembled in Würzburg in October, the issue of the Prussian franchise figured prominently in the discussions. In his opening speech a delegate from Würzburg declared that the three-class franchise must be abolished quickly and completely: 'It will be abolished because we will not allow it to continue! (strong applause). An attempt to delay it... would seal the doom of our country. In the free Prussia, the Prussia of the free franchise, there is no longer any room for that cabinet of curiosities, the "Herrenhaus"...' Another speaker demanded the vote for women and a lower voting age as well as proportional representation because parliaments should mirror the currents among the people and no political trend should be excluded from representation. In his concluding words Scheidemann warned those who intended to delay or water down the reform that they were playing with fire: 'We do not permit a delay, we do not bargain any longer about the franchise, we demand it completely equal and we demand it immediately (renewed applause).' A resolution was adopted which requested 'the immediate fulfilment of the longing of the German people for democracy', not only the equal franchise in Prussia, but also the decisive participation of the Reichstag in all the great issues of the time. Yet the demands were not fulfilled. When the decisive vote was taken in the lower house of the Prussian Diet the equal franchise was rejected with a large majority of nearly all the bourgeois parties; only the SPD, USPD, the Progressives and the deputies of the national minorities voted in favour.[31] The SPD organized a series of large public meetings to press its demand, but they too brought no result. Its collaboration with the government in war-time produced very few dividends.

Yet the moderate SPD leaders continued their cooperation with the government, not only in Berlin, but also in the provinces. This was gratefully recognized by at least some of the Prussian administrative authorities in 1917 and it also applied to the union leaders. Thus the authorities of Cologne stated that the food issues had been discussed in meetings with the leaders of the different unions and that their moves to obtain higher wages in certain factories 'were always solved to the satisfaction of those concerned'. From Trier the authorities reported later in the year that in the industries of the Saar a limited strike had occurred to gain higher wages and lower potato prices which was supported by both the Free and the Christian unions, but that economic peace was restored after a few days by some concessions. From Cassel, on the other hand, the military were informed in October that hitherto the administrative authorities had cooperated with the union leaders in influencing the working masses, but with the agitation for peace at any price the situation had changed so that the 'confidential collaboration with the union leaders seems to have suffered'. In some of the largest unions – the metal and the textile workers' – strong opposition developed to the policy of cooperation with the authorities. In June the leaders of the metal workers came under sharp attack from the Left at the union's annual general meeting, in particular for their attitude during the April strike. One delegate from Berlin accused the leaders of aiming at collaboration with the bourgeoisie, and another launched a strong personal attack on the union's leader in Berlin. Yet another speaker held the union leaders responsible for the war policy of the SPD. At the end a motion of complete confidence in the leaders was passed, but only by a small majority of 64 to 53; the leaders were reelected, but 35 blank voting slips were handed in. At the beginning of 1918 three union leaders, under pressure from their members, transferred from the SPD parliamentary party to that of the USPD although they were not political radicals.[32]

Thus the radical trend of 1917 affected the leadership of the unions, but the moves to unseat the right-wing leaders failed and they remained in control of the movement. In this they enjoyed the help of the military authorities who would take action to prevent the holding of an election by which the leaders might be ousted. In September 1917 a general meeting of the Berlin metal workers' union was to be held for the purpose of electing a new management committee, and the radicals wanted to replace the local leaders. But the military stepped in and prohibited the meeting, so that the right-wing leaders retained control.

In March 1918 the military once more intervened and forbade the members of the Berlin metal workers' union any activity aiming at the holding of a ballot on the calling of an extraordinary general meeting of the union: for this purpose the military could use their powers under the law of 1851 regulating the state of siege.[33] The union leaders were protected by the authorities when their positions were endangered, but they lost touch with their members who suffered badly from food shortages, low wages and long working hours. Many workers declared openly that they were unable to work if the food supply was not improved, and their claims were hardly ever supported by the union leaders.

The many strikes of 1917 were in their large majority entirely spontaneous and often took the union leaders entirely by surprise. Many of them disapproved of the strikes and blamed the outbreak on non-union members, for example in the Ruhr in April 1917. At Barmen in November they warned the workers not to strike for a shorter working day, but they were sharply criticized for their pro-government attitude by members of the works' committees: it was vital, they were told, to shorten the working day or to stop work unless the food situation improved. At Cologne too, the metal workers went on strike in July to win shorter working hours and the three metal workers' unions supported the demand for a working week of 51 hours and corresponding wage increases to make up for the loss, but the employers at first refused to negotiate. As men and women were collapsing every day in the factories for lack of food, many thousands of workers demonstrated in large mass meetings for their demands. They declared that, if women took a day off to try and collect a little food in the country, they were driven by hunger; other speakers asked the workers to exercise sharp pressure on their leaders so that the demands would not be watered down during the negotiations. In the end some concessions were won, the working week was reduced by three hours to a minimum of 54 per week, and a wage increase of 5 per cent was granted to compensate them for the loss.[34]

In the same month the dockyard workers of Hamburg demanded a working week of 52 hours and wage increases of 20 per cent, and more for skilled workers. The local official of the metal workers' union spoke to the striking workers and stressed that for years they had struggled with the employers without gaining any considerable concession; what they had obtained during the war was only compensation for the high food prices, but they were determined to retain the gains; nowhere were the starting wages as low as in the dockyards, for the employers were well organized and it was difficult to combat their power. Other speakers added that the demands were 'much too modest' because they would not compensate them for the high food prices, but the employers turned down the workers' demands. These are just a few glimpses of the workers' grievances and their suffering under wartime conditions: even if their demands were met by the employers no real change was achieved. This was partly due to the war, and partly to the attitude of the employers who were determined to remain the 'masters' in their own house. But at least in Bavaria it was recognized that this attitude and its support by the government was likely to undermine the influence of the union leaders and would be grist to the mill of the left-wing opposition.[35]

One new feature of the labour conflicts in Germany was noticed in many reports, the militancy of working-class women: not surprisingly because they had to feed their families in addition to all their other work, and if there was no food in the shops they had to go on hazardous expeditions into the country to forage for food. At Mannheim and at Brunswick, women took a leading part in the strikes in the armament factories. Three quarters of the strikers fined at Brunswick in August because they had continued the stoppage against military orders were women. At the beginning of the year women munition workers at Aachen demanded potatoes: when they failed to get any they demonstrated in the streets and plundered some bakers' shops. In June the majority of women employed as tram conductors and drivers in Cologne came out on strike and succeeded in gaining three free days a month without losing wages as well as a wage increase of half a mark per day. There the unions negotiated with the city and were successful in obtaining a settlement. In Reydt, also in the Rhineland, women demonstrated in June under the red flag against the food shortages. In the same month thousands of women demonstrated in the industrial towns of Upper Silesia against the shortages; when their demands were not met they looted food shops and distributed their contents.[36] In a country where women had been confined to the house and played little part in politics their arrival on the political scene and their militant spirit marked an important change. But as yet very few women occupied prominent political positions. That of Rosa Luxemburg among the Spartacists was very exceptional – and after all, she was not a German but came from Russian Poland where the traditions were very different.

The mood of the German people during the fourth year of the war was undoubtedly much influenced by the reports of soldiers who came home on leave or wrote to their families. The press section of the Bavarian War ministry attributed part of the responsibility for the change in public opinion to soldiers on leave and their violent speeches. A Bavarian deputy wrote that soldiers on leave told 'the most gruesome tales', of officers behind the front eating and drinking everything that was expensive and in large quantities, holding daily drinking bouts, etc. As these stories were told so often he felt there must be something to them, 'otherwise not all soldiers on leave would say the same'. The mayor of Aschaffenburg added that the story tellers were by no means enemy agents but genuine soldiers who in trains and pubs were spreading these tales. At Augsburg two soldiers on leave in vain went to collect coal for their families and then began to grumble: 'We have no interest in victory; only the "Prussian" who now even steals our coal would have the advantage; we are Bavarians and would be much better off with France than with the "Prussians" who now also steal our onions.' And: 'We must stand together and smash everything, then we will force "them" to make peace at last.'[37]

In 1917 Germany presented a very mixed picture. There was strong dissatisfaction and a deep longing for peace among all sections of the population, peace at almost any price. But there was no revolutionary situation and not even a revolutionary party. The new USPD attracted considerable support from sections of the working class, but it was deeply disunited, hampered by the state of siege and the interference of the authorities and, in many parts of the country, by the lack of a daily paper. As long as the bureaucratic apparatus continued to function and the armed forces remained loyal to their officers there was little prospect of a change in this situation. Russia in the same year had seen two violent revolutions, but they broke out in a country which had been defeated, whose western provinces were occupied by the Germans, in which chaotic conditions reigned. As yet, Germany was very far from reaching any such condition. Even during the German revolution of 1918 the bureaucracy on the local as well as the national level continued to function as of old. There was no breakdown as it occurred in Russia. The extreme Left – the Spartacists and Left Radicals – consisted of small, isolated groups which continued to distribute anti-war leaflets but exercised very little influence on the course of events. To overcome their isolation and to find 'a protecting roof' the Spartacists joined the USPD, but in doing so they opened up new divisions and created new internal conflicts: at best, it was a purely tactical move which did not provide them with a mass basis, and the marriage of convenience did not last long. The German Left lacked unity as well as efficient leadership.

IX

The British Left in 1917

In contrast with Germany, there was no upsurge on the Left in Britain in 1917 – apart from the exhilaration caused by the outbreak of the Russian revolution, which did not last very long. The foundation of the USPD and its repeated votes against the war credits do not seem to have produced a strong impression or a determination to follow its example. At the annual conference of the ILP, held at Leeds in April 1917 (simultaneously with the foundation conference of the USPD at Gotha), a left-wing motion that in future the ILP members of parliament should vote against the war credits received only 61 votes, 198 delegates voting against it. Bruce Glasier declared that, if the motion were carried, it would only be logical to refuse all taxes to the government. The large majority of the delegates felt that any different vote would be a motion of censure against their MPs and therefore the left-wing motion was removed from the agenda. The small group of ILP members in the House of Commons was divided on the issue. While Snowden publicly declared his support for a vote against the war credits, the majority of his colleagues were not in favour. The City of London branch of the ILP, on the other hand, stated that 'practically the whole of the rank and file of the party' endorsed the policy it had advocated for some time, to oppose the war credits, and that the time had come for the MPs to do the same. A 'soldier' writing to Lansbury in May also demanded 'something stronger than appeals to the Government' and at last a definite vote against the credits in parliament, 'as our heroic comrades on the Continent have done'.[1] Perhaps the victory of the February revolution in Russia even had a negative effect on any such resolution; for the British Left had always been reluctant to support a war for 'democracy' and against 'Prussian militarism' that was fought in alliance with the tsarist autocracy. But after February this was no longer the case, and the democracies were ranged together against German militarism and its policy of vast territorial expansion which threatened to stifle the young Russian democracy.

As to the Labour Party, its annual conference held at the beginning of 1917 rejected by 1,697,000 votes to 302,000 a motion put forward by the BSP that the war was an imperialist war and should be brought to an end immediately. An even larger majority confirmed the decision to join the wartime national government – a decision attacked at the conference in bitter speeches not only by the BSP delegates, but also by Snowden and Ernest Bevin, the delegate of the Dock, Wharf, Riverside and General Workers' Union. But, as in Germany, the majority of the union leaders were convinced of the necessity of wholehearted cooperation in the war effort and of supporting the government policy of winning the war. Yet a special Labour Party conference in August came out in favour of a negotiated peace – a course urged by the ILP for a long time – and in favour of attending the international socialist conference at Stockholm. Another special Labour Party conference held at the end of 1917 demanded by a large majority the suppression of secret diplomacy, the limitation of armaments and of national service, the establishment of a League of Nations to prevent future wars, and the abandonment of imperialism – again echoing the war aims put forward by the ILP. At the Labour Party's annual conference early in 1918 Arthur Henderson moved a resolution that the Allied governments should formulate and publish as soon as possible a precise statement of their war aims, for in his opinion the war had been unnecessarily prolonged by their refusal to do so. Peace should be brought about through negotiation. This was a remarkable change compared with previous years and showed that the ILP had been successful in influencing the policy of the Labour Party; those who still wanted to continue the war were reduced to a small, almost silent minority.[2] There was, however, very little chance that these aims could be achieved as the German military, flushed with victory over Russia, were determined to seek victory in the west by means of an all-out offensive which was to start in the spring of 1918. And when that offensive was finally brought to a standstill by the Allied armies the tide of war turned in their favour, and a compromise peace remained as remote as it had been throughout the war years. That all the left-wing parties desired a negotiated peace exercised no influence on the policy of the belligerent governments.

While there were differences in the attitude towards the war within the Labour Party and even the ILP, on one issue they were united, that of the defence of civil liberties. If Britain was fighting 'Prussianism', the establishment of some kind of militarism at home must be prevented at all costs. As Ramsay MacDonald put it at a memorial meeting for Keir Hardie in Glasgow: 'We knew that a perfect typhoon would rage round all our liberties, uprooting them, breaking, crushing and scattering them – north, south, east and west. Our appointed place was to stand by those liberties and defend them. Hardie knew that, if we lost our democratic sense, if we put on one side our democratic political instincts, militarism would come across the seas... and whilst our soldiers were fighting it on the Continent, our military authorities would give it hospitality, harbourage and welcome.' MacDonald was convinced that there was a grave danger that in the Allied countries policies would be adopted 'which will fix militarism upon Europe for generations and Prussianize Great Britain'. If the German military authorities suppressed papers and journals on political grounds and prohibited political meetings of the Left, this was considered in Britain, as he put it, 'as a proof of German Tyranny', but if the same was done in Britain, it 'was accepted as evidence of our sturdy defence of liberty' and 'the soundness of the heart of John Bull'. The same points were made even more forcefully by the BSP in a statement which was to be submitted to the Allied socialist conference to be held in March 1917. It stated that nothing had been gained by giving up the class struggle and concluding an alliance with the government: 'the governing class has taken the opportunity presented by the war to suppress free speech and the freedom of the Press, to revive the process of secret trial and imprisonment without charge, to destroy the industrial liberties for which generations of workers have nobly struggled, and to abolish Parliamentary control. Almost every vestige of liberty formerly enjoyed by the workers has been lost because the class struggle is abandoned.'[3]

These were strong words, but they were curiously enough confirmed by the findings of an official Commission for Enquiry into Industrial Unrest which reported soon after. For London and the south-east the enquiry found that 'there has gradually arisen a sense of injustice and a feeling that there is a tendency to treat them [the workers] as though they were rather the instruments of the community than members of it...'; the workers felt that, under the provisions of the Munitions of War Act of 1915, they were condemned to 'industrial servitude' as the employers were able to dismiss or retain them at their pleasure, while they were no longer able to leave their jobs freely. For the West

Midlands, the same grievances were enumerated: before the war, the worker could leave his employment at will, but now he could not do so 'unless his employer consents or the Munitions Tribunal grants a certificate... In normal times the man has the weapon of the strike and the employer that of the lock-out, now both are illegal... These changes are strongly resented as infringements of personal liberty, to which men are deeply attached... In many cases they are the renunciation of the gains of years, and what renders the renunciation more bitter is the feeling that all changes bear more hardly on the men than on the employers. This is obviously the case.' For Wales it was unequivocally stated that the growing 'antagonism between Capital and Labour' was caused at least in part by 'the indisposition of employers to concede the claims of the workers to a higher standard of living', and that this provided fuel for the propaganda of the ILP and other left-wing movements.[4]

Yet this growing industrial unrest did not bring about a corresponding growth of the political anti-war movement. As several of these reports stressed, the large majority of the British workers continued to be 'strongly loyal and patriotic', in spite of the long duration of the war, the very heavy casualties, and the ever rising food prices. Perhaps the British worker was more patriotic than his German counterpart and more determined to see the war through: a determination that must have been reinforced by the German treatment of Belgium and the other occupied countries. While the small British Socialist Party continued to stagnate and according to its own figures had only 6,435 members in 1917, the ILP – the only major anti-war party – grew, above all in Scotland where it was able to assemble and influence large crowds. There, as Kirkwood records, 'the people flocked to our meetings' and dozens of new ILP branches were founded: about 50 since the beginning of the war, most of them in 1917. Even so, the ILP did not become a mass party even where its influence was strongest. Early in 1918 it had close on 2,000 members in Glasgow and about 600 at Aberdeen, and perhaps 10,000 or so in the whole of Scotland, three times the pre-war figure.[5] Other anti-war movements also flourished in Scotland. In July 1917 the Women's Peace Crusade, which combined non-conformists, religious pacifists, ILP members and Clyde-side left-wingers, assembled 14,000 people on Glasgow Green to acclaim the peace policy of the Russian Provisional Government and to demand peace. But over the country as a whole the movement remained very small, with something like 5,000 members.[6]

Outside Scotland, however, the number of ILP branches did not

increase but declined between 1915 and 1917 from about 600 to fewer
than 500 branches. It was only in 1918 that an increase was reported
over the 1915 figures, and that was almost entirely due to Scotland. In
Lancashire, where the ILP was traditionally strong, the number of party
members declined between 1914 and 1917 and an increase to 6631
members was only reported in 1918. If the party chairman was able to
state at the Exeter conference of Easter 1918 that 158 new branches had
been founded and that the membership had gone up by 90 per cent, that
was only because he compared the 1917-18 figures with the very low
ones for the previous year. In October 1917 a worried Minister of
Labour wrote: 'The ILP not only contains wealthy individual members
but is rapidly becoming a numerically powerful organization, and so
acquiring large funds from its membership. It has certainly made great
strides during the last 12 months.' This opinion was also reflected in
Lloyd George's Memoirs when he wrote that 'the influence of the
MacDonald section of the Labour Movement was becoming greater and
their agitation was...gaining fresh adherents.' This was apparently quite
true of Scotland, where the ILP gained considerable influence in the early
war years, but with regard to England and Wales the fears seem to have
been much exaggerated.[7] Compared with the newly founded USPD,
which had to struggle against considerable persecution and had to face
the intense hostility of the SPD, the progress of the ILP was very modest
indeed. Expressed differently, in Germany war-weariness and anti-war
tendencies reached proportions quite different from those in Britain.

In contrast with Germany, the police did not interfere with ILP
meetings which often drew enthusiastic crowds; and even the
conscientious objectors were permitted to hold their meetings under the
watchful eye of the police. From Leicester it was reported that they held
religious meetings near the prison where some of their comrades were
held: there was nothing 'to warrant interference except on one occasion
when they cheered at the end of the meeting'. But the police did not
interfere either when so-called 'patriots' broke up anti-war meetings. At
Carlisle, the Labour MP Thomas Richardson intended to hold an open
air meeting in the market, but he was pelted with mud and cries arose
'put him in the dock!' He was roughly handled by the crowd but
eventually escaped to the house of the local miners' agent. For some
hours the house was besieged by an angry crowd and all the windows
were smashed with stones. Before police reinforcements arrived the
mob succeeded in breaking into the house, but Richardson and his agent
had made their escape. At Leicester, however, the ILP was able to hold

an open air meeting every Sunday in the market place, with 50 to 250 people present, without any disturbance. 'Although the speeches are anything but patriotic and not a word is ever said against Germany, no expression has ever been heard by my officers', so the Chief Constable reported, 'which would give the slightest justification for a prosecution or even a caution.' In an ILP meeting at Swansea Norman Angell declared, according to the police, 'there is no form of slavery worse than the conscription of men's bodies to put in the trenches, not only to be killed, but they are told to kill others. It is the greatest form of slavery, no slave in a plantation is told to kill...' Again the police did not interfere and the meeting passed completely peacefully. The ILP also carefully watched developments in Germany and expressed its satisfaction when Scheidemann demanded 'wholesale democratization'. From this it concluded that the SPD was 'coming over rapidly and courageously from its pro-war position', and urged the Labour Party to raise the same demand for Britain.[8] This assessment of the German situation was caused by wishful thinking, for the SPD never wavered from its pro-war attitude until the bitter end, and the same was true of the British Labour Party. In both countries, only minorities within the labour movement adopted an anti-war position and nationalism proved stronger than any feeling of international solidarity.

In Britain, as in Germany, 1917 saw considerable labour unrest, although most strikes were non-political, caused by the workers' grievances rather than by anti-war feeling. This, however, was only natural. It was only very rarely – for example, in Germany in January 1918 – that large political issues induced the working masses to take action, and then only for a few days. In Britain, there was no such occasion during the war years, the slogan of 'democratization', powerful in a country that was still very far from achieving it, only had a limited appeal, and the same applied to the demand of the vote for women which was made by Snowden and MacDonald in and out of parliament. But there were great strikes in 1917, in particular in Lancashire and the Midlands. In March the engineers struck at Barrow against a cut in the rates of piece-work. The strike was joined by about 10,000 men and lasted 11 days, but did not spread to any other town, and then it collapsed. In the same month the Minister of Munitions introduced a new bill with the purpose of extending dilution of labour, which hitherto had been limited to war work, to commercial work. The trade unions strongly objected to the bill, and their agitation coincided with the withdrawal by the government of a scheme under which the

Amalgamated Society of Engineers and certain other unions could issue their own certificates of exemption from military service to skilled workmen. A firm at Castleton near Manchester which refused to recognize any union used this opportunity to introduce dilution of labour for commercial work without consulting the men. When they refused to accept this they were discharged – and immediately conscripted by the army. Sympathy strikes were threatened, in some places strikes broke out, and elsewhere the men threatened to come out unless their demands were met within a time limit fixed by themselves. 'The burning questions of dilution and trade cards' (certificates of exemption from military service) inflamed passions in a large industrial area. At the beginning of May the Lancashire representative of the Ministry of Munitions reported that 'the strike looks like spreading not only over Lancashire but all over Great Britain'. By that time all the engineers in the Manchester district had stopped work, and at a meeting of the local shop stewards it was formally resolved that 'the methods of the Union were not drastic enough'.[9]

In May the strike movement spread like wildfire, to Liverpool, Sheffield, Derby, Coventry, and finally to the south, to London, Southampton and Bristol. In all, 48 towns and about 200,000 men were involved, and one of their principal demands was the restoration of the trade card scheme, but there were no political demands. From the Royal Arsenal at Woolwich, where guns, shells and steel for tanks were produced, it was reported that nearly all the skilled men including the assistant foremen and ratefixers joined the strike and that the position was getting worse. Nearly everywhere the strike was led by the shop stewards in opposition to the union leaders, as the movement on the Clyde had been in 1915. On 15 May their delegates met in London and resolved to ask the Minister of Munitions to receive a deputation to discuss the issue. The minister, however, refused to meet them unless they were accompanied by officials of the unions affected by the strike, thus adopting the same attitude as the German chancellor in January 1918. A few days later the leaders of the men were arrested, but it soon became evident, to quote the official history, 'that the Ministry had little prospect of maintaining the output of munitions at a satisfactory level as long as the arrested men remained in prison, and that it must either settle the dispute by discussion with the shop stewards or fail to attain a settlement.' So the shop stewards became 'the unofficial strike committee', the minister had to beat a retreat, and on 19 May a conference between them finally took place. Agreement was then reached that they would advise the men to return to work, that there would be no more arrests, that the eight men arrested would be released on their own recognizances and a pledge to be of good behaviour and to observe the agreement, and that no victimization would take place on account of the strike. But work was not resumed immediately everywhere; at Barrow, Liverpool and Crewe this was only done in the following week. It was also agreed that future negotiations would be held with the officials of the recognized unions, not with the shop stewards who were unable to preserve their short-lived position of power.[10]

The government then appointed a commission of enquiry which reported in July from the different industrial regions of the country. In Wales it found that the unrest was due to 'the rapidly increasing cost of living': indeed, by the end of June food prices had risen to more than 100 per cent above the pre-war level. But the commission also noted a deepening 'sense of antagonism between capital and labour'. In Yorkshire and the East Midlands it noticed a 'distrust of the Trade Union leaders and entire want of confidence in Government promises concerning the workers' interests and the recognition of Trade Union aims and objects'. This distrust 'has led to the formation of a vigorous defensive organization for the protection of the workmen inside their own separate workshops, known as the "Shop Committee" or "Rank-and-File" movement, with Shop Stewards elected from the workers in every shop.' Those elected were able to protect the workers' interests swiftly and effectively and threatened to become 'a most serious menace to the authority and entire work' of the trade unions. For London and the south-east the commission found that a minority among the shop stewards 'is frankly revolutionary and does not admit the possibility of improvement in the workers' condition without a radical alteration of the social and industrial systems'. In general, the skilled workers were embittered by the loss of their privileged position and the erosion of the achievements of the pre-war period. An independent enquiry, undertaken by the National War Aims Committee, however, found that in Sheffield, Barrow and Derby the principal causes of labour unrest were bad housing, long food queues and a shortage of beer. Because of the latter the pubs closed on Saturday evenings, and thus the workers stood in the streets and listened to pacifist orators, 'while in the public houses they are safe from this as the pacifists are generally teetotallers who will not show themselves in these abodes of iniquity'.[11]

Like the earlier movement on the Clyde and the Revolutionary Shop Stewards of Berlin, the shop stewards movements had above all syndicalist motives and aimed at superseding the existing unions and gaining control of the workshops, and finally at taking over the running of industry. All political issues were of secondary importance. Although it was claimed that one of the movement's aims was to terminate the war this was only true of a minority among its leaders. It was further claimed 'that certain relations subsist between the Shop Stewards Committees and such bodies as the No-Conscription Fellowship and the Union of Democratic Control'; but again this can only have applied to individual members. It was probably nearer the truth, as the statement continued, that certain agitators had tried to capture the industrial movement. But, it was admitted, 'there is no evidence that they have succeeded in doing so, and a good deal of evidence that they have not.' The aims of these various organizations were too different to allow any close cooperation or joint action, and none ever took place. Nor were the leaders of the shop stewards wild radicals. In August 1917 they held a conference in Manchester which was attended by about 120 delegates. A national council of the movement was elected, with a chairman from the Clyde and five other members, the majority from the Midlands; it marked the merging of the Clyde workers' movement with that of the shop stewards. At the conference a radical motion to call another unofficial strike was defeated and it was decided to wait until after the next wages award in October. In September a move to make the Industrial Workers of Great Britain – a syndicalist union modelled on the American Industrial Workers of the World – the controlling organization was defeated by a narrow majority, with many delegates abstaining.[12]

More strikes occurred in the autumn of 1917, but none reached the importance of the May strikes which threatened to paralyze the war industries. As in May, the government was intelligent enough to meet the men's grievances by concessions. By a new order munition workers were permitted to change their jobs, but not to transfer to work outside the industry. Churchill, the new Minister of Munitions, granted to certain groups of skilled workers a bonus of 12½ per cent on their earnings – to meet their grievance that unskilled or semi-skilled workers not doing time work could earn more than skilled men. This concession was gradually extended to all skilled men doing time work, and later to other categories. Early in 1918 a bonus of 7½ per cent was accorded to all workers doing piece work and then further extended. It thus became an ordinary increase in wages granted in a piecemeal fashion. The proposal to extend dilution of labour was quietly dropped. In this way the government hoped to reduce the influence of the shop stewards; but it was only partly successful as long as the unions adhered to their policy of industrial peace and cooperation with the government.[13]

The Union of Democratic Control, wrongly suspected of having established links with the shop stewards, possessed certain links with the labour movement, above all with the ILP which had many pacifists among its members. Links were maintained for the simple purpose of finding protection for the UDC's public meetings. After many violent incidents at meetings the executive of the UDC decided to concentrate on areas where a large labour contingent could be expected to attend because the right-wing press condemned the UDC as 'pro-German' and traitorous. The Home Office declined to take action against the UDC because it doubted whether this could be done successfully without a verdict by the courts. In September 1917, however, a reason was found to arrest and try the UDC secretary, E.D. Morel, on the flimsy charge that he had violated the Defence of the Realm Act by causing a correspondent to send two of his pamphlets to Romain Rolland who happened to live not in France but in Switzerland. Morel was sentenced to six months' imprisonment and released early in 1918. In reality, the policies of the UDC were very moderate and it was more concerned with the settlement to be reached at the end of the war than with bringing it to an end. It insisted that the independence of Belgium must be restored and Northern France be evacuated by the Germans, but also that the restoration of Belgium or that of Alsace and Lorraine to France should not be made a precondition for the opening of negotiations and that German wishes with regard to colonies should be met. The UDC welcomed the Russian revolution and claimed rather optimistically that 'the Russian Provisional Government has followed President Wilson in endorsing the principles of the UDC'. It urged that the principles of foreign policy enunciated by Wilson be accepted and later 'heartily' endorsed his Fourteen Points which envisaged a settlement based on national self-determination, reduction of armaments and 'open covenants of peace'. In September 1917 the UDC declared: 'The tide is turning towards democracy and against the suppression of liberty. The tide is turning in favour of the idea that a permanent peace can only be secured by fair treatment of all concerned' and 'against the notion that physical force is everything, that right and justice are of small account'.[14]

These were hardly revolutionary ideas, nor did the UDC pursue a revolutionary anti-war policy. But the men seeking international understanding or a compromise solution to the great conflict were as unpopular in Britain as they were in Germany; and thus Morel was sent to prison, and Bertrand Russell had to follow him. The voices preaching reason were drowned by the clash of arms. It might be argued that the mild sentences meted out to Morel and Russell – and even the more severe ones of the conscientious objectors – compared favourably with the savage sentences of Liebknecht and the German sailors. But neither Morel nor Russell, nor the large majority of the conscientious objectors, were revolutionaries, and the German sentences were those of military, not civil, courts, from which the worst might be expected in time of war. More than 60 years later it is difficult to understand the spirit of persecution and repression which permeated Britain during the first world war: it was directed against those who were considered 'traitors' to their country and to their social class. They were silenced, but only for a short time. In spite of continuing police harassment, *The Herald*, *The Labour Leader* and even *The Tribunal* of the No-Conscription Fellowship continued to be published and to bear witness that there were men and women who were opposed to the war.

X

Towards the German revolution

The most important political event in Germany during the first nine months of 1918 was no doubt the great strike of January – an entirely spontaneous movement which for a short time united the workers following the SPD and the USPD. But the strike failed and resulted in more military repression. Hence it is perhaps not surprising that there were no further such movements until the actual outbreak of the revolution. In February the military authorities reported from Magdeburg that secret propaganda for a new strike was carried on among the metal workers because the government did not seriously try to make peace with Russia but aimed at large annexations and had refused Trotsky's proposal to evacuate the occupied territories; the trade unions would submit their demands to the chancellor; if these were not accepted they would call for a strike and declare their solidarity with the radical socialists. In Berlin, the police noted in August propaganda for new strikes which emphasized that in the east peace had been achieved by force and that German soldiers suppressed the Finnish revolution (there German troops had intervened in the civil war between Whites and Reds on the side of the White armies). In the same month the military reported a 'ferment' and the planning of a general political strike among the workers of Mannheim, but succeeded in suppressing the movement 'by energetic measures', presumably arrests and conscription. Apart from Mannheim, the mood among the workers of the district was quiet; but many put forward demands for higher wages, especially the women, and the demands of the trade unions were ever increasing.[1] The important point, however, is that none of these threats materialized: 'energetic measures' were sufficient to nip the movement in the bud. The failure of the January strike and its result must have served as a warning not to repeat the experiment.

But there were plenty of other strikes, usually for higher wages and shorter working hours, without any political motive. As the press section of the Bavarian War Ministry acknowledged, the strikes were above all caused by the food shortages. At Ingolstadt in Bavaria, the women workers of the military enterprises went on strike in protest against the introduction of Sunday work and tried to prevent those willing to work from entering the premises. In March the miners of several Upper Silesian mines came out on strike to gain higher wages and were partly successful. In the summer they were followed by the women workers of the ore mines who demanded a reduction of their working day from 11 to eight hours, and by many other miners in Upper Silesia, so that the mines were 'militarized' and troops were called in to suppress the movement. In July and August tens of thousands of miners and metal workers in the Ruhr district struck, demanding a reduction of their working week because they could not work for 60 hours with so little food. But the unions persuaded the strikers to rely on the conciliation and arbitration procedures. At Kronenburg in the Rhineland a workers' deputation told the mayor that they were unable to manage with their rations of potatoes and other food. There and at nearby Remscheid and Solingen the workers demanded the introduction of the eight-hour day with equal pay, but in the end they were satisfied with a small reduction and accepted a minimum working week of 52½ hours. At a dockyard in Hamburg a strike broke out at the same time because of the potato shortage and work was resumed when bread was distributed instead. At Geestemünde near Bremen the dockyard workers struck because the rations of flour and potatoes had not been honoured for weeks. They were particularly embittered because of the rigorous police measures taken against children who brought in a few pounds of potatoes or fruit from the villages and had their purchases confiscated. From Stettin too it was reported in October that the dockyard and munition workers aimed at gaining the eight-hour day without loss of pay, a demand allegedly carried into the factories 'from outside', meaning by the unions. It is remarkable that in nearly all these cases it was not the union officials who negotiated with the employers or the authorities, but the members of the elected works' committees, and in the case of Geestemünde the chairman of the local USPD.[2] The passivity of the union officials brought new local leaders to the fore who could identify themselves with the workers' demands.

The leaders of the large unions were aware of their loss of authority and the pressure from below. In negotiations with members of the government in April 1918 the president of the German miners' union complained that no meeting was permitted to discuss the issue of the Prussian franchise, and in other meetings no discussion was allowed after the speeches; trade union trusties had suddenly been called up: measures such as these undermined the authority of the union leaders. The president of the Christian metal workers' union confirmed that the unsolved issue of the Prussian three-class franchise was causing disquiet among the rank and file, as did the call-up of union representatives and the large subsidies paid by certain employers to the 'yellow' unions (opposing any strike action). Carl Legien, the leader of the Free unions, declared that the unions hitherto had succeeded in pacifying the workers: they would not call a strike but might remain passive and neutral in case of another strike unless the government changed its policy towards the working class. Unfortunately he did not specify what he meant by this remark, but most likely he thought of the restrictions mentioned by the previous speakers and the dilatory treatment of the franchise issue. In June, at a mass meeting of the trusties of the metal workers' union at Duisburg, attended by representatives of all the factories of the area, a resolution was carried demanding a shorter working week, higher wages and the abolition of the rigorous fines levied by many enterprises, at a time when the workers were forbidden to change their jobs to improve their situation. The unions declared that, on account of the cut in the bread ration, the workers could not possibly continue working such long hours without damage to their health.[3] In the last stages of the war the union leaders were driven to take action, or at least to threaten action, by their members and their elected trusties, but a shop stewards movement on the British scale did not develop in Germany; that in Berlin remained confined to the armament factories of the capital. From Pomerania it was reported in June that for the first time the small officials of the postal services and the railways, the teachers and the white-collar employees of industry demanded higher wages, and similar tendencies existed in Berlin among the white-collar workers of large industrial firms, such as Siemens and AEG, the leading electrical firms of Germany.[4]

In spite of the exploitation of the Ukraine and other occupied countries, the food situation continued to deteriorate during the early months of 1918. In the industrialized villages of the Saxon mountains for ten days one kilogram of potatoes was distributed in May and very little bread so that the people were slowly starving; the villages were plagued by hoards of beggars who were unable to find much as the local peasants were far from wealthy. In June the authorities of Düsseldorf had to announce that the weekly bread ration would be cut from four pounds to three and a half, and that of potatoes from seven to five pounds, while the meat ration of 250 grams was unobtainable in many places. At Hamburg, the weekly potato ration of five pounds could be met in June, but was then cut to two, and finally to one pound per week, until it was stopped altogether. In late July only new potatoes were available, in very small quantities on account of the late harvest. The bread and meat rations were cut in August so that the unions bitterly complained that the government was too 'soft' in its handling of the agrarians. At Frankfurt and Munich, no potatoes at all were available in July-August, and all soft fruit went into the black market. At Gotha, crowds of women shouted for bread and potatoes. In these conditions the black market naturally flourished. Early in September the military authorities reported from Stettin that it could not be suppressed and, if they did so, 'the people would starve. There is not a single German who lives from his rations. The supplementation of [the rationed] food takes place with some through wealth which makes them indifferent to what price they pay, with others by fraud and dishonest means, with the third lot by theft, and with the rest by robbery. That is at the moment the method of food distribution in the German Empire.' According to the Berlin police, the price of one pound of butter in the black market rose to 24 M., that of one egg to 1.50 M.: the 'saviour used by all' was the black market which was legally prohibited. The industrial workers, too, benefited from it because their firms bought meat, butter and vegetables on the black market; if this stopped the workers raised hell and declared they could not work, and the radical workers of Leipzig actually threatened to strike if the authorities stopped the flow of black market food. In Baden and Württemberg, the barter trade flourished. Craftsmen and artisans demanded food instead of money from their customers and then used some of it to obtain raw materials from the wholesale trade, so that people who had no food to offer were simply not served.[5]

In these circumstances, as all reports emphasized, the mood of the population continued to be 'depressed', 'dejected' and 'bitter'. But in many parts it revived with the beginning of the 'Ludendorff offensive' in March 1918 and its initial successes, only to decline further and further when it became clear that any hope of a military victory was once more disappointed. Already in the early months of 1918 it was reported from

181

different parts of Bavaria that the people said: 'The whole war is a swindle, it only brings ruin to the small people and benefits the big ones.' Or: 'The bigwigs do not ask how long the war lasts, they live well and the longer it lasts the more money they make.' A Bavarian officer noted that the great optimism which reigned at the beginning of the negotiations of Brest-Litovsk had been replaced by an equally exaggerated pessimism. A local authority reported in February from Franconia that in the overcrowded trains incessant bitter grumbling went on about all the public institutions and measures as well as open and stealthy preaching of revolution, with remarks such as: 'We must follow the Russian example' and 'I have still got a bullet for such a bigwig'. By the summer the word 'revolution' could be heard all over Bavaria. At the beginning of September the Bavarian military authorities found 'the gravest danger for the will to hold out' in the general opinion that the war was only continued in the interest of one group or some, that the war was lost; in the trains there was such abuse of everything that it boggled the imagination, and any counter-argument was hopeless because everybody immediately pounced upon the opponent; the population had lost all confidence in the war loans and the paper money.[6]

We possess much more detailed reports from Bavaria than from any other part of Germany, but by August at the latest very similar tendencies were observed in many different areas. An army padre who during his leave travelled through the Rhineland, Westphalia and the Prussian province of Saxony wrote that everywhere the mood was one of general hopelessness: people were ready to make sweeping concessions to the enemy, sharply criticized the measures of the army and naval commands, became furious when anyone tried to preach courage and confidence, complained bitterly about the economic activities of the war societies and exploitation by the Jews; Alsace should be given to the French and the Emperor be deposed, then the war would soon be over; the idea of opposing the government by force was widely accepted, in the towns as well as in the countryside. According to the military authority responsible for Berlin and its neighbourhood, in August the mood of the population reached a veritable nadir and brought with it 'complete depression and hopelessness'; this was attributed to the failure of the last offensive and the strong attacks of the enemy which forced the German army to retreat; most regrettably, the 'unshakeable confidence in the High Command', which had previously existed was now seriously shaken. Towards the end of 1918 the authorities expected 'larger uprisings' which would be caused by the agitation of the USPD. From Frankfurt the military reported that neither the workers nor large sections of the *Mittelstand* any longer had confidence in the government and all desired a peace of compromise; and the Württemberg War Ministry attributed the very bad general mood to rumour mongering, lies and overstatements spread from mouth to mouth, to doubts, irritation, dejection and defamation of individuals or whole groups of people which apparently found general credence. In rural areas along the Rhine a further deterioration of the public mood was noticed in August, due above all to the tales of soldiers coming home on leave who no longer believed a victory possible and spread 'the most incredible rumours'.[7] These are just a few examples of the depression and hopelessness which permeated Germany by the summer of 1918, a veritable collapse of public morale, caused more by the bad military situation than by any food shortage. For many months the German public had been fed on the hope of speedy victory through the 'final' offensive; when this failed the change was all the more catastrophic. The end was near.

In their monthly returns on the mood of the population, the military authorities time and again mentioned that this was negatively influenced by soldiers coming home on leave or writing to their families. Indeed, many of the authorities were convinced that soldiers' tales were one of the major causes of the collapse of morale, in particular in the late summer of 1918. The same is confirmed by many other sources. The *Landrat* of Rüdesheim on the Rhine wrote: 'The many rumours circulating about heavy losses, refusals to obey orders, desertion of whole regiments, attempts on the life of Hindenburg, etc. are believed only too readily, in particular because many soldiers on leave from the front picture the strength of the enemy, the better quality of his material, etc. in extravagant terms and the military situation as bad for Germany.' A teacher from Kulmbach in Bavaria stated that 'unbelievable as it may sound', in the first instance soldiers were responsible for the depressed mood at home: 'if only a fraction of what they say is true it looks bad at the front'. A Bavarian military report mentioned the bad influence exercised by soldiers on leave who were agitating against the officers among their acquaintances and telling them: 'the time in which we had to suffer everything has passed, the time in which we will give orders will come soon, thus... do as you please and don't take orders from above.' From Leipzig it was reported in September that soldiers on leave were spreading 'uncontrollable rumours' about the situation at the front, the vast losses, the many traitors and deserters, which were more readily believed than before. Soldiers were responsible for similar rumours in the Rhineland about heavy casualties, desertion and bad relations between officers and men. From Baden it was reported that they simply put the word 'swindle' on their post cards, and the word was repeated by the people; even officers, especially those who had had no leave for some time, 'have acted to the same effect'. Soldiers on leave tried to persuade the women not to subscribe to the ninth war loan and told 'inflammatory stories' about the frivolous and luxurious life of the officers behind the front.[8]

As the monthly reports of the military district commands were printed and had a relatively wide circulation, at least among the senior officers, it seems inconceivable that the generals who later so assiduously propagated the legend of the 'stab-in-the-back' never heard of these many reports which indicated exactly the opposite: that the agitation was carried from the front to the rear where people had been only too gullible in the years past. To save the 'honour' of the army a legend had to be invented which turned the historical reality upside down. There existed yet another source of rumours and agitation against the authorities: the many deserters from the army in the hinterland. From Ratisbon on the Danube the garrison commandant reported in October that deserters whom the police were unable to apprehend were making life unsafe 'in the towns and in *all* villages'. At Cologne and Bonn complaints were raised about the many deserters. In the early autumn the head of the Berlin police estimated that in Berlin alone there were 40 to 50,000 deserters.[9]

From the autumn of 1917 onwards the maintenance of discipline in the army presented growing problems to the military authorities. A military order of November mentioned losses of up to 10 per cent from transports of replacements to the front. In May 1918 a division reported that out of a transport of 631 men 83 had disappeared *en route*, including three NCO's. A train carrying reinforcements to the front showed the inscription: 'We do not fight for Germany's honour, we fight for the millionaires!' In the same month a naval officer attached to the army noted: 'The mood in the army deteriorates from day to day; this cannot be doubted. All private news received from all sections of the front confirms it...Does Ludendorff not see this? does he really believe that the mere *sic jubeo* is still sufficient?' Also in May, soldiers rioted in several Bavarian towns. At Ingolstadt the cause was the maltreatment of a soldier suffering from a nervous disease by a policeman. Soldiers and civilians stormed the town hall, threw files, food coupons and money out of the windows and burnt them; then they set fire to the town hall itself, demolished near-by cafés and hotels, and the units brought in to stop the destruction made common cause with the rioters; 97 people were finally arrested, the majority under 20 years of age. From Erlangen replacements were to be sent to the front and the authorities granted them leave until midnight on the day before their departure as they feared resistance if the soldiers were not allowed to go into town. There large bawling crowds assembled outside the pubs and, when the police tried to disperse them, they were surrounded by soldiers and beaten up. Two companies sent to the scene to arrest the ringleaders were unable to do so. The windows of the town hall were smashed and then the crowd finally dispersed. In June hundreds of soldiers in Munich refused to obey the orders of their officers and shouted 'we do as we please'.[10]

Difficulties also occurred with soldiers who returned from captivity in Russia, as they did on a much larger scale in the Austrian army. At Graudenz in the east, the first three hundred men who were to be sent to the western front in July refused to obey orders. The commanding officer admonished them several times, read out the 'articles of war' and succeeded in persuading the majority to entrain. But 50 still refused to do so and were courtmartialled. The press was forbidden to mention these events. According to Ludendorff, the morale was particularly bad in the camp at Beverloo in Belgium which contained many who had been prisoners of war in Russia and were infected by Bolshevik propaganda. Also in July, Ludendorff severely criticized the 'mild sentences' imposed by the military courts in cases of absence without leave, cowardice and refusal to obey orders, cases which were tried in growing numbers. He demanded 'exemplary punishments', if necessary the death penalty, to deter soldiers from any such action. In the summer inscriptions began to appear on carriages taking soldiers to the front 'Long live Social Democracy', 'Long live Liebknecht and Haase' and 'Long live the revolution'. In September the district command for Berlin and Brandenburg for the first time mentioned 'individual cases of mutiny' which were used by propaganda to incite other units 'to similar excesses'. In September too, Bavarian crack units sent to the front to retrieve a difficult situation met retreating units shouting 'strike breakers', and other soldiers sneered why should they let themselves be used to close 'the nice hole' in the front by a counter-attack. Henceforth the term 'strike breakers', used by retreating troops for those who tried to stem the flood, occurred more and more frequently. In a military camp in Brussels the slogan was current 'if the government does not make peace we'll have to do it ourselves'. A leaflet circulated at the front in August protesting against the vast annexations of Russian territory: 'Russia offered the world peace and demanded in its open peace programme the free self-determination of the nations and rejected all conquests and indemnities... We have seen how for months the German High Command has tried to strangle the free revolutionary Russia. Livonia, Estonia, Finland, the Ukraine have systematically been brought under the power of the Prusso-German bayonets and machine guns, and every day the frontier is pushed further into Central Russia... Wake up, comrades, and use your power!'[11] Quite clearly, by the summer and early autumn of 1918 discipline in the German army was severely shaken and the military authorities were powerless to cope with the situation.

The just mentioned report about the military camp in Brussels also recounted 'that the rebellious mood of the men did not stop in front of senior officers'; when the commandant or another officer appeared he was followed by shouts from the windows and corners of the barracks 'Beat him up! Take out your knives!' A 'spirit of resistance and rebellion' was abroad. The intense dislike of the officer caste also showed itself when an officer tried to stop a soldier for not saluting properly or to ask him to identify himself. Invariably a hostile crowd collected and took sides against the officer. After one such incident the garrison commandant of Augsburg wrote rather sadly that 'large circles consider the officer an opinionated supercilious man who pays no heed to any obstacle, conducts the war for his pleasure, is divorced from the people and is on the contrary distrusted by the people simply because he is an officer... That he does his duty like everybody else, that he risks his life like the lowest soldier, that is not considered a merit for he is paid for it...' The writer expressly rejected the term 'officer caste' because all social classes were by then represented in the officer corps. The report carries enthusiastic notes written by fellow-officers. But the dislike of the officers spread to ever larger social groups. When the eminent theologian Troeltsch attended a meeting of 'patriotic' and Catholic Bavarian peasants in the summer of 1918 he was terrified by 'the fanatical hatred' of the officer corps 'as the epitome of all injustice and favouritism'. A similar frightening hatred of the officers was noticed by a correspondent who had frequent occasion to listen to the conversations of the sailors in the local trains near Bremen. Their principal complaints still were about the officers' food: they were waxing fat at the cost of the men; the latter's meat and fat rations went into the officers' kitchen; when they went home on leave the sailors got a piece of bread and a small piece of sausage for the journey, but the officers took all the food along; from occupied Belgium the officers sent large food parcels home, or their batmen were sent, allegedly on leave, with food for the officer families. The writer added that he and others 'constantly' had to listen to these tales full of bitterness and hatred which he ascribed to 'a long lasting, systematic agitation among the sailors'.[12] Only a few months later these feelings were to erupt with elemental force in the revolt of the sailors of Kiel and Wilhelmshaven and in the tearing off of the officers' epaulettes by enraged crowds.

In the course of 1918 the longing for peace became stronger and stronger. In March it was said in the Upper Palatinate that this hope was the only comfort of the despairing women who were no longer capable of coping with the heavy work and were saying: 'Whoever started the war should have his limbs cut off; the bigwigs don't notice how the small people fare'. From Munich it was reported in the same month that the people were tired and longing for the end, but were still willing to hold out on account of the 'great successes' at the western front. By August-September this was no longer the case because meanwhile the military situation had changed. According to the military authorities of Baden, there was 'a dull apathy combined with a longing for peace at any price', and large numbers looked at the war as 'a running amok of the participating states'. When the SPD parliamentary party met in September Scheidemann said that every day it was dinned into their ears 'Make peace, finish it'; the government could not finish the war because it enjoyed no confidence. Noske remarked that what was really dangerous was the total indifference towards the fate of Germany; they were arguing in the factories 'we have no interest in fighting the English' because they would recognize the value of German labour. Another deputy added that in south Germany they wanted peace at any price and were saying it did not matter whether they became French or British. A deputy from Baden confirmed that in the south there was vast bitterness against Prussia, 'not against the Prussian people but against the Junkers and the military caste'; the general feeling was that Prussia must be destroyed, and if not, Germany would be destroyed by Prussia. A journalist reported that in the Catholic villages along the Main the opinion was openly voiced that it was all the same whether they belonged to Bavaria or to France if only the war were finished; the French would be nice to the Bavarians with whom they had always had good relations. For the Rhineland the administrative

187

authorities wrote that the people wanted peace and did not care about the peace conditions, that the country population in particular wanted peace at any price; and the same was reported from the Bavarian villages.[13]

At a press conference in Berlin in May a journalist from Cologne stated that since 1866 he would have considered it impossible for an anti-Prussian mood of such strength to arise in Germany: 'Whoever visits south Germany will confirm that not a superficial, but a deep hatred of north Germany' is bred there; every measure, such as a cut in the bread ration, 'is chalked up against the bad Prussians'; he feared that German unity would suffer severe damage. No one, not even one of the Bavarian journalists present, contradicted him. In the same month the editor of a Bavarian correspondence service wrote that there was a deep distrust of Prussian policy which did not take into account the vital interests of Bavaria and did not care for justice or objectivity; in the east, Prussia would annex vast lands and thus greatly increase its territorial and political power; after the war there would be in Germany 'the grand hotel Prussia and a few neglected buildings dependent upon it'; the state governments would become the mere executive organs of the central will of Berlin which was bound to deprive the others of light, air and space.[14] Such were the feelings in Bavaria and the south after nearly four years of war. The anti-war and anti-Prussian tendencies virtually merged; the responsibility for the continuation of the war was attributed to the rapaciousness and lust for power of the Prussian ruling circles. If German unity survived the defeat of 1918 it was not their merit.

Anti-Prussian feeling also increased because of the dilatory treatment of the Prussian franchise reform which was widely interpreted as a sign that the ruling social groups of Prussia were determined to postpone the reform as long as they could. This was even true of Bavaria where the franchise had been reformed in the early twentieth century. According to the Social Democratic leader, Erhard Auer, the irritation caused among the Bavarian workers by this issue should not be underestimated. It was only due to his personal influence that a planned demonstration in front of the Prussian embassy in Munich was cancelled, or rather postponed. In January 1918 the Constitutional Committee of the Prussian Diet decided to take the reform of the first chamber before that of the franchise. The leaders of the trade union federations believed that this slowing down of the reform infuriated the workers so much that strikes would break out. This was confirmed by the town council of Frankfurt which described the mood among the workers as one of 'fever heat', partly also caused by the fear that the negotiations at Brest-Litovsk were going to fail. An underground leaflet of February began with the words 'Prussia leading the world' and ended: 'The imperialist war has borne the [promise of a] Prussian franchise reform; the proletarian peace, concluded by the German workers' democracy, will bury it together with the whole Prussian reaction.' When the Prussian Diet finally rejected the reform of the franchise there was strong indignation in Silesia because the government declined to dissolve the Diet: this was taken as proof that others (meaning the Military) were more powerful 'in all external and internal questions'. In a district conference of the SPD for Upper Silesia held in July this irritation erupted in the demand voiced by several delegates that the parliamentary party henceforth should vote against the war credits; in Germany militarism was ruling and it should be denied all financial support. The head of the Berlin police stated in August that the franchise issue was grist to the mill of the USPD and the Spartacus Group, but for the time being he did not expect any new strikes. The liberal academic Max Weber wrote that essential in wartime was the inner readiness of a nation to defend the state as *their* state; the Russian experience showed what happened if this readiness was lacking. Politically decisive, however, was in his opinion that a solemn promise to introduce the franchise reform was frustrated by allegedly clever manoeuvres, and therefore the central government must, if need be, enforce the reform even if there should be resistance.[15] But there was no progress and the three-class franchise lasted to the very end of the *ancien régime*, and with it the alienation of large sections of the population.

Yet the extreme Left was unable to profit to any significant extent from the rapid growth of anti-war feeling. This applied above all to the Spartacists who remained a small sect without much influence even among left-wing workers, not to speak of other social groups. In April 1918 the head of the Berlin police told the Admiralty that 'these numerically rather weak groups' were unable to exercise any general influence and overestimated their own possibilities, such as the claim that in Berlin they had gained influence among three or four regiments. Nothing was known, he added, of any planned mass demonstration on May Day, nothing of importance would happen on that day. Shortly after, the police of Düsseldorf confirmed that those workers 'who without exaggeration can be classified as German Bolsheviks' were convinced that it was impossible to mobilise the working class for political aims alone, that for a revolutionary uprising economic distress was essential which would be felt more strongly by the spring of 1919: a curious report, for surely economic distress was very severe in 1917 and 1918. After the experiences of the previous years, the leaders of the Spartacus Group too were still pessimistic. As late as September – eight weeks before the outbreak of the revolution – Ernst Meyer wrote to Lenin that for the time being he had nothing to report about 'larger actions', but they were planning more for the winter; opposition was on the increase in the army, and among the workers the conviction was 'slowly growing that the old methods of parliamentarian and purely demonstrative opposition' were insufficient.[16] Clearly, Meyer did not expect any revolutionary events for the time being.

Another Spartacus leader, the veteran historian Mehring, attributed the lack of success of the Left to the failure of the USPD to influence and mobilize the masses; their only slogan was not 'forward', but 'back' to the old SPD of pre-war days; the Spartacists had joined the USPD in the hope of driving it forward, but that hope they had to give up; all such attempts had failed because the USPD leaders suspected 'our best and most proven people' of being police agents. Yet, if the Spartacists had not joined the USPD, they would have been even more isolated; within the party they had ample opportunities to influence the members and to occupy leading posts on the local level. As a Spartacist from Stuttgart wrote, they were able 'under the guise of legal party work' to build up a tight organization of trusties in the factories whom they assembled every week and informed about the political situation. What infuriated Mehring most, however, was the opposition of the USPD leaders, in particular Kautsky, to the Bolsheviks and their methods of suppression, and he assured them of the 'passionate and deepest sympathy' felt by the Spartacists for the new rulers of Russia, in whom they saw the strongest protagonists of a new International. At the beginning of October the Spartacus Group held a conference together with the Left Radicals who had refused to join the USPD. The experience of working together with the USPD were discussed, which they claimed were bad eveywhere. Only where the local organization of the USPD was completely in Spartacist hands 'are the comrades satisfied with the decision to join taken at Gotha'. They also sharply criticised President Wilson's peace programme which was approved by the USPD (as it was by the UDC in Britain), for they saw in a League of Nations only a means 'to stifle the incipient proletarian world revolution'. Equally 'confusing' was in their opinion the USPD propaganda for 'parliamentarization' because it diverted energies from the 'real aim' of the movement, to foster revolution. It was resolved to establish close cooperation between the various groups represented at the conference, to start 'immediately with the formation of workers' and soldiers' councils in all places', and to send greetings of 'thanks, solidarity and brotherly sympathy' to the Russian Bolsheviks.[17] The sharp attacks on the policy of the USPD as well as the close cooperation with the Left Radicals, who had remained outside the much larger party, foreshadowed the final separation from the USPD and the foundation of an independent Communist Party which were to take place at the end of December 1918.

The work of the Spartacus Group also suffered from persecution by the authorities, and this probably partly accounted for its lack of success. In April a meeting of 15 local functionaries was surprised in a working-class district of Berlin, and the acknowledged leader and brain behind the underground organization, Leo Jogiches, was arrested together with soldiers of the Berlin garrison. Large quantities of leaflets and the type of a new *Spartacus Letter* not yet published were confiscated in the same flat. In September the underground organization received a more fatal blow, for in the suburb of Steglitz a new central office of the group was discovered in another police raid and the leader arrested with some of his helpers. This time the police found not only quantities of leaflets and correspondence, but complete lists of addresses to which propaganda material was regularly sent and – even more damaging – the addresses and addressed envelopes used for revolutionary propaganda in the army, with the leaflet 'Wake up, comrades!' ready for dispatch. The police were able to identify the students who assisted the arrested leader, but not the leader himself who used the pseudonym of 'Holz'.[18] It is impossible to say whether the police achieved these successes through informers from inside the organization or through systematic observation of the revolutionary circles. But it is certain that the underground propaganda must have been seriously disrupted. With Jogiches in prison, where Liebknecht and Luxemburg were kept throughout these years, the Spartacus Group was deprived of the intellectual and tactical leadership which it badly needed. None of the leaders still at liberty had sufficient stature to replace those in prison.

As far as the USPD was concerned, its activities were only too often directed against the SPD from which it had seceded. When Paul Hirsch, a prominent SPD leader, went to east Germany to address meetings for the reform of the Prussian franchise he was followed by Adolph Hoffmann, another deputy in the Prussian Diet under whose aegis the meetings were systematically disrupted in several towns. When another SPD deputy spoke in a small town near Frankfurt there were continuous interruptions. The USPD members present demanded first the election of the chairman from their own ranks, and then the right to have their case presented by a second speaker. The latter spoke for 90 minutes, to show, 'on the basis of facts', that the SPD had betrayed the cause of socialism ever since August 1914. At the end a resolution was voted which sharply condemned all annexations and demanded a general peace, complete democratization of all public institutions and the general, equal and secret franchise for all men and women above the age of 20. It seems ironical that the SPD deputy treated in this fashion soon after went over to the USPD. At Nuremberg, Ledebour spoke in a public meeting and declared that, if peace were not concluded by the governments soon, the result would be a general strike – a remark which caused such loud acclamations that the policeman present was unable to hear what followed. But when an SPD speaker in the discussion attempted to argue against Ledebour such whistling and heckling ensued that he could not make himself heard and was finally pulled down from the rostrum. At a USPD meeting in Munich the speaker put the question 'Is a revolution possible or not?' The audience shouted 'yes', but a soldier present called 'no', whereupon Eisner advised him to wait a few weeks and then he would see. Another speaker encouraged the 30 soldiers present to obey their conscience and not the orders of their superiors. Eisner spoke above all against militarism, not only in Prussia, and against the monarchy: both must be eliminated by revolution. In the spring of 1918, however, the USPD meetings in Munich were very badly attended, and some had to be cancelled, while a few months earlier there had always been an audience of several hundred.[19]

For southern Germany, we possess fairly reliable figures of USPD membership for 1918. In July it was given as 7009, including 1249 women, for the whole of south-west Germany with the exception of Stuttgart. The largest number was in Mannheim with 1210, followed closely by Hanau with 1208; then came Höchst (773), Frankfurt (750), Ludwigshafen (502), Cassel (356), and many other places with smaller figures. In June there were only 30 members at Wiesbaden, and the speaker from Frankfurt strongly complained about the slow progress in the whole area. For Bavaria the authorities estimated that only Nuremberg, Munich, Augsburg and Schweinfurt had more than 100 members each – with 5-600, 400, 250-300 and 140 respectively. There were none in Lower Bavaria and in the Upper Palatinate. These figures would give for the whole of south Germany – except Stuttgart but including the whole of Hesse north of the Main – fewer than 10,000 members, a rather modest number. As to north Germany, in the summer of 1918 the police estimated 630 members for Danzig, 270 for Cologne, 200 for Bremen, and only about 60 for Hanover, but about 2500 for Halle, one of the USPD strongholds, and 2060 for the duchy of Brunswick. At Chemnitz in Saxony, the regular monthly meetings of the party were only attended by 150 to 200 people; there the local leader was a well known Spartacist, and the police thought that the party had a few hundred members.[20] All these were large industrial towns, but only Halle seems to have had a large membership. Unfortunately no figures are available for Berlin or Leipzig where the membership must have been large. On the basis of these figures it must seem very doubtful whether the USPD had as many as 100,000 members (as has been estimated), and a figure of 50 or 60,000 seems more likely. Apparently the party had hardly grown since its foundation in 1917, a rather strange development considering the situation in Germany in 1918.

The propaganda of the USPD, however, was more revolutionary than the Spartacists were willing to admit. In parliament one of its deputies, Oskar Cohn, declared in February that the revolution which had started in Russia would spread to Germany, that the people would take their destiny into their own hands and end the war, against the princes and statesmen who did not know how to do it. In August Ernst Däumig, who had close connections with the Revolutionary Shop Stewards, spoke in Berlin to the socialist youth on the lessons of the Russian revolution and emphasized that it was essential to learn from them: every drop helped to undermine the structure of the state and its collapse would follow sooner or later. In September the Saxon deputy Hermann Fleissner at a district conference at Pirna allegedly stressed the necessity of underground work in the factories; in Berlin, he claimed, all was prepared for such action and the comrades there hoped that those in the provinces would not leave them in the lurch. At Frankfurt, the party secretary declared that the USPD must be ready to deal 'the last blow to militarism and capitalism' when the opportunity came. At Leipzig, the USPD agitated successfuly among the personnel of the trams whose mood was very bitter, especially the women who were much more militant than their male colleagues. In negotiations with the trade unions at Nuremberg in September it was made clear that they could only retain their influence if they obtained shorter working hours with equal pay and better food supplies: 'with promises the masses are no longer satisfied, otherwise they desert in droves to the Independent camp', as the military reported.[21] But the Independents were still far from conquering the masses.

This is confirmed by the results of the few by-elections which took place in working-class districts in 1918. After the death of the local USPD deputy a by-election became necessary in the constituency of Niederbarnim which comprised East Berlin, an old left-wing stronghold. There the USPD candidate was defeated in March by such a large majority by the SPD candidate that the USPD asked its followers to abstain in the second ballot – necessary because no candidate gained an absolute majority in the first; and Niederbarnim was considered impregnable by the party. In another working-class constituency, Crimmitschau in Saxony, the Spartacist Fritz Heckert, who was the official USPD candidate, was defeated in May by a large SPD majority. These surprising defeats showed up the true weakness of the USPD. The SPD retained the loyalty of the majority of the German working class for many years to come, in spite of its war policy. This did not change. In March the parliamentary party decided by a majority of 49 to 14 to vote once more for the war credits. In the party caucus, an equally large majority of the deputies decided not to vote in favour of the terms of the treaty of Brest-Litovsk imposed upon the Bolshevik government, but also rejected a vote against the treaty, so that the SPD abstained rather feebly when the vote was taken in the plenum and only the USPD voted against.[22] All the other parties voted in favour and thus supported the policy of Empire building in eastern Europe.

It was left to Haase, the leader of the USPD, to save the honour of the German parliament and to protest against the policy of force and annexation practised in the east: 'Russia is forced to accept a peace of violence at which the imagination boggles. It must cede straight away Courland, Riga, Lithuania, Poland... The inhabitants of these lands do not want the reactionary Prussian order with which they are to be blessed. They are able to preserve order in the country if not only the Russian, but also the German troops are withdrawn...' Haase sharply attacked the government: the old chancellor, Count Hertling, was only the fig-leaf of an all-powerful military party; 'he stands at the top but Ludendorff governs the Reich.'With regard to the treaty of Brest-Litovsk, Haase foretold correctly that Germany's policy in the east would serve to increase hatred and fear; it would prolong the war, for on the side of Germany's enemies 'the determination will be reinforced to fight on so as not to let a policy of force triumph in the whole world';

and – aiming directly at the SPD deputies – all those granting the means for the continuation of the war shared the responsibility for its prolongation; they were sowing the wind and would reap the whirlwind.[23] It only took eight months and Haase's prophecy came true, and the power wielded by General Ludendorff collapsed even earlier.

Large sections of the population were convinced that the responsibility for the policy of annexation and imperialist expansion rested with the Pan-Germans and the new *Vaterlandspartei* which enjoyed the support of the military authorities. Early in 1918 the latter reported from Baden that the Social Democrats were unwilling even to consider the aims of that party and identified it with the Pan-Germans and the Junkers whom they hated: 'therefore the *Vaterlandspartei* has not succeeded in Baden in making its aims known to the truly popular circles which look at it as a party of annexationists and of people who want to prolong the war *ad infinitum...*' A Bavarian officer writing in March remarked that the people often held the Pan-Germans and the *Vaterlandspartei* responsible for the failure of the negotiations with the Russians. A meeting of the party in Munich was broken up by workers shouting 'We are hungry, we do not want a peace of force!' and 'We do not need a king! We do not need an emperor!' In the autumn the commandant of Schweinfurt reported that the people in their bitterness blamed not only the military and the *Vaterlandspartei*, but also the government and the authorities which were too weak to call an energetic 'stop' to the policy of conquest; even those who hitherto had remained quiet now shared these feelings. In the Social Democratic press even very moderate party leaders attacked the Pan-Germans who had awakened such exaggerated hopes; their disappointment was bound to cause grave dangers.[24] Yet the SPD leaders themselves had never taken a clear stand against the annexationist plans of the government and did not even vote against the treaty of Brest-Litovsk.

Even the German pacifists were not in principle opposed to expansion and annexation. At a very well attended meeting in Stuttgart in October 1917 which was addressed by Professor Quidde a resolution was adopted which demanded a peace 'securing the vital requirements and the freedom of development of the German people', but did not say a word about those of other nations. It further stated that the Germans were 'united in their firm determination to continue with all their strength a war of defence for their independence and vital interests'. 'Vital interests' was a very elastic term, and what did these interests comprise in Eastern Europe? and was it 'a war of defence'? The Bavarian military authorities admitted that their check on the correspondence of Quidde had not produced anything incriminating and that his war aims were not all that different from those of the majority parties of the Reichstag and the Austrian Prime Minister. In their opinion, a journey of Quidde to Switzerland to attend a conference was 'less dangerous than that of the most harmless member of the USPD'. Although Ludendorff objected permission was therefore given for the journey. Yet as late as July 1918 the Prussian Minister of War tried to block any renewed activity of the German Peace Association. As they were not permitted to hold public meetings, they planned to form citizen's committees to arrange such meetings, and if that proved impossible, private meetings to make propaganda for a peace of compromise; the agenda everywhere was to be 'What kind of a peace do our people need?' But the minister was not willing to relax the restrictions imposed upon the pacifists and requested the authorities to prevent the holding of any such meeting. In Prussia and Bavaria – but not in Württemberg – the restrictions imposed on the pacifists and their leaders remained in force until October 1918.[25]

The answer of the military to pacifists and other 'troublemakers' was repression and threats. In a parliamentary speech Haase quoted a decree issued by the district command for the Prussian province of Saxony which threatened sentences of penal servitude and in certain circumstances even the death penalty for treason committed by distributing subversive leaflets: 'German men and women, repel with disdain the agitators who want to drive your fathers, brothers and wives on to the streets, allegedly to serve the cause of peace, in reality to deliver Germany into the hands of its enemies; this involves bribery by the enemy.' But, especially after the experience of the strikes of January 1918, the military also took to organizing their own propaganda. In February the military press office sent out a leaflet that every strike prolonged the war and did not help to bring peace: 'German labour has conquered the world, German labour is England's worst enemy, England wants to deprive the German worker of his bread. Whoever stops work supports this intention. "The English workers will gain the wages of which they have deprived the German workers." That the English government has promised to its workers...' The authorities in Berlin also suggested that officers or other ranks should give talks on their experiences to the workers of the armament firms to show them how their efforts contributed to the military successes. For certain military districts education officers were appointed whose task it was to arrange such lectures. The retired officer who was appointed for Württemberg then attended meetings of the works' committees of large firms to listen to the complaints and, if possible, to refute them. He also arranged a special course on war economic issues for the delegates of the armament works. The purpose of the whole exercise was 'to provide the leaders of the workers with an opportunity to discuss and air their grievances'. The union leaders supported the enterprise 'which in fact amounts to a strengthening of the moral and intellectual authority of the union leaders'. Some of the employers, however, voiced reservations, probably because they were opposed to any such strengthening and had their eye on the future. But the military insisted that the advantages of the scheme were much greater than any possible disadvantages and desired its continuation.[26] Thus political education made its debut in the service of the German war effort, but it is very difficult to say what the effect was.

There can be no doubt that in the course of 1918 the mood of the German people became more bitter and more critical of the authorities and their war policy. Even the victorious conclusion of the war against Russia did not dispel this mood for any length of time, and on the Left Brest-Litovsk only increased the hostility to the government. The mood also became more decidedly anti-monarchist. People wanted peace at any price and were not afraid of saying so. But this did not mean that a revolutionary situation developed or even that big political upheavals seemed likely. None of the leaders of the Left who made any pronouncement on this score thought so. It thus seems doubtful whether there would have been a revolution if the German army had not been defeated in France, if morale in the forces had not cracked under the impact of a vast Allied superiority, and if the military leaders – headed by General Ludendorff – had not lost their nerve and asked for the immediate conclusion of an armistice, thereby admitting that Germany was defeated. It was not the home front which stabbed the 'victorious' army in the back, but the mood of defeat was carried from the front to the rear. Yet the Left was still unable to influence the course of events. The number of revolutionaries remained pitifully small; even the USPD did not show any signs of real growth, and all the propaganda of the SPD for internal reform while there was still time was in vain.

The British Left at the
end of the Great War

As Haase in his speech on the treaty of Brest-Litovsk had quite accurately forecast, the German dismemberment of Russia was bound to strengthen the will of resistance among Germany's enemies. The great German offensive in the West which began in March 1918 was certain to have the same effect, for, if it was successful, would not Germany dictate similar peace terms to the western powers? These apprehensions were shared even by the British pacifists. As *The Herald* put it in April: 'The German treatment of Russia has emphasized the power of the military caste, and the powerlessness of the Social Democrats, in Germany. The German offensive in the West has caused everybody's first instinctive feeling to be that the German military machine is *the* enemy, the supreme danger, the unparalleled evil...A German victory would, indeed, impose upon the whole world a nightmare of militarist domination...' But the paper added that all Great Powers 'act in the same way if they get the chance', for example Japan in Korea or Britain in Africa, that a victory of the Allies would impose upon the world a similar 'nightmare', as proved by the secret treaties now revealed by the Bolshevik government, and that the Austrian and German strikes of January 1918 for 'peace and bread' had met with no response in Britain. It criticized the British government 'for its refusal to stand by the Russian Revolution' and to participate in the negotiations of Brest-Litovsk. As long as the secret treaties were not abrogated and as long as conscientious objectors languished in British prisons, Britain had no 'moral claim' to demand a decent peace. 'The German rank and file must deal with their militarists; but now is the time for us to deal with ours.'[1] This was a very forthright statement of the position of the British Left, but it acknowledged at the same time its weakness, its failure to

198

undertake any significant action against the war, its reluctance to do so while a German victory was possible.

The ILP was urged by some of its branches to do precisely this. For the annual Easter conference a resolution was proposed by the City of London branch and carried by the London divisional conference that the ILP members of parliament should dissociate themselves publicly from any support 'of conquest and Imperialist aggression', should divide the House of Commons and vote against any war credits 'on the next and any subsequent occasion' when parliament was asked to approve them. But when the conference assembled at Leicester in April it only adopted a resolution which demanded 'a democratic and unaggressive peace secured by negotiation at the earliest possible moment'. The principal attack was directed against the secret treaties 'to which governments and rulers have committed themselves behind the backs of the peoples…involving imperialist conquest and territorial aggression'; these treaties 'are the real stumbling blocks to an early and lasting peace and must be swept away with all governments that are bound by them.' In his opening address Snowden declared bluntly: 'the present British Government must go', and with it 'the equally impossible Government of France'. They must be replaced by governments which had clean hands and which could honestly say: 'We desire no territory, we desire no dominions… We desire only to live in peace and good will with all the nations of the world.' He claimed that, if the Labour Party had not joined the government and 'become so closely identified with its policy and its aims', it would now be swept into power 'to extricate the country and the world from this appalling situation' and to secure 'a genuine and democratic peace'; but as things stood a Labour government was 'neither possible nor desirable'. As the Labour Party was represented in Lloyd George's coalition government it could not possibly form an alternative government: like the German SPD it continued to support the official war policy. But the ILP, although affiliated to the Labour Party, once more emphasized its opposition in 1918, and Mrs Snowden exclaimed at the conference that the watchword should be 'Down with Lloyd George'. 'There was no hope for this country', she added, 'there was no hope for the world, whilst men like he were in office.'[2] Yet what could the ILP do to bring down the government? or to bring about a negotiated peace which was not desired by any of the belligerent governments? That the Labour Party conference held at the beginning of 1918 adopted a resolution in favour of the same aim had equally little effect.

199

The ILP also tried to determine its attitude towards the Bolshevik government of Russia. The City of London branch urged the conference to express its admiration of the Bolsheviks, their efforts to secure peace, their publication of the secret treaties, the steps taken by them to establish socialism by 'decreeing that the industries shall be owned by the community and controlled by the workers in the industry'. One of the radical delegates at the conference adopted the same line and asked why Snowden in his opening speech had not congratulated the Bolsheviks for 'having established a real Socialist Government in Russia'. Snowden replied that in 1917 the conference had sent its congratulations 'to its fellow-workers in Russia', and not to 'any particular section'. Indeed, the resolution then adopted had expressly mentioned 'the establishment – of a politically free nation...and the setting up of free political institutions'; but Snowden did not say that these no longer existed in Russia. Instead the conference of 1918 expressed 'its appreciation of the stand made for social and economic freedom by the workers of Russia, and their exposure of capitalist imperialism by the publication of the secret treaties' and pledged itself to inform the British people 'of the truth of the position adopted by our Russian comrades in the interests of International Socialism'. The resolution, like the one in favour of a negotiated peace, was carried unanimously, and thus the real issue – whether to criticize the Bolsheviks for their suppression of the Constituent Assembly and of political freedom – was avoided. At a vast May Day demonstration in Glasgow a resolution was adopted from all platforms sending greetings to the workers of all lands, including those of Germany and Russia. There James Maxton cried out: 'Peace, yes, peace, that is our insistent cry, the people want peace and the world wants socialism.'[3]

In August the National Council of the ILP issued a strong protest against the Allied intervention in Russia which 'has been undertaken without the consent of, and in direct opposition to, the wishes of the Russian Government, and is viewed with alarm and resentment by the mass of the Russian people', but was 'openly hailed in the British and foreign Jingo press as a step towards the overthrow of the Russian revolution'. Yet with regard to the Soviet government the manifesto maintained the ILP's cautious and non-committal attitude: 'We express no opinion on the merits or demerits of the present Russian Government. It is admittedly difficult to know what is the actual state of affairs in Russia.' Two factors, however, were listed which indicated that 'the general body of the Russian people' was not opposed to the

Bolshevik government: 'The first is that the Soviet Government has maintained its authority and has been carrying out great schemes of social re-organisation for nine months, and the second is that there has been no counter-revolutionary movement in Russia possessed of popular support and capable of even attempting to overthrow and supplant the Soviet Government'. The ILP therefore appealed 'to British organised Labour to express the strongest condemnation of the participation of the British Government in an act which constitutes a crime against national independence and against the Russian Revolution which has contributed, despite all its faults, so much to the hopes of human freedom – a crime which if persisted in will prove not only disastrous to Russia but to the cause of freedom and democracy throughout the world'. These were strong words, yet the manifesto did not call for a strike or any political action to halt the Allied intervention against the Bolsheviks. The ILP was still a very small party, and probably aware of its own weakness. In May 1918 an internal report of its head office showed that in April the party had at most 40,000 members, unevenly distributed over the country. Scotland and Ireland together had 7417 members, followed by the Midlands with 6359, Lancashire with 6174 and Yorkshire with 6074. London then had 5324 members, but the north-eastern counties only 2368, and the south-western ones only 540. Exclusive of Wales (the figure is missing), the total was given as 34,256:[4] not a very impressive figure after nearly four years of bitter warfare, but an increase on the very low figures of previous years.

It was only the British Socialist Party which took a much more radical line. At its conference in March one speaker claimed that Lenin and Trotsky had succeeded in driving a wedge 'between the working class and their respective governments in all the countries' and 'between the reformist section of the socialist movement and the revolutionary section'; but the only success he was able to mention was the January strike in Austria and Germany, which after all had failed. Another speaker went further and exclaimed that it was time 'to emulate the Russians and to put up and enforce the British revolution'. John Maclean declared he was confident that what had been done on the Clyde could be done throughout Britain, the miners of Lancashire were in favour of Marxism: 'We must stand by our Russian comrades and be prepared to risk our lives on behalf of our class.' The delegates were taken to task by Maclean for 'making no preparation for the contingency that would arise'. He believed that 'in the present circumstances' the passing of resolutions in favour of the Bolsheviks 'was merely a pious joke': the BSP members came to the annual conferences to pass resolutions 'and then went away and waited another year' to meet once more for the same purpose. But he did not say what the small BSP could do to promote the British revolution: at that time it had about 6 or 7000 members. It had failed to grow significantly during the war years, and its Marxist propaganda had not fallen on any fertile soil. What else could the party do but pass resolutions in favour of the Bolshevik and other revolutions? It urged 'the Socialist and Labour movement of all countries to give immediate support to the Government of the revolutionary Russian workers' and warned 'the capitalist governments that no interference with the affairs of the Russian Socialist Republic will be tolerated by the international working class'.[5] But what means did it possess to carry out the threat? Even in the trade unions its influence was minimal and the conversion of the miners to Marxism cannot have gone very far.

Indeed, what opposition there was to government policy came from the industrial side of the labour movement, and again it came above all from Scotland. At the beginning of 1918 the government decided on yet another comb-out of men employed in industry and elsewhere to increase the flow of recruits to the army, and for that purpose a Man-Power Bill was introduced. The age of men liable to compulsory military service was to be extended from 41 to 50. These plans aroused strong opposition. In Wales, the miners' leader Arthur Horner declared his opposition to the new comb-out from the mines and his solidarity with the Clyde workers. Another speaker seconded him and asked: 'Are we going to allow this war to go on?...I have two brothers in the army who were forced to join, but I say no. I'll be shot before I go to fight, and are you going to allow us to be taken to the war? I hope there will not be a ton of coal for the navy, if so'. A resolution against the comb-out was then unanimously adopted. The government sent Sir Auckland Geddes, the Minister of National Service, to Glasgow to try and persuade the local union leaders to accept the bill, for they had resolved on strike action if it were not withdrawn. He spoke to several thousands of shop stewards and workers' delegates in the city hall but met with a severe defeat. The Clyde Workers' Committee moved a resolution against the bill, pledging opposition to it 'to the very uttermost in its power'. The resolution also stated that the workers of Glasgow would 'take action to enforce the declaration of an immediate armistice', 'do nothing at all in support of carrying on the war', but 'do everything we can to bring the war to a conclusion'. There were protests against the Man-Power Bill in

London, Manchester and elsewhere; there was considerable unrest, but there was no strike. Nor was there any resistance when the bill became law in February. The government was able to point to the negotiations at Brest-Litovsk which showed what was to be expected in case of a defeat by Germany, and that clinched the issue. In this situation any resistance was hopeless and none was attempted.[6]

When the Ministry of Munitions, in July, tried to force some of the employers to release more men for military service strikes broke out at Coventry and other places, but the men returned to work when they were promised that their grievances would be considered. In the same month aircraft workers came out on strike because their shop stewards had been dismissed. The committee which led the strike consisted of shop stewards of the various works, and the Ministry of Munitions found it necessary to commandeer the factories and to run them as a national concern. In August there were more strikes. One of them was by the London policemen who demanded the recognition of their union, but only gained an increase of pay. Workers of the transport services demanded equal pay for men and women. In September a large unofficial railway strike broke out against a wage settlement which was approved by the unions but not accepted by the men, because it did not meet their full demand. The strike started on the Great Western railway in South Wales and quickly spread to Newport, Cardiff and other towns. As *The Times* wrote, 'in an incredibly brief time everything was in a state of chaos'. The movement soon affected many more towns, Birmingham, Bristol, Chester, Hereford, London and Plymouth. Coal supplies for the navy and for Britain's allies, munition and freight trains came to a halt, but the strikers agreed to work troop and hospital trains. They demanded the reopening of the negotiations, not with the recognised union officials, but with representatives elected by the strikers. It was a revival of the shop stewards movement. But the government took a strong line and declared that it would use the army for the transport of munitions, food and supplies as well as for the running of ambulance and leave trains for the army. It warned the strikers that interference with the transport of supplies needed for the war 'constituted an offence against the Defence of the Realm regulations'. The London Rifle Brigade was drafted into South Wales, the unions were forbidden to give strike pay, and the police issued a proclamation that it was illegal to interfere with men who remained at work. These strong measures caused the strike to collapse after three days. In Wales where it had started the railwaymen decided to return to work. There was more industrial unrest in the cotton industry of Lancashire and the coalfields of South Wales. Then the news of the Austrian collapse caused a lull and the strikes came to an end.[7]

Except for the Clyde, these strikes had no political purpose and were not directed against the war. The ILP and the BSP had no influence on their conduct. In that respect they differed very strongly from the January strikes in Austria and Germany in which the Social Democratic parties took a very prominent part. This was recognized in Britain at the time. *The Labour Leader* reported in glowing terms on the continental movement, claiming that in Germany it had led to 'the formation of a permanent Soviet Committee, of which both Haase and Scheidemann are members'. But this was wishful thinking, and so was the hope that 'a reunited Socialist Party will force the pace'. The ILP had always been in favour of healing the split within the labour movement and for that reason been reluctant to support the Zimmerwald movement; but in reality the German split was irrevocable and became deeper and deeper after the outbreak of the revolution. The ILP was not even in favour of using the strike weapon in wartime. In March G.D.H. Cole and another ILP member wrote that this was 'not the time for an industrial upheaval, the consequence of which would be disastrous, not only to the nation, but also to the working class...'; a strike would divide the workers, 'it would actually weaken the nation at the most critical moment of the war' and would not be forgiven by either the public or the soldiers. And in October MacDonald declared that 'during a war, purely industrial strikes have no connection with ILP policy, and are not inevitable consequences of ILP propaganda'. He specifically warned not to resort to political strikes 'as a way of paying out the Government in its own coin': to strike for higher wages was a totally different thing from striking for political change. He clearly considered such a strike impossible during the war.[8] In this respect the political scene in Britain differed strongly from that in Germany where not only the Spartacists and Left Radicals but also the USPD were committed to use the strike weapon for political purposes, as they had done in January 1918, alas without any success.

MacDonald's attitude to the war had always been rather ambiguous and he certainly did not share the anti-war sentiments of many others in the ILP. In the early stages of the war he had written: 'We are in it. We must see it through. Every step to that necessary end must be taken. Let there be no mistake about that...' His declaration about the strikes was only a logical sequel to his earlier position. But other members of the ILP adopted a much more uncompromising attitude, and leading among them were the members of the No-Conscription Fellowship. During the war, 1540 of them were sentenced to two years of hard labour and 71 of them died in prison. When Liebknecht was released under an amnesty in October 1918 *The Tribunal* wrote that in Britain 1500 men were suffering for their convictions, but in Berlin 'Karl Liebknecht, the great international socialist, who had always opposed the plans of the German militarists, was received and welcomed by cheering crowds. Germany has released her political prisoners. Are we less just and freedom-loving than Germany?' Particularly hard was the lot of the so-called 'absolutists' who while in prison refused to do any industrial or other work which would be of direct or indirect assistance to the war effort. In 1918 about 120 of them were brought to Wakefield prison and offered conditions under which they would have to do nine hours of work a day, would receive a little pocket money to be spent at the canteen and be allowed one censored letter and one visitor per week. But they rejected the scheme and refused to undertake any prison tasks and to recognize prison discipline while at Wakefield. They threatened to go on strike if they were punished, and were finally returned to various prisons in small batches.[9]

But the government also resorted to methods of repression against *The Tribunal* and its printers. In April 1918 the police raided the firm where the journal was printed. They informed the printer 'that they had instructions to break up the whole of the plant and machinery' and proceeded to do this most thoroughly, although he printed the journal as a business proposition and not out of political sympathy. As George Lansbury and the editors of other Labour journals pointed out in a leaflet appealing for funds to repair the damage, the authorities possessed ample powers under which they could have prosecuted the printer or the publishers of the paper, but had not done so, 'evidently that other printers might be terrorized' and so as 'to prevent the publication of matter that is unpalatable to the Government of the day'. But the police were unable to prevent the publication of *The Tribunal* which was henceforth printed in a wooden hut or barn on an estate at Box Hill in Surrey and taken from there to London. At the beginning of 1918 Bertrand Russell, who had taken over the running of the No-Conscription Fellowship when the younger men were called up and put in prison, published in *The Tribunal* an article which contained the sentence: 'The American Garrison which will by that time be occupying England and France, whether or not they will prove efficient against the Germans, will no doubt be capable of intimidating strikers, an occupation to which the American Army is accustomed when at home'. For this attack on an allied army he was sentenced to six months' imprisonment. Soon after the chairman and secretary of the Friends' Service Committee were tried because they refused to submit their leaflets to the censor before publication. For this offence they too were sentenced to six months' imprisonment and the one woman among them to a fine of £100. This she refused to pay and also went to prison; and their appeal against the sentence was lost.[10] These measures of repression, however, only served to strengthen the convictions of the victims; they felt they were martyrs and were ready to suffer for the cause. Nor were their tribulations over when the war came to an end. In March 1919 a leaflet published by the Friends' Service Committee stated that 1200 conscientious objectors were still in prison and another 3400 still working under a scheme arranged by the Home Office, mainly in so-called settlement camps.[11]

When the war finally reached its end there was such an outburst of patriotic and jingoist enthusiasm that the British Left had no chance to make its voice heard. In the 'Khaki' elections of December 1918 Labour was decimated and Snowden and MacDonald lost their seats. Yet after this defeat Fenner Brockway wrote to MacDonald that, although he was one of the 'young men', 'I have a feeling almost of reverence for the work you have done for the ILP, and particularly during the war', that he was confident that MacDonald would soon recover all he had lost.[12]

Like the USPD, the ILP contained many shades of left-wing opinion, from moderate to radical and revolutionary. Its core was formed by the convinced pacifists and idealists who possessed a sense of dedication and strong loyalty to their party and to their cause. They were able to face a bitterly hostile majority of the nation and to emerge from the war, if not triumphantly, with the strong conviction that they had been right and that their cause would win through in the end. This sense of dedication also distinguished the ILP from the USPD which was only founded in 1917 and never commanded the loyalty which the SPD continued to command: partly no doubt because of the many warring groups and factions within the new party which soon caused new splits, and partly because of the lack of any charismatic leaders and of efficient and clear leadership. Men like MacDonald, Snowden, James Maxton, David Kirkwood and Clifford Allen, on the other hand, while not great political leaders, held the ILP together and enjoyed great popularity among their followers and the rank and file of the party.

At its annual conference in 1918 the ILP claimed to have won 12,000 new members in the past year, but when the war came to an end it was still a small party. What then prevented its more rapid growth during the war? Perhaps MacDonald unintentionally expressed the general feeling of the nation by his 'We are in it. We must see it through'. That feeling was bound to work against a party which was opposed to the war and wanted to finish it soon by a compromise peace. Lenin and Zinoviev called the anti-war articles which they published from their Swiss exile before 1917 *Against the Current*. The ILP and similar small parties experienced how difficult it was to swim against the current during the war years.

Collapse and revolution
in Germany

During the spring of 1918 the great German offensive in France ground to a halt, and by August the military initiative passed to the Allies. In September they advanced all along the western front. Germany's allies – Bulgaria, Turkey and Austria-Hungary – one after the other admitted defeat and sued for an armistice. At the end of September the strong man of Germany, General Ludendorff, had to admit that the military situation demanded an immediate armistice. Germany declared its acceptance of President Wilson's Fourteen Points and appealed to him to bring about an armistice and to start the peace negotiations. The imminence of defeat also caused the collapse of the military autocracy which had ruled in Germany ever since the outbreak of war. A government had to be formed which enjoyed the support of the majority parties in the German parliament and – it was hoped – would impress the Allies by its liberal and constitutional character, by its willingness to carry out democratic reforms. The old Count Hertling resigned and a prince of liberal inclinations, Max von Baden, was appointed chancellor, to carry through the desired parliamentarization. His government, formed at the beginning of October, included leading members of the liberal parties, of the Catholic Centre and of the SPD. Scheidemann became one of the secretaries of state. At the end of October the German constitution, promulgated by Bismarck in 1871, was changed; for the first time, the chancellor and the members of the government became responsible to parliament, depending on the confidence of the majority in the carrying out of their duties. The semi-autocratic Hohenzollern monarchy was transformed at a stroke of the pen into a constitutional monarchy. In future a declaration of war, a peace treaty and important treaties with other states required parliamentary consent.[1] But there was no constitutional change in the bastion of tradition and conservatism, Prussia. The three-class franchise was not abrogated, in spite of all socialist attacks during the past years. The power of the Prussian bureaucracy which had ruled the country for centuries remained in force. Unchanged, too, remained the strong prerogatives of the Federal Council, which represented the governments of the federal states and was not elected. The appointment of Prince Max's government may have been a 'revolution from above', but at best it was a very incomplete revolution, for the distribution of power remained unchanged.

How did the German people react to these changes, to the resignation of Ludendorff, to the more or less open admission that the war was lost? From Hanover the authorities reported that the deterioration of the military position, the German offer of peace, Wilson's reply and the vast demands made by the enemy caused among all circles of the population a depression so deep as none previously observed, not even approximately, superseding all worries about the food shortages. But, the report added, a certain counterinfluence was created by the internal reforms, such as the confidently expected change in the Prussian franchise and the appointment of SPD leaders to the highest posts: these had been registered with satisfaction, especially among the working population – and Hanover had a large, politically very moderate working class. According to reports from Berlin, the working masses were 'dominated by a longing for peace which knew almost no limits'; here and there the idea of gaining peace by the use of force could be encountered, but it was strongly opposed by the Social Democratic press which condemned any playing with revolution; so far, the SPD and the unions had their members better in hand than they themselves had assumed. The collapse of the Habsburg monarchy at the end of October strengthened the conviction that any further resistance was pointless; it made 'a vivid impression on the workers' and was likely to strengthen radical sentiment. The collapse, the report added, was leading the Social Democrats back to the ideas of 1914 when a wave of anti-Austrian feeling swept the German socialists after the Austrian ultimatum to Serbia. In mid-October, after a discussion in the new cabinet in the presence of the generals, Scheidemann informed his parliamentary colleagues that the 'mood of the country [is] terrible, the more so the longer the negotiations drag on'; but the authorities still hoped to improve the mood 'with fat and meat and potatoes', and the military thought (rather optimistically) that the worst would be over if the army could hold out another four weeks. At the beginning of October Walther Rathenau was convinced that the country was drifting into civil war, military revolt, strikes by the producers of food, and finally 'the chaotic dissolution of the front. We can only save ourselves if we gain time.' 'The people's state' which in his opinion had now been established could only be destroyed by civil war, and even then not permanently.[2]

From Baden the military authorities reported that the offer of peace made to President Wilson by the German government was generally welcomed by the war-weary masses; when the truth slowly percolated and it was realized that the offer was made at the request of the High Command a further deterioration occurred, a veritable collapse of public morale; large circles believed that the enemy would soon occupy the country and anxious citizens sent their linen and valuable furniture away so that it could not be confiscated, while many others for the same reason were drawing money from the banks and savings acounts. In the Rhineland the Prussian authorities noticed that the people had lost all hope; the determination to hold out had disappeared; all they wanted was peace under whatever conditions it could be obtained; an early peace was considered the best way of countering the enemy's intention to destroy Germany. The mood of the workers of Ludwigshafen was described as 'anti-dynastic and secretly revolutionary' by the worried authorities. In general, the Bavarian military authorities noted that the people were saying: 'We have been lied to and have been deceived; we could have had a good peace... But a sizable section of the people had to die, and all to no purpose.' A longing for peace however bad it might be was the prevalent sentiment among the masses according to a military report from Munich. There was 'a dislike amounting to hatred of those who were considered responsible for the war and its bad end, a high degree of nervousness, total distrust of any quietening or enlightening remark'. Many desired the overthrow of the Hohenzollern dynasty, but nothing was said against the Wittelsbachs. A Social Democratic deputy found that not only the workers of Hanau demanded peace at any price, but that their wish was shared by many members of the middle classes who often added that William II and his son might as well 'unpack their top hats', i.e. disappear. Indeed, by the end of October the demand for the abdication of the Hohenzollerns was voiced by several Bavarian and other newspapers. The central censorship office in Berlin had to wire to the various press departments that 'it must be prevented at all cost that in the German press the demand is raised for the abdication of the Emperor or of the Hohenzollern dynasty.'³ Clearly, large sections considered the Emperor above all responsible for the war and the failure to bring about a compromise peace while Germany was in a strong position.

Yet the censorship, at least in Bavaria, was being relaxed. In October a leader of the Bavarian Peasant League, Karl Gandorfer, wrote in one of its papers that Germany's military power had collapsed: 'All the big words have gone; for more than four years they have lied, deceived the people, the blood of hundreds of thousands has been shed pointlessly.' The German people, he continued, could only save themselves at the last hour by taking their fate into their own hands; those who were responsible for the war and its prolongation must be eliminated; only if Germany renewed itself fundamentally was there a hope 'that we can obtain a peace with which we can live'. Everywhere in the countryside the Peasant League must take over the leadership and call to account those who had caused the war; the German people must find new forms, and the Bavarian peasant must win such power that no one would in future dare to spill the blood of his sons; a truly popular government must take over in Bavaria; the usurped power of the Catholic party (the Centre) which was in part responsible for the war must be overthrown; the first chamber of the Diet must disappear, the privileges of the nobility and the large landowners must go, together with entail and all titles of nobility 'unworthy of a free people'; 'Peasants! Your hour has come! Recognize the signs of the time!'⁴ Gandorfer was a radical; during the war he and his brother had shown courage by offering shelter to the children of Karl Liebknecht. But the article demonstrated to what extent the censorship had ceased to function. What Gandorfer wrote was a clarion call for revolutionary change.

In the Reichstag it was Haase who made himself the spokesman of the same tendency. When he commented on the changes of the constitution brought in by the new government he exlaimed: 'The crowns are rolling in the streets, the crown of the Bulgarian King Ferdinand, the crown of Tsar Nicholas, the crown of the Austro-Hungarian Emperor'; the crowns of Finland, Courland and Lithuania intended for various German princes had proved to be phantoms; all around Germany there would be republics, 'and then Germany alone, surrounded by republics, should still have a crowned head, or the wearers of many crowns and little crowns?!' A storm was shaking the world; at such a time Germany did not need an Emperor, a Federal Council, or a Reichstag with the limited competence allowed it by the constitution: 'a republic must come', and Haase added that a capitalist one was by no means his ideal. A few days later he spoke at Frankfurt to about 8000 people and declared that his goal was a socialist republic; with regard to Alsace and Lorraine he remarked that the policy of the SPD was dominated by nationalism; but if they succeeded in establishing socialism the whole national question would lose its importance. About 5000 people came to hear Haase at Mannheim where he demanded the immediate conclusion of peace, and a resolution to that effect was carried by a large majority: peace should be made without regard to any personality (meaning the Emperor) and without any further shedding of blood. On the lower Rhine – at Elberfeld, Barmen, Remscheid, Solingen, etc. – Dittmann, released from imprisonment by an amnesty, spoke at the same time to overcrowded mass meetings. At the end vast crowds demonstrated for peace in the streets of some of the towns.[5] Thanks to the more liberal policy of the new government, the leaders of the USPD were able to address mass audiences, and among them their demands found a ready echo.

In Munich, Eisner, also released from prison, in late October spoke to about 2000 people, mainly industrial workers, but also many who belonged to the middle classes 'and the best circles'; many women were present and some soldiers. Eisner sharply attacked the local SPD leader, Auer, who he claimed had stabbed the workers in the back during the January strikes, and the audience responded by calling Auer a 'scoundrel', a 'traitor' and other names. The people, Eisner continued, must be allowed to exercise democratic control in the offices of the government and the political parties, for they had been lied to long enough. From the audience the name 'Liebknecht' was shouted, and Eisner replied that, if Liebknecht were elected president, the Entente would make peace within a few days: Germany must admit that she was responsible for the war and cede Alsace and Lorraine as well as Prussian territory. There was much applause, but this diminished when Eisner said that Germany would have to pay reparations. He correctly prophesied that the war loans would become worthless paper; the workers should elect trusties and from these a workers' council should be formed. After Eisner's speech the large majority left the hall, from which the supervising police officer concluded that most of them had only come out of curiosity and that the USPD following in Munich was 'not large'. This seems to be confirmed by the fact that other USPD meetings in Munich as well as in Nuremberg in the same month were only attended by a few hundred people.[6]

Elsewhere, however, the audiences were much larger. At Hanau near Frankfurt, thousands were unable to gain admission to a mass meeting and had to stand in the streets outside the hall. A resolution demanded the abdication of the Hohenzollerns and the proclamation of a socialist republic, with Liebknecht as its president. At the end there were demonstrations with the same slogans in the streets, with the ominous addition of 'Down with the Scheidemann government! Down with the Hohenzollerns!' The police did not interfere. In Württemberg, demonstrations for peace and a republic took place at Friedrichshafen during the last week of October in which soldiers in uniform participated. Members of the works' committee informed the management that they had to take part in the demonstrations and asked for the factory gates to be closed. In Stuttgart, the trusties of the USPD met in mid-October, allegedly to discuss the possibility of a rising for a socialist republic and the winning over of the soldiers by propaganda in the barracks. On the 30th a mass meeting with the subject 'The workers and peace' was organized which was so overcrowded that a parallel meeting was arranged in the open air. About 5000 people were present, among them many soldiers and war invalids. A resolution demanded an immediate armistice, the abolition of military courts and the state of siege, the dissolution of parliament and the election of a 'people's parliament' of soldiers', workers' and agricultural workers' delegates (but not of peasants'), the annulment of all war loans above 1000 marks, the expropriation of the banks and of large landed properties, and the proclamation of an unitarian socialist republic, without dynasties and federal states. But when this resolution was put to the vote about two thirds of those present abstained. It was then decided to demonstrate at the end of the meeting in front of the royal palace and about 2000 people did so. They were addressed by a Spartacist, Fritz Rück, who concluded with cheers for a world revolution. The police tried in vain to disperse the demonstrators and had to be content to protect the entrances to the palace; but in the end the crowd dispersed and by 11 p.m. all was quiet.[7]

At Hamburg, the left-wing USPD deputy Henke spoke to the members of the party. He alluded to the fate of Nicholas II and the Austrian Emperor who were deserted by their officers and ministers; today the Emperor Charles was still 'our loyal ally', and tomorrow he was plain 'Karl Habsburg'. The people had been ruled by a minority for a long time, he continued, but this minority was unable to make peace; they no longer mentioned annexations and indemnities, because this was a time of revolution as proved by the Russian and Austrian examples: should the German people stand aside? Should they not be able to achieve what other nations had done? Henke admitted that the Bolsheviks deprived the former ruling class of all democratic rights as it had previously excluded the workers from all democratic institutions; but, he declared, he was in favour of such methods, and in Germany, too, democratic rights had been withheld from the masses in the interest of the ruling classes. He greatly preferred the Bolshevik methods to those of the German 'government socialists' who praised the new government for its measures of democratization, but what had changed in reality? A minor part of the constitution was changed, in Prussia the general franchise was allegedly secured, and in Hamburg three quarters of the members of the town council were to be elected by the voters. Yet a change of the constitutions did not consist of a piece of paper but depended on the distribution of power. The king with his soldiers was a part of the constitution, and so was the bourgeoisie. If the government socialists said that there was democratization because they were represented in the government, that was a lie, for a coalition with the bourgeois parties could not act in the interests of the working class as they were understood by the USPD. Henke concluded that this was a time when world history was made: it was necessary to stand up for their cause and if need be to sacrifice their lives for it. There was strong applause from the many hundreds present in the audience.[8]

The USPD leaders clearly felt that revolution was approaching, that it was only a question of time and the collapse of Austria would be followed by that of Germany. But what would the USPD do to bring this about? On 11 October the party executive met the district leaders in Berlin, and some days later the latter met separately in their areas. According to police reports, these meetings decided to take revolutionary action to overthrow the 'Scheidemann government'. But it seems more likely that preparations were made for another mass strike 'when the time was ripe', i.e. if no armistice was concluded by the government of Prince Max and the war was prolonged to the bitter end by the *levée en masse* which some people demanded.[9] But this contingency never arose. Nor could the Spartacists do more than distribute leaflets calling on the German workers to follow the example of their 'Russian brothers': 'they did not collect the crumbs from the table of the bourgeoisie, they did not accept alms from their enemies; they demanded "bread, peace and freedom" and, to achieve this demand, they took over the power of the government... Out of blood and tears the sun of freedom and of socialism has risen in the east.... Now the Russian revolution can already promise you help and support; and this promise it will keep.' The leaflet demanded the immediate liberation of all political prisoners, the lifting of the state of siege, the abolition of all restrictions on the press and political meetings, and above all it called for the formation of workers' and soldiers' councils.[10]

In mid-October the leaflet was distributed in some of the armament factories of Stuttgart. But workers' and soldiers' councils could at that time only have been formed in secret conventicles of determined revolutionaries, and not possibly in open mass meetings, and thus they would have been without any influence. The Spartacists now cooperated closely with the Left Radicals of North Germany whose representatives they met in October to discuss common actions, but for the time being they remained inside the USPD. The influence of the Spartacists was still small and in practice limited to a few towns, such as Berlin, Brunswick, Düsseldorf and Stuttgart. But when Liebknecht was released from prison on 23 October thanks to the new government's amnesty, about 20,000 people assembled at the station in Berlin to receive him, and he was carried shoulder-high from the platform by soldiers decorated with the Iron Cross. As a distressed Scheidemann reported to the cabinet, such a thing would have been impossible a few weeks earlier.[11] Yet such a public demonstration in honour of the famous victim of military persecution did not mean that the Spartacus Group had acquired a mass following: it was above all a demonstration against the war.

A week before thousands demonstrated in Berlin in front of the parliament building against the war and against the new government. From there they marched to the near-by Soviet embassy to express their solidarity, but the demonstrators were brutally dispersed by the police. Similar peace demonstrations took place in industrial towns of central Germany, such as Halle and Leipzig. At Brunswick, Liebknecht was expected to speak at the beginning of November but did not appear. The demonstrators preceded by the red flag of the socialist youth then marched to the market square where a speaker informed them that their demonstration was only the starting point to further actions for revolution. The police did not intervene, clearly on orders from the ducal government.[12] From all these reports it becomes clear that the influence of the USPD was rapidly growing in many industrial towns; but it was limited to the working class, and even there it was still overshadowed by the influence of the SPD which possessed a much more experienced and stronger party machine and many more daily papers.

During October the SPD too organized mass meetings in favour of peace and internal reform. The meetings were extremely well attended – 15,000 in Cologne, 5000 each in Düsseldorf and Hamburg – and several of them were disturbed by USPD followers. In Berlin, the leaders of the women organized in the SPD issued a proclamation in favour of immediate peace, without taking any notice of the views of their male comrades. In mid-October the SPD executive still published an appeal warning the 'class-conscious working class' against any strikes or demonstrations against the government 'which now serve no purpose' and were due to 'the agitation of irresponsible persons, confused by Bolshevik revolutionary phrases'. The question was how long the workers would listen to such warnings. In the meetings of the SPD parliamentary party even deputies who belonged to the right wing of the party demanded radical reforms, above all in Prussia, where a 'clean sweep of the bureaucracy' was a vital necessity. One of the deputies who put forward this demand was Gustav Noske. Yet when he went to Brunswick at the beginning of November to address a public meeting he adopted a strongly patriotic line. As Bulgaria, Turkey and Austria were eliminated from the war, he declared, Germany stood alone and the enemy was planning to attack from the south; 'Germany will victoriously withstand this colossal superiority and not permit the fatherland to become a bloody field of rubble'; their descendants would not believe what heroic deeds had been performed by army and people in this war.[13] Did Noske in November 1918 still believe in a German victory or in the possibility of a draw? At the time of his speech he must have known about the unrest which had broken out in the navy, for on the following day he went to Kiel to become the chairman of the local workers' and sailors' council: to lead the navy to final victory?

It was, however, neither the propaganda of the USPD and the extreme Left nor the strikes of hungry and exasperated workers which caused the collapse of Germany, but the vast superiority of the Allied armies on the western front. As a Bavarian military officer put it in mid-October, 'there is no doubt that our people have come to the end of their power of resistance… This is evident not only for the members of the army, especially the field army, but also for the home front. The soldiers say, tanks and aeroplanes are winning…' Units sent from the east to the western front now often refused to entrain; or they unfolded red flags and shouted 'Down with the war' and 'Long live France'. When they got to the front their attitude would undermine discipline; they were inspired by 'vague notions of freedom brought from Russia'. Allegedly soldiers sent from the east were responsible for the shouts following the officers — 'Beat him', 'Pull out your knives' — which spread 'like the plague' among the units according to a military report from the end of October. According to another, infantrymen armed with hand grenades threatened an artillery battery: 'If you fire again as you did this morning we'll kill you'. A soldier on leave from the front told a Social Democratic deputy that some units simply threw away their weapons and ran away, 'a wild, hopeless flight'. By the end of October there was open mutiny. According to General Groener, Ludendorff's successor as quartermaster-general of the army, near Metz a whole division of the territorial army refused to go back to the front, and many thousands of soldiers did not return from their leave. When Groener addressed the officers at General Headquarters he spoke of the danger that the army might completely disintegrate like the armies of Russia and Austria-Hungary. A captain from Headquarters who visited two army groups in France at the end of October and the beginning of November recorded that the soldiers were no longer willing to fight; the higher commands attributed the 'catastrophic decline of morale' to physical collapse, but a mutiny had also occurred in a regiment which was not physically exhausted; if pictures of the Emperor, Hindenburg or Ludendorff were shown in the cinemas, the soldiers whistled; they wanted peace at any price; unless there was an immediate peace, so the visitor was informed by numerous officers of both army groups, the soldiers would stop fighting. And then, he added, 'we will have revolution within a few weeks.'[14] This was written on 5 November when the revolution had already begun.

It becomes clear from these reports that the German army was no longer in a condition to resist the Allied advance, that at any moment there might be a breakthrough which would turn into a rout, that those officers who wanted to hold out until the spring to obtain better conditions were living in a pipe-dream world. How could it be different after more than four years of bitter fighting which had produced no result, faced by a much more numerous and better equipped enemy among whom the new American divisions loomed large? Much of the resentment and bitterness of the German soldiers now turned against their own officers who came from a different social class and were to a large extent still loyal to the *ancien régime*. In October the representative of the Bavarian government with the Crown Prince of Bavaria – who commanded an army group at the western front – informed his government that most of the Bavarian officers considered it not unjustified that the people were to have a decisive influence on their fate, but that almost all the Prussian officers saw in democratization 'the worst fate that might befall us'; for them, a democratic Prussia was no longer Prussia; Germany's disaster was in their opinion solely due to the rejection of the demands of the military by the left-wing parties in parliament and the attitude of those parties during the war; and some of them were indeed hoping that through force it might be possible to restore the *status quo*. Some of the officers of the cruiser *Königsberg* went further and remarked that it would be better sacrificing their ship and their lives than to serve a Scheidemann – a remark that was overheard by the sailors and aroused their indignation. Clearly, not only the extreme Left looked at the new government as a 'Scheidemann government': that leaders of the SPD for the first time were members of the cabinet caused strong hostility in conservative circles. One sailor meanwhile noticed that among his comrades Bolshevik ideas were gaining ground. 'Quite seriously, many talk about how they will soon act as "red guards".' He also asked the very pertinent question, what would happen if all peace negotiations failed and all that remained was to fight the war to the outrance?[15]

His remark proved prophetic, for at the end of October, while the armistice negotiations continued at a slow pace, the German admiralty decided to risk the high seas fleet which had remained passively in port after the battle of Jutland, in a last desperate attack on the British navy. This attack, even if partially successful, could not have exercised any influence on the outcome of the war, but it would have jeopardized the armistice negotiations and was certain to be interpreted as a sign of German bad will by the Allies now confident of victory. Indirectly the plan was also directed against the government of Prince Max which was above all interested in bringing the armistice negotiations to a speedy end. As it was put by Admiral Scheer when he informed the Emperor and the chancellor in very general terms, the attack was designed to demonstrate that the navy still possessed 'operative freedom'. But at the end of October the crews of the battleships and cruisers expected the war to end in the very near future and had no intention to sacrifice their lives for a lost cause, to save the 'honour' of the Germany navy. The sailors soon learnt of the intention of the admirals and decided to act. On 27 October the fleet at Willhelmshaven and other ports received orders to put to sea, but when the ships arrived at the point of rendezvous near Heliogoland the stokers simply extinguished the fires in the boilers. On the other ships the sailors refused to weigh anchor or, if they had done so, let the anchor drop again. When called to account by the officers the men replied: 'We do not put to sea, for us the war is over.' On some ships the sailors also declared that they were dissatisfied with the food and the conditions of leave and demanded time off. On the battleship *Baden* the sailors obeyed orders and no breaches of discipline occurred, but said that they were only willing to serve loyally in a defensive battle, not in an offensive one. They claimed that it was planned to let the fleet go down so as to prevent its being handed over to the enemy, or to thwart the armistice negotiations through an offensive; in their opinion, the officers had nothing to lose and wanted a war to the outrance in which the sailors would not participate.[16] Their action was completely successful, the enterprise against Britain was abandoned and the fleet returned to port. The deep rift between officers and men which was so clearly visible in 1917 appeared once more.

Back in harbour at Wilhelmshaven arrests were carried out. The mutineers on board the battleships were threatened by torpedo boats and submarines whose crews remained loyal. But there was much confusion and the officers did not dare to act as forcefully as they had done in 1917. Another mistake they committed was the dispatch of the Third Squadron to Kiel which only served to spread the mutiny. After the safe arrival of the ships at Kiel 47 sailors were arrested and another 200 condemned to form a penal battalion on shore. Protest meetings against these measures were prohibited by the naval authorities but took place nevertheless. The speakers urged the release of the prisoners, continued resistance to orders and an immediate armistice. On 3 November a meeting was held under the chairmanship of the military governor of Kiel, Admiral Souchon, to discuss what should be done. One admiral advocated the use of an alarm so as to bring the sailors back on board, to try and quieten them. Other admirals expressed doubt whether such tactics could be successful and suggested to use force but had to admit that even military buildings and ammunition depots were unprotected. It was decided to try persuasion and peaceful methods. The alarm was sounded but it had no effect; most sailors remained ashore. In one of the narrow streets of Kiel a crowd encountered a naval patrol the commander of which ordered the demonstrators to disperse. When this order was not heeded fire was opened. Eight men were killed and many more wounded by the volley. On 4 November Admiral Souchon was urged by naval headquarters not to make any concessions and promised that reliable troops would be sent to Kiel. But he replied that it was too late, that the situation could not be retrieved, and

obviously wanted to avoid further bloodshed. He negotiated with two
deputations, partly composed of sailors, and partly of local Social
Democrats. Both demanded the release of all prisoners, a judicial
investigation of the shooting and the cancellation of the attack on the
British navy. Souchon promised he would consider the demands
without prejudice. No demand was made for immediate peace or for any
revolutionary changes. A further meeting was arranged for the evening
in which the two emissaries sent by the government to settle the affair
and restore order – Conrad Haussmann and Gustav Noske – were to
take part.[17] Haussmann was a liberal member of the government and
Noske a right-wing Social Democrat, a specialist of his party in military
affairs and an apologist for its wartime policy.

Noske himself has described the situation which confronted him on
his arrival at Kiel. On 5 November most of the ships in the harbour
hoisted the red flag. Officers who tried to resist were disarmed or
thrown overboard. The workers of the dockyards came out on strike in
sympathy with the mutinous sailors. A large column of armed sailors
with a band and red flags marched to the military prison and freed the
arrested sailors. Admiral Souchon and his officers met the delegates of
the sailors who had constituted themselves as a soldiers' council and put
forward new demands. They consisted of 14 points among which
figured the release of all political prisoners, freedom of speech and the
press, the abolition of censorship, no punishment of the mutineers,
correct treatment of other ranks by the officers, the withdrawal of all
units not belonging to the garrison of Kiel, no further bloodshed. In
addition, the men when off duty should enjoy 'complete personal
freedom' and not be liable to carry out orders, but officers willing to
carry out the measures taken by the soldiers' council were welcome to
remain; all future measures would require the consent of this council.
There was no demand for the abdication of the Emperor and in general
no far-reaching political demand. Most of them were concerned with
the relations between officers and other ranks, and some with basic
democratic freedoms. As the military machine at the head of which they
stood no longer functioned the admiral and his officers were helpless
and conceded the demands. Their power was at an end and the soldiers'
council took over. It immediately proclaimed that 'quiet and iron nerves
are the demand of the hour', that looting and robbery were unworthy of
the men who must obey their elected leaders.[18] On his arrival Noske was
welcomed by an enthusiastic crowd who considered him their
spokesman and leader. No leader of the USPD had yet reached Kiel, and

the vast majority of the sailors looked at the differences between SPD and USPD as just minor squabbles.

In the afternoon of 5 November the elected delegates of the sailors' units met under Noske's guidance, altogether some 50 to 60 men. He then suggested that a smaller soldiers' council be elected from their midst as the group was too large for the effective conduct of business. This was agreed, and Noske selected the members according to his impression and by looking at their faces, but he admitted later that 'on this occasion' his 'insight' proved not quite right. In this curious fashion the soldiers' council proper was constituted at Kiel, with Noske as the chairman. Two days later he was also appointed governor of Germany's largest naval base in succession to Souchon. At that point Haase finally arrived at Kiel, but the speakers at the meeting felt that there was no need to wait for him as they had already elected the governor. When Haase and Noske met they agreed that it was of paramount importance for the leaders of the two Social Democratic parties to cooperate to prevent a catastrophe in Germany, and Haase departed for Berlin which he only reached after the outbreak of the revolution in the capital. The election to the post of governor was carried out by the so-called enlarged soldiers' council the majority of which consisted of naval NCO's. According to Noske's testimony, they took great pains during the following days and weeks to restore orderly conditions, and he praised several for their selfless efforts in doing so. He also persuaded the officers to remain at their posts; they were badly shaken by the events and promised him to carry on.[19] In this way, in an almost orderly and military fashion, the German revolution came to Kiel. The soldiers' council considered it one of its primary tasks to preserve law and order; there was little bloodshed and hardly any resistance by the officers. Some looting of military stores occurred, but on the whole law and order was preserved and, although there was much wild shooting, there were few casualties.

Henceforth the red sailors regarded themselves as the *avant-garde* of the German revolution – in a way similar to the red sailors of Russia who had helped the Bolsheviks into power – with the difference that the number of convinced Bolsheviks in Germany was minute and that the sailors willingly accepted a right-wing SPD deputy as their leader. If Haase or Ledebour had appeared in Kiel at the decisive moment they would as willingly have accepted them: after all, in 1917 the sailors of Wilhelmshaven had contacted the USPD deputies rather than those of the SPD. In 1918, moreover, the war was no longer a real issue, for the armistice was signed a few days after the outbreak of the naval mutiny, and it was quite clear to everybody, except the admirals, that the war was over. From Kiel the revolution spread like wildfire, first to the ports along the coast of the Baltic and the North Sea, to Lübeck, Hamburg, Bremen, Wilhelmshaven. Everywhere sailors decorated with red insignia acted as the spearhead of the movement. Everywhere workers' and soldiers' councils sprang up spontaneously.

At Bremen, huge demonstrations converged on the market square on 6 November. There they were addressed by a member of the USPD who announced the formation of the workers' and soldiers' council and its taking over of the power of command. The political prisoners were freed. On the same day an agreement was concluded between the commandant of the local garrison and the soldiers' council according to which military power in Bremen was to be exercised jointly by him and four members of the soldiers' council, and the latter undertook to preserve law, order and security. The officers were to retain their swords and epaulettes, their orders were to be carried out when the men were on duty, and looters were to be tried by courts-martial. No one seemed to fear any excesses by the red sailors and soldiers. On the next day a vast crowd was addressed by the local USPD deputy, Henke, who sharply attacked the government of Prince Max which allegedly was a 'people's government', demanded the abdication of all the dynasties and called for the preservation of discipline as essential for the success of the movement. Work was resumed on the same day. At Cologne, the revolution began on 8 November with the arrival of a group of sailors from Kiel who made propaganda among the garrison, with the result that several units came out in support of the revolution. In the morning of 8 November the local leaders of SPD and USPD met and decided to form a workers' council of 12, six from each party (i.e. not elected but self-appointed), to which the same number of soldiers was to be added. A mass demonstration in the market place then accepted demands for an immediate peace, abolition of the dynasties, release of all political prisoners, end of the call-up and annulment of the war loans. The workers' and soldiers' council called for the preservation of order; all looters and thieves would be immediately arrested by the patrols of the council and be severely punished. Subcommittees were formed for security, billeting and food, transport, health, finance, and the press. The mayor, Konrad Adenauer, put rooms in the town hall at the disposal of the council which was chaired by a soldier, one representative each of the SPD and the USPD with equal rights.[20] Thus the municipal authorities immediately reached an agreement with the organ of the revolution, which accorded to the latter the right of supervision but left the old administrative organs in control of affairs. This pattern was followed, with some local variations, in every town of the country. It was a compromise, but a compromise which left the decisive influence to the old administrators, for the large majority of the members of the workers' and soldiers' councils were not qualified to take over the administration or to control it.

In Munich, the USPD leader Eisner as early as 5 November spoke to a large crowd assembled in a meadow and told them not to march into the centre, but to wait another two days and then action would be taken, because to succeed it required not only thousands, but 'the whole of Munich, hundreds of thousands, and also the peasants'. On 7 November there was another mass meeting in the same meadow where leaders of the SPD as well as the USPD spoke. This time the crowd included many soldiers and sailors, the latter on transit from an Austrian naval base to the north, and detained in Munich on account of the mutiny. Next to Eisner stood the leader of the Bavarian Peasant League, Ludwig Gandorfer, who promised the support of the Bavarian peasants. After the speeches he and Eisner led their followers to the military barracks near-by. There some of them went inside, persuaded the soldiers to join the march, seized arms and proclaimed the revolution. Shouts for peace and the republic came from the windows. Soon all the barracks were in the hands of the revolutionaries. In the evening the king and his family left Munich as their lives might be endangered. The public buildings were occupied by armed detachments. A vast crowd of workers and soldiers moved to one of the large beer halls in the centre of Munich. In one hall a soldiers' council was formed, in another a workers' council with Eisner as the chairman. From there they marched to the Diet where Eisner opened the constituent meeting of the workers', peasants' and soldiers' council. He requested those present to remain until the provisional council had become the definitive one: it must continue to exercise its power until a national assembly could be elected by a general, equal and secret franchise to take over power in Bavaria. At about 1 a.m. it was established that the police headquarters had not yet been taken over, and a detachment was sent there to declare that the councils had seized power. The head of police was asked to continue provisionally in office until definitive arrangements could be made for the security services, provided that he declared in writing his willingness to carry out the councils' orders; after a few minutes' hesitation he accepted.[21]

During the night the workers', soldiers' and peasants' council issued a proclamation signed by Eisner informing the population that Bavaria had become a 'free state' and that a constituent assembly elected by all adult men and women would meet as soon as possible; the council would 'secure the strictest order', suppress all excesses and guarantee the right of property; officers who recognized the demands of the new time should carry on without fear of molestation, but the soldiers would 'govern themselves through soldiers' councils'. Another proclamation declared the Wittelsbach dynasty deposed and the workers', soldiers' and peasants' council the highest authority with legislative powers and in charge of army and police. The council also confirmed in office the provisional government of Bavaria which emerged from negotiations between the leaders of the SPD and the USPD, with Eisner as prime minister and foreign minister, the SPD leader Auer as minister of the interior and other SPD members in charge of education, justice and military affairs. The cabinet contained four SPD and three USPD members and one non-socialist expert. Thus Eisner and his party friends were from the outset in a minority in the government. The cooperation of some Bavarian peasants was won through the personal friendship between Eisner and Ludwig Gandorfer. When the latter was killed in a car accident on 10 November the leadership of the Bavarian Peasant League passed into the hands of his brother Karl. But the League only commanded the loyalty of a section of the Bavarian peasants, while the large majority followed the Catholic Peasant Association which was not represented in the Munich council.[22] Above all, Eisner's party, the USPD, was still very weak, and soon there was considerable friction between him and the very moderate leaders of the Bavarian SPD. In the elections held two months later, in January 1919, the Bavarian USPD only polled 2.5 per cent of the vote and gained a mere three seats in the Diet.

While these momentous events took place in the north, west and south of Germany, everything was still quiet in Berlin, although there the revolutionary groups were much stronger than in any other part of the country. After his release from penal servitude Karl Liebknecht joined the loose group of the Revolutionary Shop Stewards and suggested to them to organize for Sunday, 3 November, meetings to be followed by demonstrations in the streets. But they objected to the idea of street demonstrations, and the executive of the USPD did the same, for they considered the intention that such demonstrations should lead to the final revolutionary rising 'revolutionary gymnastics'. They also knew that the government was moving reliable units from the provinces to Berlin to cope with any revolutionary upheaval. Hence the decisive question was what attitude these units would take. One of the leaders of the shop stewards, Ernst Däumig, was entrusted with the task of winning over the soldiers of the garrison among whom he found many sympathizers. But, as the units were often moved about and new ones sent to Berlin, it was uncertain what the military would do if it came to an open clash. On 2 November the shop stewards met the leaders of the USPD and of the Spartacus Group to discuss whether to start the uprising on Monday, 4 November, but decided by a small majority to postpone it by one week because they feared that Berlin might remain isolated. As yet they had no news from Kiel and in general they were badly informed about events outside the capital. On 7 November the military authorities forbade the formation of workers' and soldiers' councils 'after the Russian pattern'. On the following day the Spartacists issued a proclamation summoning the soldiers to follow the example of the Kiel sailors and to disobey the orders of their officers; in all units and factories workers' and soldiers' councils should be elected and their delegates should take over the government; relations were to be established immediately with the international proletariat and especially with the Russian Soviet Republic; the German federal states and dynasties must disappear.[23]

On 9 November – two days earlier than planned by the revolutionaries – the revolution reached Berlin. The factories closed and huge demonstrations moved towards the centre; many were joined by soldiers in uniform. The barracks emptied, the soldiers either making common cause with the workers or packing their belongings and going home 'on leave'. Weapons were seized and the political prisoners freed from the civil and military prisons. The cockades and epaulettes were torn from the officers' uniforms. Vast crowds converged on the square in front of the parliament building, and from its balcony Scheidemann proclaimed the German Republic, probably to forestall Liebknecht who soon after proclaimed the 'German Socialist Republic' from the balcony of the royal palace. Even before these events which marked the end of the *ancien régime*, Prince Max, the last imperial chancellor, tried to hand over the government to Friedrich Ebert, the SPD leader – a breach of the constitution as only the Emperor could appoint the chancellor. But William II had left Berlin never to return, first to go to General Headquarters at Spa, and from there to seek asylum in Holland when the generals told him that the army would no longer follow his command. It was announced by special editions of the papers that Ebert was forming a new government and that a constituent assembly would soon meet to decide upon the political future: 'therewith power has passed into the hands of the people... Long live the German Republic!' A hastily formed workers' and soldiers' council proclaimed a general strike and admonished the population to preserve law and order.[24]

Ebert, however, did not become the last chancellor of Imperial Germany. In the parliament building negotiations for the formation of a coalition government were carried on by the leaders of the SPD and the USPD; they were somewhat protracted because of the absence of Haase who had gone to Kiel and was unable to return to Berlin in time. On the evening of the 9th the USPD submitted its programme to the SPD: in the German 'Social Republic' (not Socialist) the entire executive, legislative and judicial power was to be exclusively exercised by the representatives of the whole working population and the soldiers; to this the SPD replied that it must reject this demand if it meant 'the dictatorship of part of one class'. To the demand that all bourgeois ministers should be excluded from the government the SPD replied that it was unacceptable because it would endanger the food supply or even make it impossible. But the SPD accepted another demand, that the ministers responsible for a particular task were only to be 'the technical assistants of the proper and decisive cabinet'. On 10 November the USPD leaders replied that 'political power was to be in the hands of the workers' and soldiers' councils which were to be summoned as soon as possible from the whole of Germany for a plenary meeting', that the issue of a constituent assembly, topical only after the consolidation of the conditions created by the revolution, should be discussed later, that the cabinet was to consist only of Social Democrats who, as people's commissars, were to enjoy equal rights. On this basis the negotiations were concluded. The SPD nominated Ebert, Scheidemann and Otto Landsberg, a lawyer. The USPD nominated Haase and Dittmann and, as a representative of the Revolutionary Shop Stewards Emil Barth, after Liebknecht had refused to accept a seat in the government which included the SPD leaders. Ebert and Haase were to be the joint chairmen of the government.[25] The term 'people's commissar' was clearly borrowed from Soviet Russia, but otherwise the coalition government had little in common with that of Lenin. Perhaps Liebknecht made a mistake in refusing the offered cabinet post. But even in the cabinet he could not have exercised a decisive influence on the course of events. From the outset Ebert and his friends were determined to see to the election of a constituent assembly at the earliest possible moment, and there was no guarantee whatever that the election would produce a socialist majority.

On the same day that the government of the 'people's representatives' was formed by the agreement of the two Social Democratic parties the workers and soldiers of Berlin elected their councils, and in the afternoon those elected – about 3000 in number – assembled in a circus to confirm the new government in office. Ebert, Haase and Liebknecht spoke. While the first two emphasized the agreement reached and the need for unity to secure the victory of the revolution, Liebknecht sharply attacked Ebert and pointed to the danger threatening the revolution from that quarter. But his attacks met with strong opposition, especially from the side of the soldiers. Barth as the chairman of the meeting then suggested, as had been agreed upon by the Revolutionary Shop Stewards prior to the meeting, the election of an executive committee and proposed a list containing only left-wingers. He was contradicted by Ebert who demanded that the executive committee like the government should be composed of representatives of the two parties in equal numbers, while Barth wanted to exclude the members of the SPD. The soldiers shouted 'unity' and 'parity' and there were tumultuous scenes until their demand was granted. In the end the executive committee contained 14 workers' representatives – half from the SPD and half from the USPD – and 14 soldiers: parity was observed and the intended coup of the Left was abortive. Henceforth, the executive committee had the right to confirm the composition of the government and to supervise its measures; in a vague way the government was responsible to it for the time being. Its joint chairmen were Richard Müller, the leader of the Revolutionary Shop Stewards, and an official of the SPD. In the end the meeting confirmed the composition of the new government and issued a proclamation which expressed admiration for the Russian workers and soldiers, who had shown their German comrades the way to revolution, and sent them brotherly greetings; the German revolution would bring immediate peace and carry out 'the speedy and thorough socialization of the capitalist means of production'; a new economic order would arise from the ruins 'to prevent the economic enslavement of the masses, the collapse of culture'; now the workers' and soldiers' councils were exercising political power.[26] There seemed to be a complete break with the past.

From the mass meeting in the circus Ebert returned to the chancery where he had established his office, and there he received a telephone call from General Headquarters. Speaking in the name of Field-Marshal von Hindenburg, General Groener, the quarter-master general of the army, informed Ebert that the field army put itself at the disposal of the new government and that the officer corps therefore expected the government's support in the maintenance of order and military discipline. It is possible that Groener, as he wrote later, also said that the army expected from the government a common front against 'Bolshevism' and was ready to take up the fight against it. In any case, Ebert – rather shaken by his experiences in the mass meeting – accepted the offer of support, for on 10 November the German army stood far inside France and Belgium and occupied vast stretches of conquered territory in the east. It was essential to bring back the troops in orderly conditions and equally to preserve law and order at home. The new government was weak, disunited and without any proper protection if revolutionary disorders should occur. The generals in their turn needed the support of the government, otherwise soldiers' councils might dismantle the authority of the officers, as indeed happened in many units of the home army and in the navy. Thus agreement was quickly reached, but it was in the first instance an agreement with a limited purpose – the orderly return and demobilization of the army – and not the political 'alliance' as which it has figured in the literature and in Groener's later account.[27] Further steps in the same direction soon followed the agreement of 10 November. Only four weeks later Hindenburg demanded from Ebert that the soldiers' councils must disappear from the army and that the functions of the workers' councils must be curtailed. The army marched back across the Rhine in good order and under the command of its officers.

There was no disagreement among the members of the new government that it needed the services of 'experts' in many fields, experts who were not Social Democrats or democrats. Many of the former secretaries of state and even the Prussian Minister for War, General Scheüch, remained in office, as did Hindenburg and Groener at the head of the army. The new government of Prussia, also composed of representatives of the SPD and USPD in equal numbers, appealed to all Prussian authorities and officials to continue in office 'so as to contribute on their part to the preservation of law and order in the interest of the fatherland'. Even the executive committee of the Berlin workers' and soldiers' councils declared that 'all federal, state and military authorities continue their activities. All orders of these authorities are issued at the behest of the executive council of the workers' and soldiers' councils. Everybody has to carry them out.'[28] Thus the forces which had created and ruled the old Prussia, the bureaucracy and the officer corps, remained in their positions without any real change in their composition or structure. The government felt it could not do without them, because the left-wing parties did not contain a sufficiently large number of qualified people, and soon the forces of the old order were able to overcome the challenge to their power which the workers' and soldiers' councils posed for a brief time. For a few months the latter exercised a loose form of supervision over the old authorities. But with the election of representative assemblies on the local, state and federal levels in the early months of 1919 this supervision came to an end, on the whole voluntarily because the large majority of the local councils were very moderate in their political composition and considered their tasks fulfilled when 'democratization' was achieved.

On the national level, the all-German congress of the workers' and soldiers' councils held in Berlin in mid-December 1918 decided by a large majority that the elections to the constituent assembly should take place as early as 19 January 1919. A minority which wanted the elections to be held later was defeated. They were duly held on that day, all men and women over 20 years of age voting for the first time, and they did not produce a socialist majority although the SPD remained by far the largest party with 38 per cent of the vote. The USPD polled only 7.5 per cent although it must have grown considerably after the outbreak of the revolution. By then it was a small left-wing opposition party, for at the end of December its ministers had resigned from the government. Thus the future of Germany was shaped not by a socialist government but by a coalition of the SPD with the Democrats and the Catholic Centre. Germany became a bourgeois republic, but a republic in which the old bureaucracy, the old judiciary and the officer corps held sway. There was indeed a German revolution in November 1918, but the revolution was aborted. During the early months of 1919 too, the extreme Left was defeated in a series of bloody clashes, from the so-called Spartacus Rising in Berlin to the so-called Soviet Republic in Munich, by volunteer units or Free Corps; they were created at the orders of the government and commanded by members of the old officer corps. Their victories only marked the fact that the old social order, seriously shaken for a short time, had survived the revolution. The German workers' and soldiers' councils were not 'Soviets', and even the short-lived 'Soviet Republics' of Bremen, Brunswick or Munich had little in common with the Russian prototype. Many years earlier Ferdinand Lassalle had stated that constitutional questions were questions of power;[29] but his German pupils did not heed his precept. Already in October 1918 the Bavarian military representative with the High Command reported that among senior officers the opinion was widespread it was a good thing that the left-wing parties would be burdened with the odium for the conclusion of peace; thus they would suffer the storm of popular indignation.[30] Soon the legend of the stab-in-the-back was used to create this storm against the Left.

Even after the outbreak of the revolution the Bolsheviks found few convinced followers in Germany, and the German Communist Party founded at the end of 1918 was very small and rent by internal differences. In Russia, the urban masses in 1917 went over to the Bolsheviks because the Provisional Government refused to conclude an armistice and continued the war on the side of the Allies. The armistice between them and Germany was signed on the day after the government of the people's representatives was confirmed in office by the workers' and soldiers' councils of Berlin. The war-weary masses had finally achieved their goal, although hunger and unrest continued for years to come. In Germany, in contrast with Russia, there was no agrarian revolution, no movement to divide the large estates of East Germany among the peasants – another cause of the radical turn of the Russian revolution because the Bolsheviks adopted the programme of the revolutionary peasant movement. In Germany, the large majority of the peasants remained conservative and more or less hostile to the revolution, especially after its radical turn in Bavaria. There were some peasant councils but they did not develop much activity and faded out quickly. Even those sections of the peasantry who had at first sympathized with the revolution were soon alienated. When the all-German congress of the workers' and soldiers' councils met in December only two delegates out of nearly 500 represented peasant associations.[31] Otherwise the peasants did not participate in the movement. Thus with regard to the issues of peace and of land the situation in Germany differed fundamentally from Russia where the Bolsheviks could use both in their favour.

In the industrial centres too the situation was very different from Russia. Germany possessed strong and well entrenched trade unions and a well established Social Democratic Party. During the war these were able to retain the loyalty of the majority of their followers and members, in spite of all attacks from the Left – exactly as in Britain. The USPD and the ILP remained comparatively small minority parties, and the extreme left-wing groups were even smaller. This is not easily explained. Perhaps it was due to the innate patriotic feeling among the working masses, a determination to see the war through, a reluctance to separate from the large majority of the nation and to go into open opposition. Perhaps, at least in Germany, it was also due to the preoccupation of the masses with more burning issues: to get food and coal, to obtain higher wages to compensate for the increased cost of living. The vast majority of the strikes were for purely economic reasons and were above all caused by the terrible scarcity of food. As the search for food and other necessities became the primary occupation of working men and women, litte energy was left for radical politics, especially during the later years of the war. The mood of the masses became one of despair, apathetic and indifferent, not radical and revolutionary. The USPD, moreover, which was founded rather late, in April 1917, was subject to considerable police harassment and did not acquire a firm organisational structure except in a few towns. It lacked a charismatic and decisive leadership and was from the outset plagued by internal factional strife. Yet there were the political strikes of 1917-18 which demonstrated to what extent the German working class was eager to terminate the war. No political strikes on that scale occurred in Britain because there the people suffered less from the war and the nation remained on the whole more united behind the war effort.

The large majority of the German army remained loyal and obeyed orders – until the vast superiority of the Allies in France proved that the war was lost. Then the sailors of the High Seas Fleet revolted because they did not want to sacrifice their lives for a lost cause, and from the fleet the movement quickly spread to the units of the home army and the workers of the industrial towns. But it never became a national movement. The workers' and soldiers' councils which sprang up all over Germany in a vast spontaneous movement only represented certain sections of the population. Once order was restored and democratic assemblies were elected the movement quickly lost its impetus. Only a minority of the participants wanted to make the councils a permanent institution, and even fewer intended to follow the Soviet example. Thus it came to an end during the early months of 1919 and with it ended the German revolution. The strikers of January 1918 had achieved their principal aim: Germany became a democracy – but a democracy in which the bastions of power were held by the adherents of the old régime. It was the generals and the bureaucrats, the agrarians and the industrialists, who dominated the fate of the first German republic which they disliked from the outset; and finally they succeeded in destroying it by handing over political power to a lance-corporal of the Great War.

NOTES

CHAPTER I

1   E. Matthias and E. Pickart (eds.), *Die Reichstagsfraktion der deutschen Sozialdemokratie 1898 bis 1918*, Düsseldorf, 1966, II p. 3; S. Miller, *Burgfrieden oder Klassenkampf*, Düsseldorf, 1974, pp. 59-60.

2   Letter by Max König, deputy for Hagen-Schwelm, to the *Vossische Zeitung*, 5 May 1916, quoted by A. J. Ryder, *The German Revolution of 1918*, Cambridge, 1967, pp. 44-45. Interestingly enough, the other deputy was Wilhelm Dittmann, later a leader of the USPD and a very prominent left-winger. Clearly, at this stage the differences between Right and Left were not very clearly marked.

3   Institut für Marxismus-Leninismus (ed.), *Dokumente und Materialien zur Geschichte der deutschen Arbeiterbewegung*, I, Berlin, 1958, Nr. 8, pp. 20-21; F. Klein and others, *Deutschland im Ersten Weltkrieg*, I, Berlin, 1968, p. 459: Liebknecht's letter of 18 January 1915.

4   *Ausserordentlicher Internationaler Sozialisten-Kongress zu Basel am 24 und 25 November 1912*, Berlin, 1912, p. 23; D. Groh, *Negative Integration und revolutionärer Attentismus*, Frankfurt-Berlin-Vienna, 1974, pp. 238, 429.

5   Ph. Scheidemann, *Der Zusammenbruch*, Berlin, 1921, p. 3: diary entry of 25 July 1914; facsimile print of *Vorwärts* 25 July, in R. Müller, *Vom Kaiserreich zur Republik*, I, Vienna, 1924, p. 27 (emphasis in the original); Kautsky to Adler, 25 July, in F. Adler (ed.), *Victor Adler – Briefwechsel mit August Bebel und Karl Kautsky*, Vienna, 1954, p. 596.

6   *Vorwärts*, 29 July: *Dokumente und Materialien zur Geschichte*, I, Nr. 5, pp. 14-15.

7   Groh, *Negative Integration* ... ,pp. 638-39; Scheidemann, *Zusammenbruch*, p. 3; report by Büro für Sozialpolitik, Berlin, 1 November 1918: Bundesarchiv-Militärarchiv, RM3/v.2612; C. Geyer, *Die revolutionäre Illusion*, Stuttgart, 1976, p.43.

8   Groh, *Negative Integration* ..., pp. 653, 656; A. Balabanoff, *Erinnerungen und Erlebnisse*, Berlin, 1927, p. 57.

9   The quotations are from Henri de Man to Pierre Renaudel, 29 February 1915, in support of the latter's version published in *l'Humanité* on 26

February. A translation into English in Ramsay MacDonald Papers, PRO 30/69, 5/ 104. The letter gives a fuller account than Renaudel's article and quotes Müller's remarks in German. Müller's own report written from memory in 1915 may be found in Scheidemann, *Zusammenbruch*, pp. 12-18. Emphasis in the original. The French protocol quotes Müller more briefly as saying: 'La question du vote *pour* ne se posera pas. Ou contre, ou abstention unanime...et on ne votera pas les crédits. En aucun cas.' G.A. Ritter (ed.), *Die II. Internationale 1918/1919*, Berlin-Bonn, 1980, p. 224.

10   Akt des Königl. Kriegsministeriums, Bayer. Hauptstaatsarchiv, M. Kr. 11528; Geyer, *Revolutionäre Illusion*, p. 43; Groh, *Negative Integration...*, pp. 675, 677 note 86.

11   Ibid., pp. 660-61, 663; *Protokoll über die Verhandlungen des Parteitages der Sozialdemokratischen Partei Deutschlands abgehalten in Würzburg vom 14 bis 20 Oktober 1917*, Berlin, 1917, p. 63; William II on 14 May 1889 and 2 September 1895, quoted by M. Balfour, *The Kaiser and his Times*, London, 1975, p. 159; Konrad Haenisch in a pamphlet written in late 1915, quoted by Groh, *Negative Integration...*, p. 707 note 188; in general, ibid., pp. 725-26. 'Deutschland, Deutschland, über alles...' is still the German national anthem.

12   Adolph Hoffmann at the Zimmerwald conference in September 1915: H. Lademacher (ed.), *Die Zimmerwalder Bewegung*, The Hague-Paris, 1967, I p. 82; Julian Borchardt, *Vor und nach dem 4. August 1914 – Hat die deutsche Sozialdemokratie abgedankt?* Berlin, 1915, p. 22; N. Leser, *Zwischen Reformismus und Bolschewismus*, Vienna-Frankfurt-Zürich, 1968, p. 271.

13   *Berliner Volkszeitung*, 4 August 1914, filed by the Hamburg political police in the file on Luise Zietz: Staatsarchiv Hamburg, Politische Polizei, S 5883; 'Kriegsflugblatt der Deutschen Friedensgesellschaft', Stuttgart, 15 August: Bundesarchiv Koblenz, Nachlass Quidde, Nr. 96.

14   Groh, *Negative Integration...*, pp. 712-13; Miller, *Burgfrieden und Klassenkampf*, p. 81; J.P. Nettl, *Rosa Luxemburg*, Oxford, 1966, p. 610; Klein, *Deutschland im Ersten Weltkrieg*, I p. 460.

15   Groh, *Negative Integration...*, pp. 212-13; Klein, *Deutschland im Ersten Weltkrieg*, I p. 461; Institut für Marxismus-Leninismus, *Geschichte der deutschen Arbeiterbewegung*, II, Berlin, 1966, p. 227; E. Prager, *Geschichte der USPD*, Berlin, 1921, p. 32, with the declaration of Dr Herz, Dr Laufenberg and F. Wolffheim.

16   Eduard David's diary entry, 25 September 1914: E. Matthias and S. Miller (eds.), *Das Kriegstagebuch des Reichstagsabgeordneten Eduard David 1914 bis 1918*, Düsseldorf, 1966, pp. 42-43; W. Heine to G. von Vollmar, October 1914: Lademacher, *Zimmerwalder Bewegung*, I p. 97 note 81; report by the Berlin director of police, 12 October: *Dokumente und Materialien zur Geschichte...*, I, Nr. 22, p. 44.

17   Liebknecht to the party executive, October 1914: Klein, *Deutschland im Ersten Weltkrieg*, I p. 474; Institut für Marxismus-Leninismus, *Geschichte der deutschen Arbeiterbewegung*, II. Nr. 76, pp. 442-43; F. Adler (ed.), *Victor Adler – Briefwechsel*, pp. 603, 606-7.

18   Matthias and Pikart (eds.), *Die Reichstagsfraktion...*, II, pp. 7, 12 note 19; *Dokumente und Materialien zur Geschichte...*, I, Nr. 30 p. 64; H. von Gerlach, *Von Rechts nach Links*, Zürich, 1937, p. 245; Liebknecht to the party

executive, October 1914: Klein, *Deutschland im Ersten Weltkrieg*, I p. 474. According to P. Frölich, *10 Jahre Krieg und Bürgerkrieg*, Berlin, 1924, p. 144, even Rosa Luxemburg and Mehring advised Liebknecht not to vote against the war credits because they feared that such a demonstration would do more damage than good if he remained alone.

19   *The Labour Leader*, 31 December 1914.

20   Later report by one of the participants, Jakob Walcher, on the meeting of 21 September 1914: *Dokumente und Materialien zur Geschichte...*, I p. 35 n. 1; *Protokoll des Parteitages der SPD...in Würzburg...*, pp. 54-56; E. Kolb and K. Schönhoven, *Regionale und lokale Räteorganisationen in Württemberg 1918/19*, Düsseldorf, 1976, pp. xxxiv-xxxviii; both with many details; Miller, *Burgfrieden und Klassenkampf*, pp. 85-87. In the later years of the war Stuttgart was no longer one of the centres of left-wing strength; it is still puzzling why the first bitter clashes should have taken place there.

21   E. Lucas, *Die Sozialdemokratie in Bremem während des Ersten Weltkrieges*, Bremen, 1969, pp. 12-14, 28, 33; *Weser-Zeitung* Bremen, 15 November 1914; H. Laufenberg and F. Wolffheim, *Imperialismus und Demokratie*, Hamburg, 1914, pp. 5, 34.

22   M. Rauh, *Die Parlamentarisierung des Deutschen Reiches*, Düsseldorf, 1977, pp. 301-2; Stellv. Generalkommando III. bayer. A.K. to Regierung von Oberfranken, 28 November 1914: Bayer. Hauptstaatsarchiv, M.Kr. 13858; Prussian law of 4 June 1851: E.R. Huber, *Dokumente zur Deutschen Verfassungsgeschichte*, I, Stuttgart, 1961, Nr. 169, pp. 414-18. The law, like so many Prussian institutions and the constitution itself, had never been modified.

23   L. Quidde, *Der deutsche Pazifismus während des Weltkrieges 1914-1918*, ed. by K. Holl, Boppard, 1979, p. 68; Klein, *Deutschland im Ersten Weltkrieg*, I pp 480-86; J.D. Shand, 'Doves among the Eagles', *Journal of Contemporary History*, X 1, January 1975, p. 97.

24   F. Williams, *Fifty Years' March – The Rise of the Labour Party*, London, s.a., pp. 217-18; *The Daily Herald*, 1 August 1914.

25   Williams, *Fifty Years' March*, pp. 222-26; S. Bünger, *Die sozialistische Antikriegsbewegung in Grossbritannien 1914-1917*, Berlin, 1967, pp. 18-19.

26   *The Labour Leader*, 6 August 1914; F. Brockway, *Inside the Left*, London, 1947, pp. 45-46. Emphasis in the original.

27   Text in British Library of Political Science, Coll. Misc. 464 (M 890); quoted by A.F. Brockway, *Socialism for Pacifists*, Manchester-London, s.a. (1916) pp. 49-51, and *Inside the Left*, p. 47; J. McNair, *James Maxton*, London, 1955, pp. 46-47.

28   Brockway, *Inside the Left*, pp. 47, 52-53; he estimates that about one fifth of the ILP adopted an 'intense patriotism'; Williams, *Fifty Years' March*, p. 237; ILP Divisional Council London to branches and members, s.d.: British Library of Political Science, Coll. Misc. 314, ILP Papers IV B file 4; *The Labour Leader*, 22 October 1914; T. Bell, *John Maclean*, 1944, p. 27.

29   Minutes of special meeting of the ILP National Administrative Council, 31 August – 1 September 1914: Brit. Libr. of Political Science, Coll. Misc. 464 (M 890), 1/7; Bünger, *Sozialistische Antikriegsbewegung...*, p. 26; W. Kendall, *The Revolutionary Movement in Britain 1900-1921*, London, 1969,

p.88; J. Paton, *Proletarian Pilgrimage*, London, 1935, pp. 245-46.

30 Ibid., p. 248; Kendall, *Revolutionary Movement*..., pp. 88-90; K. Robbins, *The Abolition of War*, Cardiff, 1976, p.34.

31 M. Swartz, *The Union of Democratic Control in British Politics during the First World War*, Oxford, 1971, p. 86; Clifford Allen, *Is Germany right and Britain wrong?*, London, November 1914, p. 5; Bünger, *Sozialistische Antikriegsbewegung*...,pp. 33, 48; Williams, *Fifty Years' March*, p. 223.

32 MacDonald to Laidler, 3 November 1914: MacDonald Papers, PRO/30/69, 5/24; leaflet, s.d. (autumn 1914), ibid., PRO/30/69, 5/98.

33 Resolution passed by the Leicester ILP branch, 3 November 1914, ibid. Many similar resolutions by ILP branches, ibid., 5/98 and 5/100. Private letters supporting MacDonald's attitude to the war, are in ibid., 5/99.

34 Swartz, *Union of Democratic Control*..., pp. 11-14, 25; N. Angell, *After All*, London, 1951, p. 193; A.J.A. Morris, *C.P. Trevelyan 1870-1958*, London, 1977, p. 121.

35 Swartz, *Union of Democratic Control*..., pp. 42-44; H. Hanak, 'The Union of Democratic Control', *Bulletin of the Institute of Historical Research*, XXXVI, 1963, p. 170; Morris, *C.P. Trevelyan*, pp. 121-25.

36 J. Ramsay MacDonald, *War and the Workers*, London, s.a., p. 15; Swartz, *Union of Democratic Control*..., p. 48 n. 7; Hanak 'Union of Democratic Control', p. 178.

37 Minutes of Special Council Meeting of National Peace Council, 4 August 1914; Brit. Libr. of Political Science, Minutes 1/1; Robbins, *Abolition of War*, p. 32; *The Autobiography of Bertrand Russell*, London, 1975, pp. 240-41.

38 ILP 'Road to Peace Leaflet, No. 3', s.d.; R.E. Dowse, *Left in the Centre – The Independent Labour Party*, London, 1966, p. 22.

39 Chief Constable of Cornwall to Home Office, 25 September 1914: PRO, HO 45/10741, file 263275, no 17; MacDonald Papers, PRO 30/69, 5/110; W. Gallacher, *Revolt on the Clyde*, London, 1940, p. 32.

40 Swartz, *Union of Democratic Control*..., p. 89; Allen, *Is Germany right and Britain wrong?* November 1914, p. 14; M. Gilbert, *Plough my Own Furrow*, London, 1965, pp. 36-37.

41 Paton, *Proletarian Pilgrimage*, p. 246. In 1906 Charles Trevelyan wrote contemptuously of 'Nicholas the Last': Morris, *C.P. Trevelyan*, p. 105.

42 G.D.H. Cole, *British Working Class Politics 1832-1914*, London, 1941, pp. 151, 228.

CHAPTER II

1 Letter of 3 December 1914: Lademacher, *Zimmerwalder Bewegung*, II p. 10.

2 N. Lenin, 'Uber den Kampf mit dem Sozialchauvinismus', 1 June 1915, in: N. Lenin and G. Sinowjew, *Gegen den Strom*, Hamburg, 1921, p. 102.

3 Report by Clara Zetkin, s.d.: *Dokumente und Materialien zur Geschichte*..., I, Nr. 64, pp. 119ff.; Lademacher, *Zimmerwalder Bewegung*, II p. 72 note 1.

4 J. Humbert-Droz, *Der Krieg und die Internationale*, Vienna, 1964, pp. 121-22; reports by stellv. Generalkommando I. bayer. A.K. and II. bayer. A.K., 22

June 1915: Bayer. Hauptstaatsarchiv. M.Kr. 13864; Angelica Balabanoff, *Erinnerungen und Erlebnisse*, pp. 101-2.

5   Grimm's recollections quoted by Humbert-Droz, *Der Krieg...*, pp. 130-32; Lademacher, *Zimmerwalder Bewegung*, I pp. 117ff. Emphasis in the original.

6   Ledebour and Lenin at Zimmerwald on 7 September: ibid., I pp. 127-30.

7   Thus Zinoviev on Zimmerwald in: Lenin and Sinowjew, *Gegen den Strom*, pp. 283-86.

8   Merrheim and Ledebour on 7 September: Lademacher, *Zimmerwalder Bewegung*, I, pp. 144-45, 147.

9   Thalheimer, Meyer and Trotsky on 7 September 1915: ibid., I pp. 132, 134, 141; M. Fainsod, *International Socialism and the World War*, Cambridge, Mass., 1935, p. 69.

10 A. Balabanoff, *Die Zimmerwalder Bewegung 1914-1919*, Leipzig, 1928 (reprint 1969), pp. 13-14, 19-20; Lademacher, *Zimmerwalder Bewegung*, I pp. 168-69, 175-76; Fainsod, *International Socialism and the World War*, p. 80.

11 Report from Germany, 27 November: Lademacher, *Zimmerwalder Bewegung*, II pp. 152-53; *Volksfreund*, 13 November 1915: Staatsarchiv Wolfenbüttel, Herzogl. Geheime Kanzlei, 12 A neu Fb. 5, Nr. 6235.

12 Thalheimer to Grimm, 4 and 15 November 1915: Lademacher, *Zimmerwalder Bewegung*, II pp. 244, 299. 'Our opposition' meant the circle of Rosa Luxemburg.

13 Borchardt to Grimm, 15 November 1915, Thalheimer to Grimm, 20 January 1916: ibid., II p. 297 and note 1, p. 407.

14 Williams, *Fifty Years' March*, p. 256; minutes of the National Administr. Council of the *ILP*, 24-25 January 1916: Brit. Libr. of Political Science, Coll. Misc. 464 (M 890), 1/7; *Report of the Annual Conference of the ILP, April 1916*, London, 1916, p. 11.

15 *Report of the Annual Conference of the ILP, April 1915*, London 1915, p. 46 (Chairman's address); Bünger, *Sozialistische Antikriegsbewegung...*, pp. 106-7.

16 Rathenau to Harden, 25 January 1915: Bundesarchiv Koblenz, Nachlass Harden, Nr. 85a. Rathenau was the head of the 'Kriegs-Rohstoff-Abteilung' in the War Ministry and thus possessed ample inside information.

17 Oberzensurstelle to Bavarian Ministry of War, 16 October 1915: Bayer. Hauptstaatsarchiv, M.Kr. 13869; M. Schumacher, *Land und Politik*, Düsseldorf, 1978, p. 40; J. Kocka, *Klassengesellschaft im Krieg*, Göttingen, 1973, p. 17; W. Schumann, 'Die Lage der deutschen und polnischen Arbeiter in Oberschlesien...' *Zeitschrift für Geschichtswissenschaft*, IV, 1956, p. 500.

18 Institut für Marxismus-Leninismus (ed.), *Spartakusbriefe*, Berlin, 1958, p. 42; Klein, *Deutschland im Ersten Weltkrieg*, II, Berlin, 1968, p. 308; *Dokumente und Materialien zur Geschichte...*, I, Nr. 85, pp. 246-48 and n. 1; Lademacher, *Zimmerwalder Bewegung*, II p. 249.

19 Quotation by General von Kuhl from a pamphlet 'Fünf Jahre Dresdener USP' in: *Die Ursachen des Deutschen Zusammenbruches im Jahre 1918*, Vierte Reihe, VI, Berlin, 1928, p. 7; Polizeipräsident Frankfurt to Regierungspräsident Wiesbaden, 19 May 1915, reporting that the leaflet had been distributed 'in several hundred copies': Staatsarchiv Wiesbaden, Abt. 405, Nr. 2773.

20 E. Matthias and E. Pikart (eds.), *Die Reichstagsfraktion der deutschen Sozialdemokratie 1898 bis 1918,*, Düsseldorf, 1966, II pp. 116, 119, 128; police report, Düsseldorf, 5 March 1915: Staatsarchiv Düsseldorf, Regierung Düsseldorf, Nr. 15985. According to a report of 30 May, ibid., the SPD had only about 4500 members left in Düsseldorf and its meetings were badly attended.

21 Miller, *Burgfrieden und Klassenkampf*, pp. 107-8; *Dokumente und Materialien zur Geschichte...*, I, Nr. 144, p. 407; Matthias and Miller, *Das Kriegstagebuch des Reichstagsabgeordneten David*, p. 117; *Dokumente und Materialien zur Geschichte...*, I, Nr. 66, pp. 187-88; resolution of 20 October 1915, accepted 'almost unanimously': Friedr.-Ebert-Stiftung, Nachlass Giebel, Kassette 2, Mappe 9.

22 Ledebour on 5 September, and Zetkin to Grimm, 29 April 1915: Lademacher, *Zimmerwalder Bewegung*, I p. 80, II pp. 55-56; Polizeipräsident Frankfurt to Regierungspräsident Wiesbaden, 19 May, 2 June 1915; Prussian War Ministry to stellv. Generalkommando XVIII. A.K., 25 May: Staatsarchiv Wiesbaden, Abt. 405, Nr. 2773.

23 *Volksfreund*, Brunswick, 3 September 1915; R. Gast, 'Die Spaltung der SPD in Braunschweig während des Ersten Weltkrieges', Brunswick thesis 1949, pp. 59, 84f., 115; F. Boll, 'Spontaneität der Basis...', *Archiv für Sozialgeschichte*, XVII, 1977, p.349.

24 F. Adler (ed.), *Victor Adler – Briefwechsel...*, p. 611; Prager, *Geschichte der USPD*, pp. 73-74; K.-P. Schulz, *Proletarier – Klassenkämpfer – Staatsbürger*, Munich, 1963, p. 118: manifesto of the party executive of June 1915.

25 Matthias and Pikart, *Die Reichstagsfraktion...*, II, pp. 29, 31, 66, 74-75, 99; *Dokumente und Materialien zur Geschichte...*, I, Nr. 92, pp. 263-64.

26 Liebknecht in December 1915: Friedr.-Ebert-Stiftung, Nachlass Dittmann, Kassette 1; 'Die Dezember-Männer von 1915': *Spartakusbriefe*, pp. 86-89; leaflet of May: *Dokumente und Materialien zur Geschichte...*, I, Nr. 62, pp. 162-66.

27 Later report by Pieck: ibid., I, Nr. 57, p. 135; Klein, *Deutschland im Ersten Weltkrieg*, II p. 286.

28 *Documente und Materialien zur Geschichte*, I, Nr. 57, pp. 135-37, 146; Klein, *Deutschland im Ersten Weltkrieg*, II pp. 286-88.

29 Thus Berta Thalheimer on 6 February 1916 at the International Socialist Commission's meeting: Lademacher, *Zimmerwalder Bewegung*, I, pp. 229-30.

30 Mehring to Herzfeld, 19 February, and to Henke, 15 June 1916: Klein, *Deutschland im Ersten Weltkrieg*, II pp. 424-25; Friedr.-Ebert-Stiftung, Nachlass Henke, Kassette 1; police report, Düsseldorf, 14 February 1918, Bundesarchiv-Militärarchiv, RM 33/v.282, giving the foundation date of the 'allgemeine Arbeiterverband' as May 1915; *Dokumente und Materialien zur Geschichte...*, I. Nr. 47, p. 108.

31 *Unter dem Belagerungszustand. Stenographischer amtlicher Bericht über die Reden der Abgeordneten Stadthagen und Ledebour im Reichstag am 20 März 1915*, s.a., pp. 23, 25-27. Ledebour was a very effective and popular speaker.

32 Prussian Ministry of War to the stellv. Generalkommandos, 18 August 1915: Staatsarchiv Berlin-Dahlem, Rep. 84a, Nr. 8211; Prussian Minister of

the Interior to Prime Minister, 22 October: *Dokumente und Materialien zur Geschichte...*, I pp. 243-44; leaflet of the Munich SPD inviting to nine mass meetings on 8 February 1915: Bayer. Hauptstaatsarchiv, M.Kr. 13862; G.D. Feldman, *Army, Industry and Labor in Germany 1914-1918*, Princeton, 1966, p. 101.

33 Police reports on meetings of 2 October, 12, 26 and 29 November, 3, 10 and 17 December 1915: Bayer. Hauptstaatsarchiv, M.K. 19301a, M.Kr. 13366 and 13367.

34 L. Quidde, *Der deutsche Pazifismus während des Weltkrieges 1914-1918*, Boppard, 1979, pp. 78-79, 97-99, 254; report on the general meeting of November 1915: Bayer. Hauptstaatsarchiv, M.Kr. 13366; J.D. Shand, 'Doves among the eagles', *Journal of Contemporary History*, X, 1975, pp. 98, 101.

35 Quidde to Baron von Puttkammer, 20 January 1917: Bayer. Hauptstaatsarchiv, M.Kr. 13371; Quidde, *Der deutsche Pazifismus...*, p.101; Klein, *Deutschland im Ersten Weltkrieg*, I p. 487; W. Benz, 'Der Fall Muehlon', *Vierteljahrshefte für Zeitgeschichte*, XVIII, 1970, pp. 345-46; Shand, loc.cit., p. 101.

36 Prussian Ministry of War to the Militärbefehlshaber, 7 November 1915: W. Deist, *Militär und Innenpolitik im Weltkrieg 1914-1918*, Düsseldorf, 1970, Nr. 113, pp. 261-63.

37 *The Herald*, 16 January 1915; minutes of the NAC of the ILP, 8-9 January 1915: Brit. Libr. of Political Science, Coll. Misc. 464 (M 890), 1/7; H. Bryan to W.C. Anderson, MP, 24 January: ibid., City of London branch correspondence, file no. 9; new members elected at annual meeting, 25 March 1915, ibid.; Minute Book no. 2 of the City of London branch, ILP Papers IIA, ibid. The branch then had 120 members.

38 ILP, *Report of the Annual Conference held at Norwich, April 1915*, pp. 53, 95-96, 100; MacDonald to Roden Buxton, 8 October, and to Simons, 16 April 1915: Robbins, *Abolition of War*, p. 57; MacDonald Papers, PRO 30/69, 5/104. The continuation of the letter is missing from the file.

39 ILP, *Report of the Annual Conference held at Norwich*, p. 91; *The Herald*, 10 April 1915.

40 Clifford Allen in *The Labour Leader*, 27 May; Ellen Wilkinson, ibid., 3 June 1915.

41 *The Herald*, 10 April 1915; Robbins, *Abolition of War*, pp. 140-41; Archibald Fenner Brockway transcript: Imperial War Museum, Department of Sound Records, Anti-war Movement 1914-1918.

42 Resolution of 26 June 1915: MacDonald Papers, PRO 30/69, 5/104; *The Herald* 16 October 1915, with the headline 'Rebellion in Scotland'.

43 Territorial Force, Liverpool, to War Office, 9 July 1915: PRO, HO 45/10741, file 263275, no. 61; First of May Celebration Committee, ibid., no. 28.

44 Minutes of meeting of NAC of the ILP, 2-3 April and 21-22 October 1915: Brit. Libr. of Political Science, Coll. Misc. 464 (M 890), 1/7; *The Labour Leader*, 19 August and 2 September 1915; P. Snowden, *An Autobiography*, London, 1934, I pp. 421-22; Home Office to Norwich Chief Constable, 1 April: PRO, HO 45/10741, file 263275, no. 29.

45   F.B. Booth to Lt. Col. Kell at the War Office, 27 July 1915: ibid., no. 73; the Hampstead branches of the ILP and BSP to 'Dear Comrandes', s.d.: Brit. Libr. of Political Science, Coll. Misc. 314, ILP City of London branch correspondence, file no. 10.

46   J. Bruce Glasier, *The Peril of Conscription*, published by the ILP, London, 1915, pp. 11, 21; J.V. Crangle and J.O. Baylen, 'Emily Hobhouse's peace mission 1916', *Journal of Contemporary History*, XIV, October 1979, p. 733.

47   Minutes of meeting of NAC of the ILP, 27-29 July and 21-22 October 1915: Brit. Libr. of Political Science, Coll. Misc. 464 (M 890), 1/7.

48   Resolution of the Yorkshire branches, 10 July 1915: MacDonald Papers, PRO 30/69, 5/104; City of London branch leaflet, s.d.: Brit. Libr. of Political Science, Coll. Misc. 314, Minute Book no.3; *Labour Leader*, 23 September 1915; *The Herald*, 1 January 1916.

49   ILP, *Report of the Annual Conference held at Newcastle-upon-Tyne, April 1916*, London, 1916, p. 16; Bünger, *Sozialistische Antikriegsbewegung . . .*, pp. 95-97; Williams, *Fifty Years' March*, pp. 235-36.

50   Appendix I to 'The History of the Clyde Strikes Feb. 1915 – April 1916', prepared in the Historical Records Section: PRO MUN 5, no., 346; E. Shinwell, *Conflict without Malice*, London, 1955, p. 54; B. Pribićević, *The Shop Stewards Movement and Workers Control*, Oxford, 1959, pp. 33-35; A.J.P. Taylor, *English History 1914-1945*, Oxford, 1965, pp. 38-39.

51   Thus the semi-official 'History of the Clyde Strikes', quoted in note 50, p.6. It contains a very detailed, fascinating account of the strikes and their causes, written in 1918 by the Historical Section of the Ministry of Munitions.

52   Lansbury in *The Herald*, 6 March 1915. In general, D. Kirkwood, *My Life of Revolt*, London, 1935, pp. 89-91; Gallacher, *Revolt on the Clyde*, pp. 40-42, 47-49; Kendall, *The Revolutionary Movement . . .*, pp. 113-14; Shinwell, *Conflict without Malice*, p.54.

53   Bell, *John Maclean*, pp. 50-51, 54; Bünger, *Sozialistische Antikriegsbewegung . . .*, pp. 87, 142; Kirkwood, *My Life of Revolt*, p. 120; Gallacher, *Revolt on the Clyde*, pp. 43, 51-53; Pribićević, *Shop Stewards Movement . . .*, p.85.

54   'The History of the Clyde Strikes . . .', pp. 39-42, 65, PRO MUN5, no. 346; Bell, *John Maclean*, pp. 35-36; Kendall, *The Revolutionary Movement . . .*, p. 121; Pribićević, *Shop Stewards Movement . . .*, pp. 112, 124, quoting the Constitution of the Clyde Workers' Committee, dating from 1915.

55   'The History of the Clyde Strikes . . .', pp. 67-74, PRO MUN5, no. 346; Kirkwood, *My Life of Revolt*, pp. 111-12; Shinwell, *Conflict without Malice*, p.55.

56   Lynden Macassey, K.C. 'Memorandum on Certain Causes of Unrest Among Munition Workers on Clyde and Tyne-side which are Peculiar to those Districts', 16 December 1915: PRO, MUN5, no. 73.

57   Kendall, *Revolutionary Movement . . .*, p. 151; Bünger, *Sozialistische Antikriegsbewegung . . .*, pp. 65-67; *The Labour Leader*, 22 July 1915; Commission of Enquiry into Industrial Unrest, No. 7 Division, Wales, 12 July 1917, p. 22, PRO MUN5, no. 49.

CHAPTER III

1   ILP, *Report of the Annual Conference held at Newcastle-on-Tyne, April 1916,* London, 1916, pp. 54, 60, 62, 72; Robbins, *Abolition of War,* p. 73; John Scurr, in *The Herald,* 16 September 1916.

2   Annual report of the branch, 9 March 1916: Brit. Libr. of Political Science, Coll. Misc. 314, Minute Book no. 3, and Correspondence File no. 11 (letter of 2 April 1916).

3   Police reports of 1 February, 10 and 12 December 1916: PRO, HO45/10782, file 278537, no. 83; HO45/10742, file 263275, nos. 208 and 209.

4   *Western Mail* and *Wales Daily News,* 13 November 1916; Ivor Thomas to MacDonald, 31 October: all in MacDonald Papers, PRO 30/69, 5/117; police report on Snowden's speech on 2 December 1916, s.d.: PRO,HO45/10814, file 312987, no. 10.

5   BSP, *Report of Fifth Annual Conference, 23-24 April 1916,* London, 1916, pp. 11-12, 15; *Report of Sixth Annual Conference, 8-9 April 1917,* London, 1917, p. 11; Bünger, *Sozialistische Antikriegsbewegung...,* p.125.

6   F. Brockway, *Inside the Left,* pp. 67-69; interview with Fenner Brockway, 15 November 1978; Robbins, *Abolition of War,* pp. 77-78.

7   Clifford Allen, *Presidential Address to the National Convention of the No-Conscription Fellowship,* 27 November 1915, pp. 11-12; Allen to H. Bryan, 10 August 1916: Brit. Libr. of Political Science, Coll. Misc. 314, ILP Papers V, general correspondence.

8   Interview with Fenner Brockway, 15 November 1978; M. Gilbert, *Plough My Own Furrow – The Story of Lord Allen of Hurtwood,* London, 1965, pp. 3-4.

9   Special Branch Report, 6 June 1916: PRO, HO45/10801, file 307402, no. 74; *The Tribunal,* 28 September 1916, quoted by Robbins, *Abolition of War,* p. 90; undated leaflet 'Why we object' in the Library of Friends' House, London (clearly from 1916).

10 Undated leaflet 'The position of the conscientious objector', ibid.; Arthur Watts, 'The way to end war', 28 March 1919, ibid.; Snowden, *An Autobiography,* I p. 410; Bünger, *Sozialistische Antikriegsbewegung...,* p.98.

11 The above is a summary of several recordings of former members of the No-Conscription Fellowship from the Department of Sound Records, Imperial War Museum, especially those of H.F. Bing (Croydon), A.F. Brockway, H.C. Marten (Harrow), Helen B. Pease née Wedgwood (Cambridge and Stoke-on-Trent).

12 *Autobiography of Bertrand Russell* (1975 edtn.). p. 247; Brockway, *Inside the Left,* p. 70; interview with Fenner Brockway, 15 November 1978; Bünger, *Sozialistische Antikriegsbewegung...,* pp. 78, 98.

13 Letter from K.E. Otley, in *The Labour Leader,* 11 May 1916; Aylmer Rose to H. Bryan from RDC Headquarters, 6 January, and Mordecai Goldberg to the same, Winchester, 22 February 1917: both in Brit. Libr. of Political Science, Coll. Misc. 314, ILP Papers V, general correspondence. The file contains many other letters from conscientious objectors, many of great personal interest.

14 'The History of the Clyde Strikes...', pp. 111-12, PRO MUN 5, no. 346; *The Labour Leader*, 10 February 1916; McNair, *James Maxton*, p.60; Gallacher, *Revolt on the Clyde*, pp. 99-102.

15 'The History of the Clyde Strikes...', pp. 109-12, PRO MUN5, no. 346; 'Summary of the Position on the Clyde', s.d., ibid., no. 79; Kirkwood, *My Life of Revolt*, pp. 129 ff.; Shinwell, *Conflict without Malice*, p. 56.

16 Bell, *John Maclean*, pp. 62-64; Gallacher, *Revolt on the Clyde*, pp. 117-20; Pribićević, *Shop Stewards Movement...*, p. 87.

17 ILP *Report of the Annual Conference held at Newcastle-on-Tyne, April 1916*, pp. 75-76; 'Undertaking to be signed by the Clyde Deportees', s.d., protest of Glasgow Trades Council, 2 February 1917, and other documents in Scottish Record Office, Edinburgh, HH/31/22 (a file on the Clyde deportations); Bell, *John Maclean*, p. 67.

18 *The Labour Leader*, 20 and 27 April 1916; 'Estimates 1916: Strike at Barrow', s.d., PRO, MUN5, no. 79.

19 'Notes on the Shop Stewards Movement', 29 May 1917, pp. 2-4, PRO MUN5, no. 54; Kendall, *Revolutionary Movement in Britain*, pp. 154-55; J.T. Murphy, *New Horizons*, London, 1941, pp. 50-52; Bünger, *Sozialistische Antikriegsbewegung...*, pp. 131-32; Williams, *Fifty Years' March*, p. 238.

CHAPTER IV

1 G. Bry, *Wages in Germany, 1871-1945*, Princeton, 1960, pp. 209-11; Feldman, *Army, Industry and Labor...*, p. 117; W. Dittmann, *Belagerungszustand, Zensur und Schutzhaft – Drei Reichstagsreden...*, Leipzig, 1917, p. 9.

2 Stellv. Generalkommando X. A.K. to government of Brunswick, 13 September, and Police Directorate of Brunswick to the same, 30 September 1916: Staatsarchiv Wolfenbüttel, Herzogl. Geh. Kanzlei, 12 A Neu, Fb. 7a, Nr. 2932.

3 Reports by stellv. Generalkommando IV. A.K. in Prussian War Ministry, Monatsberichte über Volksstimmung und Volksernährung, 15 July and 16 December 1916: Bayer. Hauptstaatsarchiv, M.Kr. 12851; Captain Boyd-Ed to chief of the naval staff, 25 August 1916: Deist, *Militär und Innenpolitik im Weltkrieg*, Nr. 170, p. 420; Matthias and Miller, *Das Kriegstagebuch des Reichstagsbageordneten David*, p. 198.

4 Report by Polizeipräsident of Hanover, 16 May 1916: Staatsarchiv Hannover, Hannover Des. 122a xxxiv Nr. 365; Klein, *Deutschland im Ersten Weltkrieg*, II p. 630.

5 Reports by the Kommission für Kriegsversorgung Hamburg, 24 June, 25 August, and the Kriegsversorgungsamt, s.d.: Staatsarchiv Hamburg, I a 19 b and c; *Illustrierte Geschichte der Deutschen Revolution*, Berlin, 1929, p. 125.

6 H. Drüner, *Im Schatten des Weltkrieges*, Frankfurt, 1934, pp. 188-90; Oberzensurstelle to Bavarian War Ministry, 15 June; Linienkommandantur P. to stellv. Generalkommando II. bayer. A.K., 23 October; Prussian War Ministry, Monatsberichte der stellv. Generalkommandos, 17 November 1916: Bayer. Hauptstaatsarchiv, M.Kr. 13878, 12842 and 12851.

7 Police report, Berlin, 16 May: *Dokumente und Materialien zur Geschichte...*,I, Nr. 138, p. 392; *Spartakusbriefe*, Berlin, 1958, p. 193; report by XVIII. A.K. in Monatsberichte der stellv. Generalkommandos, 15 July: Bayer. Hauptstaatsarchiv. M.Kr. 12851; the mayor of Hamborn on 24 August: Staatsarchiv Koblenz, Abt. 403, Nr. 12696; Hamburg police report, 30 August: Staatsarchiv Hamburg, A II p 233; underground leaflet 'Die Kosaken in Hamburg', ibid., Polit. Polizei, Bestand 9, Abt.38, Nr. 44.

8 M. Schumacher, *Land und Politik - Eine Untersuchung über politische Parteien und agrarische Interessen*, Düsseldorf, 1978, pp. 45-46; A. Hundhammer, *Geschichte des bayerischen Bauernbundes*, Munich, 1924, pp. 121-22.

9 Faulhaber to Staatsminister für Kirchen - und Schulangelegenheiten, 4 April 1916; reports to the Bavarian Ministry of the Interior, 20 October; Heim to Bavarian War Ministry, 17 February, and Minister of the Interior to the same, 5 February: Bayer. Hauptstaatsarchiv, M.K1. 9288, M.Inn. 66327; Aktennotiz of 8 November, ibid., M.Kr. 2331.

10 Reports by Bezirkskommando Landau, 28 September, stellv. Generalkommando XI. A.K., Cassel, 13 October, Landrat of Düsseldorf, 23 March, Deputation für Handel, Schiffahrt und Gewerbe, 20 October 1916: ibid., M.Kr. 12842; Staatsarchiv Wiesbaden, Abt. 405, Nr. 2776; Staatsarchiv Karlsruhe, stellv. Generalkommando XIV. A.K., Abt. IIe, Bd. 70; Staatsarchiv Hamburg. Kriegsversorgungsamt, I a 19 c.

11 There are many such reports in Bayer. Hauptstaatsarchiv. M.Kr. 2330 and 2331; decree of the Bavarian War Ministry, 1 February 1916: Deist, *Militär und Innenpolitik...*, Nr. 127, p. 300.

12 'Zusammenstellung der Monatsberichte der stellv. Generalkommandos vom 3.10. 1916', 14 October 1916: Staatsarchiv Karlsruhe, Stellv. Generalkommando XIV. A.K., Abt. IIe, Bd. 70.

13 SPD Parteivorstand, 8 August: Staatsarchiv Wiesbaden, Abt. 405, Nr. 2776; stellv. Generalkommando IX. A.K. to Hamburg Senate, 17 August: Staatsarchiv Hamburg, Senatsakten, A II p 129; the Bavarian envoy in Dresden, 8 November: Bayer. Hauptstaatsarchiv, M.Kr. 2331; *Die Ursachen des Deutschen Zusammenbruches*, VI p. 7.

14 K. Weller, *Die Staatsumwälzung in Württemberg*, Stuttgart, 1930, p. 87; L. von Köhler, *Zur Geschichte der Revolution in Württemberg*, Stuttgart, 1930, p. 42; *Spartakusbriefe*, p. 201; underground leaflets, s.d.: Bundesarchiv Koblenz, Zeitgeschichtl. Sammlung, 2/41; *Dokumente und Materialien zur Geschichte...*, I, Nr. 97, pp. 286-88.

15 Military hospital of Ingolstadt to Festungskommandantur, 26 June 1916, with text of leaflet: Bayer. Hauptstaatsarchiv, M.Kr. 13879.

16 Cases mentioned by Dittmann in the Reichstag, 18 January and 28 October 1916: Dittmann, *Belagerungszustand, Zensur und Schutzhaft...*, pp. 12-13, 40, 46. Hence Dittmann spoke of 'the nightmare of military despotism' which was oppressing Germany: ibid., p. 19.

17 Ströbel to M. Harden, 27 April: Bundesarchiv Koblenz, Nachlass Harden, Nr. 103; report of 10 January 1916 in Matthias and Pikart, *Die Reichstagsfraktion...*, II p. 151; Miller, *Burgfrieden und Klassenkampf*, pp. 125-26.

18   Berlin police report, 30 May: *Dokumente und Materialien zur Geschichte...*, I, Nr. 140, pp. 395-96; resolution of SPD Neukölln, 27 May, ibid., Nr. 144, p. 408; report of Büro für Sozialpolitik, 29 July: Bayer. Hauptstaatsarchiv, M.K. 19291; Lucas, *Sozialdemokratie in Bremen...*, pp. 71, 79; *Volksfreund*, Brunswick, 21 December; *Dokumente und Materialien zur Geschichte...*, I, Nr. 120, p. 146; D.W. Morgan, *The Socialist Left and the German Revolution*, Ithaca, 1975, pp. 50-51; Toni Sender, *The Autobiography of a German Rebel*, London, 1940, pp. 59-60; Drüner, *Im Schatten des Weltkrieges*, p. 203.

19   Rühle in *Vorwärts*, 12 January, and *Der Kampf*, Duisburg, 7 October 1916: *Dokumente und Materialien zur Geschichte...*, I, Nr. 101, pp. 304-5, Nr. 164, p. 478; Kautsky to Adler, 7 August 1916; F. Adler, *Victor Adler – Briefwechsel...*, pp. 630-31. Coming from Kautsky who was no great admirer of Liebknecht, the statement of his popularity in the trenches is particularly valuable.

20   Matthias and Pikart, *Die Reichstagsfraktion...*, II p. 154; H. Trotnow, *Karl Liebknecht*, Cologne, 1980, pp. 240, 247-48; *Spartakusbriefe*, pp. 166-67; *Karl Liebknecht – Das Zuchthausurteil*, Berlin, 1919, pp. 105-8.

21   Müller, *Vom Kaiserreich zur Republik*, I pp. 63-64; Haase's letter of 2 July: E. Haase, *Hugo Haase*, Berlin, 1929, p. 124; report to Bavarian War Minister, 24 July: Bayer. Hauptstaatsarchiv, M.Kr. 2330; Brunswick resolution, 28 June: Staatsarchiv Wolfenbüttel, Herzogl. Geh. Kanzlei, 12 A neu Fb. 5, Nr. 6234.

22   Bremen police report, 5 July: Institut für Marxismus-Leninismus, *Geschichte der deutschen Arbeiterbewegung*, II, Nr. 95, p. 475; *Spartakusbriefe*, pp. 198-200, 294; *Dokumente und Materialien zur Geschichte...*, I, Nr. 142, pp. 401-2; Ströbel to Harden, 12 May: Bundesarchiv, Nachlass Harden, Nr. 103.

23   C. Beradt, *Paul Levi*, Frankfurt, 1969, p. 18; O.K. Flechtheim, *Die KPD in der Weimarer Republik*, Frankfurt, 1969, p.109; K. Retzlaw, *Spartacus – Aufstieg und Niedergang*, Frankfurt, 1976, pp. 39-41, 51; Dissmann to Henke, 28 October: Friedr.-Ebert- Stiftung, Nachlass Henke, Kassette 2.

24   'Leitsätze', 3 February 1916, *Spartakusbriefe*, pp. 113-15; report about the second conference, 30 March 1916, ibid., pp. 134-35, 141.

25   *Spartacus* of 9 March and 13 April 1916, ibid., pp. 118-20, 152; Mehring to Herzfeld, 19 February, and to Henke, 15 June 1916: Klein, *Deutschland im Ersten Weltkrieg*, II p. 424, Friedr.-Ebert-Stiftung, Nachlass Henke, Kassette I. Liebknecht's bitter attack on 'Die Dezember-Männer von 1915' is in *Spartakusbriefe*, pp. 86-92 (27 January 1916).

26   Lademacher, *Zimmerwalder Bewegung*, I pp. 362-63, 369-70, 406; Fainsod, *International Socialism and the World War*, pp. 95-96.

27   Jogiches' circular, 26 September 1916: *Dokumente und Materialien zur Geschichte...*, I, Nr. 162, p. 472; Lademacher, *Zimmerwalder Bewegung*, I, pp. 286, 297, 343; the SPD Parteiausschuss contra Spartacus, December 1916: Friedr.-Ebert-Stiftung, Nachlass Giebel, Kassette 2, Mappe 9.

28   Knief to Henke, 28 September 1915: Friedr.-Ebert-Stiftung, Nachlass Henke, Kassette 1; later report on the conference of 1 January 1916: *Dokumente und Materialien zur Geschichte...*, I p. 283; reports of the Büro für Sozialpolitik, 8 and 21 October 1916: Bayer. Hauptstaatsarchiv, M.K. 19291; Lucas, *Sozialdemokratie in Bremen...*, pp. 62-63; P. Frölich, *10 Jahre*

Krieg und Bürgerkrieg, Berlin, 1924, p. 155. Frölich was one of the Bremen leaders.

29 Ms. by Knief 'Haltung der Arbeiterpolitik', confiscated by the Bavarian police at his arrest: Zentralpolizeistelle Bayern, 25 February 1918: Bayer. Hauptstaatsarchiv, M.Inn. 66283; Radek's articles from *Arbeiterpolitik* in his *In den Reihen der Deutschen Revolution*, Munich, 1921, pp. 325, 332.

30 Gruppe Arbeiterpolitik, *Die Bremer Linksradikalen*, Bremen, 1969, p. 13; Lademacher, *Zimmerwalder Bewegung*, I, p. 297; Lenin and Sinowjew, *Gegen den Strom*, pp. 417, 426, with Lenin's attacks on *Junius* of October 1916.

31 W. Schumann, 'Die Lage der deutschen und polnischen Arbeiter in Oberschlesien...', *Zeitschrift für Geschichtswissenschaft*, IV, 1956, p. 500; report by Kommando der Marinestation der Ostsee, 16 June 1916: Bundesarchiv-Militärarchiv, RM 31/v.2388; Bremen police report, 5 July: Institut für Marxismus-Leninismus, *Geschichte der deutschen Arbeiterbewegung*, II, Nr. 95, p. 475; Hamburg police reports, 27 October: Staatsarchiv Hamburg, Polit. Polizei, S 20230, Bd. 1.

32 Reports of 3, 25 and 26 August: Staatsarchiv Koblenz, Abt. 403, Nr. 12696; reports of 11 and 15 October, ibid., Nr. 13536; report from Düsseldorf, 11 December: Staatsarchiv Düsseldorf, Regierung Nr. 9081; 'Braunschweiger Anzeiger', 26 April 1916, quoting the decree of 22 April, and police report, 24 July: Staatsarchiv Wolfenbüttel, Herzogl. Polizeidirektion, 133 neu 2320; *Spartakusbriefe*, 28 May 1916, pp. 190-91; Gast, 'Die Spaltung der SPD in Braunschweig', Examensarbeit of Kant-Hochschule 1949, pp. 129-32.

33 Quidde, *Der deutsche Pazifismus...*, p. 104; Klein, *Deutschland im Ersten Weltkrieg*, II pp. 445-48; leaflet Nr. 2 of 'Zentralstelle Völkerrecht', December 1916: Geh. Staatsarchiv Berlin-Dahlem, Zeitgeschichtl. Sammlung, IV 275.

CHAPTER V

1 Reports of stellv. Generalkommando IX. A.K. and Württemberg War Ministry, 3 April: Zusammenstellung der Monatsberichte der stellv. Generalkommandos, 16 April 1917: Staatsarchiv Karlsruhe, Abt. IIe, Bd.70; stellv. Generalkommando I. bayer. A.K., 7 April 1917: Bayer. Hauptstaatsarchiv, M.Kr. 12844.

2 Prof. Alois Ries and O. Nebeck to Bavarian Ministry of Interior, 16 April and 3 May 1917: Bayer. Hauptstaatsarchiv, M.Inn. 66328; A. Schreiner and G. Schmidt, 'Die Rätebewegung in Deutschland bis zur November-revolution', in *Revolutionäre Ereignisse und Probleme in Deutschland während der Periode der Grossen Sozialistischen Oktoberrevolution 1917/18*, Berlin, 1957, pp. 244, 254; report from Magdeburg to the Emperor, 25 April: L. Stern (ed.), *Die Auswirkungen der grossen sozialistischen Oktoberrevolution auf Deutschland*, Berlin, 1959, vol. 4/II, Nr. 71, p. 479; stellv. Generalkommando XVII. A.K. on 3 May 1917: Zusammenstellung der Monatsberichte der stellv. Generalkommandos, 15 May: Staatsarchiv Karlsruhe, Abt. IIe, Bd. 70.

3   Reports of the stellv. Generalkommando IV. A.K., 3 August: Zusammenstellung der Monatsberichte der stellv. Generalkommandos, 15 August; Staatsarchiv Karlsruhe, Abt. IIe, Bd. 70; and Karlsruhe, 19 August: ibid., stellv. Generalkommando XIV. A.K., Abt. V, Nr. 99; report of 1 August by Büro für Sozialpolitik: Stern, *Die Auswirkungen...*, vol. 4/I, p. 85.

4   Spartacus leaflets, s.d. (April 1917): *Dokumente und Materialien zur Geschichte...*, I, Nr. 222, pp. 637-38, Nr. 220, p. 631. A very similar leaflet in Bundesarchiv Koblenz, Zeitgeschichtl. Sammlung, 2/41 .

5   Prussian Minister of the Interior to the higher administrative authorities, 6 September: *Dokumente und Materialien zur Geschichte...*, I, Nr. 235, p.674; Retzlaw, *Spartacus*, pp. 62-63. Banknotes with similar inscriptions were circulating in Bavaria: police report of 12 July 1917, Bayer. Hauptstaatsarchiv, M.Inn. 71700.

6   O.K. Flechtheim (ed.), *Rosa Luxemburg: Die Russische Revolution*, Frankfurt, 1963, p. 9; Heckert at Gotha: Eichhorn (ed.), *Gründungsparteitag der USPD*, p. 78; report by mayor of Düsseldorf, 17 April 1917: Staatsarchiv Düsseldorf, Regierung Düsseldorf Präs., Nr. 29, Bd. 16.

7   Haase on 6 April and 30 March: Eichhorn, *Gründungsparteitag der USPD*, p. 8, and H. Haase, *Reichstagsreden gegen die deutsche Kriegspolitik*, Berlin, 1919, pp. 65-66; Berlin police report, 20 November: Stern, *Die Auswirkungen...*, vol. 4/II, Nr. 233, p. 767; *Leipziger Volkszeitung*, 19 March 1917.

8   Resolution unanimously adopted on 19 April 1917: *Protokoll über die Verhandlungen des Parteitages der SPD in Würzburg vom 14. bis 20 Oktober 1917, p. 36*; ibid. p. 70, the declaration in parliament of July; Scheidemann, *Zusammenbruch*, pp. 40-41, 119.

9   *Vorwärts*, 13 November, quoted in Institut für Marxismus-Leninismus, *Geschichte der deutschen Arbeiterbewegung*, II p. 442; Ebert at Elberfeld on 18 and at Hamburg on 23 November 1917: K. Mammach, 'Das erste Echo der Grossen Sozialistischen Oktoberrevolution', *Zeitschrift für Geschichtswissenschaft*, V, 1957, p. 1024; police report, 23 November, Staatsarchiv Hamburg, Polit. Polizei, V 880.

10 Dr Einhauser to Ministry of Interior, 26 April: Bayer. Hauptstaatsarchiv, M.Inn. 66328, M.Kr. 2332; Ay, *Entstehung einer Revolution*, p. 55.

11 Report by Pressereferat of Bavarian War Ministry, 30 October: Bayer. Hauptstaatsarchiv, M.K. 19289; E. Haase, *Hugo Haase*, p. 43.

12 Eichhorn (ed.), *Gründungsparteitag der USPD*, pp. 81-82; Scheidemann, *Memoirs of a Social Democrat*, London, 1929, p. 337; Stern, *Die Auswirkungen...*, vol. 4/I, Nr. 49, p. 451; report by stellv. Generalkommando II. A.K., 3 May 1917: Zusammenstellung der Monatsberichte der stellv. Generalkommandos, 15 May, Staatsarchiv Karlsruhe, Abt. IIe, Bd. 70.

13 A. Balabanoff, *Zimmerwalder Bewegung*, pp. 69-70; J. Stillig, *Die russische Februarrevolution 1917 und die Sozialistische Friedenspolitik*, Cologne-Vienna, 1977, pp. 131-32; *Leipziger Volkszeitung*, 27 June 1917, quoting the *Internationale Korrespondenz*; Staatsarchiv Hamburg, Polit. Polizei, S 20570.

14 Fainsod, *International Socialism and the World War*, pp. 144-45; Stillig, *Russische Februarrevolution...*, p. 151; Haase's letters of 24 May and 13 June 1917, in E. Haase, *Hugo Haase*, pp. 144-47; Bernstein to MacDonald, 30 September 1917: PRO, MacDonald Papers, 30/69, 5/27.

15 Scheidemann, *Zusammenbruch*, pp. 135-37; Balabanoff, *Erinnerungen und Erlebnisse*, pp. 169-70.

16 USPD manifesto, 12 November 1917: *Dokumente und Materialien zur Geschichte...*, II, Nr. 7, p. 19; *Vorwärts*, 26 November: ibid., Nr. 13, p. 31; Mammach, 'Das erste Echo der Grossen Sozialistischen Oktoberrevolution', pp. 1024-26, 1029-31.

17 Lenin and Trotsky 'An die deutschen Soldaten', s.d.: Bundesarchiv Koblenz, Zeitgeschichtl. Sammlung, 2/64; Ebert in the meeting of the parliamentary party on 4 January 1918: Matthias and Pikart, *Die Reichstagsfraktion...*, II p. 353. For Brest-Litovsk in general see W. Hahlweg (ed.), *Der Friede von Brest-Litowsk*, Quellen zur Geschichte des Parlamentarismus und der politischen Parteien, 1. Reihe, vol. 8, Düsseldorf, 1971.

18 Henke on 20 February: Lucas, *Sozialdemokratie in Bremen...*, pp. 98-99; Munich police report, 24 January on USPD meeting: Bayer. Hauptstaatsarchiv, M.Inn. 66283; Kriegspresseamt report, Berlin, 17 September: ibid., M.Kr. 13909.

19 *Spartacus*, Nr. 8, January 1918: *Spartakusbriefe*, p. 409.

20 Memorandum by Drews, Prussian Minister of the Interior, 13 February 1918, quoted by E.O. Volkmann, *Der Marxismus und das deutsche Heer im Weltkriege*, Berlin, 1925, pp. 297, 304.

21 Russell, 'Russia Leads the Way' in *The Tribunal*, 22 March; Lansbury, 'The Russian Programme', in *The Herald*, 24 March; *The Labour Leader*, 29 March and 5 April 1917, with the ILP resolution signed by five MPs and 12 other leading ILP members.

22 'The Revolution at the Albert Hall' in *The Herald*, 7 April 1917; Bünger, *Sozialistische Antikriegsbewegung...*, p. 148; transcript of recording by Helen B. Pease, pp. 79-80, Imperial War Museum, Anti-War Movement 1914-1918; 'A Soldier and a Democrat' to Lansbury, 8 May: Brit. Libr. of Political Science, Lansbury Collection, vol. 7.

23 ILP, *Report of the Annual Conference held at Leeds, April 1917*, London, 1917, pp. 43-45; MacDonald to Petrograd Soviet, 15 June 1917 (copy), PRO MacDonald Papers, 30/69, 5/27; B. Sacks, *J. Ramsay MacDonald in Thought and Action*, Albuquerque, New Mexico, 1952, pp. 499-500.

24 BSP, *Sixth Annual Conference, Salford 8-9 April 1917*, London, 1917, pp. 6-7, 10-11; meeting of National Peace Council, 18 April 1917: Brit. Libr. of Political Science, National Peace Council, Minutes 1/2.

25 Bünger, *Sozialistische Antikriegsbewegung...*, pp. 184, 187; Gallacher, *Revolt on the Clyde*, pp. 137-38, 144, 147, 157-58; Williams, in *The Herald*, 28 July; special branch report on ILP meeting at Woolwich, 30 July 1917: PRO, HO 45/10814, file 312987, no. 12.

26 *Mercury*, 11 March 1918, in PRO, HO 45/10743, file 263275, no. 345; Birmingham police reports, 12 June and 17 September 1917: ibid., nos. 232

and 246; an unknown soldier to Lansbury, 8 May 1917: Brit. Libr. of Political Science, Lansbury Collection, vol. 7.

27 Kendall, *Revolutionary Movement...*, p. 174; Bünger, *Sozialistische Antikriegsbewegung...*, pp. 159-63; S.R. Graubard, *British Labour and the Russian Revolution 1917-1924*, Cambridge Mass., 1956, pp. 36-37; Snowden *An Autobiography*, I p. 454; *The Labour Leader*, 7 June 1917.

28 'What happened at Leeds', in *The Herald*, 9 June 1917; Bünger, *Sozialistische Antikriegsbewegung...*, p. 164; Snowden, *An Autobiography*, I pp. 455-56; F. Brockway, *Socialism over Sixty Years*, p. 153; Kendall, *Revolutionary Movement...*, p. 175. It should be made clear that the Leeds Convention met before the Bolshevik revolution and had nothing to do with alleged 'Bolshevik' influences.

29 Minutes of special meetings, 30 June and 25 October 1917: Brit. Libr. of Political Science, Coll. Misc. 464 (M 890), 1/7.

30 *The Herald*, 28 June 1917; *Autobiography of Bertrand Russell*, 1975 edn., pp. 254-55; A. Linklater, *Unhusbanded Life*, London, 1980, p. 194.

31 All documents quoted above in Scottish Record Office, HH/31/19 (July-August 1917).

32 *The Labour Leader*, 29 November and 6 December 1917; Salter, 'The ILP and the Bolsheviks', ibid., 7 March 1918. For the figures of the elections to the Constituent Assembly, see L. Schapiro, *The Communist Party of the Soviet Union*, London, 1970, p. 183: 175 Bolsheviks against 370 Social Revolutionaries.

33 Police reports on ILP meetings in May and August 1918: PRO, HO 45/10744, file 263275, nos. 362, 418; Gilbert, *Plough My Own Furrow*, p. 118.

34 Graubard, *British Labour and the Russian Revolution*, pp. 57-58; BSP, *Report of Seventh Annual Conference, Leeds 31 March - 1 April 1918*, London, 1918, pp. 8-9, 16-17; Kendall, *Revolutionary Movement...*, pp. 177-78.

CHAPTER VI

1 Quotations from the diary of Richard Stumpf, printed in *Die Ursachen des Deutschen Zusammenbruches im Jahre 1918*, Vierte Reihe, X 2, Berlin, 1928, pp. 47, 63, 66, 80-81, 97, 204-5; W. Dittmann, *Die Marine-Justizmorde von 1917 und die Admiralsrebellion von 1918*, Berlin, 1926, p. 13.

2 Thus sailors heard as witnesses by the parliamentary committee investigating the causes of the German collapse in 1918: *Ursachen des Deutschen Zusammenbruches*, 4. Reihe, IX 1, pp. 11-12, IX 2, p. 293; Dittman, *Marine-Justizmorde...*, pp. 7, 13-14.

3 Reports by commanding officers of First and Third Squadron, 9 and 25 July, 30 September 1917: Bundesarchiv-Militärarchiv, RM 47/v.458, RM 47/v.424; 'S.M.S. Ostfriesland', 18 August, and verdict of Feldkriegsgericht contra Sachse, Reichpietsch and others, 25 August 1917: ibid., F. 4078/64923; *Ursachen des Deutschen Zusammenbruches*, 4. Reihe, IX 1, pp. 8-10, IX 2, p. 264, X 1, pp. 48-49, X 2, pp. 247-49.

4 Verdict of Feldkriegsgericht contra Sachse etc., loc. cit.; Oberreichsanwalt Zweigert to Ministry of Justice, 18 February 1918: Bundesarchiv-Militärarchiv, RM 27XIII/v.424; Stumpf's diary, 2 August 1917: *Ursachen des Deutschen Zusammenbruches*, X 2, p. 252.

5 Stumpf's diary: *Ursachen des Deutschen Zusammenbruches*, X 2, pp. 81, 190, 215, 235, 250, 251.

6 The stoker Rebe in March 1917: H.-J. Bernhard, 'Die Entstehung einer revolutionären Friedensbewegung in der deutschen Hochseeflotte im Jahre 1917', in *Revolutionäre Ereignisse und Probleme in Deutschland...*, Berlin, 1957, p. 102; Dittmann, *Marine-Justizmorde...*, p. 18; Sachse as a witness: *Ursachen des Deutschen Zusammenbruches*, IX 2, pp. 244-45.

7 In the parliamentary committee investigating the causes of the German collapse the historian Arthur Rosenberg asserted that the sailors had no idea that more radical groups existed to the Left of the USPD (*Ursachen des Deutschen Zusammenbruches*, IV p. 104); this is not correct: but they had no contact with them. For the following, see Rosenberg's remarks, ibid., pp. 103-4.

8 The above according to Oberreichsanwalt Zweigert to Ministry of Justice in the case against Luise Zietz and others, 18 February 1918: Bundesarchiv-Militärarchiv, RM 27XIII/v.424 (a detailed summary of the evidence).

9 Ibid.; 'Aufruf der USPD', s.d., found 4 August 1917, ibid., F 4078/64923; and testimony of sailors quoted in *Ursachen des Deutschen Zusammenbruches*, IX 1, pp. 25, 514-15, by Dittmann and by Dr Loesch. Text of the *König Albert* leaflet in Bundesarchiv-Militärarchiv. RM 27XIII/v.424.

10 Reports by Vice-Admiral Mauve and the court over which he presided, 11 August: Deist, *Militär und Innenpolitik*, Nr. 375, pp. 1000-1, p. 999 n. 4; Kommando der Hochseestreitkräfte, 7 October: *Ursachen des Deutschen Zusammenbruches*, X 1, pp. 141-44; and 'S.M.S. Ostfriesland', 18 August 1917: Bundesarchiv-Militärarchiv. F 4078/64923.

11 Thus D. Horn, *The German Naval Mutinies*, New Brunswick, 1969, pp. 99-100; Bernhard, 'Die Entstehung einer revolutionären Friedensbewegung...', p. 140; and Klein, *Deutschland im Ersten Weltkrieg*, II pp. 703-7.

12 Oberreichsanwalt Zweigert to Ministry of Justice, 18 February 1918: Bundesarchiv-Militärarchiv. RM 27XIII/v.424; interrogations of Beckers, Bräuner, Köbis, Reichpietsch and Sachse in August 1917, ibid. They were all stokers.

13 The witness Weber: *Ursachen des Deutschen Zusammenbruches*, IX 2, p. 303; the witness Beckers, on the other hand, claimed in 1926 that on *Prinzregent Luitpold* there had been a complete Soldiers' League with a central leader and leaders for external and internal affairs: ibid., p. 268.

14 *Ursachen des Deutschen Zusammenbruches*, IX 2, pp. 276-77, 324; Kommando der Hochseestreitkräfte, 7 October 1917, ibid., X 1, pp. 143-44; Dr Dobring as a witness in Munich in 1925: *Der Dolchstossprozess in München 1925*, Munich, 1925, pp. 59-60; Deist, *Militär und Innenpolitik*, Nr. 374, p. 997; Stumpf's diary, 2 August: *Ursachen des Deutschen Zusammenbruches*, X 2, pp. 252-53.

15 Stumpf's diary, 4 September 1917: ibid., p. 256; military court sentences, 23 and 25 August 1917: Bundesarchiv-Militärarchiv, F 4078/64923; Ubersicht der Straftaten, s.d., ibid.; Scheidemann and Stresemann letters, November 1917, ibid., RM 20/9.

16 Leaflet 'Folgt ihrem Beispiel!': Bundesarchiv, Zeitgeschichtl. Sammlung, 2/41. Possibly a Spartacist leaflet.

17 SPD parliamentary party report on military affairs: *Protokoll über die Verhandlungen des Parteitages der SPD... Oktober 1917*, pp. 90-91, 94; Erhard Auer as a witness in the stab-in-the-back trial in Munich in 1925, declaring that he had received up to 2,000 letters per week from serving soldiers: *Der Dolchstoss-Prozess in München...*, p. 150.

18 von Riedl, Divisional Staff of 39th Bavarian Division, to War Ministry, June 1917, and anonymous letters sent by the *Münchener Post* to the same: Bayer. Hauptstaatsarchiv, M.Kr. 13372 and 2332; Scheidemann, *Memoirs of a Social Democrat*, London, 1929, p. 413.

19 Ay, *Entstehung einer Revolution*, p. 101 (report of 8 December 1917); letter of 9 July 1917: Institut für Marxismus-Leninismus, *Geschichte der deutschen Arbeiterbewegung*, II, Nr. 115, pp. 499-500.

20 Memorandum, Berlin, 3 October 1917: Geh. Staatsarchiv Berlin-Dahlem, Rep. 84a, Nr. 8211; Gast, *Die Spaltung der SPD in Braunschweig*, p, 65; R. Wenzel, *Das Revolutionsjahr 1918-19 in Braunschweig*, Brunswick, 1949, p. 16.

21 All details from D. Gill and G. Dallas, 'Mutiny at Étaples in 1917', *Past and Present*, no. 69, November 1975, pp. 89-98, 106. The paper also mentions strikes by labour companies at Boulogne in the autumn of 1917, companies which were unarmed and consisted of Chinese and Egyptian workers. They were brutally suppressed by troops.

CHAPTER VII

1 The strike figures according to Schumann, 'Die Lage der deutschen und polnischen Arbeiter...', *Zeitschrift für Geschichtswissenschaft*, IV, 1956, p. 500; M. Scheel, 'Der Aprilstreik 1917 in Berlin', *Revolutionäre Ereignisse und Probleme in Deutschland während der Periode der Grossen Sozialistischen Oktoberrevolution*, Berlin, 1957, p. 13.

2 Prussian Ministry of War, Berlin, 3 May 1917, with copy of the leaflet, s.d.: Staatsarchiv Wiesbaden, Abt. 405, Nr. 2777; Retzlaw, *Spartacus*, p. 53.

3 Müller, *Vom Kaiserreich zur Republik*, I pp. 81-82; Scheidemann, *Zusammenbruch*, p. 63; report by Oberkommando in den Marken, Berlin, 19 April 1917: *Dokumente und Materialien zur Geschichte...*, I, Nr. 212, p. 611. Müller gives the number of 300,000 strikers as an estimate 'that may not have been too high'.

4 Scheel, 'Der Aprilstreik 1917 in Berlin', pp. 39, 48-49, 53, 60; Stern, *Die Auswirkungen...*, vol. 4/II, Nr. 42 and 49, pp. 445, 451; Nr. 56, p. 549; *Dokumente und Materialien zur Geschichte...*, I, Nr. 214, p. 613; Deist; *Militär und Innenpolitik*, Nr. 298, p. 754.

5 Ibid., Nr. 298, p. 753; Stern, *Die Auswirkungen...*, vol. 4/III, Nr. 429, p. 1127; 4/II, Nr. 98a, pp. 511-12; Scheel, 'Der Aprilstreik...' p. 49; Müller,

Vom Kaiserreich zur Republik, I p. 84, with the exact demands of the Leipzig strikers.

6   Minutes of conference of Brunswick Minister of the Interior and workers' representatives, 7 April 1917: Staatsarchiv Wolfenbüttel, 12 A neu, Fb. 7a, Nr. 3402; Boll in *Archiv für Sozialgeschichte*, VII, 1977, p. 360.

7   'General-Anzeiger', Hamburg, 18 April 1917, reprinting a detailed article from *Vorwärts:* Staatsarchiv Hamburg, Polit. Polizei, S 20510, Bd. 1.

8   Groener addressing the Reichstag Hauptausschuss on 26 April: Bundesarchiv-Militärarchiv, Nachlass Groener, N 46/16; and to Bavarian War Ministry, 25 April: Bayer. Hauptstaatsarchiv, M.Kr. 13890.

9   Scheidemann's diary notes: *Zusammenbruch*, p. 66; notes about conference in the *Kriegsamt* on 23 April: Deist, *Militär und Innenpolitik*, Nr. 289, pp. 725-26; the Oberkommando in den Marken on 3 May 1917: Zusammenstellung der Monatsberichte der stellv. Generalkommandos, 15 May 1917: Staatsarchiv Karlsruhe. Abt.IIe, Bd. 70.

10   Scheel, 'Der Aprilstreik...', p. 53; Spartacist circular, 22 April 1917: Institut für Marxismus-Leninismus, *Geschichte der deutschen Arbeiterbewegung*, II, Nr. 113, p. 498; Müller, *Vom Kaiserreich...*, I pp. 84-85.

11   Police reports, Brunswick, 22 August, 1 October 1917, note with the strikers' demands, s.d.: Staatsarchiv Wolfenbüttel, 12 A neu, Fb. 7a, Nr. 3402, 133 neu 2320, 133 neu 2322; report of Merseburg Regierungspräsident, 15 August: *Dokumente und Materialien zur Geschichte...*, I, Nr. 231, p. 661, p.662 note 1.

12   Generaloberst von Bertel, Oberbefehlshaber in den Marken, to William II, 6 February 1918: Bundesarchiv-Militärarchiv, Acta des Konigl. Militär-Cabinets, PH2/14.

13   *Arbeiter-Zeitung*, 9 and 15 November, 1 December 1917, quoted by R. Löw, *Otto Bauer und die russische Revolution*, Vienna, 1980, pp. 26-27.

14   *Arbeiter-Zeitung*, 16 January 1918; R.G. Plaschka, H. Haselsteiner and A. Suppan, *Innere Front*, Munich, 1974, pp. 61-66, 68-69, 71, 74-75; Leser, *Zwischen Reformismus und Bolschewismus*, p. 286.

15   The Prussian Minister of War to the Emperor, 5 February 1918: Deist, *Militär und Innenpolitik*, Nr. 437, p. 1158; Müller, *Vom Kaiserreich zur Republik*, I p. 101; Stern, *Die Auswirkungen...*, vol. 4/III, Nr. 334, p. 953 (manifesto of the USPD deputies, 10 January 1918); slightly different versions in Bundesarchiv Koblenz, Zeitgeschichtl. Sammlung, 2/41.

16   Bavarian Ministry of the Interior, 21 January, and report about Eisner's speech, 27 January: Bayer. Hauptstaatsarchiv, M.Inn. 66283; Berlin police report, 6 February 1918, quoted by A. Schreiner and G. Schmidt, 'Die Rätebewegung in Deutschland bis zur Novemberrevolution', p. 279.

17   The Prussian Minister of War to the Emperor, 5 February 1918: Bundesarchiv-Militärarchiv, PH2/14; Müller, *Vom Kaiserreich zur Republik*, I pp. 103-5, 204; Rosenberg, *Die Entstehung der deutschen Republik 1871-1918*, Berlin, 1928, pp. 197-98.

18   Müller, *Vom Kaiserreich zur Republik*, I pp. 103-4; report of SPD executive of February 1918: Matthias and Pikart, *Die Reichstagsfraktion...*, II pp. 366-67; Saxon envoy to Saxon foreign minister, 8 March 1918: Stern, *Die Auswirkungen...*, vol. 4/III, Nr. 479, p. 1225.

19 Berlin director of police to Minister of Interior, 29 January, and Minister of War to the Emperor, 5 February 1918: ibid., Nr. 361, p. 989; Bundesarchiv-Militärarchiv, PH2/14; leaflet of January 1918: Matthias and Pikart, *Die Reichstagsfraktion*..., II p. 366; Spartacus report found by police during a search, probably written by Jogiches: Stern, *Die Auswirkungen*..., vol. 4/III, Nr. 437, p. 1149.

20 Müller, *Vom Kaiserreich zur Republik*, I pp. 105-6, 205; Scheidemann, *Zusammenbruch*, pp. 77-79, with the full text of the SPD declaration of 30 January 1918; Konferenz der Vertreter der Verbandsvorstände abgehalten am 1 February 1918, in *Beschlüsse der Konferenzen von Vertretern der Zentralverbandsvorstände*, Berlin, 1919, p. 84.

21 Müller, *Vom Kaiserreich zur Republik*, I pp. 106-7, 205-6; W. Bartel, 'Der Januarstreik 1918 in Berlin' in *Revolutionäre Ereignisse und Probleme*..., p. 163, with quotations from Ebert's speech; private letter of Dittmann, 23 October 1918: Friedr.-Ebert-Stiftung, Nachlass Dittmann, Kassette 1; report of Prussian Minister of War, 5 February: Deist, *Militär und Innenpolitik*, Nr. 437, p. 1160.

22 Müller, *Vom Kaiserreich zur Republik*, I pp. 108-9; Ebert on 5 February: Matthias and Pikart, *Die Reichstagsfraktion*..., II pp. 363-64; *Beschlüsse der Konferenzen von Vertretern der Zentralverbandsvorstände*, 1 February 1918, pp. 82-83.

23 Müller, *Vom Kaiserreich zur Republik*, I pp. 109-10; Spartacist leaflet, s.d.: Bundesarchiv Koblenz, Zeitgeschichtl. Sammlung, 2/41. Emphasis in the original.

24 Reports by Oberkommando in den Marken, 4 February, and Generaloberst von Bertel to the Emperor, 6 February 1918: Bundesarchiv-Militärarchiv, RM 33/v.282 and PH2/14; in general Müller, *Vom Kaiserreich zur Republik*, I pp. 110, 206-7.

25 The Prussian War Minister, 5 February: Deist, *Militär und Innenpolitik*, Nr. 437, p. 1161; resolution of the strikers, 29 January: *Dokumente und Materialien zur Geschichte*..., II, Nr. 30, p. 79; Kriegstagebuch der I. Werftdivision, 27 January: Bundesarchiv-Militärarchiv, F 4078/64923; *Beschlüsse der Konferenzen von Vertretern der Zentralverbandsvorstände*, p. 82 (Legien on events in Kiel).

26 Report by stellv. Generalkommando IX. A.K., 9 February: Bundesarchiv.Militärarchiv, RM 33/v.282; police reports on strike meetings, 29-30 January: Staatsarchiv Hamburg, Polit Polizei, S 20510, Bd. 2.

27 'Übersicht über Verlauf und Umfang des Streiks...', Berlin 9, February, with exact figures for Bremen, Hamburg, Kiel and Wilhelmshaven: Bundesarchiv-Militärarchiv, RM 27 XIII/v. 425; Kaiserl. Werft Wilhelmshaven, 15 February, ibid., RM 33/v.281; stellv. Generalkommando IX. A.K., Altona, 9 and 11 February, ibid., RM 33/v.282; Regierungspräsident of Aurich, 7 February: Staatsarchiv Hannover, Oberpräsidium, 122a xxxiv Nr. 365.

28 Klein, *Deutschland im Ersten Weltkrieg*, II pp. 166-67; Stern, *Die Auswirkungen*..., vol. 4/III, Nr. 374 and 539, pp. 1020, 1320: Regierungspräsidenten of Münster and Arnsberg. 31 January and 27 April 1918.

29 Reports by Regierungspräsident Cologne, 25 April, Düsseldorf police, 11 February, Regierungspräsident Coblenz, 27 April, and Regierungspräsident Trier, 28 April 1918: Staatsarchiv Düsseldorf, Regierung Aachen Präsidium Nr. 856 and 872, Regierung Düsseldorf Nr. 14966.

30 The Prussian Minister of War, 5 February: Deist, *Militär und Innenpolitik*, Nr. 437, p. 1162; Regierungspräsident of Cassel, 1 February: Stern, *Die Auswirkungen*..., vol. 4/III, Nr. 387, 389 and 402, pp. 1037, 1041, 1076; Schreiner and Schmidt, 'Die Rätebewegung in Deutschland...', p. 284.

31 Regierungspräsident of Danzig, 1 May: Stern, *Die Auswirkungen*..., vol. 4/III, Nr. 547, p. 1329; stellv. Generalkommando I. A.K., 3 February: Zusammenstellung der Monatsberichte der stellv. Generalkommandos, 15 February 1918: Bundesarchiv-Militärarchiv, RM 3/v.7794.

32 Ay, *Entstehung einer Revolution*, p. 198; reports by Regierung Mittelfranken, Bezirksamt Fürth, Magistrat Nürnberg and Lt.-Col. von Kress, all of 28 January, Magistrat Fürth, 30 January, III. bayer. A.K., 2 February 1918: Bayer. Hauptstaatsarchiv, M. Inn. 66283, M.Kr. 12846.

33 Müller, *Vom Kaiserreich zur Republik*, I p. 111; Ay, *Entstehung einer Revolution*, pp. 199-200; Pressereferat of Bavarian War Ministry, 25 February: Bayer. Hauptstaatsarchiv, M.K. 19289; speech by Karsten on 30 January: ibid., M.Inn. 66283.

34 Stellv. Generalkommando XIV. A.K., 1 February 1918: Staatsarchiv Karlsruhe, Abt. 236/23079; B. Brandt and R. Rürup, *Arbeiter-, Soldaten- und Volksräte, in Baden*, Düsseldorf, 1980, p. liii.

35 Report by Regierung der Pfalz, 4 February 1918: Bayer. Hauptstaatsarchiv, M.Inn. 66283.

36 E. Kolb and K. Schönhoven, *Regionale und lokale Räteorganisationen in Württemberg*, Düsseldorf, 1976, p. xliv.

37 Bernstein to MacDonald, 30 September 1917: PRO, MacDonald Papers, 30/69, 5/27. The letter was written in English when Bernstein was on his way to Stockholm, as a member of the USPD delegation.

38 The USPD parliamentary party on 27 February: Müller, *Vom Kaiserreich zur Republik*, I p. 211.

39 Assessment of the strike by Jogiches (?), March 1918: *Dokumente und Materialien zur Geschichte*...., II, Nr. 55, p. 136; Bartel, 'Der Januarstreik 1918 in Berlin', pp. 165, 178 and note 115. According to E. Barth, *Aus der Werkstatt der deutschen Revolution*, Berlin 1919, p. 23, 40 to 50,000 strikers were called up in Berlin alone, and more than 200 sentenced to terms of imprisonment.

CHAPTER VIII

1 Reports by Regierungspräsident of Schwaben und Neuburg, 9 July, Unteroffizier Adam, 8 November, Bavarian War Ministry, 24 October, Bavarian Ministry of Interior, 7 July, and Pressereferat of War Ministry, 12 August 1917: Bayer. Hauptstaatsarchiv, M.Inn. 66328, M.Kr. 2333, 2335-36, 12844.

2 Pressereferat of Bavarian War Ministry (Lt.-Col. Falkner von Sonnenburg), 12 August, 12 September and 1 November 1917: ibid., M.Kr. 12844-45,

M.K. 19288-89. The author was a middle-aged officer who was re-activated during the war.

3   Report of 12 September 1917: ibid., M.Kr. 12845, M.K. 19289.

4   Reports by stellv. Generalkommando XVIII. A.K., 3 October, stellv. Generalkommando XIX. A.K., 3 August 1918, Lt.-Col. Bauer, July 1918: ibid., M.Kr. 112852; Bundesarchiv. Militärchiv, RM 3$v.7796; Deist, *Militär und Innenpolitik*, Nr. 464, p. 1240.

5   Bry, *Wages in Germany...*, p. 211; J. Kocka, *Klassengesellschaft im Krieg*, Göttingen, 1973, pp. 15, 17.

6   Resolution of Mittelstandsvereinigung für Mitteldeutschland, 18 August 1916: Staatsarchiv Wiesbaden, Abt. 408, Nr. 121; Feldman, *Army, Industry and Labor...*, pp. 465-67; Kocka, *Klassengesellschaft im Krieg*, pp. 76-77.

7   Berlin police report, 15 March 1917: Scheel, 'Der Aprilstreik 1917 in Berlin', p. 6; reports by stellv. Generalkommando XVII. A.K. and Gouvernement Mainz, 3 August; Zusammenstellung der Monatsberichte der stellv. Generalkommandos, 15 August 1917, Staatsarchiv Karlsruhe, Abt. IIe, Bd. 70; reports from Mannheim, 16 May and 12 July 1917, ibid., Abt. V, Nr. 99, Beilageheft.

8   Reports by president of Trierischer Bauernverein: Zusammenstellung der Monatsberichte der stellv. Generalkommandos, 15 November 1917, Bayer. Hauptstaatsarchiv, M.Kr. 12852; by stellv. Generalkommando II. A.K., ibid.; reports from Limburg, 16 September, and Rüdesheim, 17 March, 20 June, 16 August, 16 November 1917: Staatsarchiv Wiesbaden, Abt. 405, Nr. 6358-59; by stellv. Generalkommando XIV. A.K., 1 December: Staatsarchiv Karlsruhe, Abt. 236/23079; Ay, *Entstehung einer Revolution*, p. 118.

9   Klein, *Deutschland im Ersten Weltkrieg*, III p. 139; report of 3 March: Deist, *Militär und Innenpolitik*, Nr. 254, pp. 666-67; reports from Düsseldorf, 15 November, Munich, 11 February and 5 March, Wiesbaden, 19 July, and Hamburg, 23 April 1917: Staatsarchiv Düsseldorf, Regierung Nr. 29; Bayer. Hauptstaatsarchiv, M.Kr. 12843; Staatsarchiv Wiesbaden, Abt. 405, Nr. 6358; Staatsarchiv Hamburg, Kriegsversorgungsamt, I a 19b, Bd.2; Polit. Polizei, Bestand 9, Ablieferung 38, Nr. 45.

10 *Protokoll über die Verhandlungen des Parteitages der SPD... Oktober 1917*, p. 463; report by stellv. Generalkommando XX. A.K.: Zusammenstellung der Monatsberichte der stellv. Generalkommandos, 15 November 1917, Bayer. Hauptstaatsarchiv, M.Kr. 12852; Regierungspräsident Stade, 22 March: Staatsarchiv Hannover, Oberpräsidium, 122a xxxiv Nr. 365; Drüner, *Im Schatten des Weltkrieges*, pp. 215, 223.

11 Police reports, Harburg, 13 January, and Hanover, 30 January: Staatsarchiv Hannover, Oberpräsidium, 122a xxxiv Nr. 365; report by Landrat of Harburg, 28 February, ibid.; stellv. Generalkommando X. A.K..: Zusammenstellung der Monatsberichte der stellv. Generalkommandos, 17 February 1917, Staatsarchiv Karlsruhe, Abt. IIe, Bd. 70; Hamburg police report, 28 February: Staatsarchiv Hamburg, Polit. Polizei, Bestand 9, Ablieferg, 38, Nr. 45; Regierungspräsident Düsseldorf, 28 February and 22 April: Staatsarchiv Düsseldorf, Regierung Nr. 29, Staatsarchiv Koblenz, Abt. 403, Nr. 13536; reports by stellv. Generalkammando II. A.K. and VII.

A.K.: Zusammenstellung der Monatsberichte der stellv. Generalkommandos, 15 July 1917, Staatsarchiv Karlsruhe, Abt. IIe, Bd. 70; report by Kriegsamtsstelle Frankfurt, 3 May, ibid.; Schumann, 'Die Lage der deutschen und polnischen Arbeiter in Oberschlesien...', pp. 484-85; Stern, *Die Auswirkungen...*, vol. 4/II, Nr. 146, p. 603.

12 Reports, Karlsruhe, 19 May, and Mannheim, 16 May 1917: Staatsarchiv Karlsruhe, stellv. Generalkommando XIV. A.K., Abt. V, Nr. 99; report from Frankfurt, 17 December: Staatsarchiv Wiesbaden, Abt. 405, Nr. 6359; and by Kriegsamtsstelle Danzig, 3 August: Zusammenstellung der Monatsberichte der stellv. Generalkommandos, 15 August, Staatsarchiv Karlsruhe, Abt. IIe, Bd. 70; Ay, *Entstehung einer Revolution*, p. 118; report from Bayreuth, 30 October: Bayer. Hauptstaatsarchiv, M.K. 19289; ibid., M.Kr. 2332; from Düsseldorf and Essen, 10 and 13 August: Staatsarchiv Koblenz, Abt. 403, Nr. 13534. These are just a few examples of the 'Friedenssehnsucht' reported from many parts of Germany.

13 E. Haase (ed.), *Hugo Haase*, p. 43; G. Ledebour, *Proletariat und Frieden!* – *Zwei Reichstagsreden* (USPD pamphlet 1917), pp. 12, 19; *Protokoll über die Verhandlungen des Parteitages der SPD abgehalten in Würzburg...*, pp. 36, 350; Staatsarchiv Hamburg, Polit. Polizei, Bestand 9, Ablieferung 38, Nr. 45, and leaflet, s.d., ibid.; Drüner, *Im Schatten des Weltkrieges*, p. 204.

14 F. Fischer, *Griff nach der Weltmacht*, Düsseldorf, 1961, pp. 560-61; notes by Lt.-Col. von Sonnenburg, 27 March 1918: Bayer. Hauptstaatsarchiv, M.Kr. 2340; report by Nürnberg Town Council, 28 January, ibid., M.Inn. 66283; *Protokoll über die Verhandlungen des Parteitages der SPD in Würzburg...*, p. 488; Deist, *Militär und Innenpolitik*, Nr. 444, p. 1178; Geyer, *Revolutionäre Illusion*, p. 66; Weller, *Staatsumwälzung in Württemberg*, p. 87.

15 Reports of 27 January, 23 February, late June and 9 July 1917: Bayer. Hauptstaatsarchiv, M.Inn. 66328, M.K. 19288, M.Kr. 13887; Ay, *Entstehung einer Revolution*, pp. 137, 147; Rupprecht's letter of 19 July: *Der Dolchstossprozess in München...*, p. 101; Bischöfliches Ordinariat Limburg, 11 June: Staatsarchiv Wiesbaden, Abt. 405, Nr. 2777.

16 The minutes of the January conference are printed by Eichhorn (ed.), *Gründungsparteitag der USPD...*, pp. 84ff. Ibid., pp. 89, 92, 98-99.

17 Ibid., pp. 107-8, 110, 118-19; Miller, *Burgfrieden und Klassenkampf*, p. 152; Prager, *Geschichte der USPD*, pp. 129-30, with the text of the SPD resolution of 16 January 1917.

18 Eichhorn (ed.), *Gründungsparteitag der USPD...*, pp. 8, 10, 20-21, 25, 38, with the geographical distribution of the 124 delegates.

19 Ibid., pp. 24, 26-28, 46, 72.

20 Ibid., pp. 47-49, 72. Cp. the very different 'organisational guidelines' of the opposition from the same year: Staatsarchiv Hamburg, Polit. Polizei, S 20570.

21 Miller, *Burgfrieden und Klassenkampf*, pp. 176-77; Morgan, *The Socialist Left...*, pp. 67-68, 71, 75; Flechtheim, *Die KPD...*, p. 109; *Protokoll über die Verhandlungen des Parteitages der SPD in Würzburg...*, pp. 235-36; *Spartakusbriefe*, p. 402 (November 1917). For more detailed membership figures of the USPD in 1918, see above, p. 192-93.

22 Berlin police report, 25 March: Stern, *Die Auswirkungen...*, vol. 4/I, Nr. 16, p. 393; K. Obermann, 'Bemerkungen über die Entwicklung der Arbeiterbewegung in Berlin 1916/17...' *Zeitschrift für Geschichtswissenschaft*, V, 1957, p. 1019; Brunswick police report, 19 April: Staatsarchiv Wolfenbüttel, 133 neu 2279; report by stellv. Generalkommando XVIII. A.K., 3 February: Zusammenstellung der Monatsberichte der stellv. Generalkommandos, 17 February 1917, Staatsarchiv Karlsruhe, Abt. IIe, Bd. 70; Düsseldorf police reports, 17 April, 15 November 1917, 2 January 1918: Staatsarchiv Düsseldorf, Präs. Nr. 29, Regierung Nr. 15061; report from Elberfeld, 17 April 1917: ibid., Präs. Nr. 29.

23 Reports by stellv. Generalkommando XIV. A.K., 2 June and 1 December: Staatsarchiv Karlsruhe, Abt. V, Nr. 99, Abt. 236/23079; reports from Munich, 19 and 21 July, 3 September and 22 December: Bayer. Hauptstaatsarchiv, M.Kr. 11528-29, M. Inn. 71700; press section of Bavarian War Ministry, 26 November: ibid., M.Kr. 19289; Deist, *Militär und Innenpolitik*, Nr. 289, p. 733; Stern, *Die Auswirkungen...*, vol. 4/II, Nr 308, pp. 908-9.

24 *Der Dolchstossprozess in München...*, pp. 200-1; manifesto, s.d.: Prager, *Geschichte der USPD*, pp. 158-60. For the attitude of the SPD to Poland, see above, p. 99.

25 The Prussian Minister of War, von Stein, to the Militärbefehlshaber, 14 June 1917: Deist, *Militär und Innenpolitik*, Nr. 303, pp. 761-63; the chancellor to the state governments, 3 July: Bayer. Hauptstaatsarchiv, M.Kr. 13894.

26 Flechtheim, *Die KPD...*, p. 103; Spartacus circular of 22 April 1917: Institut für Marxismus-Leninismus, *Geschichte der deutschen Arbeiterbewegung*, II, Nr. 113, pp. 497-98; *Volksfreund*, Brunswick, 20 March 1917, 'Wo stehen die Massen?'; Spartacus leaflets, s.d. (1917): *Dokumente und Materialien zur Geschichte...*, I, Nr. 222, p. 637, and Bundesarchiv Koblenz, Zeitgeschichtl. Sammlung, 2/41.

27 Reports by Düsseldorf police and stellv. Generalkommando VII. A.K., 17 April and 3 May 1917: Staatsarchiv Düsseldorf, Präs. Nr. 29, Staatsarchiv Karlsruhe, Generalkommando XIV. A.K., Abt. IIe, Bd. 70; *Vorwärts*, 24 February, *Der Grundstein*, 2 March, *Arbeiterpolitik*, 20 April, *Hamburger Echo*, 24 April 1917: all in Staatsarchiv Hamburg, Polit. Polizei, S. 20570.

28 Büro für Sozialpolitik, Berlin, 30 May 1917 and 15 May 1918: Bayer. Hauptstaatsarchiv, M.K. 19290-91; J. Borchardt in *Arbeiterpolitik*, 10 March 1917; the Hamburg Left Radicals on 28 February 1917: *Dokumente und Materialien zur Geschichte...*, I, Nr. 195, p. 572; Radek, *In den Reihen der deutschen Revolution*, pp. 410-11; letter from Hamburg to Berlin, s.d. (ca. May 1918): Staatsarchiv Hamburg, Polit. Polizei, S 13424.

29 G. Feldmeier to Frau Ahrens, Essen, 8 September 1918: Staatsarchiv Wolfenbüttel, 133 neu 2253; stellv. Generalstab der Armee, Abt. IIIb, Berlin, 23 February 1918: Bundesarchiv-Militärarchiv, RM 33/v.275, with copies of *Arbeiterpolitik* of November-December 1917.

30 Saxon Ministry of the Interior, 15 April 1917: Stern, *Die Auswirkungen...*, vol. 4/II, Nr. 36, p. 436; Scheidemann, *Zusammenbruch*, pp. 41-42, 119;

'Easter Message' of 7 April and decree of 11 July: E.R. Huber (ed.), *Dokumente zur deutschen Verfassungsgeschichte*, II, Stuttgart, 1964, pp. 467-69; P. Hirsch, *Der Weg der Sozialdemokratie zur Macht in Preussen*, Berlin, 1929, pp. 89-92.

31 Meeting of SPD parliamentary party, 3 May: Matthias and Pikart, *Die Reichstagsfraktion...*, II p. 256; Hirch, *Der Weg...*, pp. 87-88; *Protokoll über die Verhandlungen des Parteitages der SPD... in Würzburg*, pp. 140, 227, 454, 488.

32 Reports by Regierungspräsidenten of Cologne, 30 April, Trier, 29 October, and Cassel, 23 October: Staatsarchiv Düsseldorf, Regierung Aachen, Präsidium Nr. 872; Stern, *Die Auswirkungen...*, vol. 4/II, Nr. 219, p. 737; report by the Kriegsamt, 31 July: Bundesarchiv-Militärarchiv, RM 33/v.257; Matthias and Pikart, *Die Reichstagsfraktion...*, II p. 349 note 2.

33 G. Ledebour, *Proletariat und Frieden!* – *Zwei Reichstagsreden* (1917), p. 28; Oberkommando in den Marken to director of Berlin police, 9 March 1918: Deist, *Militär und Innenpolitik*, Nr. 448, p. 1202. Ledebour intervened several times in vain on behalf of the union members: ibid., note 2.

34 Reports by stellv. Generalkommando VII. A.K., 3 May and 3 December 1917: Zusammenstellung der Monatsberichte der stellv. General kommandos, 15 May and 15 December: Staatsarchiv Karlsruhe, Abt. IIe, Bd. 70, Bayer. Hauptstaatsarchiv, M.Kr. 12852; Mamach, 'Das erste Echo...', p. 1033; *Rheinische Zeitung*, 22 August, and report, Cologne, 1 September 1917: Staatsarchiv Koblenz, Abt. 403, Nr. 13536.

35 Hamburg police report on meeting of dockyard workers in trade union house, 16 July: Staatsarchiv Hamburg, Polit. Polizei, S 20510; report by Third Bavarian A.K., 2 December 1917: Bayer. Hauptstaatsarchiv, M.Kr. 12846.

36 Brandt and Rürup, *Arbeiter-, Soldaten- und Volksräte in Baden*, p. lii; Boll, 'Spontaneität der Basis... Das Beispiel Braunschweig', pp. 361-62; stellv. Generalkommando VIII. A.K., 3 February: Zusammenstellung der Monatsberichte der stellv. Generalkommandos, 17 February 1917: Staatsarchiv Karlsruhe, Abt. IIe, Bd. 70; Cologne police report, 20 June: Staatsarchiv Koblenz, Abt. 403, Nr. 13536; report from Reydt, 13 October: Staatsarchiv Düsseldorf, Präs. Nr. 29; Schumann, 'Die Lage der deutschen und polnischen Arbeiter in Oberschlesien...', pp. 484-85.

37 Reports by press section of Bavarian War Ministry, 12 August, and K. Puffer, 9 July 1917: Bayer. Hauptstaatsarchiv, M.K. 19288, M.Kr. 2333; report by Unteroffizier Adam, 8 November 1917: ibid., M.Kr. 2336; Ay, *Entstehung einer Revolution*, p. 55.

CHAPTER IX

1 ILP, *Report of the Annual Conference held at Leeds, April 1917*, London, 1917, pp. 70-71; Bünger, *Sozialistische Antikriegsbewegung...*, pp. 137, 151; City of London Branch Annual Report for the year ending 28 February 1917: Brit. Libr. of Political Science, Coll. Misc. 314, ILP Papers IIc; 'A Soldier and a Democrat' to Lansbury, 8 May 1917: ibid., Lansbury Collection, vol. 7.

2   Williams, *Fifty Years' March*, pp. 237, 244, 270, 279; Bünger, *Sozialistische Antikriegsbewegung*..., p. 142; Dowse, *Left in the Centre*, p. 26; Robbins, *Abolition of War*, p. 153; Snowden, *Autobiography*, I pp. 480-81; Morris, *C.P. Trevelyan*, p. 139. In Scotland, the labour movement adopted the slogan of a negotiated peace considerably earlier than in England: *The Herald*, 5 May 1917.

3   Williams, *Fifty Years' March*, pp. 252-53; draft of a letter by MacDonald, s.d., and article in *Forward*, 22 September 1917: PRO, MacDonald Papers, 30/69, 3a/23 and 3a/64; BSP, *Sixth Annual Conference, Salford, 8-9 April 1917*, London, 1917, p. 27. MacDonald's letter clearly is from the year 1917.

4   Reports by Commission for Enquiry, 12 July 1917, no. 4, 5 and 7 Divisions: PRO, MUN5/no. 49.

5   Kendall, *Revolutionary Movement*..., p., 312;Kirkwood, *My Life of Revolt*, p. 168; Paton, *Proletarian Pilgrimage*, pp. 288-89; *The Herald*, 29 December 1917, 16 March and 13 April 1918.

6   Linklater, *Unhusbanded Life*, pp. 195, 197.

7   Dowse, *Left in the Centre*, pp. 28-29; Snowden, *Autobiography*, I p. 484; Swartz, *Union of Democratic Control*, pp. 182, 197. In 1918 12,000 new ILP members were reported: ILP, *Report of the Annual Conference held at Leicester*, London, 1918, p. 25.

8   Leicester Chief Constable to Home Office, 29 December; *The Carlisle Journal*, 17 August 1917, both in PRO HO 45/10743, file 263275; police report on Swansea meeting on 28 January 1917: PRO HO 45/10734, file 328752; *The Herald*, 30 June 1917, adding 'it will be the most burning disgrace if we lag behind' the Germans.

9   Murphy, *New Horizons*, pp. 54-55; Kendall, *Revolutionary Movement*..., p. 156; G.D.H. Cole and R. Postgate, *The Common People*, London, 1938, p. 515; 'History of the Strike of the Amalgamated Society of Engineers in May 1917', pp. 24-32: Ms. in PRO, MUN 5/no. 79 (written in August 1917).

10   'History of the Strike of the Amalgamated Society of Engineers in May 1917', pp. 33-38, 43-45, loc.cit.; Strike of Engineers May 1917: PRO MUN 4/no.2213; Kendall, *Revolutionary Movement*..., pp. 158-60; Bünger, *Sozialistische Antikriegsbewegung*..., p. 155.

11   Reports by Commission for Enquiry, 12 July 1917, no. 3, 5 and 7 Divisions: PRO, MUN 5/no. 49; Swartz, *Union of Democratic Control*, p. 195 note 86, with report by G. Fiennes of November 1917.

12   'Notes on the Shop Stewards Movement', 29 May 1917, and 'Rank and File Movement', s.d., both in PRO, MUN 5/no. 54; Murphy, *New Horizons*, pp. 59, 64.

13   Cole and Postgate, *The Common People*, pp. 516-17; Bünger, *Sozialistische Antikriegsbewegung*,... p. 193.

14   Morris, *C.P.Trevelyan*, p. 134; Swartz, *Union of Democratic Control*, pp. 76, 79, 88, 121, 135, 138, 157, 178; Hanak, 'Union of Democratic Control', *Bulletin of the Institute of Historical Research*, xxxvi, 1963, pp. 179-80; Russell, *Autobiography*, pp. 255-56.

CHAPTER X

1 Reports by stellv. Generalkommando IV. A.K., Magdeburg, 20 February, and stellv. Generalkommando XIV. A.K., Karlsruhe, 1 August 1918: Bundesarchiv-Militärarchiv, RM 33/v.282, RM 3/v.7796; Berlin police report of August, quoted by Schreiner and Schmidt, 'Die Rätebewegung in Deutschland bis zur Novemberrevolution', p. 303.

2 Reports by press section of Bavarian War Ministry, 9 March, Bezirksamt Ingolstadt, 20 January, stellv. Generalkommando VI. A.K., 3 April: Bayer. Hauptstaatsarchiv, M.Kr. 12846, M.Inn. 66283, Bundesarchiv-Militärarchiv. RM 3/v. 7794; Institut für Marxismus-Leninismus, *Geschichte der deutschen Arbeiterbewegung*, II pp. 66-67; Feldman, *Army, Industry and Labor*, pp. 508-9; reports, Kronenberg, 24 July, and Remscheid, 17 August: Staatsarchiv Düsseldorf, Regierung Nr. 9081; Staatsarchiv Wolfenbüttel, 133 neu 2323; police reports, Hamburg, 17-18 July, and Geestemünde, 4-5 October: Staatsarchiv Hamburg, Polit. Polizei, S 20510; Bundesarchiv-Militärarchiv, RM 31/v.2372, RM 33/v.283; stellv. Generalkommando II. A.K., Stettin, 3 October: Bayer. Hauptstaatsarchiv, M.Kr. 12853.

3 Conference in the Ministry of Economics, 26 April 1918: *Dokumente und Materialien zur Geschichte...*, II, Nr. 59, pp. 143-48; the metal workers' unions to the Regierungspräsident, 21 June: Staatsarchiv Düsseldorf, Regierung, Nr. 9081.

4 Report by stellv. Generalkommando II. A.K., Stettin 2 June: Bundesarchiv-Militärarchiv, RM 33/v.282; Kocka, *Klassengesellschaft im Krieg*, p. 77.

5 Letter of 27 May and report of 23 June: Stern, *Die Auswirkungen...*, vol.4/III, Nr. 572, 599, pp. 1361, 1401; Kriegsversorgungsamt Hamburg. 24 July and 24 August: Staatsarchiv Hamburg. I a 19 b and c; reports, Frankfurt, 17 August, and Munich, 3 August: Staatsarchiv Wiesbaden, Abt. 405 Nr. 6360, Bayer. Hauptstaatsarchiv, M.Kr. 12849; stellv. Generalkommando II. bayer. A.K., 3 September, ibid.; Berlin police report, 29 October: Stern, *Die Auswirkungen...*, 4/III, Nr. 757, p. 1698; Düsseldorf police report, 6 May: Staatsarchiv Düsseldorf, Präs. Nr. 29; stellv. Generalkommando XIX. A.K., 3 March, XIV.A.K., and Württemberg War Ministry, 3 January: Bundesarchiv-Militärarchiv, RM 3/v.7794.

6 Reports by stellv. Generalkommando I. bayer. A.K., 18 January, Lt.-Col. Falkner v. Sonnenburg, 30 January, Bezirksamt Schwabach, 2 February, Freiherr Poschinger von Frauenau, 19 February, stellv. Generalkommando I. bayer. A.K., 15 September: Bayer. Hauptstaatsarchiv, M.Kr. 12846, M.Kr. 2338, M.Inn. 66283, M.Kr. 12847 and 12849; *Der Dolchstossprozess in München...*, p. 306.

7 Reports by Feldgeistlicher Ostendorf, Münster, 2 September, Oberkommando in den Marken, stellv. Generalkommando XVIII. A.K. and Württemberg War Ministry, 3 September: Bayer. Hauptstaatsarchiv, M.Kr. 2346; Zusammenstellung der Monatsberichte der stellv. Generalkommandos, 15 September, Staatsarchiv Berlin-Dahlem, Rep. 90J Nr. 6; reports from Limburg and Rüdesheim, 16 August, and St

Goarshausen, 16 September 1918: Staatsarchiv Wiesbaden, Abt. 405, Nr. 6360.

8   Reports from Rüdesheim, 16 August, Kulmbach, 28 August, Weilheim, 19 September, Koblenz and Leipzig, 3 September, Karlsruhe 3 September and 1 October: Staatsarchiv Wiesbaden, Abt. 405, Nr. 6360; Bayer. Hauptstaatsarchiv, M.Kr. 2345, M.Kr. 12849; Zusammenstellung der Monatsberichte der stellv. Generalkommandos, 15 September 1918, Staatsarchiv Berlin-Dahlem, Rep. 90J Nr. 6; Staatsarchiv Karlsruhe, Abt. 236/23079.

9   Reports from Ratisbon, s.d., Koblenz, 3 October 1918: Bayer. Hauptstaatsarchiv, M.Kr. 12850; Zusammenstellung der Monatsberichte der stellv. Generalkommandos, 15 October: ibid., M.Kr. 12853; *Der Dolchstossprozess in München...*, p. 46.

10 Deist, *Militär und Innenpolitik*, p. 1226 note 1, with many details; General von Kuhl in *Ursachen des Deutschen Zusammenbruches*, 4. Reihe, VI p. 15; letter by F. Oerter, Fürth, 21 May: Staatsarchiv Wolfenbüttel, 133 neu 2154 (file Sepp Oerter); report from Erlangen, 25 May: Bayer. Hauptstaatsarchiv, M.Inn. 66284; Ay, *Entstehung einer Revolution*, pp. 186-87.

11 Report by Gouvernement Graaudenz, 13 July, telegram to Bavarian War Ministry, 11 July: Stern, *Die Auswirkungen...*, vol. 4/III, Nr. 619, p. 1439, Bayer. Hauptstaatsarchiv, M.Kr. 13907; E. Ludendorff, *Kriegführung und Politik*, Berlin, 1922, p. 153; Ludendorff's report of 9 July: Volkmann, *Marxismus und das deutsche Heer...*, p. 313; Oberkommando in den Marken, September 1918: Deist,, *Militär und Innenpolitik*, Nr. 472, p. 1278; General von Kuhl in *Ursachen des Deutschen Zusammenbruches*, VI p. 54; leaflet of August 1918 in Müller, *Vom Kaiserreich zur Republik*, I pp. 213-14. The above are just some examples. There would no doubt be many more if the German army archives had not been destroyed at the end of the Second World War.

12 Report of 6 February 1919 and quotation from Troeltsch: *Ursachen des Deutschen Zusammenbruches*, VI p. 55; IV p. 129; Garnisonkommando Augsburg to Generalkommando I. bayer. A.K., 24 May 1918: Bayer. Hauptstaatsarchiv, M.Kr. 12848; H. Hincke to stellv. Generalkommando X. A.K., s.d.: Bundesarchiv-Militärarchiv, RM 31/v.2372.

13 Reports, Amberg, 20 March, Munich, 30 March, stellv. Generalkommando XIV. A. K., 3 September: Bayer. Hauptstaatsarchiv, M.Kr. 12847; Zusammenstellung der Monatsberichte der stellv. Generalkommandos, 15 September, Staatsarchiv Berlin-Dahlem, Rep. 90J Nr. 6; Matthias and Pikart, *Die Reichstagsfraktion...*, II pp. 428, 434-35; 458; the editor of *Generalanzeiger*, Wesel, s.d.: Bayer. Hauptstaatsarchiv, M.Inn. 66332; the Landräte of Biedenkopf, St Goarshausen and Usingen, 18 October: Staatsarchiv Wiesbaden, Abt. 405, Nr. 6360; Bayer. Hauptstaatsarchiv, M.Kr. 12850 (reports of 22-23 October 1918).

14 Reports by the Bavarian delegate with the Prussian *Kriegsamt* and the editor of *Bayerische Provinzial-Korrespondenz*, both of 25 May 1918: Bayer. Hauptstaatsarchiv, M.Kr. 2342, M.Inn. 66331.

15 Notes on conversation with Auer, 14 June: Bayer. Hauptstaatsarchiv, M.Inn. 66284; Matthias and Pikart, *Die Reichstagsfraktion...*, II p. 372;

reports by Magistrat Frankfurt, 17 February, and Gouvernement Mainz, 13 February: Staatsarchiv Wiesbaden, Abt. 405, Nr. 6539 and 2749; by stellv. Generalkommandos V. and VI. A.K., 3 June: Zusammenstellung der Monatsberichte der stellv. Generalkommandos, 15 June, Staatsarchiv Berlin-Dahlem, Rep. 90J Nr. 6; Schumann, 'Die Lage der deutschen und polnischen Arbeiter in Oberschlesien', p. 495; Berlin Polizeipräsident on 3 August: Zusammenstellung der Monatsberichte...15 August, Bundesarchiv-Militärarchiv. RM 3/v. 7796; M. Weber, *Wahlrecht und Demokratie in Deutschland*, Berlin, 1918, p. 44 (written December 1917).

16 Berlin Polizeipräsident to Admiralty, 26 April: Bundesarchiv-Militärarchiv, RM 33/v. 282; Düsseldorf police report, 6 May: Staatsarchiv Düsseldorf, Präs. Nr. 29; Meyer to Lenin, 5 September: *Dokumente und Materialien zur Geschichte*..., II, Nr. 77, p. 195.

17 Mehring's 'Open Letter' to the Bolsheviks was printed in *Pravda*, 13 June, *Münchener Post*, 25 June, *Leipziger Volkszeitung*, 4 July: *Illustrierte Geschichte der Deutschen Revolution*, pp. 163-64; conference of 7 October: *Spartakusbriefe*, pp. 469-71.

18 Oberkommando in den Marken, 7 April: Stern, *Die Auswirkungen*..., vol. 4/III, Nr. 513, p. 1283; Berlin Polizeipräsident to Reichsmarineamt, 11 September: Bundesarchiv-Militärarchiv. RM 33/v.283. One of the arrested students was Susanne Leonhard, later the author of a well known autobiography, *Gestohlenes Leben*, Frankfurt, 1956, describing her experiences in Soviet labour camps.

19 Hirsch, *Weg der Sozialdemokratie*..., p. 80; 'Aus der USPD', 12 February, Nachlass Hoch Nr. 20, Friedr.-Ebert-Stiftung; Nuremberg police report, 22 January, and Munich police reports, 24 January, 2 May and 27 June: Bayer.Hauptstaatsarchiv, M.Inn., 66283, M.Kr. 11529, M.Inn. 66284.

20 Polizeipräsident Frankfurt, 11 July, apparently based on internal USPD figures: Staatsarchiv Wolfenbüttel, 133 neu 2278; Gouvernement Festung Mainz, 3 June: Bundesarchiv-Militärarchiv. RM 3/v.7795; reports by the Bavarian Regierungspräsidenten, 13 September, ibid., F1685; reports from Halle, 10 May, Danzig, 6 July, Hanover, 13 July, Bremen, 19 July, Chemnitz, 12 September, Brunswick, 30 September, and Cologne, 24 October: Staatsarchiv Wolfenbüttel, 133 neu 2277, 2279 and 2282; Staatsarchiv Hanover, Des. 122a xxxiv Nr. 366; Bundesarchiv-Militärarchiv. RM 33/v.258 and RM 31/v.2372. Morgan, *The Socialist Left*..., p. 67, suggests about 100,000 USPD members in Germany.

21 Ryder, *The German Revolution of 1918*, p. 119; speech by Däumig on 1 August: Stern, *Die Auswirkungen*..., vol. 4/III, Nr. 639, p. 1494; Abwehr report on Fleissner's speech, 30 September: Bundesarchiv-Militärarchiv, RM 31/v. 2372; Frankfurt police report, 20 October, ibid.; stellv. Generalkommando XIX. A.K., 3 January, ibid., RM 3/v.7794; stellv. Generalkommando III. bayer. A.K., Nuremberg, 2 October: Bayer. Hauptstaatsarchiv, M.Kr. 12850.

22 Miller, *Burgfrieden und Klassenkampf*, p. 381; *Leipziger Volkszeitung*, 15 March and 14 May, *Hamburger Echo*, 16 March and 15 May, *Vorwärts*, 14 May 1918, all in Staatsarchiv Hamburg, Polit. Polizei, S 20570; Matthias and Pikart, *Die Reichstagsfraktion*..., II p. 392.

23 Haase, *Reichstagsreden gegen die deutsche Kriegspolitik,* pp. 133-34, 161-62 (speeches of 27 February and 22 March 1918).

24 Reports by stellv. Generalkommando XIV. A.K., 1 February, and Lt.-Col. von Sonnenburg, 27 March: Staatsarchiv Karlsruhe, Abt. 236/23079, Bayer. Hauptstaatsarchiv, M.Kr. 2340; Ay, *Entstehung einer Revolution,* p. 132; Garnisonältester of Schweinfurt, 19 October 1918: Bayer. Hauptstaatsarchiv, M.Kr. 12850; Büro für Sozialpolitik, 21 August 1918: Bundesarchiv-Militärarchiv, RM 3/v.2612.

25 *Der Völker-Friede,* Nr. 9. October 1917, pp. 14-15; notes by Lt.-Col. von Sonnenburg, 10 October: both in Bayer. Hauptstaatsarchiv, M.Kr. 13373; Prussian War Minister, Berlin, 8 July 1918: Staatsarchiv Wiesbaden, Abt. 405, Nr. 2778; Shand, 'Doves among the Eagles', *Journal of Contemporary History,* X 1, pp. 104-5.

26 Haase, *Reichstagsreden gegen die deutsche Kriegspolitik,* pp.118-19; leaflet of February 1918 and report by stellv. Generalkommando XIII. A.K., Stuttgart, 25 April 1918: both Staatsarchiv Karlsruhe, Abt. V, Nr. 84; Deist, *Militär und Innenpolitik,* Nr. 352 and 354, pp. 930-31, 937-41.

CHAPTER XI

1 'The Peace Position', leader in *The Herald,* 6 April 1918.

2 Resolution carried by Divisional London Conference, 2 February 1918: Brit. Libr. of Political Science, Coll. Misc. 314, ILP Papers IV C; ILP, *Report of the Annual Conference held at Leicester, April 1918,* London, 1918, pp. 46, 67-68, 72.

3 Resolution carried by London Divisional Conference, 2 February: Brit. Libr. of Political Science, Coll. Misc. 314, ILP Papers IV C; *Report of the Annual Conference held at Leeds, April 1917,* pp. 43-44; *Report of the Annual Conference held at Leicester, April 1918,* pp. 48, 58; McNair, *James Maxton,* p. 82.

4 Manifesto of the ILP National Council, s.d. (August 1918), and report by ILP Head Office, 17 May 1918: Brit. Libr. of Political Science, Minutes of ILP National Administrative Council for 1918. The total membership for March 1918 was given as 28,278, again without Wales. No other figures seem to be available.

5 BSP, *Report of Seventh Annual Conference, Leeds 31 March - 1 April 1918,* London, 1918, pp. 9, 15-16; Kendall, *Revolutionary Movement...,* p. 312.

6 Report by Deputy Chief Constable of Glamorgan, 22 January 1918: PRO, HO 45/10743, file 263,275, no. 315; Gallacher, *Revolt on the Clyde,* pp. 177, 179, 184; Bünger, *Sozialistische Antikriegsbewegung...,* pp. 195-97.

7 Cole and Postgate, *The Common People,* p. 528; *The Herald,* 20 July and 14 September; *The Times,* 24 to 27 September 1918: PRO, HO 45/10884, file 346,578.

8 *The Labour Leader,* 7 February; G.D.H. Cole and W.H. Hutchinson, in *The Herald,* 30 March; MacDonald, 'Strikes!', in *The Labour Leader,* 10 October 1918.

9 Leaflet by MacDonald, s.d.: PRO, MacDonald Papers, 30/69, 5/98; *The Tribunal,* no. 131, 31 October 1918; 'The Absolutists', in *The Herald,* 28 September 1918; Williams, *Fifty Years' March,* pp. 254-55.

10 Leaflet signed by Lansbury and nine others, 1 June 1918, Friends' House Library; *The Tribunal*, no. 110, 30 May 1918; Russell, *Autobiography*, pp. 256, 309; H.F. Bing transcript, Department of Sound Records, Imperial War Museum.
11 A. Watts, *The Way to end War*, 28 March 1919, Friends' House Library.
12 Brockway to MacDonald, s.d.: PRO, MacDonald Papers, 30/69, 6/21.

CHAPTER XII

1 Law of 28 October 1918; Huber, *Dokumente zur deutschen Verfassungsgeschichte*, II, Nr. 350, pp. 484-85; Rosenberg, *Entstehung der Deutschen Republik*, pp. 224-29.
2 Reports by Regierungspräsident of Hanover, 25 October, and Büro für Sozialpolitik, 18 October and 1 November: Staatsarchiv Hannover, Des. 122a xxxiv Nr.366; Bundesarchiv-Militärarchiv, RM 3/v.2612; Matthias and Pikart, *Die Reichstagsfraktion...*, II p. 495; Rathenau to Harden, 8 October 1918: Bundesarchiv, Nachlass Harden, Nr. 85a.
3 Reports by stellv. Generalkommando XIV. A.K., 1 November, by the Landräte of Usingen, Biedenkopf and St Goarshausen, 17-18 October, by stellv. Generalkommando II. bayer. A.K., 2 November, and stellv. Generalkommando I. bayer. A.K., 4 November: Staatsarchiv Karlsruhe, Abt. 236/23079; Staatsarchiv Wiesbaden, Abt. 405, Nr. 6360; Bayer. Hauptstaatsarchiv, M.Kr. 12850; G. Hoch on 15 October, Friedr.-Ebert-Stiftung, Nachlass Hoch, Kassette 20; Oberzensurstelle to press section of Bavarian War Ministry, 29 October: Bayer. Hauptstaatsarchiv. M.Kr. 13910.
4 Gandorfer in the *Landauer Volksblatt*, organ of the Bavarian Peasant League, 23 October 1918: Bayer. Hauptstaatsarchiv, M.Inn. 66338.
5 Haase on 23 October: *Hugo Haase – Reichstagsreden gegen die deutsche Kriegspolitik*, pp. 193, 201; Drüner, *Im Schatten des Weltkrieges*, p. 325; stellv. Generalkommando XIV. A.K., 1 November, Staatsarchiv Karlsruhe, Abt.236/23079; S. Miller, *Die Bürde der Macht*, Düsseldorf, 1978, p. 66.
6 Police report on Eisner meeting on 25 October, and reports on USPD meetings on 8-10 and 26 October: Bayer. Hauptstaatsarchiv, M.Inn. 66285, M.Kr. 11529.
7 USPD report on Hanau meeting: *Dokumente und Materialien zur Geschichte...*, II, Nr. 106, p. 272; von Köhler, *Zur Geschichte der Revolution...*, pp. 78, 88-89, 108-12, with the police report of 30 October 1918; Rück's diary in *Illustrierte Geschichte der Deutschen Revolution*, p. 182. Both supplement each other.
8 Police report on USPD meeting on 1 November 1918: Staatsarchiv Hamburg, Polit. Polizei, V 1066.
9 Police report based on information by an agent, Düsseldorf, 15 October: Bundesarchiv-Militärarchiv, RM 31/v.2372; Morgan, *The Socialist Left...*, p. 111, with a more cautious assessment.
10 Leaflet sent by the Württemberg Landespolizeiamt, 18 October, as distributed 'during the past days': Bundesarchiv-Militärarchiv, RM 31/v.2372.

11 *Ursachen des Deutschen Zusammenbruches*, 4. Reihe, VI p. 272; Trotnow, *Karl Liebknecht*, p. 249; Institut für Marxismus-Leninismus, *Geschichte der deutschen Arbeiterbewegung*, II p. 82.

12 Institut für Marxismus-Leninismus, *Geschichte der deutschen Arbeiterbewegung*, II p. 82; Klein, *Deutschland im Ersten Weltkrieg*, III p. 461; Wenzel, 'Das Revolutionsjahr 1918/19 in Braunschweig', Brunswick thesis 1949, p. 31.

13 Report by Büro für Sozialpolitik, 1 November: Bundesarchiv-Militärarchiv. RM 3/v-2612; Miller, *Bürde der Macht*, p. 66; Matthias and Pikart, *Die Reichstagsfraktion...*, II pp. 473, 480; police report on Noske's speech, 4 November: Staatsarchiv Wolfenbüttel, 133 neu 2279.

14 Reports by Wirtschaftsstelle of stellv. Generalkommando III. bayer. A.K., 18 October, stellv. Generalstab, 15 October, 87th Infantry Division, 31 October: Bayer. Hauptstaatsarchiv, M.Kr. 12850; Klein, *Deutschland im Ersten Weltkrieg*, III p. 448; *Ursachen des Deutschen Zusammenbruches*, 4. Reihe, VI pp. 15, 22, 350; Hoch's diary, 15 October, Friedr.-Ebert-Stiftung, Nachlass Hoch, Kassette 20; Groener as a witness, in *Dolchstossprozess in München*, pp. 213-14; report from General Headquarters, 1 November, in Stern, *Die Auswirkungen...*, vol. 4/IV, Nr. 769, p. 1721; report by Captain Loose, 5 November, in Deist, *Militär und Innenpolitik*, Nr. 500, p. 1356 note 4.

15 Reports by Legationsrat Krafft von Dellmensingen, Tournai, 7 October, and by Police Inspector Wilotzki, Wilhelmshaven, 1 November: Deist, *Militär und Innenpolitik*, Nr. 481, p. 1308, Bundesarchiv-Militärarchiv, RM 47/v.555; diary of Richard Stumpf, 12 October, in *Ursachen des Deutschen Zusammenbruches*, X 2, p. 297. As the navy had remained safely in port, it could still be used for an offensive operation in contrast with the army.

16 Reports by officers of *Regensburg*, 29 October and 15 November, *Karlsruhe*, 31 October, *Baden*, 4 November, and Police Inspector Wilotzki, 1 November: Bundesarchiv-Militärarchiv, RM 47/v.549, 550, 551 and 555. In general, W. Deist, 'Die Unruhen in der Marine 1917/18', *Marine-Rundschau*, 1971, Heft 6, pp. 340-42; Horn, *German Naval Mutinies...*, pp. 219-24.

17 Report by Captain von Waldeyer-Hartz, 8 January 1919: Bundesarchiv.Militärarchiv, Nachlass Waldeyer-Hartz, Nr.2; Reichs-Marine-Amt to Admiral Küsel and his reply, 4 November 1918: ibid., RM 31/v.2390; Horn, *German Naval Mutinies...*, pp. 235-42.

18 Ibid., pp. 248-52, with some different demands; G. Noske, *Von Kiel bis Kapp*, Berlin, 1920, pp. 10-13; proclamations of the Kiel soldiers' council, 4 and 5 November: Frölich, *10 Jahre Krieg und Bürgerkrieg*, p. 251; Huber, *Dokumente zur deutschen Verfassungsgeschichte*, II, Nr. 366, p. 500. Noske, p. 13, claims that the first point in the demands was 'the abdication of the Hohenzollerns', but it is not mentioned in the two proclamations.

19 Noske, *Von Kiel bis Kapp*, pp. 19, 26-29. There is no reason to doubt his description although it was written two years after these events.

20 P. Müller, 'November – Januar', in W. Breves (ed.), *Bremen in der deutschen*

Revolution, Bremen, 1919, pp. 11-12, 15, 17; W. Sollmann, *Die Revolution in Köln*, Cologne, 1918, pp. 7-12.

21 Ay, *Entstehung einer Revolution*, pp. 206-7; F. Schade, *Kurt Eisner und die bayerische Sozialdemokratie*, Hanover, 1961, pp. 59-60; G. Schmolze (ed.), *Revolution und Räterepublik in München 1918/19*, Düsseldorf, 1969, pp. 97-102; A. Mitchell, *Revolution in Bavaria 1918-19*, Princeton, 1965, pp. 92-96, 99-100.

22 *Münchner Neueste Nachrichten*, 8 November 1918; Schmolze, *Revolution und Räterepublik...*, p. 109, with the text of the proclamations of 8 November; Mitchell, *Revolution in Bavaria*, pp. 101, 106. Schade, *Kurt Eisner...*, p. 127 note 32, gives 10,000 members for the Bavarian Peasant League and 140,000 for the Catholic Peasant Association.

23 Müller, *Vom Kaiserreich zur Republik*, I pp. 137-41; Trotnow, *Karl Liebknecht*, pp. 252-53; Spartacus leaflet of 8 November signed by Liebknecht and Ernst Meyer, photocopy; *Illustrierte Geschichte der Deutschen Revolution*, pp. 199, 203-4; Barth, *Aus der Werkstatt der deutschen Revolution*, pp. 47, 51.

24 Müller, *Vom Kaiserreich zur Republik*, II pp. 11-13, 22-24; special editions of *Vorwärts* of 9 November in Friedr.-Ebert-Stiftung, Nachlass Barth, II Nr. 339-41.

25 Huber, *Dokumente zur deutschen Verfassungsgeschichte*, III, Stuttgart, 1966, Nr. 3-4, pp. 2-3; Müller, *Vom Kaiserreich zur Republik*, II pp. 27-29.

26 Müller, *Vom Kaiserreich zur Republik*, II pp. 36-40, 234-35, with the text of the proclamation; G.A. Ritter and S. Miller (eds.), *Die deutsche Revolution 1918-1919*, Frankfurt, 1968, Nr. 5, pp. 85-87 (*Vorwärts* of 11 November).

27 Groener's diary for 10 November, Bundesarchiv-Militärarchiv, Nachlass Groener, and his *Lebenserinnerungen*, ed. by F. Hiller von Gaertringen, Göttingen, 1957, p. 467.

28 Proclamations of 11 and 12 November 1918: Müller, *Vom Kaiserreich zur Republik* II p. 235; Ritter and Miller, *Die deutsche Revolution*, Nr. 4d, p. 94.

29 F. Lassalle, 'Über Verfassungswesen', in *Reden und Schriften*, Berlin, 1892, I pp. 476, 481, 491.

30 Report of 7 October 1918: Deist, *Militär und Innenpolitik*, p. 1308 note 17.

31 *Allgemeiner Kongress der Arbeiter- und Soldatenräte Deutschlands vom 16 bis 21 Dezember 1918 im Abgeordnetenhause zu Berlin*, Berlin, 1919, pp. 203, 207.

BIBLIOGRAPHY

A. UNPUBLISHED SOURCES

Public Record Office, London
Home Office 45/10741, File 263275; 45/10742, File 263275;
45/10743, File 263275; 45/10744, File 263275; 45/10782, File
278537; 45/10801, File 30740; 45/10814, File 312987;
45/10834, File 328752; 45/10884, File 346578;
Ministry of Munitions, nos. 5/49, 5/54, 5/73, 5/79, 5/346, 4/2213;
Ramsay MacDonald Papers, 30/69, 5/24; 30/69, 5/27-28; 30/69,
5/98-100; 30/69, 5/104; 30/69, 5/110; 30/69, 5/117; 30/69,
3a/23; 30/69, 3a/64A; 30/69, 6/21; 30/69, 7/17.

British Library of Political and Economic Science, London
Coll. Misc. 314, ILP Papers IIA, ILP Papers, IIB, ILP Papers IIC, ILP
Papers IVB, ILP Papers IVC, ILP Papers V;
Coll. Misc. 464 (M 890), ILP Papers 1/7;
Lansbury Collection, vol. 7;
National Peace Council, Minutes 1/1, Minutes 1/2.

Friends' House Library, London
Collection of leaflets and pamphlets from 1914-18.

Imperial War Museum, Department of Sound Records, London
Transcripts of 'Anti-War Movement 1914-1918', recorded in the
1970s, in particular H. F. Bing, A. F. Brockway, D. Grant,
H. C. Marten, Helen B. Pease, and Claire Winsten.

Scottish Record Office, Edinburgh
HH/31/19, HH/31/22.

Bayerisches Hauptstaatsarchiv, Munich
M.Inn. 66283, 66284, 66285, 66327, 66328, 66329, 66330,
    66331, 66332, 66338, 71700;
M.K. 19288, 19289, 19290, 19291;
Kriegsarchiv M.Kr. 2330-2346, M.Kr. 11528-11529, M.Kr. 12842-
    12853, M.Kr. 13366-13374, M.Kr. 13858-13910.

Bundesarchiv, Koblenz
Nachlass Maximilian Harden, Nr. 49, 85a, 103, 147;
Nachlass Ludwig Quidde, Nr. 96;
Zeitgeschichtliche Sammlung, 2/41, 2/64.

Bundesarchiv-Militärarchiv, Freiburg
Acta des Königl. Militär-Cabinets, PH 2/14, PH 2/17;
Reichs-Marine-Amt, RM 3/v.2612, 3/v.7794, 3/v.7795, 3/v.7796,
    20/9, 27XIII/v.424, 27XIII/v.425, 31/v.2372, 31/v.2383,
    31/v.2388, 31/v.2390, 33/v.257, 33/v.275, 33/v.258, 33/v.281,
    33/v.282, 33/v.283, 47/v.424, 47/v.458, 47/v.551, 47/v.555,
    47/v.549, 47/v.550;
Reichswehrministerium Marineleitung, F 4078/64923; F 1685;
Nachlass Wilhelm Groener, N 46/16, N 46/32, N 46/113;
Nachlass von Waldeyer-Hartz, Nr. 2.

Staatsarchiv, Berlin-Dahlem
General-Akten des Preussischen Justizministeriums betr. Hochverrat
    und Landesverrat, Rep. 84a, Nr. 8211;
Preussisches Staatsministerium, Rep. 90J, Nr. 6;
Zeitgeschichtliche Sammlung, IV 275.

Staatsarchiv, Düsseldorf
Regierung Aachen Präsidium, Nr. 856, Nr. 872;
Regierung Düsseldorf Präsidium, Nr. 29;
Regierung Düsseldorf, Nr. 9081, Nr. 14935, Nr. 15061, Nr. 14966,
    Nr. 15985.

Friedrich-Ebert-Stiftung, Bonn
Nachlass Wilhelm Dittman, Kassette I;

Nachlass Carl Giebel, Kassette 2;
Nachlass Alfred Henke, Kassette I and II;
Nachlass Gustav Hoch, Kassette 2 and 20.

Staatsarchiv, Hamburg
Kriegsakten des Senats, A II p 129; A II p 233;
Kriegsversorgungsamt, I a 19 b, Band 1 and Band 2; I a 19 c;
Politische Polizei, V 880, V 1066, Nr. 20565, S 20570, S 5883,
    S 13613, S 19561, S 13424, S 20230, Band 1 and Band 2, S 20510,
    Band 1 and Band 2, S 20510, Band 4, S 20923; Bestand 9, Ablieferung
    38, Nr. 44 and 45.

Hauptstaatsarchiv, Hannover
Oberpräsidium Hannover, Des. 122a xxxiv Nr. 365, Nr. 366.

Staatsarchiv, Karlsruhe
Badisches Ministerium des Innern, Kriegssachen, Abt. 236/23079;
Stellv. Generalkommando XIV. A.K., Abt. IIe, Band 70; Abt. V,
    Nr. 52, Nr. 84, Nr. 99 and Beilageheft.

Staatsarchiv, Koblenz
Oberpräsidium der Rheinprovinz, Abt. 403, Nr. 12696, Nr. 13536,
    Nr. 14152, Nr. 13534

Haupstaatsarchiv, Wiesbaden
Abt. 405, Nr. 2749, Nr. 2773, Nr. 2776, Nr. 2777, Nr. 6358,
    Nr. 6359, Nr. 6360; Abt. 408, Nr. 121

Staatsarchiv, Wolfenbüttel
Herzogliche Geheime Kanzlei, 12 A neu Fb. 7a, Nr. 598, Nr. 3402,
    Nr. 2932; 12 A neu Fb. 5, Nr. 6234, Nr. 6235, Nr. 6236, Nr. 6238;
Herzogliche Polizeidirektion Braunschweig, 133 neu 2154, 133 neu
    2253, 133 neu 2277, 133 neu 2278, 133 neu 2279, 133 neu 2282, 133
    neu 2320, 133 neu 2322, 133 neu 2323.

B. PUBLISHED SOURCES

Adler, Friedrich (ed.), *Victor Adler – Briefwechsel mit August Bebel und
    Karl Kautsky*, Vienna, 1954.
Allen, Clifford, *Is Germany right and Britain wrong?* A Reprint of a
    Speech, second edition, London, 1914.

Presidential Address to the National Convention of the No-Conscription Fellowship, on 27 November 1915, London, 1916.

Allgemeiner Kongress der Arbeiter- und Soldatenräte Deutschlands vom 16. bis 21. Dezember 1918 im Abgeordnetenhause zu Berlin, Berlin, s.d. (1919).

Ausserordentlicher Internationaler Sozialisten-Kongress zu Basel am 24. und 25. November 1912, Berlin, 1912.

Beschlüsse der Konferenzen von Vertretern der Zentralverbandsvorstände, Berlin, 1919.

Borchardt, Julian, *Vor und nach dem 4. August 1914 – Hat die deutsche Sozialdemokratie abgedankt?* Berlin-Lichterfelde, 1915.

British Socialist Party, *Report of Fifth Annual Conference, Salford 23-24 April 1916*, London, 1916.

Sixth Annual Conference, Salford 8-9 April 1917, London, 1917.

Report of Seventh Annual Conference, Leeds 31 March – 1 April 1918, London, 1918.

Brockway, A. Fenner, *Socialism for Pacifists*, Manchester-London, s.a. (1916).

Deist, Wilhelm (ed.), *Militär und Innenpolitik im Weltkrieg 1914-1918*. Quellen zur Geschichte des Parlamentarismus und der politischen Parteien, 2. Reihe, Band 1, Düsseldorf, 1970.

Dittman, Wilhelm, *Belagerungszustand, Zensur und Schutzhaft – Drei Reichstagsreden, gehalten am 18. Januar, 24. Mai und 28. Oktober 1916*, Leipzig, 1917.

Dokumente und Materialien zur Geschichte der deutschen Arbeiterbewegung, ed. by Institut für Marxismus-Leninismus beim Zentralkomitee der Sozialistischen Einheitspartei Deutschlands, 2 vols., Berlin, 1957-58.

Dolchstossprozess in München, Oktober-November 1925 – Eine Ehrenrettung des deutschen Volkes, Munich 1925.

Eichhorn, Emil (ed.), *Protokoll über die Verhandlungen des Gründungsparteitags der U.S.P.D. vom 6. bis 8. April 1917 in Gotha*, Berlin, 1921.

Glasier, J. Bruce, *The Peril of Conscription*, published by the ILP, London, 1915.

Haase, Ernst (ed.), *Hugo Haase – Sein Leben und Wirken*, Berlin, s.a. (1929).

Haase, Hugo, *Reichstagsreden gegen die deutsche Kriegspolitik*, Berlin, s.a. (1919).

Herald, Daily, 1 to 4 August 1914.

Herald, The, 1915 to 1918.

Huber, Ernst Rudolf, *Dokumente zur Deutschen Verfassungsgeschichte,* 3 vols., Stuttgart, 1961-66.

Independent Labour Party, *Report of the Annual Conference held at Norwich, April 1915,* London 1915.

Report of the Annual Conference held at Newcastle-upon-Tyne, April 1916, London, 1916.

Report of the Annual Conference held at Leeds, April 1917, London, 1917.

Report of the Annual Conference held at Leicester, April 1918, London, 1918.

Labour Leader, The, 1914 to 1918.

Lademacher, Horst (ed.), *Die Zimmerwalder Bewegung – Protokolle und Korrespondenz,* 2 vols., The Hague-Paris, 1967.

Ledebour, Georg, *Unter dem Belagerungszustand – Stenographischer amtlicher Bericht über die Reden der Abgeordneten Stadthagen und Ledebour im Reichstage am 20. März 1915,* s.a. (1915).
Proletariat und Frieden – Reichstagsrede des Abgeordneten Ledebour am 10. Oktober 1917, Unabhängige Genossenschaftsdruckerei, s.a. (1917).

Lenin, N., and Sinowjew, G., *Gegen den Strom – Aufsätze aus den Jahren 1914-1916,* Hamburg, 1921.

Liebknecht, Karl, *Das Zuchthausurteil – Wörtliche Wiedergabe der Prozessakten, Urteile und der Eingaben Karl Liebknechts,* Berlin Wilmersdorf, 1919.

Luxemburg, Rosa, 'Die Krise der Sozialdemokratie', in: *Politische Schriften,* ed. by Ossip K. Flechtheim, II, Frankfurt-Vienna, 1966.
Die Russische Revolution, ed. by Ossip K. Flechtheim, Frankfurt, 1963.

Matthias, Erich, and Miller, Susanne (eds.), *Das Kriegstagebuch des Reichstagsabgeordneten Eduard David 1914 bis 1918.* Quellen zur Geschichte des Parlamentarismus und der politischen Parteien, 1. Reihe, Band 4, Düsseldorf, 1966.

Matthias, Erich, and Pikart, Eberhard (eds.), *Die Reichstagsfraktion der deutschen Sozialdemokratie 1898 bis 1918.* Quellen zur Geschichte des Parlamentarismus und der politischen Parteien, 1. Reihe, Band 3/II, Düsseldorf, 1966.

Radek, Karl, *In den Reihen der deutschen Revolution 1909-1919,* Munich, 1921.

Renaudel, Pierre, 'La Voix de Londres', in: *l'Humanité,* 26 February 1915.

Ritter, Gerhard A. and Miller, Susanne (eds.), *Die deutsche Revolution 1918-1919 – Dokumente*, Frankfurt, 1968.

Sozialdemokratische Partei Deutschlands, *Protokoll über die Verhandlungen des Parteitages der* SPD *abgehalten in Würzburg vom 14. bis 20. Oktober 1917*, Berlin, 1917.

Spartakusbriefe, ed. by Institut für Marxismus-Leninismus beim Zentralkomitee der Sozialistischen Einheitspartei Deutschlands, Berlin, 1958.

Stern, Leo (ed.), *Die Auswirkungen der grossen sozialistischen Oktoberrevolution auf Deutschland*, Archivalische Forschungen zur Geschichte der deutschen Arbeiterbewegung, Band 4/I, 4/II, 4/III and 4/IV, Berlin, 1959.

Stumpf, Richard, Erinnerungen aus dem deutsch-englischen Seekriege, in: *Ursachen des Deutschen Zusammenbruches im Jahre 1918*, 4. Reihe, 10. Band, 2. Halbband, Berlin, 1928.

Tribunal, The, published by the No-Conscription Fellowship, 1916-1918.

Ursachen des Deutschen Zusammenbruches im Jahre 1918, 4. Reihe im Werk des Parlamentarischen Untersuchungsausschusses, 4. Band, 6. Band, 9. Band, 10. Band, Berlin, 1928.

C. SECONDARY AUTHORITIES

Ay, Karl Ludwig, *Die Entstehung einer Revolution – Die Volksstimmung in Bayern während des Ersten Weltkrieges*, Berlin, 1968.

Balabanoff, Angelica, *Erinnerungen und Erlebnisse*, Berlin, 1927.
Die Zimmerwalder Bewegung 1914-1919, Leipzig, 1928 (reprint 1969).

Balfour, Michael, *The Kaiser and His Times*, London, 1975.

Bartel, Walter, 'Der Januarstreik 1918 in Berlin', in: *Revolutionäre Ereignisse und Probleme in Deutschland während der Periode der Grossen Sozialistischen Oktoberrevolution 1917/1918*, Berlin, 1957, pp. 141-83.

Barth, Emil, *Aus der Werkstatt der deutschen Revolution*, Berlin, s.a. (1919).

Bell, Tom, *John Maclean – a Fighter for Freedom*, Scottish Committee of Communist Party, 1944.

Benz, Wolfgang, 'Der "Fall Muehlon" – Bürgerliche Opposition im Obrigkeitsstaat während des Ersten Weltkriegs', *Vierteljahrshefte für Zeitgeschichte*, xviii, 1970, pp. 343-65.

271

Bibliography

Beradt, Charlotte, *Paul Levi – Ein demokratischer Sozialist in der Weimarer Republik*, Frankfurt, 1969.

Bernhard, Hans-Joachim, 'Die Entstehung einer revolutionären Friedensbewegung in der deutschen Hochseeflotte im Jahre 1917' in: *Revolutionäre Ereignisse und Probleme in Deutschland während der Periode der Grossen Sozialistischen Oktoberrevolution 1917/1918*, Berlin, 1957, pp. 89-140.

Boll, Friedhelm, 'Spontaneität der Basis und politische Funktion des Streiks 1914-1918 – Das Beispiel Braunschweig', *Archiv für Sozialgeschichte*, xvii, 1977, pp. 337-66.

Brandt, Peter, and Rürup, Reinhard, *Arbeiter-, Soldaten- und Volksräte in Baden 1918/19*, Düsseldorf, 1980.

Brandt, Willy, and Löwenthal, Richard, *Ernst Reuter – Ein Leben für die Freiheit*, Munich, 1957.

Brockway, Fenner, *Inside the Left – Thirty Years of Platform, Press, Prison and Parliament*, London, 1947.

Bry, Gerhard, *Wages in Germany, 1871-1945*, Princeton, 1960.

Bünger, Siegfried, *Die sozialistische Antikriegsbewegung in Grossbritannien 1914-1917*, Berlin, 1967.

Cole, G.D.H., *British Working Class Politics 1832-1914*, London, 1941.

Cole, G.D.H., and Postgate, Raymond, *The Common People 1746-1938*, London, 1938.

Crangle, John V., and Baylen, Joseph O., 'Emily Hobhouse's Peace Mission 1916', *Journal of Contemporary History*, xiv, 1979, pp. 731-43.

Deist, Wilhelm, 'Die Unruhen in der Marine 1917/18', *Marine-Rundschau*, Heft 6, 1971, pp. 325-43.

Dittman, Wilhelm, *Die Marine-Justizmorde von 1917 und die Admirals-Rebellion von 1918*, Berlin, 1926.

Dowse, Robert E., *Left in the Centre – The Independent Labour Party 1893-1940*, London, 1966.

Drüner, Hans, *Im Schatten des Weltkrieges – Zehn Jahre Frankfurter Geschichte*, Frankfurt, 1934.

Fainsod, Merle, *International Socialism and the World War*, Cambridge, Mass., 1935.

Feldman, Gerald D., *Army, Industry and Labor in Germany 1914-1918*, Princeton, 1966.

Fischer, Fritz, *Griff nach der Weltmacht – Die Kriegszielpolitik des kaiserlichen Deutschland 1914/18*, Düsseldorf, 1961.

Flechtheim, Ossip K., *Die KPD in der Weimarer Republik*, Frankfurt, 1969.

Frölich, Paul, 10 Jahre Krieg und Bürgerkrieg, 2nd edtn., Berlin, 1924.
Illustrierte Geschichte der Deutschen Revolution, Berlin, 1929
(published without the name of the author).

Gallacher, William, Revolt on the Clyde - An Autobiography,
London, 1949.

Gast, Renate, Die Spaltung der SPD in Braunschweig während des ersten
Weltkrieges. Examensarbeit der Kant-Hochscule in Braunschweig,
1949 (copy of 1960).

Gerlach, Hellmut von, Von Rechts nach Links, Zürich, 1937.

Geyer, Curt, Die revolutionäre Illusion - Zur Geschichte des linken
Flügels der USPD, ed. by Wolfgang Benz and Hermann Graml,
Stuttgart, 1976.

Gilbert, Martin, Plough My Own Furrow - The Story of Lord Allen
of Hurtwood as told through his writings and correspondence,
London, 1965.

Gill, Douglas, and Dallas, Gloden, 'Mutiny at Étaples Base in 1917',
Past and Present, no. 69, November 1975, pp. 88-112.

Graubard, Stephen Richard, British Labour and the Russian Revolution
1917-1924, Cambridge, Mass., 1956.

Groener, Wilhelm, Lebenserinnerungen, ed. by Friedrich Hiller von
Gaertringen, Göttingen, 1957.

Groh, Dieter, Negative Integration und Revolutionärer Attentismus - Die
deutsche Sozialdemokratie am Vorabend des Ersten Weltkrieges,
Frankfurt-Berlin-Vienna, 1974.

Gruppe Arbeiterpolitik Bremen, Die Bremer Linksradikalen - Aus der
Geschichte der Bremer Arbeiterbewegung, Bremen, 1969.

Hanak, Harry, 'The Union of Democratic Control during the First
World War', Bulletin of the Institute of Historical Research,
xxxvi, November 1963, pp. 168-80.

Hirsch, Paul, Der Weg der Sozialdemokratie zur Macht in Preussen,
Berlin, 1929.

Horn, Daniel, The German Naval Mutinies of World War I, New
Brunswick, 1969.

Humbert-Droz, Jules, Der Krieg und die Internationale - Die
Konferenzen von Zimmerwald und Kienthal, Vienna, 1964.

Institute für Maxismus-Leninismus beim Zentralkomitee der
Sozialistischen Einheitspartei Deutschlands, Geschichte der
deutschen Arbeiterbewegung, Band 2, Berlin, 1966, Band 3,
Berlin, 1966.

Kendall, Walter, The Revolutionary Movement in Britain 1900-21 -
The Origins of British Communism, London, 1969.

Kirkwood, David, *My Life of Revolt*, London, 1935.

Klein, Fritz, and others, *Deutschland im Ersten Weltkrieg*, 3 vols., Berlin, 1968-1969.

Klein, Fritz (ed.), *Politik im Krieg 1914-1918 – Studien zur Politik der deutschen herrschenden Klassen im ersten Weltkrieg*, Berlin, 1964.

Kocka, Jürgen, *Klassengesellschaft im Krieg – Deutsche Sozialgeschichte 1914-1918*, Göttingen, 1973.

Köhler, Ludwig von, *Zur Geschichte der Revolution in Württemberg*, Stuttgart, 1930.

Kolb, Eberhard, and Schönhoven, Klaus, *Regionale und lokale Räteorganisationen in Württemberg 1918/19*, Düsseldorf, 1976.

Leser, Norbert, *Zwischen Reformismus und Bolschewismus – Der Austromarxismus als Theorie und Praxis*, Vienna-Frankfurt-Zürich, 1968.

Linklater, Andro, *Unhusbanded Life – Charlotte Despard, Suffragette, Socialist and Sinn-Feiner*, London, 1980.

Löw, Raimund, *Otto Bauer und die russische Revolution*, Vienna, 1980.

Lucas, Erhard, *Die Sozialdemokratie in Bremen währen des Ersten Weltkrieges*, Bremen, 1969.

Ludendorff, Erich, *Kriegführung und Politik*, 2nd edtn., Berlin, 1922.

McGovern, John, *Neither Fear nor Favour*, London, 1960.

McNair, John, *James Maxton – The Beloved Rebel*, London, 1955.

Mammach, Klaus, 'Das Erste Echo der Grossen Sozialistischen Oktoberrevolution in der deutschen Arbeiterklasse im November 1917', *Zeitschrift für Geschichtswissenschaft*, v, 1957, pp. 1021-33.

Miller, Susanne, *Burgfrieden und Klassenkampf – Die deutsche Sozialdemokratie im Ersten Weltkrieg*, Düsseldorf, 1974.
Die Bürde der Macht – Die deutsche Sozialdemokratie 1918-1920, Düsseldorf, 1978.

Mitchell, Allan, *Revolution in Bavaria 1918-1919*, Princeton, 1965.

Morgan, David M., *The Socialist Left and the German Revolution – A History of the German Independent Social Democratic Party 1917-1922*, Ithaca-London, 1975.

Morris, A.J.A., *C.P. Trevelyan 1870-1958 – Portrait of a Radical*, London, 1977.

Müller, Paul, 'November-Januar', in: Breves, Wilhelm (ed.), *Bremen in der deutschen Revolution*, Bremen, 1919, pp. 9-61.

Müller, Richard, *Vom Kaiserreich zur Republik*, 2 vols., Vienna, 1924-25.

Murphy, J.T., *New Horizons*, London, 1941.

Nettl, J.P., *Rosa Luxemburg*, 2 vols., London, 1966.

Noske, Gustav, *Von Kiel bis Kapp*, Berlin, 1920.

Paton, John, *Proletarian Pilgrimage – An Autobiography*, London, 1935.

Plaschka, Richard Georg, Haselsteiner, Horst, and Suppan, Arnold, *Innere Front – Militärischer Widerstand und Umsturz in der Donaumonarchie*, Munich, 1974.

Prager, Eugen, *Geschichte der USPD – Entstehung und Entwicklung der Unabhängigen Sozialdemokratischen Partei Deutschlands*, Berlin, 1921.

Pribićević, Branko, *The Shop Stewards Movement and Workers' Control 1910-1922*, Oxford, 1959.

Quidde, Ludwig, *Der deutsche Pazifismus währen des Weltkrieges 1914-1918*, ed. by Karl Holl, Boppard am Rhein, 1979.

Rauh, Manfred, *Die Parlamentarisierung des Deutschen Reiches*, Düsseldorf, 1977.

Retzlaw, Karl, *Spartacus – Aufstieg und Niedergang. Erinnerungen eines Parteiarbeiters*, 4th edtn., Frankfurt, 1976.

Robbins, Keith, *The Abolition of War – The 'Peace Movement' in Britain 1914-1919*, Cardiff, 1976.

Rosenberg, Arthur, *Die Entstehung der Deutschen Republik 1871-1918*, Berlin, 1928.

Russell, Bertrand, *Autobiography*, London, 1975.

Ryder, A.J., *The German Revolution of 1918 – A Study of German Socialism in War and Peace*, Cambridge, 1967.

Sacks, Benjamin, *J. Ramsay MacDonald in Thought and Action*, Albuquerque, 1952.

'The Independent Labour Party and International Socialism during the World War', *The University of New Mexico Bulletin, Sociological Series*, ii 4, July 1936.

Schade, Franz, *Kurt Eisner und die bayerische Sozialdemokratie*, Hanover, 1961.

Scheel, Heinrich, 'Der Aprilstreik 1917 in Berlin', in: *Revolutionäre Ereignisse und Probleme in Deutschland während der Periode der Grossen Sozialistischen Oktoberrevolution 1917/1918*, Berlin, 1957, pp. 1-88.

Scheidemann, Philipp, *Der Zusammenbruch*, Berlin, 1921.

Memoirs of a Social Democrat, London, 1929.

Schmolze, Gerhard, *Revolution und Räterepublik in München 1918/19*, Düsseldorf, 1969.

Schreiner, Albert, and Schmidt, Günter, 'Die Rätebewegung in Deutschland bis zur Novemberrevolution', in: *Revolutionäre Ereignisse und Probleme in Deutschland während der Periode der Grossen Sozialistischen Oktoberrevolution*, Berlin, 1957, pp. 229-308.

Schulz, Klaus-Peter, *Proletarier – Klassenkämpfer – Staatsbürger – 100 Jahre deutsche Arbeiterbewegung*, Munich, 1963.

Schumacher, Martin, *Land und Politik – Eine Untersuchung über politische Parteien und agrarische Interessen 1914-1923*, Düsseldorf, 1978.

Schumann, Wolfgang, 'Die Lage der deutschen und polnischen Arbeiter in Oberschlesien im Kampf gegen den deutschen Imperialismus in den Jahren 1917 und 1918', *Zeitschrift für Geschichtswissenschaft*, iv, 1956, pp. 466-500.

Sender, Toni, *The Autobiography of a German Rebel*, London, 1940.

Shand, James D., 'Doves among the Eagles – German Pacifists and their Government during World War I', *Journal of Contemporary History*, x, 1975, pp. 95-108.

Shinwell, Emanuel, *Conflict without Malice*, London, 1955.

Snowden, Philip, *An Autobiography*, London, 1934.

Sollmann, Wilhelm, *Die Revolution in Köln*, Cologne, 1918.

Stillig, Jürgen, *Die russische Februarrevolution 1917 und die Sozialistische Friedenspolitik*, Cologne-Vienna, 1977.

Swartz, Marvin, *The Union of Democratic Control in British Politics during the First World War*, Oxford, 1971.

Trotnow, Helmut, *Karl Liebknecht – Eine politische Biographie*, Cologne, 1980.

Volkmann, Erich Otto, *Der Marxismus und des deutsche Heer im Weltkriege*, Berlin, 1925.

Watts, Arthur, *The Way to end War*, London, 1919.

Weber, Max, *Wahlrecht und Demokratie in Deutschland*, Berlin, 1918.

Wehler, Hans-Ulrich, *Das deutsche Kaiserreich 1871-1918*, 2nd edtn., Göttingen, 1975.

Weller, Karl, *Die Staatsumwälzung in Württemberg 1918-1920*, Stuttgart, 1930.

Wenzel, Hans, Das Revolutionsjahr 1918/19 in Braunschweig. Examensarbeit der Kant-Hochschule in Braunschweig 1949.

Williams, Francis, *Fifty Years' March – The Rise of the Labour Party*, London, s.a.

Winkler, Erwin, 'Die Berliner Obleutebewegung im Jahre 1916', *Zeitschrift für Geschichtswissenschaft*, xvi, 1968, pp. 1422-36.

INDEX

INDEX

Index

Index

Index